# A VIEW OF THE SWAMP

## Foreign Impressions of Washington, D.C.

## From the Founding Era to the Civil War

Edited with an Introduction

by

Christopher Lee Philips

WASHINGTON, D.C.
Cloud Light Publishing
2020

*A View of the Swamp: Foreign Impressions of Washington, D.C. From the Founding Era to the Civil War* is published by Cloud Light Publishing of Washington, D.C.

Copyright 2020 by Christopher Lee Philips.

ISBN: 978-1-0966-4071-4


Cover Illustration: *George Town and Federal City, or City of Washington* by T. Cartwright and George Beck. Published in London and Philadelphia by Atkins and Nightingale, 1801. [Image via Library of Congress: #2002695146].

For HAP and WHP

## CONTENTS

PREFACE ........................................................................................1
INTRODUCTION .........................................................................3
"A Town of Any Importance" ....................................................13
"An Elegant Building" ................................................................23
"Influx of Speculations" .............................................................29
"Obelisks in Trees" .....................................................................37
"A Place of Commerce" ..............................................................41
"Drain the Swamp" .....................................................................51
"Spoil of the Conqueror" ............................................................57
"America is Young" ....................................................................69
"Our Enlightened Countrymen" .................................................77
"The Aspect of the House" .........................................................85
"Punishment is 20 Dollars" .......................................................105
"The Custom is to Shake Hands" .............................................125
"God Bless the American People" ...........................................137
"Nobody Would Inhabit Such a Town" ...................................151
"Do You Mean to Buy the Lad, Sir?" ......................................161
"It Reminded Me Much of a Russian City" ............................179
"The Spitting was Incessant" ...................................................191
"To Dazzle with False Glitter" .................................................211
"The Road to Washington" ......................................................219

"Ladies of America are Uncommonly Frank" ...................................... 227

"The Bottom of an Old Lake" ............................................................. 241

"The President Offered Me Bonbons" ................................................ 251

"A Subject of Grave Reflection" ......................................................... 275

"Just One Month" ................................................................................ 287

"Magnificent ... Magnificent" ............................................................. 295

"Every Species of Alcoholic Beverage" .............................................. 315

"A Fit Act of Hero Worship" ............................................................... 339

"We are the Same People" ................................................................... 351

"No! No! ... No! No!" .......................................................................... 359

"In Charge was a Door-Keeper" .......................................................... 375

"The Saddest Spot on Earth" ................................................................ 385

"Fishing in Troubled Waters" .............................................................. 411

SOURCES ............................................................................................ 419

NOTES ................................................................................................. 433

# A VIEW OF THE SWAMP

# PREFACE

*A View of the Swamp: Foreign Impressions of Washington, D.C. from the Founding Era to the Civil War* is an anthology of writings excerpted from larger works by select foreign authors who visited the United States and its fledgling capital city from the 1790s through the 1860s.

The original works reproduced herein were published in different, albeit mostly English-speaking countries at different times and under different editorial standards. With this in mind, the editor has sought to present a general-interest work for a modern audiences while remaining faithful to the original texts. For example, the various spellings of Georgetown (George Town) and Potomac (Patomack) have generally been retained as originally presented. English spellings (expence, flavour, neighbour) have also been retained, even where they would be considered archaic (visiters), but that most visually jarring habit of the era, spelling "any thing" and "every thing" as such, proved entirely too much for this editor to bear. Consequently, something had to be done. Variations in capitalization (Pennsylvania avenue) have often been made consistent with contemporary editorial standards. Numbers (55,000), fractions (⅝) and prices in dollars and pounds sterling ($500; £4,500) have been made uniform. Punctuation, especially the comma, the semi-colon and the hyphen, has been selectively refined. Linguistic distinctions (attaché) have been retained as originally presented, as have instances of *italics*. The inevitable [*sic*] is used sparingly.

Language and meaning change over time but the intention of the writer usually remains clear to the attentive reader. Archaic, culturally insensitive and pejorative references regarding class, gender, national origin, race and religion have been retained as originally presented. No effort has been made to expurgate the text.

Chapter titles ("Drain the Swamp") have been devised from lines within the original text, lines that will perhaps reveal to the reader what is to come. Brief biographical and contextual information has been provided for each author. Explanatory notes have been provided where they are considered helpful or necessary and may be expanded or repeated in subsequent sections of the text. A descriptive list of sources is provided at the end of the text for reference and for further reading.

The editor welcomes comments for future editions.


CLP
Washington, D.C.
June, 2020

## INTRODUCTION

In 1774, a group of revolutionaries, British subjects residing in the North American colonies, banded together to end monarchical rule by a despotic king and create a free and independent nation. In 1776 they presented to King George III a Declaration of Independence which outlined their grievances and stated their intentions. What followed was bloody revolution, with the attendant loss of life and property inevitable in military conflict. But in the midst of this upheaval, these American revolutionaries were able to create and maintain the essential mechanisms of self-government. They established a Congress, and this legislative body met in various places and usually under difficult circumstances until victory had been achieved in 1783, whereupon the former colonies united as one nation upon the eventual ratification, by decade's end, of the Constitution of the United States.

During the American Revolution, Congress had met, for all practicable purposes, when and where it could. Travel took time and there were vexing issues to consider; geographical proximity, the necessity of a suitable building, and the ever-present threat of the British army. Even after the Revolution, Congress had, on one embarrassing occasion, run from its *own* army. In short, during the revolutionary era the nation's capital was mobile, moveable of necessity, subject to the circumstances of the moment and more a waystation in the pursuit of liberty than a permanent place from which to govern. During the period between 1774 and 1790, Congress met in the following locations:

The Congress of the Revolution first met in Philadelphia, Pennsylvania on September 5th, 1774, and remained there until Wednesday, December 12th, 1776, when it adjourned to Baltimore, Maryland in consequence of the approach of the British army.

Congress met in Baltimore Friday, December 20th, 1776, and remained there until February 27th, 1777, when it adjourned to Philadelphia, where it met on March 4th and adjourned from day to day until March 12th.

On September 18th, 1777, military necessity again led to the removal of Congress from Philadelphia. It thereupon adjourned to Lancaster, Pennsylvania, where it met on Saturday, September 27th, and on the same day adjourned to meet at York, Pennsylvania, at which place it assembled on Tuesday, September 30th.

Congress remained in York until Saturday, June 27th, 1778, when, in view of the evacuation of Philadelphia by the British, it adjourned to that city, where it held its next session on Thursday, July 2nd, 1778.

Congress remained in Philadelphia until June 21st, 1783, when in consequence of the menacing demonstration toward it by the unpaid soldiers of the Revolutionary Army, it adjourned to meet either at Trenton or Princeton, New Jersey, as the President might direct.

Upon the summons of the President, Congress met at Princeton on June 30th and continued to hold its sessions there until November 4th, 1783.

On November 26, 1783, Congress met in Annapolis, Maryland, where it remained until June 3rd, 1784.

Congress next met in Trenton, New Jersey from November 1st, 1784, until December 24th, 1784, when it adjourned to meet in the city of New York.

It met in New York City on January 11th, 1785, and continued to meet there until March 4th, 1789, when it was succeeded by the Congress provided for in the Constitution.

The Congress provided for by the Constitution first met in New York City. The first Wednesday, which was the 4th day of March, 1789, was the day appointed by the resolution of September 12th, 1788, for "commencing proceedings" by the Congress provided for by the Constitution, and several members of each House were present on that day, but no quorum appeared in the House of Representatives until April 1st, 1789, nor in the Senate until April 6th. On December 6th, 1790, Congress removed to Philadelphia.[1]

Thus far, the notion of a capital city had perhaps been an afterthought in the minds of many in Congress. But eventually, the need for a permanent capital became a reality to be confronted. Where would these United States choose to locate their seat of government?

Northern cities like Philadelphia and New York had been agreeable meeting places during the Revolution, in part because of their infrastructure. These were older, well-established cities, at least by American standards, with roads, buildings, business districts and neighborhoods. The traveler could find lodging and a hot meal. These cities in no way compared to European capitals, but still there was culture, even if much of it was imported.

Members of Congress from the southern states no doubt grew weary of such travel demands, and who could blame them? After all, in a country originally stretching merely from New Hampshire to Georgia along the eastern seaboard of North America, the logical center was arguably somewhere in the mid-Atlantic region.

The Constitution had addressed the need for a capital, a "district" of "ten miles square," but at the time of ratification there had been no commitment to a specific location. As ratified, the United States Constitution authorized Congress:

> To exercise exclusive Legislation in all Cases whatsoever, over such District (not exceeding ten Miles square) as may, by Cession of particular States, and the Acceptance of Congress, become the Seat of the Government of the United States, and to exercise like Authority over all Places purchased by the Consent of the Legislature of the State in which the Same shall be, for the Erection of Forts, Magazines, Arsenals, Dock-Yards, and other needful Buildings....[2]

But by the cession of which states? Where would these "needful buildings" be built? By the time the Constitution was ratified, over a dozen possible locations had been suggested, the most popular of which were in the more urban areas of Philadelphia, Pennsylvania and Trenton, New Jersey, both on the Delaware River. There were two possible sites in Pennsylvania along the Susquehanna River, and another location somewhere along the Potomac River, the waterway which divided Maryland from Virginia.[3] Wherever the location, James Madison of Virginia had argued in *Federalist* XLIII against an individual state hosting the new capital and instead promoted the virtues of a separate and independent federal district, hence the "cession of particular states."

> The indispensable necessity of complete authority at the seat of government, carries its own evidence with it. It is a power exercised by every legislature of the Union,

I might say of the world, by virtue of its general supremacy. With out it, not only the public authority might be insulted and its proceedings interrupted with impunity; but a dependence of the members of the general government on the State comprehending the seat of the government, for protection in the exercise of their duty, might bring on the national councils an imputation of awe or influence, equally dishonorable to the government and dissatisfactory to the other members of the Confederacy. This consideration has the more weight, as the gradual accumulation of public improvements at the stationary residence of the government would be both too great a public pledge to be left in the hands of a single State, and would create so many obstacles to a removal of the government, as still further to abridge its necessary in dependence. The extent of this federal district is sufficiently circumscribed to satisfy every jealousy of an opposite nature. And as it is to be appropriated to this use with the consent of the State ceding it; as the State will no doubt provide in the compact for the rights and the consent of the citizens inhabiting it; as the inhabitants will find sufficient inducements of interest to become willing parties to the cession; as they will have had their voice in the election of the government which is to exercise authority over them; as a municipal legislature for local purposes, derived from their own suffrages, will of course be allowed them; and as the authority of the legislature of the State, and of the in habitants of the ceded part of it, to concur in the cession, will be derived from the whole people of the State, in their adoption of the Constitution, every imaginable objection seems to be obviated.

The necessity of a like authority over forts, magazines, etc., established by the general government, is not less evident. The public money expended on such places, and the public property deposited in them, require that they should be exempt from the authority of the particular State. Nor would it be proper for the places on which the security of the entire Union may depend, to be in any degree dependent on a particular member of it. All objections and scruples are here also obviated, by requiring the concurrence of the States concerned, in every such establishment. [4]

While Congress wrestled with the issue of a permanent location for the new capital, longstanding sectional differences among the states remained an undercurrent in the debate. Pennsylvania, for example, was moving toward the gradual abolition of slavery, but Virginia's slave population was steadily increasing. Polarized north and south, the country's sectional factions each needed a *quid pro quo*.

The final decision on the location of the permanent seat of government in the United States was borne of compromise, a compromise reached in a gentleman's agreement over dinner and Madeira in the New York home of Thomas Jefferson, then George Washington's Secretary of State.

In 1790, Secretary of the Treasury Alexander Hamilton had proposed that Congress should assume the debts incurred by the states during the Revolution, a financial measure which arguably favored the northern states. Hamilton was a New Yorker, a Federalist, and prone to fiscal responsibility. The southern states, however, vigorously opposed Hamilton's assumption bill and it went down to defeat. As a consequence, another factional debate between north and south reared its head. The assumption of state debts and the selection of a site for the new capital were now two political stalemates existing in tandem, stalemates that threatened the future of an already fragile nation.

Secretary of State Thomas Jefferson was well aware of the potential international repercussions of a fiscal crisis in the young republic. A Virginian, a slaveholder and a member of the southern faction seeking to win the debate over locating the new capital, Jefferson, the budding Democratic-Republican, was politically in conflict with the Federalist Hamilton. And yet, it was Jefferson who moved the opposing parties toward resolution of these tandem stalemates over dinner one evening in June, 1790. Among those in attendance were Alexander Hamilton and future president James Madison, then a member of the House of Representatives from Virginia. In what became known as the Compromise of 1790, Madison agreed to support Hamilton's assumption bill and Hamilton agreed to support the location the capital of the United States along the banks of the Potomac River. The Residence Act was subsequently signed into law in July and the Funding Act became law the following August. Congress also agreed that Philadelphia would serve as the temporary capital from 1790 until 1800, by which time the new capital was expected to be finished.

By now, Maryland and Virginia had ceded land and pledged funds for the development of the new capital along the banks of the Potomac River. The general location having finally been agreed to, Congress bestowed upon George Washington the authority to choose the specific site and to shepherd development of the capital toward completion. Washington was in familiar territory. His estate, Mount Vernon was just downriver from Alexandria, Virginia and its cross-river rival, Georgetown in Maryland, both thriving 18th century Potomac River port towns. The General, as many admirers called him, was now President of the United States, and he took on the development of the new Federal City with the same vigor, leadership and determination he had shown during his military career. After so much debate over the site of the new capital, now perhaps there would be a sense of urgency.

Among Washington's first steps were to select a young French engineer, Pierre Charles L'Enfant, to design the Federal City. L'Enfant, who had first come to Washington's attention during the Revolution, had previously supervised the renovations of Federal Hall in New York, where Washington had been inaugurated President in 1789. Washington also selected three capable lieutenants (Daniel Carroll, Thomas Johnson and David Stuart) to serve as Commissioners of the Federal City. Contests were announced for the designs of a capitol building and a residence for the president.

The building of the new Federal City would be an ambitious undertaking, one conducted over the following decade while Congress met in Philadelphia. But subsequent events wrought new challenges. Pierre Charles L'Enfant produced a brilliant plan for the new city, but personal difficulties in working with others rendered his tenure short-lived. Luckily, Andrew Ellicott was able to pick up where L'Enfant left off. Ellicott was assisted by Benjamin Banneker, a free African American mathematician and almanac publisher whose astrological observations were essential to the accuracy of Ellicott's surveys. In another major challenge, construction of the new capitol initially proved so haphazard that only one wing of the building would be finished by 1800.

Once the new city had been surveyed, lots were to be sold by auction to fund the construction of the highly anticipated metropolis. But in spite of personal involvement by George Washington himself, the initial land auction was a failure, and ready speculators subsequently exploited every new opportunity that arose. On a practical level, skilled labor was in short supply, and the most back-breaking work would inevitably be performed by the local enslaved population. And then, in perhaps the greatest national loss of the era, the recently retired George Washington would die at Mount Vernon, only a year before

Congress was expected to remove from Philadelphia and inhabit its new capital.

In spite of overwhelming odds, and often at great personal sacrifice, citizens of the newly formed United States had secured their freedom and independence. They were Americans now. They had held together a fragile coalition of thirteen states, a coalition that by the dawn of the 19th century was already growing in number. And now, as new visitors began to come to their shores, they would experience the first foreign criticisms of their evolving national character, and of Washington, D.C., their nascent capital city.

"A Town of Any Importance"

From *Travels Through the States of North America, and the Provinces of Upper and Lower Canada, During the Years 1795, 1796, and 1797* by Isaac Weld, Jr.

The inveterate Irish traveler, topographical writer and artist Isaac Weld, Jr. (1774-1856) was named for Isaac Newton, who was a friend of Weld's great grandfather, Dr. Nathaniel Weld, a Dublin minister. Like his predecessors, young Isaac enjoyed the benefits of a quality education, first studying under schoolmaster Samuel Whyte in Dublin, then in England under the Reverend Rochemont Barbauld at Palgrave Academy in Suffolk and finally with Dr. William Enfield in Norwich.

In 1795, shortly after his twenty-first birthday, Isaac Weld set sail for the United States with the intention of determining the merits of potential Irish emigration to the former English colonies. Weld's voyage across the Atlantic was a difficult one, encompassing some fifty-nine days by his own account. After landing in Philadelphia in November, 1795, Weld began an adventuresome two-year journey through the United States and Canada. Traveling south from Philadelphia, then the temporary capital of the United States, he reached Washington, D.C. toward the end of the month.

Weld's *Travels* was well-received upon its publication and appeared in subsequent editions including translations into French and German. In this excerpt, Weld provides a highly detailed and arguably well-informed summary of Washington, D.C. during the first decade of its existence. He also addresses the continuing rivalry between north and south over the preferred location of the capital of the United States.

---

Washington, November [1795].

The City of Washington, or the Federal City, as it is indiscriminately called, was laid out in the year 1792, and is expressly designed for being the metropolis of the United States, and the seat of the federal government. In the year 1800 the congress is to meet there for the first time. As the foundation of this city has attracted the attention of so many people in Europe, and as such very different opinions are entertained about it, I shall, in the following pages, give you a brief account of its rise and progress.

Shortly after the close of the American war, considerable numbers of the Pennsylvanian line, or of the militia, with arms in their hands, surrounded the hall in which the congress was assembled at Philadelphia, and with vehement menaces insisted upon immediate appropriations of money being made to discharge the large arrears due to them for their past services. The members, alarmed at such an outrage, resolved to quit a state in which they met with insult in instead of protection, and quickly adjourned to New York, where the session was terminated. A short time afterwards, the propriety was strongly urged in congress, of fixing upon some place for the meeting of the legislature, and for the seat of the general government, which should be subject to the laws and regulations of the congress alone, in order that the members, in future, might not have to depend for their personal safety, and for their freedom of deliberation, upon the good or bad police of any individual state. This idea of making the place, which should be chosen for the meeting of the legislature, independent of the particular state to which it might belong, was further corroborated by the following argument: That as the several states in the union were in some measure rivals to each other, although connected together by certain ties, if any one of them, was fixed upon for the seat of the general government in preference, and thus raised to a state of pre-eminence, it might perhaps be the occasion of great jealousy amongst the others. Every person was convinced of the expediency of preserving the union of the states entire; it was apparent, therefore, that the greatest precautions ought to be taken to remove every source of jealousy from amongst them, which might tend, though remotely, to produce a separation. In fine, it was absolutely necessary that the seat of government should be made permanent, as the removal of the public offices and the archives from place to place could not but be attended with many and very great inconveniences.

However, notwithstanding this measure appeared to be beneficial to the interest of the union at large, it was not until after the revolution, by which the present federal constitution was established, that it was acceded to on the part of all the states. Pennsylvania, in particular, conscious of her being a principal and central state, and therefore likely to be made the seat of government if this new project was not carried into execution, was foremost in the opposition. At last she complied; but it was only on condition that the congress should meet at Philadelphia until the new city was ready for its reception, flattering herself that there would be so many objections afterwards to the removal of the seat of government, and so many difficulties in putting the project into execution, that it would finally be relinquished. To the discriminating judgment of General Washington, then president, it was left to determine upon the spot best calculated for the federal city. After mature deliberation he fixed upon a situation on the banks of the Patowmac River, a situation which seems to be marked out by nature, not only for a large city, but expressly for the seat of the metropolis of the United States.

In the choice of the spot there were two principal confederations: First, that it should be as central as possible in respect to every state in the union; secondly, that it should be advantageously situated for commerce, without which it could not be expected that the city would ever be distinguished for size or for splendour; and it was to be supposed, that the people of the United States would be desirous of having the metropolis of the country as magnificent as it possibly could be. These two essential points are most happily combined in the spot which has been chosen.

.... The city is laid out on a neck of land between the forks formed by the eastern and western or main branch of Patowmac River. This neck of land, together with an adjacent territory, which is in the whole ten miles square, was ceded to congress by the states of Maryland and Virginia. The ground on which the city immediately stands was the property of private individuals, who readily relinquished their claim to one half of it in favour of congress, conscious that the value of what was left to them would increase, and amply compensate them for their loss. The profits arising from the sale that part of which has thus been ceded to congress will be sufficient, it is expected, to pay for the public buildings, for the watering of the city, and also for paving and lighting of the streets. The plan of the city was drawn by a Frenchman of the name of L'Enfant, and is on a scale well suited to the extent of the country, one thousand two hundred miles in length, and one thousand in breadth, of which it is to be the metropolis; for the ground already marked out for it is no less than fourteen miles in circumference. The streets run north, south, east, and west; but to prevent that sameness necessarily ensuing from the streets all crossing each other at right angles, a number of avenues are laid out in different parts of the city, which run transversely; and in several places, where these avenues intersect each other, are to be hollow squares. The streets, which cross each other at right angles, are from ninety to one hundred feet wide, the avenues one hundred and sixty feet. One of these is named after each state, and a hollow square also allotted to each, as a suitable place for statues, columns, &c. which, at a future period, the people of any one of these states may wish to erect to the memory of great men that may appear in the country. On a small eminence, due West of the capitol, is to be an equestrian statue of General Washington.

The capitol is now building upon the most elevated spot of ground in the city, which happens to be in a very central situation. From this spot there is a complete view of every part of the city, and also of the adjacent country. In the capitol are to be spacious apartments for the accommodation of congress; in it also are to be the principal public offices in the executive department of the government, together with the courts of justice. The plan on which this building is begun is grand and extensive; the expense of building it is estimated at a million of dollars, equal to two hundred and twenty-five thousand pounds sterling.

The house for the residence of the president stands north-west of the capitol, at the distance of about one mile and a half. It is situated upon a riling ground not far from the Patowmac, and commands a most beautiful prospect of the river, and of the rich country beyond it. One hundred acres of ground, towards the river, are left adjoining to the house for pleasure grounds. South of this there is to be a large park or mall, which is to run in an easterly direction from the river to the capitol. The buildings on either side of this mall are all to be elegant in their kind; amongst the number it is proposed to have houses built at the public expense for the accommodation of the foreign ministers, &c. On the eastern branch a large spot is laid out for a marine hospital and gardens. Various other parts are appointed for churches, theatres, colleges, &c. The ground in general, within the limits of the city, is agreeably undulated; but none of the risings are so great as to become objects of inconvenience in a town. The soil is chiefly of a yellowish clay mixed with gravel. There are numbers of excellent springs in the city, and water is readily had in most places by digging wells. Here are two streams likewise, which run through the city, Reedy Branch and Tiber Creek.[1] The perpendicular height of the source of the latter, above the level of the tide, is two hundred and thirty-fix feet.

By the regulations published, it was settled that all the houses should be built of brick or stone; the walls to be thirty feet high, and to be built parallel to the line of the street, but either upon it or withdrawn from it, as suited the taste of the builder. However, numbers of wooden habitations have been built; but the different owners have all been cautioned against considering them as permanent. They are to be allowed for a certain term only, and then destroyed. Three commissioners, who reside on the spot, are appointed by the president, with a salary, for the purpose of superintending the public and other buildings, and regulating everything pertaining to the city.

The only public buildings carrying on as yet are the president's house, the capitol, and a large hotel. The president's house, which is nearly completed on the outside, is two stories high, and built of free stone.[2] The principal room in it is of an oval form. This is undoubtedly the handsomest building in the country, and the architecture of it is much extolled by the people, who have never seen anything superior; but it will not bear a critical examination. Many persons find fault with it, as being too large and too splendid for the residence of any one person in a republican country; and certainly it is a ridiculous habitation for a man who receives a salary that amounts to no more than £5,625 sterling per annum, and in a country where the expences of living are far greater than they are even in London.

The hotel is a large building of brick, ornamented with stone; it stands between the president's house and the capitol. In the beginning of the year 1796, when I last saw it, it was roofed in, and every exertion making to have it finished with the utmost expedition. It is anything but beautiful. The capitol, at the same period, was raised only a very little way above the foundation.

The stone, which the president's house is built with, and such as will be used for all the public buildings, is very similar in appearance to that found at Portland in England; but I was informed by one of the sculptors, who had frequently worked the Portland stone in England, that it is of a much superior quality, as it will bear to be cut as fine as marble, and is not liable to be injured by rain or frost. On the banks of the Patowmac they have inexhaustible quarries of this stone; good specimens of common marble have also been found; and there is in various parts of the river abundance of excellent slate, paving stone, and lime stone. Good coal may also be had.

The private houses are all plain buildings; most of them have been built on speculation, and still remain empty. The greatest number, at any one place, is at Greenleaf's Point,[3] on the main river, just above the entrance of the eastern branch. This spot has been looked upon by many as the most convenient one for trade; but others prefer the shore of the eastern branch, on account of the superiority of the harbour, and the great depth of the water near the shore. There are several other favourite situations, the choice of any one of which is a mere matter of speculation at present. Some build near the capitol, as the most convenient place for the residence of members of congress, some near the president's house; others again prefer the west end of the city, in the neighbourhood of George Town, thinking that as trade is already established in that place, it must be from thence that it will extend into the city. Were the houses that have been built situated in one place all together, they would make a very respectable appearance, but scattered about as they are, a spectator can scarcely perceive anything like a town. Excepting the streets and avenues, and a small part of the ground adjoining the public buildings, the whole place is covered with trees. To be under the necessity of going through a deep wood for one or two miles, perhaps, in order to see a next door neighbour, and in the same city, is a curious, and, I believe, a novel circumstance. The number of inhabitants in the city, in the spring of 1796, amounted to about five thousand, including artificers,[4] who formed by far the largest part of that number. Numbers of strangers are continually passing and repassing through a place which affords such an extensive field for speculation.

In addition to what has already been said upon the subject, I have only to observe, that notwithstanding all that has been done at the city, and the large sums of money which have been expended, there are numbers of people in the United States, living to the north of the Patowmac, particularly in Philadelphia, who are still very adverse to the removal of the seat of government thither, and are doing all in their power to check the progress of the buildings in the city, and to prevent the congress from meeting there at the appointed time. In the spring of 1796, when I was last on the spot, the building of the capitol was absolutely at a stand for want of money; the public lots were at a very low price, and the commissioners were unwilling to dispose of them; in consequence they made an application to congress, praying the house to guaranty a loan of three hundred thousand dollars, without which they could not go on with the public buildings, except they disposed of the lots to great disadvantage, and to the ultimate injury of the city; so strong, however, was the opposition, that the petition was suffered to lie on the table unattended to for many weeks; nor was the prayer of it complied with until a number of gentlemen, that were very deeply interested in the improvement of the city, went round to the different members, and made interest with them in person to give their assent to the measure. These people, who are opposed to the building of the city of Washington maintain, that it can never become a town of any importance, and that all such as think to the contrary have been led astray by the representations of a few enthusiastic persons; they go so far even as to assert, that the people to the eastward will never submit to see the seat of government removed so far from them, and the congress assembled in a place little better than a forest, where it will be impossible to procure information upon commercial points; finally, they insist, that if the removal from Philadelphia should take place, a separation of the states will inevitably follow. This is the language held forth; but their opposition in reality arises from that jealousy which narrow minded people in trade are but too apt to entertain of each other when their interests clash together. These people wish to crush the city of Washington while it is yet in its infancy, because they know, that if the seat of government is transferred thither, the place will thrive, and enjoy a considerable portion of that trade which is centered at present in Philadelphia, Baltimore, and New York. It is idle, however, to imagine that this will injure their different towns; on the contrary, although a portion of that trade which they enjoy at present should be drawn from them, yet the increase of population in that part of the country, which they must naturally supply, will be such, that their trade on the whole will, in all probability, be found far more extensive after the federal city is established than it ever was before.

A large majority, however, of the people in the United States is desirous that the removal of the seat of government should take place; and there is little doubt that it will take place at the appointed time. The discontents indeed, which an opposite measure would give rise to in the south could not but be alarming and if they did not occasion a total separation of the southern from the northern states, yet they would certainly materially destroy that harmony which has hitherto existed between them.

"An Elegant Building"

From *Struggles Through Life, Exemplified in the Various Travels and Adventures in Europe, Asia, Africa, & America* by John Harriott.

The English adventurer and master mariner John Harriott (1745-1817) led a colorful and peripatetic life. As a youth, he served in the Royal Navy during the Seven Years War. Subsequent service with the merchant marine brought the young Harriott to the English Colonies in America in the 1760s. At twenty-three, he was awarded a military commission and joined the East India Company, but during his India service, Harriott suffered a leg wound which brought an end to his military career.

Harriott returned home to Essex, England and dabbled in various business pursuits. Through his own industry and cleverness, he reclaimed nearby Rushley Island from the sea and converted it into a sustainable farm. This enterprising effort earned Harriott a gold medal from the Society of Arts. But Harriott's success as a farmer was short-lived. Fire destroyed his farm in 1790. Shortly thereafter, Harriott sailed once again for the United States where he lived briefly with his family during the next few years. His residence in the United States did not prove fruitful, and Harriott eventually returned home again. Toward the end of the century, Harriott joined forces with London magistrate Patrick Colquhoun to found the Thames

River Police, an organization dedicated to combating crime along the city's historic river.

John Harriott was a practical man of little formal education, yet during his lifetime he was awarded patents for several maritime inventions, including improvements to capstans, fire escapes and windlasses. He also authored several books, including *Tables for the Improvement of Landed Estates*, *The Religion of Philosophy as Contradistinguished from Modern French Philosophy*, and his memoir, *Struggles Through Life*, which proved to be a popular work. In this excerpt from May, 1796, Harriott reflects upon his visit to Washington, D.C., during which he observed a city in embryo, the growing capital of a new nation of independent states whose collective future was at that time far from certain.

---

.... We stopped a few days at Baltimore to see some friends, and then set off in the mail-coach, at six in the morning, for George-town; the fare, four dollars each. The first seven miles until we came to Patapsco-ferry, was a clayey soil, over un-cultivated hills. At Elkridge,[1] the land improves all the way to Spurrier's,[2] a substantial farmer and tavern-keeper, where we had a comfortable clean breakfast for forty cents each.

Five miles further brought us to the Patuxent,[3] where, near the river side, I noticed some of the best land on this road. From Spurrier's to Bladensburg,[4] where we dined, the distance is twenty-one miles; the soil in general either a cold clay or a sand, with a few interval bottoms of tolerable land. Bladensburg is a neat town, situated at the head of the east branch of the Patowmac, four miles above ship navigation.

From Bladensburg to George-town is eight miles, where you travel most of the way through the new city. When we first entered this city we were shewn by the citizen driver, one or two of the main streets. These were long wide avenues, cut through woods and across fields, without a house to be seen; until, travelling on a few miles, we saw a few new-built brick houses, in various directions; some of them a quarter of a mile, and others half a mile distant from each other, which, with intervening woods and fields of grass or grain, had an appearance of pleasant farm houses.

Continuing thus for a mile or more we came to the capitol, an *intended* building, of which one wing only was about one third erected; promising, when the whole should be completed, to be a noble edifice. The hotel soon came in view, a handsome large house, then just covered in, built to ensure accommodations for the members of congress; the money for it was raised by public auction. Still keeping on for George-town, at the distance of a mile or more from the capitol, we passed the President's intended house; and, except half a dozen houses that were covering in, and the foundations of six more level with the ground, there really was nothing to be seen that had the smallest appearance of forming a street.

At George-town, which is close adjoining the City of Washington, we were set down at a large new inn, built on speculation, for the purpose of entertaining visiters and others coming to view the new city. We stopped here a few days before we passed the Patowmac river into Virginia, and met with more attention from the landlord of this house, than from any other during the whole journey, and he found his account in it. When will be a sufficient number of houses built to entitle it to the name of a great city. It is true, the public buildings are erecting on a grand scale, possibly too much so for so young a country. — A century hence, should the Union of the States continue so long, they might correspond; at present, they do not. It is to be remembered that these remarks were made on the spot, in 1796.

The President's house is 180 feet in front and 88 deep, built of free-stone[5] of an excellent quality. Not more than a fourth part is built, but when finished it promises to be an elegant building. The capitol, building with the same materials, is 380 feet in front, by 120 in depth; of which one wing only is just raised high enough for the first scaffolding. But few men were at work, either at the public or private buildings, and several of them told me they could get more work than money. Brick-making was the principal business going forward; and for this purpose, the whole body of earth that I examined, where they had dug for cellars, seems well adapted, and the well-water good.

If any part of the whole might be said to have the appearance of a town, or rather a village, it is at the eastern point, nearly three miles from the President's, and where Mr. Law[6] and Mr. Duncason,[7] two gentlemen of fortune, from India,[8] were the only individuals actually engaged in building private houses. The workmen told me, that these gentlemen were the only people whom they could depend on for money; one or two others that had begun, having left off. Here again, as I have before observed respecting the usual mistake of Englishmen, I fear these gentlemen will find, to their cost, that they have calculated on English ideas, unnecessarily magnified by eastern habits.

In this part of the city there are four or five groups of houses, of four or six in a group, at no great distance from each other, in different stages of finishing, with but few that are inhabited; and reckoning up all the houses I could see or hear of, as belonging to the new City of Washington, they did not amount to eighty. I was the more particular in remarking this, from the extravagant false accounts that had been sent to and published in the London papers, as before mentioned. Had they described them as house lots, it might have passed, but would not have answered their purpose, as it was these lots, to build houses on, that they wished to sell by such puffs of the rapid progress which the new city was making.

Bad as I apprehend it is, and will turn out to be, to the purchasing speculators, it has proved of great advantage to the old proprietors of the land. When congress first determined to build a Federal city, General Washington was desired to fix on the most eligible spot. He chose the present, the land of which was not then worth more than five pounds an acre, Maryland money. — Treating with the proprietors it was agreed, that all the streets, avenues, squares, grounds for public buildings and uses, should be paid for at twenty-five pounds an acre: the remainder of their respective lands to be divided into equal lots, one-half to be sold for the benefit of the public, by commissioners, the other at the disposal of the original proprietor.

On an average, an acre of ground is now estimated at £1,500 and a Mr. B[9], — whose estate of nearly 500 acres was not worth more than £3,000 more than which he was said to owe, has hereby realised a property of £80,000.

Having seen and examined everything, and gained all the information I could concerning this so-much-talked-of city, I sat down between the President's house and the capitol, and entered the following in my minute-book, as my opinion, viz.

"Should the public buildings be completed, and enterprising individuals risk considerably in building houses; should the Union of the States continue undisturbed; should congress assemble for a number of years, until the national bank and other public offices necessarily draw the monied interests to it; the City of Washington, in the course of a century, may form a focus of attraction to mercantile and trading people, sufficient to make it a beautiful commercial city, deserving the name of its founder; but I apprehend so many hazards as to be most unwilling to venture any part of my property in the undertaking."

The price of provisions at George-town is much the same as at Baltimore. The good people in this town, as well as every other sea-port I was at on the continent of North America, are remarkably fond of dress. At one chapel in George-town, I noticed, Presbyterian service performed in the morning and Episcopal in the afternoon.

On our return from a short excursion in Virginia, back through George-town and Washington-city, I was informed that congress had guaranteed a loan, to enable them to go on with the public buildings, which renovated the hopes of the speculators. But I did then, and do still, recommend emigrants and foreign speculators to be on their guard against the delusive flattering accounts that for many years will be spread abroad.

"Influx of Speculations"

From *Travels Through the United States of North America: the Country of the Iroquois, and Upper Canada, in the Years 1795, 1796, and 1797* by François Alexandre Frédéric, duc de la Rochefoucauld-Liancourt.

François Alexandre Frédéric, duc de la Rochefoucauld-Liancourt (1747-1827) is primarily known as a social reformer in his native France. A member of the French nobility, he supported the loyalists during the French Revolution. The Duke fled Paris in 1792 and spent several years in exile, first in England and then in the United States, where he travelled extensively during the latter part of the decade. Upon his return to France in 1799, the Duke published a reminiscence of his experiences in the United States and Canada. An English edition appeared in 1800.

In this excerpt from his *Travels*, the Duke comments upon the rampant land speculation taking place in the nation's capital during its early years. He identifies several of the major players in the game of boom and bust, including Robert Morris, John Nicholson and James Greenleaf, speculators who the Duke clearly realized might or might not make a fortune in the 1790s era Washington, D.C. real estate market.

In America, where, more than in any other country in the world, a desire for wealth is the prevailing passion, there are few schemes which are not made the means of extensive speculations; and that of the erecting of Federal-City presented irresistible temptations, which were not in fact neglected.

Mr. Morris[1] was among the first to perceive the probability of immense gain in speculations in that quarter; and, in conjunction with Messrs. Nicholson and Greenleaf,[2] a very short time after the adoption of the plan purchased every lot he could lay hold on, either from the commissioners[3] or individual proprietors; that is to say, every lot that either one or the other would sell at that period. Of the commissioners he bought six thousand lots at the price of eighty dollars per lot, each containing five thousand two hundred and sixty-five square feet. The conditions of his bargain with the commissioners, which was concluded in 1793, were, that fifteen hundred of the lots should be chosen by him in the north-east quarter[4] of the city and the remaining four thousand five hundred wherever Mr. Morris and his partners chose to select them; that he should erect an hundred and twenty houses of brick, and with two stories, on these lots within the space of seven years; that he should not sell any lot before the first of January 1790, nor without the like condition of building; and finally, that the payment for the lots should be completed within seven years, to commence on the 1st of May 1794; a seventh part to be paid annually — that is to say, about sixty-eight thousand dollars yearly, the purchase money for the whole being four hundred and eighty thousand dollars.

The lots purchased by Mr. Morris from individuals amounted to nearly the same number, and were bought at the same price. The periods for payment varied with the different proprietors, and are not of importance in this general history of Federal-City.

The sale made to Mr. Morris was the only one of like extent made either by the commissioners or individuals. Expecting a higher price, the commissioners waited for a time when demands for habitations would be more numerous. The private proprietors acted on the same principle, and both one and the other, in the sale made to Mr. Morris, considered it chiefly as the means of hastening the completion of the city, by the inducement he would have to sell part of his lots, and so augment the number of persons interested in the rapid progress of the undertaking. Mr. Morris, in fact, sold about a thousand of his lots within eighteen months of his purchase. The building of a house for the president, and a place for the sittings of the Congress, excited, in the purchasers of lots, the hope of a new influx of speculations. The public papers were filled with exaggerated praises of the new city; accounts of the rapidity of its progress towards completion; in a word, with all the artifices which trading people in every part of the world are accustomed to employ in the disposal of their wares, and which are perfectly known, and amply practised in this new world.

Mr. Law[5] and Mr. Dickinson;[6] two gentlemen that had lately arrived from India, and both with great wealth, General Howard, General Lee,[7] and two or three wealthy Dutch merchants, were the persons who bought the greatest number of lots of Mr. Morris; but none more than Mr. Law, who purchased four hundred and forty-five lots. The lowest they gave was two hundred and ninety-three dollars per lot — or rather five pence for each square foot, of Maryland money; for all the lots were not absolutely of the same extent. Many of the lots sold for six, eight, and ten pence per square foot; the last comers constantly paying a higher price, and the situation of the lots also making a difference in their value. Some of the more recent purchasers, in order to have one or more of the entire squares into which the whole was divided, or for other purposes of their speculations, made their purchases of the commissioners, paying at the same rate for them. The bargains were all clogged with the same conditions to build as that of Mr. Morris. The number of lots sold in this manner amounted to six hundred. Each of the purchasers chose his ground according to the opinion he had of its general advantages, and of its being in a neighbourhood that would the most readily be filled with houses. The neighbourhood of the president's house, of the *Capitol*, of George-Town,[8] the banks of the Potowmack, the Point, and the banks of the East-branch, were the places chiefly chosen by the first purchasers.

The opinion that the ground marked out for the whole city would soon be filled was so general, and the president of the United States and the commissioners were so much of the same opinion, that in their regulations they prohibited the cultivating any portion of the ground otherwise than for gardens; or to build houses with less than two stories, or even to build houses of wood.

These regulations were, however, speedily afterwards withdrawn; and the original proprietors had liberty to inclose and cultivate at their pleasure the ground they had not disposed of.

Mr. Blodget,[9] one of the most considerable and intelligent speculators of Philadelphia, having purchased a large quantity of lots, under the pretence of forwarding the building of the city, but more probably with the real motive of disposing most securely and advantageously of his acquisitions, made two lotteries for the disposal of them. The principal lot of the first was a handsome tavern built between the capitol and the President's house, valued at fifty thousand dollars; the three principal lots of the second were three houses to be erected near the capitol, of the respective value of twenty-five thousand, fifteen thousand, and ten thousand, dollars. These lotteries were made before the prohibition of the state of Maryland to make private lotteries, without the authority of the legislature. They were powerfully patronized by the commissioners, who considered them as the means of advancing the building of the city. It appears that these lotteries were attended with the effect proposed to himself by Mr. Blodget, that of gaining a large profit on the disposal of his lots, and that he was the only person not deceived in the transaction.

The speculations of Mr. Morris, and the succeeding purchasers, had not the same rapid success. After the plan of the city had been for a while admired for its beauty and magnificence, people began to perceive that it was too extensive, too gigantic, for the actual circumstances of the United States, and even for those which must follow for a series of years, admitting that no intervening accidents arrested the progress of their prosperity. It was discovered that the immense extent of ground marked out for the city would not be so speedily covered with houses as was expected; and every proprietor of lots intrigued to get the neighbourhood of his lots first inhabited. From that instant the common interest ceased, and the proprietors became rivals. Each began to build in his own quarter, with the hope of drawing thither the new-comers. Each vaunted of the advantages of that side of the city where his property lay, and depreciated others. The public papers were no longer filled with the excellencies of Federal-City, but with those of one or other of its quarters.

The commissioners were not altogether clear from this venal contest. Two of them possessed lots near George-Town; and if that had not been the case, their habits and prejudices relative to the city would have determined their opinion as to the advantage of beginning to build in one quarter or another, and would not have permitted them to remain indifferent spectators of the emulation of the several proprietors.

There were four principal quarters to which different interests had drawn the greatest number of houses. The inhabitants of George-Town, who had purchased a great many lots in their neighbourhood, maintained that a small town already built was the proper spot to begin the new city, by facilitating and augmenting its resources. They boasted of the port of George-Town, and represented the commerce already belonging to the place as a favourable opening to the general commerce of the city.

The proprietors of lots near the Point[10] declared that situation to be the most airy, healthy, and beautiful in the city; advantageous to commerce, as it lay along the banks of both rivers, and as being a central situation between the capitol and the President's house, from each of which it was equally distant.

The proprietors of the East-branch contemned the port of George-Town, and the banks of the Potowmack, which are not secure in winter from shoals of ice; they decried the Point, which, placed between the two rivers, was far from being able completely to enjoy the advantage of either; and boasted of their own port, because of its great depth, and its security from ice, and from the most prevailing winds. They vaunted of their vicinity to the capitol, which must be the common centre of affairs, it being the place of the sittings of the Congress, and in which all the members must meet, at least once in the day, and from which their distance was not more than three quarters of a mile.

The proprietors in the neighbourhood of the Capitol contended, that Federal-City was not necessarily a commercial town; that the essential point was to raise a city for the establishment of the Congress and government; that the natural progress was, first to build houses round the capitol, and then to extend them towards the President's house, which, although of a secondary consideration, was nevertheless next in importance to the capitol; and that every effort should be made, for the convenience of Congress and the facilitating of public affairs, to unite, by a continuation of streets and buildings, these two principal points of the government.

Thus each proprietor supported with his arguments the interests of the quarter where the mass of his property lay; but he built notwithstanding with great caution, and with a constant fear of some of the opposite interests prevailing.

The commissioners, to whom was entrusted the erection of public edifices, were accused by the proprietors that lay at a distance from George-Town of paying an undue attention to the completion of the President's house, which was in their neighbourhood; of designing to establish the public-offices there, and, consequently, to neglect the capital; in a word, of being partial to George-Town to the injury of the three other quarters of the town.

Each of these opinions relative to the spot at which they should begin to build the city might find advocates, even among disinterested people, regarding only the public advantage; but the public advantage was no motive of any of the rival parties.

"Obelisks in Trees"

From *Epistles, Odes, and Other Poems* by Thomas Moore.

The prolific Irish poet and balladeer Thomas Moore (1779-1852) often referred to himself as Anacreon after the Greek poet. He was fond of drinking songs and likely not one to mince words. Moore toured the United States and Canada in 1803-1804 and met President Thomas Jefferson during a visit to Washington, D.C., where he stayed in the company of Anthony Merry, then Great Britain's minister to the United States. By then, Merry had little use for America. Moore's sentiments soon followed.

In 1806, the London publisher James Carpenter produced the edition from which the following is excerpted. Moore's own footnotes are reproduced here in part with minor [additional comments].

---

*Epistle VII*
To Thomas Hume Esq. M.D.[1]
From The City Of Washington.

'Tis evening now; the heats and cares of day
In twilight dews are calmly wept away.
The lover now, beneath the western star,
Sighs through the medium of his sweet segar,
And fills the ears of some consenting she

With puffs and vows, with smoke and constancy!
The weary statesman for repose hath fled
From halls of council to his negro's shed,
Where blest he woos some black Aspasia's grace,
And dreams of freedom in his slave's embrace![2]

    In fancy now, beneath the twilight gloom,
Come, let me lead thee o'er this modern Rome,[3]
Where tribunes rule, where dusky Davi bow,
And what was Goose-Creek once is Tiber now![4] —
This fam'd metropolis, where Fancy sees
Squares in morasses, obelisks in trees;
Which travelling fools and gazetteers adorn
With shrines unbuilt and heroes yet unborn.
Though nought but wood[5] and ********* they see,
Where streets should run and sages *ought* to be!

    And look, how soft in yonder radiant wave,
The dying sun prepares his golden grave! —
Oh great Potowmac! oh yon banks of shade!
Yon mighty scenes, in nature's morning made,
While still, in rich magnificence of prime,
She pour'd her wonders, lavishly sublime,
Nor yet had learn'd to stoop, with humbler care,
From grand to soft, from wonderful to fair!

    Say, were your towering hills, your boundless floods,
Your rich savannas and majestic woods,
Where bards should meditate and heroes rove,
And woman charm and man deserve her love!
Oh! was a world so bright but born to grace
Its own half-organiz'd, half-minded race[6]
Of weak barbarians, swarming o'er its breast,
Like vermin, gender'd on the lion's crest?
Were none but brutes to call that soil their home,
Where none but demi-gods should dare to roam?

Or worse, thou mighty world! oh! doubly worse,
Did heaven design thy lordly land to nurse
The motley dregs of every distant clime,
Each blast of anarchy and taint of crime,
Which Europe shakes from her perturbed sphere,
In full malignity to rankle here?

But, hush! — observe that little mount of pines,
Where the breeze murmurs and the fire-fly shines,
There let thy fancy raise, in bold relief,
The sculptur'd image of that veteran chief,[7]
Who lost the rebel's in the hero's name,
And stept o'er prostrate loyalty to fame;
Beneath whose sword Columbia's patriot train
Cast off their monarch, that their mob might reign!

How shall we rank thee upon glory's page?
Thou more than soldier and just less than sage!
Too form'd for peace to act a conqueror's part,
Too train'd in camps to learn a statesman's art,
Nature design'd thee for a hero's mould,
But, ere she cast thee, let the stuff grow cold!

While warmer souls command, nay make their fate,
Thy fate made thee and forc'd thee to be great.
Yet Fortune, who so oft, so blindly sheds
Her brightest halo round the weakest heads,
Found *thee* undazzled, tranquil as before.
Proud to be useful, scorning to be more;
Less prompt at glory's than at duty's claim,
Renown the meed, but self-applause the aim;
All thou hast been reflects less fame on thee,
Far less than all thou hast forborn to be!

Now turn thee, Hume, where faint the moon-light falls
On yonder dome — and in those princely halls.

If thou canst hate, as oh ! that soul must hate,
Which loves the virtuous and reveres the great,
If thou canst loath and execrate with me
That Gallic garbage of philosophy,
That nauseous slaver of these frantic times,
With which false liberty dilutes her crimes!
If thou hast got, within thy free-born breast,
One pulse, that beats more proudly than the rest,
With honest scorn for that inglorious soul,
Which creeps and winds beneath a mob's controul,
Which courts the rabble's smile, the rabble's nod,
And makes, like Egypt, every beast its god!
There, in those walls — but, burning tongue, forbear!
Rank must be reverenc'd, even the rank that's there:
So here I pause — and now, my Hume! we part;
But oh! full oft, in magic dreams of heart.
Thus let us meet, and mingle converse dear
By Thames at home, or by Potowmac here!
O'er lake and marsh, through fevers and through fogs,
Midst bears and yankees, democrats and frogs.
Thy foot shall follow me, thy heart and eyes
With me shall wonder, and with me despise!
While I, as oft, in witching thought shall rove
To thee, to friendship, and that land I love,
Where, like the air that fans her fields of green,
Her freedom spreads, unfever'd and serene;
Where sovereign man can condescend to see
The throne and laws more sovereign still than he!
Once more, adieu! — my weary eye-lid winks,
The moon grows clouded and my taper sinks.

———

"A Place of Commerce"

From *The Stranger in America: Containing Observations Made During a Long Residence in that Country, on the Genius, Manners and Customs of the People of the United States* by Charles William Janson.

Curiously little is known about Englishman Charles William Janson, who by his own account came to the United States intrigued by the possibilities presented in the new country and intent on a lengthy stay. Janson spent some thirteen years in the United States, roughly 1793-1806, but left the country discouraged, having suffered numerous disappointments, including financial losses from various business pursuits and in land speculation, and, one imagines, at horse racing.

In the Preface to his book, *The Stranger in America*, Janson suggests that Americans are prejudiced toward the English and possess a basic incompatibility with them. The United States, he writes, is "in every respect uncongenial to English habits, and to the tone of an Englishman's constitution." Honing his criticism, Janson states that the Americans "make a point of denying every truth that in any way tends to expose a defective habit, or a national error."

In an unsigned article appearing in *The Critical Review*, one of Janson's countrymen suggested that perhaps the author protests too much in his descriptions of America. "The manners of the Anglo-Americans appear to have been little suited to the taste of our author, who in vain expected that deference and civility to which he had been accustomed in his intercourse with his inferiors in wealth in the ancient world." The reviewer observes that Janson "grumbles throughout... and loses no opportunity of saying ill both of the citizens, the government and the country of America." As the expression goes, there it is.

---

To return to the city of Washington — I have remarked, that on my return to London, the first general enquiry of my friends is respecting this far-famed place. The description given of it by interested scribblers, may well serve to raise an Englishman's curiosity, and lead him to fancy the capital of Columbia a terrestrial paradise.

The entrance, or avenues, as they are pompously called, which lead to the American seat of government, are the worst roads I passed in the country; and I appeal to every citizen who has been unlucky enough to travel the stages north and south leading to the city, for the truth of the assertion. I particularly allude to the mail stage road from Bladensburg[1] to Washington, and from thence to Alexandria[2]. In the winter season, during the sitting of Congress, every turn of your waggon [sic] wheel (for I must again observe, that there is no such thing in the country as what we call a stage coach, or a post-chaise), is for many miles attended with danger. The roads are never repaired; deep ruts, rocks, and stumps of trees, every minute impede your progress, and often threaten your limbs with dislocation.

Arrived at the city, you are struck with its grotesque appearance. In one view from the capitol hill, the eye fixes upon a row of uniform houses, ten or twelve in number, while it faintly discovers the adjacent tenements to be miserable wooden structures, consisting, when you approach them, of two or three rooms one above another.

Again, you see the hotel,[3] which was vauntingly promised, on laying the foundation, to rival the large inns in England. This, like every other private adventure, failed: the walls and the roof remain, but not a window! and, instead of accommodating the members of Congress, and travellers of distinction, as proposed, a number of the lowest order of Irish have long held the title of *naked possession*, from which, were it ever to become an object, it would be difficult to eject them. Turning the eye, a well finished edifice presents itself, surrounded by lofty trees, which never felt the stroke of the axe. The president's house, the offices of state, and a little theatre, where an itinerant company repeated, during a part of the last year, the lines of Shakespeare, Otway, and Dryden, to empty benches, terminate the view of the Pennsylvania, or Grand Avenue.

Speculation, the life of the American, embraced the design of the new city. Several companies of speculators purchased lots, and began to build handsome streets, with an ardor that soon promised a large and populous city. Before they arrived at the attic story, the failure was manifest; and in that state at this moment are the walls of many scores of houses begun on a plan of elegance. In some parts, purchasers have cleared the wood from their grounds, and erected temporary wooden buildings: others have fenced in their lots, and attempted to cultivate them; but the sterility of the land laid out for the city is such, that this plan has also failed. The country adjoining consists of woods in a state of nature, and in some places of mere swamps, which give the scene a curious patch-work appearance. The view of the noble river Potomack, which the eye can trace till it terminates at Alexandria, is very fine. The navigation of the river is good from the bay of Chesapeak, till the near approach to the city, where bars of sand are formed, which every year encroach considerably on the channel. The frigate which brought the Tunisian embassy, grounded on one of these shoals, and the barbarians were obliged to be landed in boats. This is another great disadvantage to the growth of the city. It never can become a place of commerce, while Baltimore lies on one side, and Alexandria on the other; even admitting the navigation to be equally good — nor can the wild and uneven spot laid out into streets be cleared and levelled for building upon, for many years, even with the most indefatigable exertions.

The Capitol, of which two wings arc now finished, is of hewn stone, and will be a superb edifice, worthy of its name. The architect who built the first wing, left the country soon after its completion; the corresponding part was carried on under the direction of Mr. Latrobe, an Englishman; from whose taste and judgment much may be expected in finishing the centre of the building; the design of which, as shown to me by Doctor Thornton, is truly elegant.

The president's house... is situated one mile from the Capitol, at the extremity of Pennsylvania Avenue. The contemplated streets of this embryo city are called avenues, and every state gives name to one. That of Pennsylvania is the largest; in fact I never heard of more than that and the New Jersey Avenue, except some houses uniformly built, in one of which lives Mr. Jefferson's printer, John Harrison Smith, a few more of interior note, with some public-houses, and here and there a little *grog-shop*, this boasted avenue is as much a wilderness as Kentucky, with this disadvantage, that the soil is good for nothing. Some half-starved cattle browzing [*sic*] among the bushes, present a melancholy spectacle to a stranger, whose expectation has been wound up by the illusive description of speculative writers. So very thinly is the city peopled, and so little is it frequented, that quails and other birds are constantly shot within a hundred yards of the Capitol, and even during the sitting of the houses of congress.

Ten years ago Mr. Weld[4], speaking of the president's house, tells us of its being then erected; and of an hundred acres of land left for pleasure-ground, and a park or mall, to run in an easterly direction towards the Capitol — that the buildings on either side of this mall, were all to be elegant of their kind, and that among the number it was *proposed* to have houses built at the public expence for the accommodation of public ministers. This traveller then proceeds with informing us that other parts of this city are appointed for churches, theatres, colleges, &c. In nearly the same state as Mr. Weld saw the city so long ago, it still remains, except indeed that some of the few houses which were then building, are now falling to ruin, the unfortunate owner having been ruined before he could get them roofed.

Neither park, nor mall, neither churches, theatres, nor colleges, could I discover so lately as the summer of 1806. A small place has indeed been erected since Mr. Weld[5] visited Washington, in the Pennsylvania Avenue, called a theatre, in which Mr. Green[6] and the Virginia company of comedians were nearly starved the only season it was occupied, and were obliged to go off to Richmond during the very height of the sitting of congress. Public offices on each side of the president's house, uniformly built of brick, may also, perhaps, have been built subsequent to that period. That great man who planned the city, and after whom it is named, certainly entertained the hopes that it would at some future period equal ancient Rome in splendor and magnificence. Among the regulations for building were these — that the houses should be of brick or stone — the walls to be at least thirty feet high, and to he built parallel to the line of the street.

The president's house is certainly a neat but plain piece of architecture, built of hewn stone, said to be of a better quality than Portland stone[7], as it will cut like marble, and resist the change of the seasons in a superior degree. Only part of it is furnished; the whole salary of the president would be inadequate to the expence of completing it in a style of suitable elegance. Rooms are fitted up for himself, an audience chamber, and apartments for Mr. Thomas Man [*sic*] Randolph,[8] and Mr. Epps,[9] and their respective families, who married two of his daughters, and are members of the house of representatives.

The ground around it, instead of being laid out in a suitable style, remains in its ancient rude state, so that, in a dark night, instead of finding your way to the house, you may, perchance, fall into a pit, or stumble over a heap of rubbish. The fence round the house is of the meanest sort; a common post and rail enclosure. This parsimony destroys every sentiment of pleasure that arises in the mind, in viewing the residence of the president of a nation, and is a disgrace to the country.

Though the permanent seat of government has been fixed at Washington, its progress has been proved to be less rapid than any other new settlement supported only by trade. The stimulus held out by the presence of congress has proved artificial and unnatural. After enumerating the public buildings, the private dwelling-houses of the officers of government, the accommodations set apart for the members of the legislature, and the temporary tenements of those dependent on them, the remainder of this boasted city is a mere wilderness of wood and stunted shrubs, the occupants of barren land. Strangers after viewing the offices of state, are apt to enquire for the city, while they are in its very centre.

"The golden dreams of the speculator," says an American writer in describing the city of Washington, "ended in disappointment. His houses are untenanted, and going to ruin, and his land either lies a dead burthen on his hands, or he disposes of it, if not at a less price than his fond imagination had anticipated. The present proprietor is obliged to moderate his views of profit, and to centre all his hopes in the continuance of the government where it now is."

Another writer in Philadelphia says, "The increase of Washington is attributed by sensible Americans to its true cause, SPECULATION; a field for which being once opened to the land-jobbers, who swarm in the United States, they made large purchases, and bent all their resources towards running up buildings, and giving the city an eccentric appearance of prosperity. So industriously have those purchases been pursued, that in London five hundred pounds sterling was at one time asked for about the sixth part of a single lot, many of the prime of which, in point of situation, were originally purchased for twenty, and at three years credit. If this sudden increase had arisen from actual settlement alone, a more undeniable proof would be given of the prosperity of Washington, than by the magic appearance of uninhabited structures like mushrooms after a shower."

It has been asserted that a seventy-four gun ship was building on the waters of the Potomack, from which circumstance no doubt was entertained of its channel being deep enough for ships of any burthen. This like most travellers' exaggerations, is not true — no ship of the line, nor even a frigate, was ever constructed on the Potomack. The ship carpenters employed by government have enough to do to repair those already built, most of which are in a state of decay. I saw the plank and some of the timbers of the frigate called the United States, built at Philadelphia not twelve years ago, so rotten, that they crumbled to powder on being handled. The timber of America is not so durable as that of Europe.

The only part of this city which continues to encrease [*sic*] is the navy-yard, but this circumstance is entirely owing to the few ships of war which the Americans have in commission, being ordered there to be fitted out and paid off. Tippling shops, and houses of rendezvous for sailors and their doxies, with a number of the lowest order of traders, constitute what is called the navy-yard.

Among the sufferers by the Washington speculation is Mr. Thomas Law[10], brother to Lord Ellenborough, who, as has been already observed, invested the greatest part of the money he obtained in India, in building near the capitol, where he still resides, under the mortifying circumstance of daily witnessing whole rows of the shells of his houses gradually falling to pieces.

In November, in each year, there are horse-races in the capital of America. I happened to arrive just at this time on horseback at George Town, which is about two miles from the race-ground. After an early dinner, served up sooner on the occasion, a great bustle was created by the preparations for the sport. It had been my intention to pass the remainder of the day at the far-famed city, but, stimulated by curiosity I determined to mingle with the sporting group. Having paid for my dinner, and the refreshment for my horse, I proceeded to the stable. I had delivered my beast to a yellow fellow, M'Laughlin, the landlord's head ostler[11]. This name reminds me of an anecdote of Macklin, the English theatrical Nestor. It is said that his proper name was M'Laughlin, but dissatisfied with the harsh pronunciation, he sunk the uncouth letters, and called himself Macklin. Be that as it may, I went for my horse, to attend the race, and repeatedly urged my dingy ostler to bring him out. I waited long with great patience at the stable-door, and saw him lead out a number without discovering mine. I again remonstrated, and soon heard a message delivered to him to saddle the horses of Mr. A. Mr. B. Mr. C. and so on. He now appeared with the horses according to the recent order, leading them by their bridles. Previous to this, I had saddled my own horse, seeing the hurry of the time, yet I thought it a compliment due to me that the servant should lead him to me. I now spoke in a more angry tone, conceiving myself insulted by neglect.

The Indian sourly replied, "I must wait upon the gentlemen," (that is the sporting sharpers). "Then," quoth I, "a gentleman neglected in his proper turn, I find, must wait upon you." I was provoked to knock the varlet to the ground. The horses which he led, startled at the sudden impulse, ran off, and before the ostler recovered from the effects of the blow, or the horses were caught, I led out my nag, and leisurely proceeded to the turf.

Here I witnessed a scene perfectly novel. I have been at the races of Newmarket, Epsom, York, in short I have seen, for aught I know to the contrary, one hundred thousand pounds won and lost in a single day, in England. On coming up to an enclosed ground, a quarter of a dollar was demanded for my admission. Rather than turn back, though no sportsman, I submitted. Four-wheeled carriages paid a dollar, and half that sum was exacted for the most miserable single-horse chaise. Though the day was raw, cold, and threatening to rain or snow, there were abundance of ladies, decorated as if for a ball. In this year (1803) congress was summoned very early by President Jefferson, upon the contemplated purchase of Louisiana, and to pass a bill in order to facilitate his election again, as president. Many scores of American legislators, who are all allowed six dollars a day, besides their travelling expences, went on *foot* from the Capitol, above four English miles; to attend the sport. Nay, it is an indisputable fact, that the houses of congress adjourned at a very early hour to indulge the members for this purpose. It rained during the course, and thus the law-makers of the country were driven into the booths, and thereby compelled to eat and pay for what was there called a dinner; while their contemplated meal remained untouched at their respective boarding-houses. Economy is the order of the day, in the Jeffersonian administration of that country, and the members pretend to avail themselves of it, even in their personal expences.

I saw on the race-ground, as in other countries, people of every description, sharpers in abundance, and *grog*, the joy of Americans, in oceans. Well mounted, and a stranger, I was constantly pestered by these sharks; and had I been idiot enough to have committed myself to them, I should soon have been stripped of all my travelling cash.

"Drain the Swamp"

From *Travels in the United States of America, in the Years 1806 & 1807, and 1809, 1810, & 1811* by John Melish.

Scottish geographer and mapmaker John Melish (1771-1822) was apprenticed as a youth to a textile manufacturer in his native Glasgow. After distinguishing himself at the University of Glasgow, his subsequent career in the textile business brought him to the United States, where he traveled extensively along the east coast and throughout the western territories. Melish eventually chose to emigrate with his family from Scotland to America. He initially considered agricultural pursuits but chose instead to settle in Philadelphia and launch what became a highly successful business as a mapmaker.

Among his publications, often accompanied by detailed maps, were *Travels in the United States of America* (1812), *A Military and Topographical Atlas of the United States* (1813), and *The Travellers' Directory through the United States* (1815), the latter being one of the first American travel guides. Though his career as a mapmaker was relatively brief, he is considered by the late cartographic historian Walter Ristow to be "one of the founders of American commercial map publishing."

In the following selection from his *Travels*, Melish recounts a meeting at the White House with President Thomas Jefferson and their conversations on a variety of subjects, including manufactures, ports, roads, and the scourge of yellow fever.

---

Washington, October 5 [1806]. In pursuance of the recommendation of my friends, I set out, this morning, at 8 o'clock, for the purpose of waiting on Mr. Jefferson. On my arrival at the president's house, I delivered my address to a servant, who in a few minutes returned with an answer, that Mr. Jefferson would be with me presently, and showed me into an elegant apartment. Mr. Jefferson soon entered by an inner door, and requesting me to be seated, sat down himself; and immediately, and very frankly, entered into conversation, by asking where I had landed, and how long I had been in the country. Having informed him, he remarked that I would probably be travelling to the northward; I replied that I had been to the north, and was now travelling to the southward. "And how do you like New York?" "Very much," said I; "it is one of the finest sea-ports I have seen, and, I presume, will always continue to be the first commercial city in the United States." He observed that he found that idea generally entertained by strangers; that New York was a very fine situation, and would unquestionably continue always to be a great commercial city; but it appeared to him that *Norfolk* would probably, in process of time, be the greatest sea-port in the United States, New Orleans perhaps excepted. He pointed out the circumstance of the vast confluence of waters, that constituted the outlet of the Chesapeake bay, on which Norfolk is situated, and remarked that these rivers were as yet but partially settled; but they were rapidly settling up, and, when the population was full, the quantity of surplus produce would be immense, and Norfolk would probably become the greatest depot in the United States, except New Orleans.

The conversation next turned upon the climate and season; on which the president remarked, that the country had this summer been remarkably healthy; that no case of epidemical sickness had come to his knowledge, some few of *bilious fever* and *fever and ague* excepted, at the foot of the mountains on James river, not far from where he lived; and which country was never known to experience any cases of the kind before. As this appeared singular, I inquired whether there was any way of accounting for it. He replied, that the way he accounted for it was this: "In ordinary seasons, there is a sufficiency of water to keep the rivers in a state of circulation, and no more; but this season there has been a long and very severe drought, which, in many places, has dried them up. The water has stagnated in pools, and sends out a putrid effluvia to some distance; which, being lighter than the atmosphere, ascends even some little way up the mountains, and reaches the abodes of those who thought themselves heretofore free from attack."

I was struck with the force of this remark, and applied it to a circumstance that had come under my observation at Washington. The Capitol Hill is elevated above the river upwards of 70 feet. Between this and the river there is a low meadow, about a mile broad, abounding with swamps and small shrubbery. In the autumn these swamps send out an effluvia, which often affects the health of those who live on the hill. I noticed this circumstance and the president remarked that it was a case exactly in point. He said he had frequently observed from his windows, in the morning, the vapour to rise, and it seemed to have sufficient buoyancy to carry it to the top of the hill, and no further; there it settled, and the inhabitants, coming out of their warm rooms, breathed this cold contaminated vapour, which brought on agues and other complaints. He said he had frequently pointed out this to the people, and urged them to drain the swamp, but it was still neglected, although they had, besides suffering in their health, probably expended more in doctor's bills than it would have cost. "But, indeed," he continued, "mankind are exceedingly slow in adopting resolutions to prevent disease, and it is very difficult to convince them where they originate; particularly when the reasoning applied is the result of philosophical deduction."

The transition from this subject to that of the yellow fever was natural, and I introduced it by noticing Paine's essay[1] on the subject. The president observed that it was one of the most sensible performances on that disease that had come under his observation. The remarks were quite philosophical, and, not being calculated to excite any party-feeling, they might have a very useful tendency.

…. He then made a few remarks on the nature of the yellow fever itself. He observed that it evidently arose from breathing impure air, and impure air may be either generated in the country or imported. A case had come under his observation where it was imported. A vessel arrived at Norfolk, and the air in her hold was so pestilential, that every person who went into it was affected, and some of them died; but, on the discovery being made, the vessel was purified, and the fever did not spread. This was a local circumstance, he observed, and there may be many others, which are pernicious as far as they go, and care should be taken to prevent them. But a ship can never import a sufficient quantity of impure air to pollute a whole city, if that city be otherwise healthy, and, therefore, the origin of the yellow fever, *on an extended scale*, must be sought for in an impure air, generated from filth collected in and about great cities; and it was very expedient that this view of the subject should be enforced, in order to induce mankind to attend to one of the most important concerns in life — cleanliness.

I took notice of the bad state of the road between Baltimore and Washington, and expressed my surprise that it should remain in this state, so near the capital of the United States. The president observed, that the removal of the seat of government[2] was a recent measure, and the country was so extensive, that it would necessarily be a considerable time before good roads could be made in all directions, but as it was a most important subject, it would be attended to as fast as circumstances would permit; and the road to Baltimore, being the great thoroughfare to the northern states, would probably be one of the first that would undergo a thorough repair. He then informed me, that both this subject and that of internal navigation by canals, were under consideration at the present time, upon a very extended scale, and probably a report would soon be published relative to them; and he had little doubt, but that in less than 20 years, turnpike roads would be general throughout the country; and a chain of canals would probably be cut, which would complete an inland navigation from Massachusetts to Georgia; and another to connect the eastern with the western waters.

I remarked that these would be most important improvements, and would greatly facilitate internal intercourse; and as to manufactures, I presumed it would long continue to be the policy of the country to import them. He replied, that this, like other branches, would of course find its level, and would depend upon the genius of the people; but it was astonishing, the progress that had been made in manufactures of late years. It would hardly be believed, he said, by strangers, but he had it on the best authority, that the manufactures of Philadelphia were greater in value annually, than were those of Birmingham 20 years ago; and he had no doubt but that manufactures, of articles of the first necessity, would increase until they became quite general through the country.

As the non-importation act[3] was then in dependence, I was naturally anxious to ascertain, whether matters were likely to be adjusted with Britain, and, as modestly as possible, endeavoured to turn the conversation that way. I was urged to this by two considerations. I was not sure but that part of our fall importation would come under the operation of the non-importation act, if it took place; and being fully satisfied of the friendly disposition of the whig party in Britain towards America, I would gladly have availed myself of an opportunity of expressing that opinion to the president. But on this subject Mr. Jefferson was, of course, reserved; though, from the few observations he made, I concluded that matters would ultimately be amicably adjusted. I was highly gratified by the expression of his opinion, on the character of my great favourite statesman Mr. Fox.[4] Accounts had that morning reached Washington that Mr. Fox was in the last stage of his illness. — I noticed the circumstance. "Poor man," said Mr. Jefferson, "I fear by this time he is no more, and his loss will be severely felt by his country — he is a man of the most liberal and enlightened policy — a friend to his country, and to the human race."

A gentleman then called upon him, I believe general Eaton,[5] and I took my leave, highly pleased with the affability, intelligence, and good sense, of the President of America.

"Spoil of the Conqueror"

From *A Narrative of the Campaigns of the British Army at Washington and New Orleans, Under Generals Ross, Pakenham, and Lambert, in the Years 1814 and 1815* by George Robert Gleig.

George Robert Gleig (1796-1888) was a Scot and a bishop's son who was ostensibly following in his father's footsteps until his studies at Oxford were interrupted by a period of military service. As a young soldier in the British Army, Gleig participated in several battles on American soil during the War of 1812, including the Battle of Bladensburg in the Maryland suburbs of Washington, D.C. This action is also known as the Bladensburg Races, a pejorative phrase coined at the Americans' expense which describes their hasty retreat in the face of advancing British troops.

    Although Gleig accompanied the army in late August, 1814 as it set its sights on Washington, D.C., his participation in the burning of Washington, D.C. was by his account more as an observer, and he confesses that his recounting of a certain episode in the culinary history of the White House is a second-hand retelling. Nevertheless, George Robert Gleig's *Narrative* demonstrates the author's flair for rousing detail, a talent he would continue to demonstrate in numerous biographies and military histories during a prolific writing career.

....The hour of noon was approaching, when a heavy cloud of dust, apparently not more than two or three miles distant, attracted our attention. From whence it originated there was little difficulty in guessing, nor did many minutes expire before surmise was changed into certainty; for on turning a sudden angle in the road, and passing a small plantation, which obstructed the vision towards the left, the British and American armies became visible to one another. The position occupied by the latter was one of great strength, and commanding attitude. They were drawn up in three lines upon the brow of a hill, having their front and left flank covered by a branch of the Potomac, and their right resting upon a thick wood and a deep ravine. This river, which may be about the breadth of the Isis at Oxford, flowed between the heights occupied by the American forces, and the little town of Bladensburg. — Across it was thrown a narrow bridge, extending from the chief street in that town to the continuation of the road, which passed through the very centre of their position; and its right bank (the bank above which they were drawn up) was covered with a narrow stripe of willows and larch trees, whilst the left was altogether bare, low, and exposed. Such was the general aspect of their position as at the first glance it presented itself; of which I must endeavour to give a more detailed account, that my description of the battle may be in some degree intelligible.

I have said that the right bank of the Potomac was covered with a narrow stripe of willow and larch trees. Here the Americans had stationed strong bodies of riflemen, who, in skirmishing order, covered the whole front of their army. Behind this narrow plantation, again, the fields were open and clear, intersected, at certain distances, by rows of high and strong palings. About the middle of the ascent, and in the rear of one of these rows, stood the first line, composed entirely of infantry; at a proper interval from this, and in a similar situation, stood the second line; while the third, or reserve, was posted within the skirts of a wood, which crowned the heights. The artillery, again, of which they had twenty pieces in the field, was thus arranged: on the high road, and commanding the bridge, stood two heavy guns; and four more, two on each side of the road, swept partly in the same direction, and partly down the whole of the slope into the streets of Bladensburg. The rest were scattered, with no great judgment, along the second line of infantry, occupying different spaces between the right of one regiment, and the left of another; while the cavalry showed itself in one mass, within a stubble field, near the extreme left of the position. Such was the nature of the ground which they occupied, and the formidable posture in which they waited our approach; amounting, by their own account, to nine thousand men, a number exactly doubling that of the force which was to attack them.

In the meantime, our column continued to advance in the same order which it had hitherto pre served. The road conducted us for about two miles in a direction parallel with the river, and of consequence with the enemy's line; when it suddenly turned, and led directly towards the town of Bladensburg. Being of course ignorant whether this town might not be filled with American troops, the main body paused here, till the advanced guard should reconnoitre. The result proved that no opposition was intended in that quarter, and that the whole of the enemy's army had been withdrawn to the opposite side of the stream, whereupon the army was again put in motion, and in a short time arrived in the streets of Bladensburg, and within range of the American artillery. Immediately on our reaching this point, several of their guns opened upon us, and kept up a quick and well directed cannonade, from which, as we were again commanded to halt, the men were directed to shelter themselves as much as possible behind the houses. The object of this halt, it was conjectured, was to give the General an opportunity of examining the American line, and of trying the depth of the river; because at present there appeared to be but one practicable mode of attack, by crossing the bridge, and taking the enemy directly in front. To do so, however, exposed as the bridge was, must be attended with bloody consequences, nor could the delay of a few minutes produce any mischief which the discovery of a ford would not amply compensate.

But in this conjecture we were altogether mistaken; for without allowing time to the column to close its ranks or to be formed by some of the many stragglers, who were now hurrying, as fast as weariness would permit, to regain their places, the order to halt was countermanded, and the word given to attack; and we immediately pushed on at double quick time, towards the head of the bridge. While we were moving along the street, a continued fire was kept up, with some execution, from those guns which stood to the left of the road; but it was not till the bridge was covered with our people that the two-gun battery upon the road itself began to play. Then, indeed, it also opened, and with tremendous effect; for at the first discharge almost an entire company was swept down; but whether it was that the guns had been previously laid with measured exactness, or that the nerves of the gunners became afterwards unsteady, the succeeding discharges were much less fatal. The riflemen likewise now galled us from the wooded bank, with a running fire of musketry; and it was not without trampling upon many of their dead and dying comrades, that the fight brigade established itself on the opposite side of the stream.

When once there, however, everything else appeared easy. Wheeling off to the right and left of the road, they dashed into the thicket, and quickly cleared it of the American skirmishers; who falling back with precipitation upon the first line, threw it into disorder before it had fired a shot. The consequence was, that our troops had scarcely shown themselves when the whole of that line gave way, and fled in the greatest confusion, leaving the two guns upon the road in possession of the victors.

But here it must be confessed that the light brigade was guilty of imprudence. Instead of pausing till the rest of the army came up, they lightened themselves by throwing away their knapsacks and haversacks; and extending their ranks so as to show an equal front with the enemy, pushed on to the attack of the second line. The Americans, however, saw their weakness, and stood firm, and having the whole of their artillery, with the exception of those captured on the road, and the greater part of their infantry in this line, they first checked the ardour of the assailants by a heavy fire, and then, in their turn, advanced to recover the ground which was lost. Against this charge, the extended order of the British troops would not permit them to offer an effectual resistance, and they were accordingly borne back to the very thicket upon the river's brink; where they maintained themselves with determined obstinacy, repelling all attempts to drive them through it; and frequently following, to within a short distance of the cannon's mouth, such parts of the enemy's line as gave way.

In this state the action continued till the second brigade had likewise crossed, and formed upon the right bank of the river; when the 44th Regiment moving to the right, and driving in the skirmishers, debouched upon the left flank of the Americans, and completely turned it. In that quarter, therefore, the battle was won; because the raw militia-men, who were stationed there as being the least assailable point, when once broken could not be rallied. But on their right, the enemy still kept their ground with much resolution; nor was it till the arrival of the 4th Regiment, and the advance of the British forces in firm array, to the charge, that they began to waver. Then, indeed, seeing their left in full flight, and the 44th getting in their rear, they lost all order, and dispersed, leaving clouds of riflemen to cover their retreat; and hastened to conceal themselves in the woods, where it would have been vain to follow them. The rout was now general throughout the whole line. The reserve, which ought to have supported the main body, fled as soon as those in its front began to give way; and the cavalry, instead of charging the British troops, now scattered in pursuit, turned their horses' heads and galloped off, leaving them in undisputed possession of the field, and of ten out of the twenty pieces of artillery.

This battle, by which the fate of the American capital was decided, began about one o'clock in the afternoon, and lasted till four. The loss on the part of the English was severe, since, out of two-thirds of the army, which were engaged, up wards of five hundred men were killed and wounded; and what rendered it doubly severe was, that among these were numbered several officers of rank and distinction. Colonel Thornton who commanded the light brigade; Lieutenant Colonel Wood commanding the 85th Regiment, and Major Brown who had led the advanced guard, were all severely wounded; and General Ross himself had a horse shot under him. On the side of the Americans the slaughter was not so great. Being in possession of a strong position, they were of course less exposed in defending, than the others in storming it; and had they conducted themselves with coolness, and resolution, it is not conceivable how the day could have been won. But the fact is, that, with the exception of a party of sailors from the gun boats, under the command of Commodore Barney, no troops could behave worse than they did. The skirmishers were driven in as soon as attacked, the first line gave way without offering the slightest resistance, and the left of the main body was broken within half an hour after it was seriously engaged. Of the sailors, however, it would be injustice not to speak in the terms which their conduct merits. They were employed as gunners, and not only did they serve their guns with a quickness and precision which astonished their assailants, but they stood till some of them were actually bayonetted, with fuses in their hands; nor was it till their leader was wounded and taken, and they saw themselves deserted on all sides by the soldiers, that they quitted the field. With respect to the British army, again, no line of distinction can be drawn. All did their duty, and none more gallantly than the rest; and though the brunt of the affair fell upon the light brigade, this was owing chiefly to the circumstance of its being at the head of the column, and perhaps, also, in some degree, to its own rash impetuosity. The artillery, indeed, could do little; being unable to show itself in presence of a force so superior; but the six-pounder was nevertheless brought into action, and a corps of rockets proved of striking utility.

Our troops being worn down from fatigue, and of course as ignorant of the country, as the Americans were the reverse, the pursuit could not be continued to any distance. Neither was it at tended with much slaughter. Diving into the recesses of the forests, and covering themselves with riflemen, the enemy was quickly beyond our reach; and having no cavalry to scour even the high road, ten of the lightest of their guns were carried off in the flight. The defeat, however, was absolute, and the army, which had been collected for the defence of Washington, was scattered beyond the possibility of, at least, an immediate reunion; and as the distance from Bladensburg to that city does not exceed four miles, there appeared to be no farther obstacle in the way, to prevent its immediate capture.

....An opportunity so favourable was not endangered by any needless delay. While the two brigades which had been engaged, remained upon the field to recover their order, the third, which had formed the reserve, and was consequently unbroken, took the lead, and pushed forward at a rapid rate towards Washington.

As it was not the intention of the British government to attempt permanent conquests in this part of America; and as the General[1] was well aware that, with a handful of men, he could not pretend to establish himself, for any length of time, in an enemy's capital, he determined to lay it under contribution, and to return quietly to the shipping. Nor was there anything unworthy of the character of a British officer, in this determination. By all the customs of war, whatever public property may chance to be in a captured town, becomes, confessedly, the just spoil of the conqueror; and in thus proposing to accept a certain sum of money in lieu of that property, he was showing mercy, rather than severity, to the vanquished. It is true, that if they chose to reject his terms, he and his army would be deprived of their booty, because, without some more convenient mode of transporting it than we possessed, even the portable part of the property itself could not be removed. But, on the other hand, there was no difficulty in destroying it; and thus, though we should gain nothing, the American government would lose probably to a much greater amount than if they had agreed to purchase its preservation by the money demanded.

Such being the intention of General Ross, he did not march the troops immediately into the city, but halted them upon a plain in its immediate vicinity, whilst a flag of truce was sent in with terms. But whatever his proposal might have been, it was not so much as heard; for scarcely had the party bearing the flag entered the street, than they were fired upon from the windows of one of the houses, and the horse of the General himself, who accompanied them, killed. You will easily believe, that conduct so unjustifiable, so direct a breach of the law of nations, roused the indignation of every individual, from the General himself down to the private soldier. All thoughts of accommodation were instantly laid aside; the troops advanced forthwith into the town, and having first put to the sword all who were found in the house from which the shots were fired, and reduced it to ashes, they proceeded, without a moment's delay, to burn and destroy everything in the most distant degree connected with Government. In this general devastation were included the Senate-house,[2] the President's palace, an extensive dock-yard and arsenal, barracks for two or three thousand men, several large store-houses filled with naval and military stores, some hundreds of cannon of different descriptions, and nearly twenty thousand stand of small arms. There were also two or three public rope-works which shared the same fate, a fine frigate pierced for sixty guns, and just ready to be launched, several gun-brigs and armed schooners, with a variety of gun-boats and small craft. The powder magazines were of course set on fire, and exploded with a tremendous crash, throwing down many houses in their vicinity, partly by pieces of the walls striking them, and partly by the concussion of the air; whilst quantities of shot, shell, and hand-grenades, which could not otherwise be rendered useless, were thrown into the river. In destroying the cannon, a method was adopted which I had never before witnessed, and which, as it was both effectual and expeditious, I cannot avoid relating. One gun of rather a small calibre, was pitched upon as the executioner of the rest; and being loaded with ball, and turned to the muzzles of the others, it was fired, and thus beat out their breechings. Many, however, not being mounted, could not be thus dealt with; these were spiked, and having their trunions knocked off, were afterwards cast into the bed of the river.

All this was as it should be, and had the arm of vengeance been extended no farther, there would not have been room given for so much as a whisper of disapprobation. But, unfortunately, it did not stop here; a noble library, several printing-offices, and all the national archives were likewise committed to the flames, which, though no doubt the property of Government, might better have been spared. It is not, however, my intention to join the outcry, which will probably be raised, against what they will term a line of conduct at once barbarous and unprofitable. Far from it; on the contrary, I cannot help admiring the forbearance and humanity of the British troops, since, irritated as they had every right to be, they spared as far as was possible, all private property, not a single house in the place being plundered or destroyed, except that from which the general's horse had been killed; and those which were accidentally thrown down by the explosion of the magazines.

While the third brigade was thus employed, the rest of the army, having recalled its stragglers, and removed the wounded into Bladensburg, began its march towards Washington. Though the battle was ended by four o'clock, the sun had set before the different regiments were in a condition to move, consequently this short journey was performed in the dark. The work of destruction had also begun in the city, before they quitted their ground; and the blazing of houses, ships, and stores, the report of exploding magazines, and the crash of falling roofs, informed them, as they proceeded, of what was going forward. You can conceive nothing finer than the sight which met them as they drew near to the town. The sky was brilliantly illumined by the different conflagrations; and a dark red light was thrown upon the road, sufficient to permit each man to view distinctly his comrade's face. Except the burning of St. Sebastian's,[3] I do not recollect to have witnessed, at any period of my life, a scene more striking or more sublime.

Having advanced as far as the plain, where the reserve had previously paused, the first and second brigades halted; and, forming into close column, passed the night in bivouac. At first, this was agreeable enough, because the air was mild, and weariness made up for what was wanting in comfort. But towards morning, a violent storm of rain, accompanied with thunder and lightning, came on, which disturbed the rest of all those who were exposed to it. Yet in spite of the disagreeableness of getting wet, I cannot say that I felt disposed to grumble at the interruption, for it appeared that what I had before considered as superlatively sublime, still wanted this to render it complete. The flashes of lightning seemed to vie in brilliancy, with the flames which burst from the roofs of burning houses, while the thunder drowned the noise of crumbling walls, and was only interrupted by the occasional roar of cannon, and of large depots of gunpowder, as they one by one exploded.

I need scarcely observe, that the consternation of the inhabitants was complete, and that to them this was a night of terror. So confident had they been of the success of their troops, that few of them had dreamt of quitting their houses, or abandoning the city; nor was it till the fugitives from the battle began to rush in, filling every place as they came with dismay, that the President himself thought of providing for his safety. That gentleman, as I was credibly informed, had gone forth in the morning with the army, and had continued among his troops till the British forces began to make their appearance. Whether the sight of his enemies cooled his courage or not, I cannot say, but, according to my informer, no sooner was the glittering of our arms discernible, than he began to discover that his presence was more wanted in the senate than with the army; and having ridden through the ranks, and exhorted every man to do his duty, he hurried back to his own house, that he might prepare a feast for the entertainment of his officers, when they; should return victorious. For the truth of these details, I will not be answerable; but this much I know, that the feast was actually prepared, though instead of being devoured by American officers, it went to satisfy the less delicate appetites of a party of English soldiers. When the detachment, sent out to destroy Mr. Maddison's [*sic*] house, entered his dining parlour, they found a dinner-table spread, and covers laid for forty guests. Several kinds of wine, in handsome cut-glass decanters, were cooling on the side-board; plate-holders stood by the fire-place, filled with dishes and plates; knives, forks and spoons, were arranged for immediate use; in short, everything was ready for the entertainment of a ceremonious party. Such were the arrangements in the dining-room, whilst in the kitchen were others answerable to them in every respect. Spits, loaded with joints of various sorts, turned before the fire; pots, saucepans, and other culinary utensils, stood upon the grate; and all the other requisites for an elegant and substantial repast, were exactly in a state which indicated that they had been lately and precipitately abandoned.

You will readily imagine, that these preparations were beheld, by a party of hungry soldiers, with no indifferent eye. An elegant dinner, even though considerably over-dressed, was a luxury to which few of them, at least for some time back, had been accustomed; and which, after the dangers and fatigues of the day, appeared peculiarly inviting. They sat down to it, therefore, not indeed in the most orderly manner, but with countenances which would not have disgraced a party of aldermen at a civic feast; and having satisfied their appetites with fewer complaints than would have probably escaped their rival *gourmands*, and partaken pretty freely of the wines, they finished by setting fire to the house which had so liberally entertained them.

"America is Young"

From *Travels in Canada, and the United States, in 1816 and 1817* by Francis Hall.

Francis Hall (d. 1833) dedicated his *Travels* to "brother Wykehamists," being those students who attended Winchester College in Hampshire, England, where by indication of his writing and its many literary allusions, the young Hall must have received an excellent education.

Hall departed Liverpool on January 20th, 1816, bound for New York, sailing on an America vessel he describes as "excellently built and commanded." After spending most of the year traveling throughout New York and Canada, he began the southern leg of his journey, traveling down the eastern seaboard, making numerous stops in Pennsylvania and Maryland, and finally reaching Washington, D.C. toward the end of the year.

Francis Hall found Washington, D.C. a city both under construction and under renovation. Scarcely two years after the burning of the capital by the British, the Congress was meeting in a temporary building, not the capitol, and the President was living in a temporary residence, not the White House. But in spite of the British attack in August, 1814, and in spite of his nationality, Francis Hall found Americans to be generally hospitable, a fact he takes the opportunity to mention in his *Travels*.

The traveller, having passed through Bladensburg, on the east branch of the Patuxent, where the action was fought, which the Americans have nick-named the "Bladensburg races,"[1] crosses a sandy tract, interspersed with oak barrens and pine woods, until suddenly mounting a little rise, close to a poor cottage with its Indian corn patch, he finds himself opposite to the Capitol of the Federal city. It stands on an ancient bank of the Patomac, about eighty feet above the present level of the river; the course of which it commands, as well as the adjacent country, as far as the Alleghany Ridges. The edifice consists of two wings, intended to be connected by a centre, surmounted by a dome or cupola. The design is pure and elegant, but the whole building wants grandeur. Each wing would not be a large private mansion: the interiour has consequently a contracted appearance, a kind of economy of space disagreeably contrasting with the gigantick scale of nature without, as well as with our ideas of the growing magnitude of the American nation. The staircase, which is a kind of vestibule to the impression to be produced by the whole building, is scarcely wide enough for three persons to pass conveniently. The chambers of the senate and representatives are of very moderate dimensions, and the judgment hall, with its low-browed roof, and short columns, seems modelled after the prison of Constance in Marmion.[2] Some of the decorations, too, are of very dubious taste. Mr. Latrobe[3] has modelled a set of figures for the Chamber of Representatives, to personify the several states of the Union; but as it is not easy to discover an attribute, to say nothing of a poetical characteristick, by which Connecticut may be distinguished from Massachusetts, North Carolina from South Carolina, or Kentucky from Ohio, recourse must be had to the ungraceful expedient of a superscription to point out his own tutelary saint to each representative. Mr. Latrobe has, indeed, hit upon one device for Massachusetts; she is leading by the hand an ugly cub of a boy, representing Maine, which boy becomes a girl when Maine assumes her proper state; — a puerile conceit.[4] One cannot help regretting the Americans should have neglected to give their new Capitol a character of grandeur worthy of their territory and ambition. Private edifices rise, decay, and are replaced by others of superiour magnificence, as the taste or growing opulence of the nation require; but publick buildings should have a character answerable to their purpose; they bear upon them the seal of the genius of the age, and sometimes prophetically reveal the political destinies of the nations by which they are raised. The Romans communicated to their erections the durability of their empire. The Americans, in "their aspirations to be great," seem sometimes to look towards Roman models, but the imitation must be of things, not names; or instead of a noble parallel, they are in danger of producing a ludicrous contrast.

From the foot of the Capitol hill there runs a straight road,[5] (intended to be a street), planted with poplars, for about two miles, to the President's house, a handsome stone mansion, forming a conspicuous object from the Capitol Hill: near it are the publick offices, and some streets nearly filled up: about half a mile further is a pleasant row of houses, in one of which the President at present resides: there are a few tolerable houses still further on the road to Georgetown, and this is nearly the sum total of the City for 1816. It used to be a joke against Washington, that next door neighbours must go through a wood to make their visits; but the jest and forest have vanished together: there is now scarcely a tree betwixt Georgetown and the Navy Yard, two miles beyond the Capitol, except the poplars I have mentioned, which may be considered as the *locum tenentes*[6] of future houses. I doubt the policy of such thorough clearing; clumps of trees are preferable objects to vacant spaces, and the city in its present state, being commenced from the extremities instead of the centre, has a disjointed and naked appearance. The fiery ordeal has, however, fixt [sic] its destiny. Land and houses are rising in value, new buildings are erecting, and with the aid of the intended university,[7] there is little doubt that Washington will attain as great an extent as can be expected for a city possest [sic] of no commercial advantages, and created, not by the natural course of events, but by a political speculation. The plan, indeed, supposes an immense growth, but even if this were attainable, it seems doubtful how far an overgrown luxurious capital would be the fittest seat for learning, or even legislation. Perhaps the true interest of the union would rather hold Washington sacred to science, philosophy, and the arts: a spot in some degree kept holy from commercial avarice, to which the members of different states may repair to breathe an atmosphere untainted by local prejudices, and find golden leisure for pursuits and speculations of publick utility. Such fancies would be day dreams elsewhere, and are so perhaps here; but America is young in the career of political life; she has the light of former ages, and the sufferings of the present to guide her; she has not crushed the spirits of the many, to build up the tyranny of the few, and, therefore, the prophetick eye of imagination may dwell upon her smilingly.

I fell into very pleasant society at Washington. Strangers who intend staying some days in a town, usually take lodgings at a boarding house, in preference to a tavern: in this way, they obtain the best society the place affords; for there are always gentlemen, and frequently ladies, either visitors or temporary residents, who live in this manner to avoid the trouble of housekeeping. At Washington, during the sittings of Congress, the boarding houses are divided into messes, according to the political principles of the inmates, nor is a stranger admitted without some introduction, and the consent of the whole company. I chanced to join a democratick mess, and name a few of its members with gratitude, for the pleasure their society gave me: — Commodore Decatur[8] and his lady, the Abbé Correa,[9] the great botanist and plenipotentiary of Portugal, the Secretary of the Navy,[10] the Secretary of the Navy Board,[11] known as the author of a humorous publication, entitled "John Bull, and Brother Jonathan," with eight or ten members of Congress, principally from the Western states, which are generally considered as most decidedly hostile to England, but whom I did not on this account find less good-humoured and courteous. It is from thus living in dally intercourse with the leading characters of the country, that one is enabled to judge with some degree of certainty of the practices of its government; for to know the paper theory is nothing, unless it be compared with the instruments employed to carry it into effect. A political constitution may be nothing but a cabalistick form to extract money and power from the people; but then the jugglers must be in the dark, and "no admittance behind the curtain." This way of living affords too the best insight into the best part of society; for if in a free nation the depositaries of the publick confidence be ignorant, or vulgar, it is a very fruitless search to look for the opposite qualities in those they represent; whereas, if these be well informed in mind and manners, it proves at the least an inclination towards knowledge and refinement, in the general mass of citizens, by whom they are selected. My own experience obliges me to a favourable verdict in this particular. I found the little circle into which I had happily fallen, full of good sense and good humour, and never quitted it without feeling myself a gainer on the score, either of useful information or of social enjoyment.

The President, or rather his lady, holds a drawing-room weekly, during the sitting of Congress. He takes by the hand those who are presented to him; shaking hands being discovered in America to be more rational and manly than kissing them. For the rest, it is much as such things are everywhere, chatting, and tea, compliments and ices, a little musick, (some scandal, I suppose, among the ladies), and to bed. Nothing in these assemblies more attracted my notice, than the extraordinary stature of most of the western members; the room seemed filled with giants, among whom moderately sized men crept like pigmies. I know not well, to what the difference may be attributed, but the surprising growth of the inhabitants of the Western slates is matter of astonishment to those of the eastern, and of the coast line generally. This phenomenon, which is certainly a considerable stumbling-block to the Abbé Raynal's[12] theory, may probably be resolved into the operation of three positive causes, and one negative, namely, plentiful but simple food, a healthy climate, constant exercise in the open air, and the absence of mental irritation. In a more advanced stage of society, luxurious and sedentary habits produce in the rich that enfeeblement of vitality, which scanty food, and laborious or unwholesome occupations bring upon the poor. The only persons to be compared with these Goliahs[13] of the West, were six Indian chiefs from Georgia, Chactaws [*sic*] or Chickasaws, who, having come to Washington on publick business, were presented at Mrs. Madison's drawing-room. They had a still greater appearance of muscular power than the Americans; and while looking on them, I comprehended the prowess of those ancient knights, whose single might held an army in check, "and made all Troy retire."[14]

The sittings of Congress are held in a temporary building,[15] during the repair of the Capitol: I attended them frequently, and was fortunate enough to be present at one interesting debate on a change in the mode of Presidential elections: (most of the principal speakers took a part in it: Messrs. Gaston,[16] Calhoun,[17] and Webster[18] in support of it; Randolph[19] and Grosvenor[20] against it. The merits of the question were not immediately to be comprehended by a stranger, but their style of speaking was, in the highest degree, correct and logical, particularly that of Mr. Webster of New Hampshire, whose argumentative acuteness extorted a compliment from Mr. Randolph himself, "albeit unused to the complimenting mood." Mr. Grosvenor, both in action and language, might be considered a finished orator, as far as our present notions of practical oratory extend, Mr. Randolph, whose political talents, or rather political success, is said to be marred by an eccentrick turn of thought, which chimes in with no party, seems rather a brilliant than a convincing speaker; his elocution is distinct and clear to shrillness, his command of language and illustration seems unlimited; but he gave me the idea of a man dealing huge blows against a shadow, and wasting his dexterity in splitting hairs: his political sentiments are singular: he considers the government of the United States as an elective monarchy; "Torture the constitution as you will," said he, in the course of the debate, "the President will elect his successor, and that will be his son whenever be has one old enough to succeed him." No expressions are used, either of approbation or the contrary; whatever may be the opinion of the House, the most perfect attention is given to each member; nor, however long he may speak, is he ever interrupted by those indications of impatience so common in our House of Commons. This may reasonably be accounted for by supposing, that their average speeches are, in themselves better; or more agreeably, by conjecturing, that the American idea of excellence is put at a lower standard than our own. Both the talents, however, and behaviour of the members, seem worthy of the government, and of what America is, and may be. Their forms of business and debate nearly resemble those of our parliament; always excepting wigs and gowns, a piece of grave absurdity well omitted: for it is surely an odd conceit, to fancy the dignity of the first officers of States attached to, or supported by, large conglomerations of artificial hair.

"Our Enlightened Countrymen"

From *Sketches of America* by Henry Bradshaw Fearon.

Henry Bradshaw Fearon (1793-1842) provides perhaps the best description of the purpose of his visit to the United States in the sub-title of his *Sketches of America*, further delineating the work as: *A Narrative of a Journey of Five Thousand Miles through the Eastern and Western States of America; Contained in Eight Reports Addressed to the Thirty-nine English Families by Whom the Author was Deputed, in June 1817, to Ascertain Whether Any, and What Part of the United States Would be Suitable for their Residence.* Although records of subsequent residence among those thirty-nine families are wanting, Fearon was clearly up to the task. As is the case with many travelers, Fearon takes the opportunity to acknowledge those who came to Washington, D.C. before him.

---

It has been so fashionable with natives, as well as foreigners, to ridicule the federal city, that I had anticipated the reality of Moore's description of...

"This famed metropolis, where fancy sees
Squares in morasses, obelisks in trees"

But in this I was pleasingly disappointed.

The river Potowmac, at this place, is only navigable for small craft near its banks. Besides the Potowmac, the River "Tiber" runs through the city; its stream is about the width of the Paddington canal.[1] The ridiculous, though characteristic vanity displayed in altering it from the original name of "Goose Creek," to that of the Tiber, has been happily exposed by Moore.

The President's palace, and the Capitol, situated on opposite hills, are the chief public buildings, both of which were nearly destroyed by the buccaneering incursions of our country-men, who acted, perhaps, agreeably to their orders, but certainly in opposition to the feelings, judgment, and character of the British people. These buildings are now rapidly rising into increased splendour. The Capitol, in which are both houses of the legislature, and several public offices, stands on a bank of the Potowmac, seventy feet above the level of that river: it as yet consists of but two wings, intended to be connected by a centre, surmounted by a dome.[2] The architect is Mr. Latrobe: In the internal construction of this building, he has not evinced even a common knowledge of what contributes to convenience, and still less to elegance of appearance. The apartments are small, crowded, and without unity of design: the exterior, when completed, will, however, produce a really grand effect. Some of the pillars are of a native marble, of a peculiarly novel and beautiful description, bearing some resemblance to the finest specimens of mosaic. The Americans, however, are not content with the productions of their own country: they have made large imports from Italy of its most expensive marble; and so anxious is even the President himself for "foreign ornament," that he has imported chairs at one hundred dollars each, though the cabinet-makers of Baltimore would have equalled, and I believe surpassed them in every particular, at the price of sixty dollars!

The President's house is at the opposite end of "Pennsylvania Avenue," commanding a most beautiful prospect. On each side of it stands a large brick building; one of which is the treasury, the other the war and navy offices. These are to be connected with the palace, which, when completed, would form an ornament even to St. Petersburgh itself. Upon a second visit to the Capitol, I explored nearly all its recesses. Marks of the late conflagration are still very apparent, while the walls bear evidence of public opinion in relation to that transaction, which seems to have had the singular fate of casting disgrace upon both the Americans and British. Some of the pencil drawings exhibit the military commander hanging upon a tree; others represent the President running off without his hat or wig; some, Admiral Cockburn robbing hen-roosts: to which are added such inscriptions as, "The capital of the Union lost by cowardice;" "Curse cowards;" "A — sold the city for 5000 dollars;" "James Madison is a rascal, a coward, and a fool;" "Ask no questions," &c.

The post-office is a large brick building, situated at about equal distances from the president's house and the Capitol. Under the same roof is the patent-office, and also the national library, for the use of members of congress. In the first of these departments, I witnessed upwards of nine hundred specimens of native mechanical genius. This would appear to afford decisive proof that Americans are not deficient in inventive talent, though it cannot be extensively, or with profit, called into action, until you little island ceases to be the universal workshop. The library is small, consisting of but 3000 volumes; but it is select and well chosen, and includes various classes of literature, having been the property of Mr. Jefferson, for which he obtained from the United States 20,000 dollars.[3] The former library, containing from 7 to 8000, was destroyed by our *enlightened* countrymen. So great has been, at some periods, the depreciation of property in this city, that in

1802, what had originally cost 200,000 dollars, was sold for 25,000. This decay continued to go on, until the visit of General Ross, and the subsequent signature of peace: since that time it seems to have risen, like the phoenix from the flames, and is once more partially increasing in prosperity. There are now a number of two and three story brick buildings, none of which are uninhabited; and also some small wooden houses, though, according to the original plan, none were to be built less than three stories high, and all to have marble steps. But the childish folly of this scheme was soon subverted by the natural course of events; and though the existence of "*lower orders,*" even in the capital of the republic, may not accord with the vanity of its legislators, they ought to be told, that neither prosperity nor population can be possessed by any nation, without a due admixture of the *natural classes* of society.

The population of Washington city is about 9000; of Georgetown, 6000; of Alexandria, 8000; and of all other parts of the district of Columbia, 7000; making a total of 30,000. *Alexandria*, which is seven miles from the city, may be considered the sea-port. *Georgetown* is the residence of shopkeepers, and *Washington* the depôt for office-holders, place-hunters, and boarding-house keepers; none of whom would appear to be in possession of too much of this world's goods. Between these three divisions of this district there exists considerable jealousy.

.... There are three market-houses in Washington, and I believe, four market days per week. Negroes are the chief sellers. The supplies at this time are neither good nor various. Beef is from 4½d. to 6½d. per pound; pork the same; potatoes, 3s. 4½d. per bushel; bread, 2d. per. pound; beer, 6½d. per bottle; milk, 5½d, per quart; tea, 4s. 6d. to 13s. 6d. per pound; coffee, 12¾d. to 16d.; sugar, from 54s. to 90s. per hundred. Rents are as high as elsewhere. Mechanics are fully employed, and well paid. Shopkeepers are too numerous, and none of them remarkably successful. British goods abound, as in every other part of America. When I had been here a few hours, I went to a store to purchase a pair of worsted gloves: they were of the commonest kind, such as are sold in London at 8s, 6d. per dozen. The price was half a dollar per pair. I presented a Philadelphia one dollar note; it would not be taken without a discount of 2½ per cent. I then tendered a Baltimore bank, of the same amount. This being one hundred miles nearer was accepted. The store-keeper had no silver change; to remedy which, he took a pair of scissors and divided the note between us: I enquired if the half would pass, and being answered in the affirmative, took it without hesitation, knowing the want of specie throughout the country, and being previously familiarized with Spanish dollars cut into every variety of size. I now find that demi-notes are a common circulating medium. Capital is generally wanted, though my enquiries do not lead me to believe that it can be employed here with anything more than ordinary advantage. The increase of the federal city cannot be rapid. Here is fine natural scenery, but no decidedly great natural advantages; little external commerce, a barren soil, a scanty population, enfeebled too by the deadly weight of absolute slavery, and no direct means of communication with the Western country. For the apparently injudicious selection of such a spot, upon which to raise the capital of a great nation, several reasons are given. Some have even gone so far as to attribute to Gen. Washington the influence of pecuniary interest, his property being in the neighbourhood.[4] But the most common argument adduced in support of the choice is that it is central, or rather that it *was* so; for the recent addition of new States has removed the centre very far west, so much so indeed, that the inhabitants of Lexington affirm, that *their* town must on that ground soon become the capital; and even the people of St. Louis, in the Missouri, put in their claim, that city being said to be geographically the exact centre of the Union.⁵ But assuming that Washington were central, I do not see much validity in the argument, — at least if we are to be influenced in our judgment by any country in the old world — where is the important nation, whose capital is placed exactly in the centre of its dominions? Spain is perhaps the only country which can be adduced, and no very favourable conclusion can be drawn from such an instance: though unquestionably if rivers and soil, if roads and canals, all united to recommend that situation, it would be in some other respects extremely convenient; but this not being the case, the knowledge of Euclid must be dispensed with for something of more practical, though perhaps more vulgar utility.

There may be other objections to this capital: among them I would venture to suggest, that the legislators, and rulers pf a nation, ought to reside in that city which has the most direct communication with all parts of their country, and of the world at large they ought to see with their own eyes, and hear with their own ears, without which, though possessed of the best intentions, they must often be in error. Newspaper communications, letters and agents, are but substitutes, and sometimes very poor ones; besides which, I conceive that mere expedients should not be admitted in national legislation. Unless this city increases with a rapidity unsanctioned by the most sanguine anticipation, the American lawmakers will be half a century behind what they would become by a residence in New York or Philadelphia. Another objection to Washington may suggest itself to some minds, in its neighbourhood to Virginia. The "Virginian dynasty," as it has been called, is a subject of general, and I think very just, complaint throughout other parts of America. This State has supplied four of the five presidents, and also a liberal number of occupants of every other government office. The Virginians very modestly assert, that this monopoly does not proceed from corrupt influence, but is a consequence of the buoyancy and vigour of their natural talent. Without entering into the controversy, whether or not seventeen States can supply a degree of ability equal to that of Virginia single-handed, I must express my want of respect for a State in which every man is either a slave-holder, or a defender of slavery — a State in which landed property is not attach able for debt — a State in which human beings are sold in the streets by the public auctioneer, are flogged without trial at the mercy of their owner or his agents, and are killed almost without punishment: — yet these men dare to call themselves democrats, and friends of liberty! — from such democrats, and such friends of liberty, good Lord deliver us!

The customs of society at this season differ, I presume, in some degree, from those portions of the year when congress is not sitting. Tea parties, and private balls, are now very frequent. Mr. Bagot, the English ambassador, and his lady, are particularly assiduous in their attentions to all classes, and maintain a strict conformity with the habits of the place. Their cards of invitation are left at my boarding-house for different gentlemen every day. The speaker (Mr. Clay) gives public periodical dinners. A drawing-room is held weekly at the President's house: it is generally crowded. There is little or no difficulty in getting introduced on these occasions. Mr. Munroe is a very plain, practical man of business. The custom is shaking, and not the degrading one of kissing, hands. Conversation, tea, ice, music, chewing tobacco, and excessive spitting, afford employment for the evening. The dress of the ladies is very elegant, though that of the gentlemen is too frequently rather ungentlemanly.

The theatre is a miserable building. I have, attended several representations in it by the same company which I saw when in Pittsburgh, Incledon has been here — the

Washington critics think him too vulgar, and also an indifferent singer![6]

In this city I witnessed also the exhibitions of *Sema Sama*, the Indian juggler, from London.[7] My chief attention was directed to the audience; their disbelief of the possibility of performing the numerous feats advertised, and their inconceivable astonishment at witnessing the actual achievement, appeared extreme, — approaching almost to childish wonder and astonishment.

The few private families to which I have had introductions, do not evince a more accurate knowledge of that English word *comfort* than I have remarked elsewhere; indeed, I would class them a century inferior to Boston and half a century behind New York. The boarding-houses and inns partake of the same characteristics. I first applied at the chief, which is Davis's Indian Queen tavern: most of the door-handles are broken; the floor of the coffee-room is strewed with bricks and mortar, caused by the crumbling of the walls and ceiling; and the character of the accommodations is in unison with this unorganized state of things: the charges are as high as at the very first London hotel.

"The Aspect of the House"

From *Travels through Part of the United States and Canada in 1818 and 1819* by John M. Duncan.

Author John Morison Duncan (c1795-1825) was at the time of his travels to the United States involved in printing and bookselling in partnership with his father Andrew in their native Glasgow. Andrew Duncan held the position of University Printer in Glasgow from 1811 until the year after his son's early death when financial woes rendered the company bankrupt. During their more prosperous years the father and son produced many fine books, including works by Xenophon, Euripides and Sir Isaac Newton.

John Morison Duncan's *Travels* recounts his visits to several American cities, including Albany, Baltimore, Boston, New Haven, New York, Philadelphia, Princeton and Washington, D.C. He records many detailed observations on his visit to the capital, covering topics such as the width of the streets, the duration of copyright, the energetic pace of the local printing presses and the footwear of members of Congress. Duncan is often critical but on occasion refreshingly forthright regarding his own potential fallibility.

Washington, September, 1818.

I have now the honour of addressing you from the metropolis of the United States. It is common here to call Washington "the city in the woods." I was therefore somewhat surprised to find that there is little or no wood near it. The aspect of the city indeed would have been much improved by a few trees, to fill up the vacancies, and thus afford something for the eye to rest upon between one group of buildings and another. The soil however is poor, and the probability is that there has never been much timber on this spot; I have noticed none of the stumps which are usually left when the forests are felled.

The position which was selected for the Federal city, is a point of land embraced by the forking of the river Potowmak, about one hundred and twenty miles from its junction with the Chesapeake, and about two hundred and fifty miles from the sea. The principal branch of the river flows down upon the west, arid unites with the smaller one from the eastward in front of the city. Ships of war of the largest size can float in safety three or four miles above the junction of the streams. It was expected that this situation would have been found particularly favourable to commercial enterprize, and consequently that the population would rapidly increase; hitherto however these hopes have not been realized. Georgetown, about a mile above upon the principal branch of the river, monopolizes the inland trade, and Alexandria seven miles below intercepts the foreign; while the barrenness of the surrounding country is discouraging to settlers. The prosperity of Washington therefore seems to be in a great measure dependent on its advantages as the seat of government, and these in a new government, economical even to penuriousness in the salaries of its public officers, cannot as yet be very important.

Great however or trifling as they may be the city did not till very lately enter upon the full enjoyment of them. Great doubts were entertained whether it was to continue to enjoy the presence of the chief magistrate, and supreme legislature; and capitalists felt no inclination to invest their money in property which was not otherwise valuable, and which might therefore be suddenly and irretrievably depreciated. But what the natives were at a loss to decide, the British may be said to have decided for them. The burning of the Capitol and the President's house during last war, has settled the question, and it seems to be now ascertained to the satisfaction of speculators, that Washington is to continue, at least for a considerable time to come, in the undisturbed enjoyment of her metropolitan privileges. How an event so disastrous should lead to consequences so propitious, may seem to be in some measure a paradox, but it is one of easy explanation. When the rebuilding of these edifices came to be the subject of deliberation in Congress, the question as to the removal of the seat of the legislature was necessarily discussed; national feeling however cooperated powerfully with other considerations to influence the decision, the proposal was at once scouted, and the requisite amount was enthusiastically voted to efface the memorials of British triumph. Preparations were instantly made to rebuild the Capitol and President's house with more than their original splendour, the value of building ground and of houses took an immediate start, and Washington now exhibits abundant proof of the enterprize and elasticity of the national character.

The original plan of the city was on a most extensive scale. A parallelogram more than four miles and a half long, and two miles broad, was regularly divided into streets, avenues, and squares, and should the anticipations of its founders be realized, this will after all be but the nucleus of the future metropolis. The streets are laid out towards the cardinal points, crossing each other at right angles; the avenues intersect these diagonally, so as to avoid the tiresome sameness which is observable in Philadelphia, and extensive squares are to be placed at the crossings of these transverse lines. The avenues are from 130 to 160 feet wide, the streets from 80 to 110.[1]

To lay out the plan of a city however is one thing, and to build it is another; of all the regularity and system which the engraved plan exhibits, scarcely a trace is discernible upon the ground. Instead of beginning this gigantic undertaking in a central spot, and gradually extending the buildings from a common focus, they appear to have commenced at once in twenty or thirty different places, without the slightest regard to concentration or the comforts of good neighbourhood; and a stranger looking round him for Washington, sees two houses here, and six there, and a dozen yonder, scattered in straggling groups over the greater part of three or four square miles. Hitherto the city does not contain above fourteen thousand inhabitants, but these have taken root in so many different places, that the public crier, a black man whom I have just seen performing the duties of his calling, is obliged to make the circuit on horseback. Pennsylvania Avenue is almost the only place where the line of communication can be traced. This stretches from the Capitol to the President's house, a distance of rather more than a mile, with double rows of gravel walks and poplar trees; and a good many buildings have been erected on both sides of it, with considerable attention to neatness and continuity. This however is but a small portion of the intended avenue, which according to the plan is to stretch out in both directions, till it is eventually about four miles in length.

A short way from the Capitol, Pennsylvania Avenue is crossed by the Tiber, a little muddy stream, or creek according to American phraseology, which filters through flags and rushes into the Potowmak. A wooden bridge is thrown over it, but the stage driver who brought me from Baltimore preferred fording the stream, to cool the feet of his horses. Moore in one of his poetical epistles dated from the "Modern Rome," makes a sarcastic allusion to this classic stream, but, if Weld is correct, the name was given it by some early settler, before the site was chosen for the Federal city, and therefore its founders are not answerable for what at first seems a piece of ridiculous affectation.

As the Capitol and the President's house are both of freestone, we are rather disappointed to find them covered with white paint. The grain of the stone is indeed rather coarse, and a good many hard white pebbles are imbedded in it, yet the walls would certainly have looked better in their natural colour. The truth is, the buildings were both originally unpainted; but the unceremonious usage which they received from our troops at the capture of the city, so effectually begrimmed their visages that it was found impossible to eradicate the defilement. To have demolished and rebuilt the walls, would have been a very costly expedient, and as the least of two evils, the painter's brush was resorted to; here and there however, above some of the windows, the black wreathings of the smoke are still discernible through the white covering.

Of all the errors committed on our part during that unhappy war, this was undoubtedly one of the greatest. Setting aside the question as to its abstract defensibility, on the ground of retaliation or otherwise, it is obvious that it was in the highest degree impolitic; because its immediate effect, as might have been anticipated, was to break down party spirit among the Americans, and to unite them as one man in support of the measures of their government. The firebrand was no sooner applied to their Chief Magistrate's Palace, and the National Senate House, than thousands who had from the beginning maintained a systematic opposition to the contest, at once came forward and took up arms to maintain it; their national feelings were roused into powerful excitement, and they joined in one loud voice of execration at the destruction of their national edifices. Our ministers, had such been their object, could not have devised a more effectual way of strengthening Mr. Madison's hands. Had our troops recorded their triumph upon the front of the buildings, and left them uninjured, the indignant feeling of humiliation would have wreaked itself on those by whose imbecility the capture of the city had been occasioned, and who escaped so nimbly when it fell into the enemy's hands. But the burning of the buildings saved Mr. Madison; a thirst for revenge of the insult overcame every other feeling, and the war became thenceforward, what it had not been before, decidedly popular and national.

No more than the wings of the Capitol had been completed when the city was captured. They have risen from their ashes, and are again roofed in; the centre also is beginning to appear above the ground. Each wing is pretty nearly square, and consists of a basement and principal story, surmounted with a low circular dome bearing a small lantern. The basement is rusticated, and between the windows of the principal story is a row of Corinthian pilasters. The centre is to resemble the wings in its general features, but will project considerably beyond them. The building wants simplicity very much.

The House of Representatives will occupy a magnificent hall in the right wing of the building. The Speaker's chair is to be placed near the wall, and the seats and desks of the members will be disposed in semicircular lines round it, rising as they recede. Beyond the members' seats will be an extensive gallery for spectators. Twenty-two splendid Corinthian columns with corresponding pilasters are to surround the outline of the semicircle, and the wall behind the Speaker's chair. Part of these are already erected. The shaft of the columns is of a kind of puddingstone from the banks of the Potowmak, composed of numerous pebbles of various sizes and colours, and admitting of a good polish. The capitals, which were executed in Italy, are of white marble, and it is said cost upwards of a hundred pounds sterling each. The appropriate foliage of this splendid order is most exquisitely elaborated. I am disposed to think, however, that had the columns been altogether of white marble, the effect would have been much more pleasing. As the workmen are still busy with this hall, I am unable to be more minute in my description.

Among a multitude of workmen who are now employed on the building, I chanced to enter into conversation with an Irish marble cutter, who has been here for some months. He said that a large proportion of the workmen were from Scotland and Ireland; their wages are from one to two dollars a day, it costs them about three dollars a week for board and lodging, and he is able to save about one half of his wages.

The President's House is a handsome building of considerable dimensions, occupying the brow of a rising ground near the bank of the river and commanding a most extensive and beautiful prospect. In the centre of the side towards the river is a semicircular projection, and Corinthian pilasters,[2] rising between the windows to the full height of the building, support a balustrade which goes completely round. The principal front however is on the other side, rather a singular arrangement I think, where a plain but lofty portico of four columns rises above the entrance door. Among heaps of rubbish around the building I saw several fragments of the old capitals of the pilasters, which had been cracked by the conflagration and thoroughly blackened with smoke.

The walls of the President's House are now restored to their former condition, and carpenters and upholsterers are busied in giving to the interior more than its original splendour. The walls of some of the rooms which have been finished are covered with very rich French paper studded with gilt flowers. I saw in one of them a full length copy in oil of Stuart's portrait of Washington; the original is, or at least was, in the possession of the Marquis of Lansdown,[3] and is the same from which the beautiful engraving by Heath was executed.

Along with the Capitol and the President's House the public offices were also destroyed. There were at that time only two, which have been rebuilt, and other two have been added; they are appropriated to the departments of the treasury, state, navy, and war, and stand near the President's House, two on each side.

No less than five libraries perished in that ill-fated conflagration, two of which were of considerable value. Many public documents and some curious papers connected with the history of the revolution were also destroyed. As a recommencement of a national library, Congress has purchased from Mr. Jefferson the whole of his private collection, containing about ten thousand volumes. In turning over a few of Mr. Jefferson's books I found a copy of Professor Dalzel's Collectanea Græca Majora which bore the following inscription in the autograph of the editor:

Ad virum honoratissimum
et doctissimum
THOMAM JEFFERSON S. R. S. Edin.
a fœderatis Americae civitatibus
ad Regiam Majestatem Christianissimam
cum plenâ potestate legatum
hunc librum observationis causâ
misit

ANDREAS DALZEL.

A similar one appeared on the Minora.

The models in the Patent Office would have shared the fate of the Capitol, but for the intercession of the person who had charge of them.[4] He strenuously pled with our officers that they might be spared, representing that they had no relation to warlike affairs, that many of them were ingenious and useful, and that to destroy them would be to wage war against the arts, and against general improvement. This appeal was effectual, and the models were left uninjured. Its success makes one regret that no such intercession took place on behalf of the libraries and national archives, to which the same argument applied with tenfold force. A gentleman who witnessed the whole process of destruction, stated to me his opinion that General Ross would probably have been induced to abstain from the destruction of the Capitol and the President's House, had suitable exertions been made by the civil authorities. The whole of these however, officers of state and local magistrates, regardless of all but their personal safety, took to their heels by common consent, and left the public buildings to their fate. Old Anchises should have shamed them all: —

> "Vos agitate fugam!
> Me si cœlicolæ voluissent ducere vitam,
> Has mihi servassent sedes. Satis una, superque,
> Vidimus excidia, et captæ superavimus urbi."

The Patent Office exhibits a singular assemblage of nick-knacks, for the greater part of the models seemed to me to deserve no better appellation, though I dare say they are quite as important as many of those useful inventions which are every month recorded in the corresponding office in London. A boat was pointed out to us which was to be propelled by machinery, but it unfortunately turned out that the machinery was a sufficient load for the boat without any other cargo. The frame of a tent bed made of iron graced another shelf; but the originality of the invention was more than questioned by some wag, who had written on the label affixed to it "Og King of Bashan had an iron bedstead." Patent churns were numerous; and if you search minutely, patent cradle-rockers and patent brooms may also be discovered. Our conductor particularized as an invention of real utility, a machine for cutting iron nails; the introduction of which has completely superseded, throughout the United States, the use of hammered ones.

The expense of obtaining a patent here is only thirty dollars; £6, 15s sterling. The securing of copyright is a still cheaper process. One copy of the book is deposited in the Secretary of State's office, and a fee of sixty cents, about half a crown, is paid to the clerk of the District where the author resides, for an entry of the claim; another half crown is paid for a certified copy of this entry, which must be advertised for four weeks in the newspapers, and copied at full length on the back of the title page of the book. The term of copyright is fourteen years, but in the event of the author's surviving, a repetition of the same process secures it for other fourteen. There is a good deal of cumbrous and unnecessary machinery in all this, but it is much more favourable to authors and enterprizing publishers than the exaction, as with us, of eleven copies of the work however voluminous and expensive. There is one impolitic regulation on this subject; an alien cannot hold copyright until he has resided in the country at least two years at one time. Poor encouragement this for an emigration of authors, to give a start to the national literature! Not only is an alien deprived of the power of personally holding copyright, he cannot even convey a title to another person. Were the "Great Unknown" to cross the Atlantic, and to continue the manufacture of his literary ware at the usual rate of three publications per year, by which he would at home, according to report, net at least three or four times as many thousands of pounds sterling, for two whole years he could not gain a dollar by his writings; he might publish them, but before three days flew past,[5] two or three pirated editions would make their appearance without his having it in his power to suppress them. There is at least a semblance of good policy in most of the American statutes respecting foreigners, and by some of them considerable advantages are offered to emigrants, but the framers of this law seem to have regarded *quilldrivers* as a race by no means likely to increase the energies or resources of the nation; and therefore as an effectual barrier to the importation of such learned lumber, they have rendered them incapable of benefiting themselves or even of earning a subsistence by their peculiar art, for two years after their arrival, proclaiming all that they may produce during this period to be lawful prey to depredators of every kind. The same law applies to patents.

The navy yard, which is about a mile south east of the Capitol, occupies nearly forty acres of ground on the margin of a small inlet of the eastern branch of the river. Before visiting it I had neglected to provide myself with an introduction to the commanding officer, and reached the gate before I recollected that this would be necessary. As the only remaining chance, I walked boldly past the sentinel hoping to get in unchallenged; ere I had gone many paces, however, the serjeant [*sic*] of the guard hailed me, and having ascertained that I was an interloper ordered me to turn. I made no remonstrance, but observing at a short distance from the gate a marble monument, I asked and obtained permission to inspect it. It proved to be a monument to the memory of some American naval officers, who fell several years ago in an attack on Tripoli. It consists of a column upon a square base, surmounted with an eagle and surrounded by allegorical figures as large as life. The shaft of the column bears the beak and stern of three vessels of the antique form, projecting from it at equal distances from each other. The figures are allegorical of

History, Fame, Commerce, and America. History is in the act of recording on her tablet the heroic achievements of the departed warriors; Fame has mounted upon the base to crown them with laurel; Mercury carrying the cornucopiæ, as the representative of Commerce, bewails their untimely fate; and Columbia, a beautiful female decorated with feathers, is pointing two little chubby boys, one of whom carries the Roman fasces, to the commemorative device. On the front of the base is a sculptured basso relievo representation of the bombardment. The other three sides are occupied with inscriptions; one contains the names of those who fell, another intimates that the monument was erected by their brother officers, and on the third is inscribed —

> FAME HAS CROWNED THEIR DEEDS,
> HISTORY RECORDS THE EVENT,
> THE CHILDREN OF COLUMBIA ADMIRE,
> AND COMMERCE LAMENTS THEIR FALL.

This last inscription is, to say the least of it, superfluous, for the art of the sculptor is worth nothing if it cannot suggest the same ideas more expressively than words. The monument was executed in Italy and is very beautiful, but the spectator regrets to observe that the fingers of some of the figures have been broken off. We are not left in doubt as to the perpetrators of this outrage, for a small square tablet bears the mortifying information —

> MUTILATED
> BY BRITONS,
> 25TH AUGUST, 1814.

This inscription might also have been spared. It is not at all improbable that some of our soldiers, in the wantonness of victory, may have been the guilty individuals, for the monuments in Westminster Abbey abundantly manifest the propensity which prevails in the inferior classes of our countrymen to similar acts of vandalism; many of the smaller figures there, have been deprived not only of their fingers, but of their heads, and the real cause of wonder with respect to this one is, not that so much but that so little mischief was done. The person who ordered the inscription, however, should have reflected that it immediately suggests the question "How came 'Britons' to be here?" and it is possible, if the answer to this question is followed up by others which naturally occur, that the disgrace of allowing the fingers to be taken off, might eventually appear to be at least as great as that of having done it. A few years hence, nothing could have been seen in Washington to remind a visitor of its having been once in an enemy's hands, but so long as this monument remains in its present state, the humiliating fact is conspicuously recorded.

*Postscript, February*, 1819.

A second visit to this city has given me an opportunity of visiting Congress, which was not in session when I was here formerly.

The Senate and House of Representatives meet at present in plain brick buildings close by the Capitol, where temporary halls have been fitted up for them.[6] The galleries of both houses are open to every person; I found in them auditors of every description, workmen without their coats in one place, and elegantly dressed females in another. The utmost quietness and decorum however prevailed.

The President of the Senate wears no costume; he appeared in a blue coat with gilt buttons, and occupied a plain elbow chair with a small canopy over it. Each senator has a writing desk before him, and many of them were either writing letters or reading newspapers. They were all in plain dresses, and many wore jockey boots.

I found the Senate discussing the propriety of making compensation to a British subject in Upper Canada, for a small vessel which had been captured by an American cruiser on Lake Ontario, before the declaration of war. The vessel had been sold, and the proceeds paid to the clerk of one of the Districts of the State of New York, to await the decision of a court; the court decided that the capture was illegal and ordered restitution, but in the meantime the clerk had become a defaulter and eloped. A bill had in consequence been brought into the Senate, containing a provision for making good to the owner of the vessel the sum which he had thus lost. Various individuals spoke shortly on both sides of the question. Some opposed the bill, on the footing that the individual aggrieved ought to have recourse upon the legal securities of the District Clerk, and said that it would be giving to a British subject an advantage which would not have been conceded to a citizen of the United States. I had however the pleasure of hearing the Hon. Rufus King, one of the senators for the State of New York, speak warmly in favour of the bill. He said that the nation was bound in honour to make good to a foreigner the decision of the court; that in similar circumstances an American citizen would have most certainly obtained redress in Great Britain, and that he had never known an instance of such a decision there, in which prompt and ample compensation had not been made. The question was ultimately carried in the affirmative.[7]

The house of Representatives was in committee, and I found Mr. Sargeant[8] of Philadelphia concluding a long speech, which had been begun the preceding day, on the subject of the United States' Bank. A committee, which had been appointed to investigate some alleged misconduct on the part of the Bank Directors, had reported an opinion to the House that the charter of the Bank had been violated, and consequently forfeited entirely. Mr. Sargeant combated this opinion, and was arguing while I was present, that although the facts were proved to be exactly as the committee had reported, the charter was still good, for such delinquencies had all been provided for in that charter, and specific penalties attached to them; the penalties he said were incurred, but the charter was still perfectly valid. I left this gentleman speaking, and his opinion in the end prevailed.

The aspect of the House of Representatives is still less dignified than that of the Senate. The house was pretty full, but many of the members were lounging beside the fire reading newspapers, others were clustering round the windows, and few even of those who remained at their desks were attending to the orator, most of the others being busily engaged in writing letters, and some carefully weighing them to ascertain that the enclosures did not exceed the weight which their franks covered. In the House of Commons, it struck me that the members showed a good deal of indifference to the discussions which were going forward; the triple bows of the wigged messengers between the door and the bar, seemed sufficiently childish; the peremptory order of the Speaker, "strangers withdraw," somewhat uncivil to strangers; the confusion which took place in clearing the gallery, and the elbowing and pushing at filling it again, not a little annoying and vexatious; but after all there is more senatorial decorum in the House of Commons than in the House of Representatives. It appeared singular that so many members should attend the debates while so few seemed to be interested in them, and I thought that those whose legislative exertions were confined to gazing out at the window, or toasting their toes at the fire, might with more propriety so enjoy themselves at home. I have since learned from a member of the House, as some explanation of this, that in place of forty members constituting a quorum as in our House of Commons, it requires in the House of Representatives a majority of the whole number. The total number of members, which is increasing every year, is at present 118, consequently at least 59 must be assembled at every deliberation, and as a great many subjects are necessarily of a local nature and interesting to very few, it is no wonder that many should avail themselves of the newspapers, or of pen and ink, "to give time a shove." The question which I heard discussed was one that regarded the existence of the national bank, which had been established but two or three years before, chiefly with a view to facilitate the financial operations of government; and in which a great deal of money had been made and lost, by sudden and unprecedented fluctuations in the value of its stock, which after rising from 100 to upwards of 150, had recently fallen to 93. It was however no way surprising that they should be tired of a speech which had lasted two days, and that on a subject which had engrossed a great part of the session, to very little purpose; the orator, is esteemed one of the ablest men in the house, but an animated debate is one thing, and a lecture another. Instances are not wanting of members occupying the floor for three successive days; the house adjourning when they get tired, to resume the thread of discourse the following day. The writing desks are bad things, were it for no other reason than that they encourage indolence and inattention; the benches of the House of Commons scarcely admit of lounging; besides it is to speak and not to write that the members are sent to Congress.

It would not however be fair to try the American Congress by a comparison with the British Parliament. There is little similarity either in the materials or in the manner of their construction. In America, a young, thinly peopled, and republican country, almost every person is engaged in the active business of life, and the equality of succession to property, and the necessarily frequent division of it, prevents almost entirely the accumulation of large fortunes. A great proportion of those who compose her representative assemblies are men of no wealth and sometimes of little education, many of them second rate lawyers, others merchants, well stored with commercial information, and a few who find a seat in Congress a convenient thing were it only for the salary which is connected with it.[9] Great Britain on the other hand is an old country, overflowing with population, where a monarchy, hereditary nobility, and feudal tenures, are necessarily connected with large fortunes, and with the entire leisure of their possessors for legislative or other pursuits; a country where many receive an education expressly intended to qualify them for the service of the state, and where many members of the representative assembly, so far from requiring a stipendiary compensation for their attendance, are able to expend immense sums in procuring their election. Yet with all these disadvantages the wisdom and integrity of the American Congress have ere now put to shame the more practised politicians of Europe, and her diplomatic agents have often evinced themselves more than a match for the starred and titled plenipotentiaries of our own and other countries.

The building of the Capitol has advanced so considerably since the period of my former visit that several apartments in the right wing have been finished, and one of them is now occupied by the Supreme Court of the United States.

This Court is almost the only one which has adopted an official costume; in all the inferior courts throughout the country, except I believe those of South Carolina, the judges are to be distinguished from the counsel or the jury, only by their position on the bench. This is probably a point on which the Americans have mistaken the reverse of wrong for right. It was all very well to lay aside the antiquated and grotesque wig, which buries the intellectual organ under curls and pomatum, but to strip the administrator of justice of every distinctive garb was depriving the judicial office of an accessory which has a very powerful influence on the human mind.

The Supreme Court is composed of five judges, and I found them like the House of Representatives engaged upon the subject of the United States' Bank.[10] This national establishment is by no means popular throughout the Union, and some of the State legislatures imposed a very heavy tax upon the branches which were established by it within their jurisdiction. The payment of this tax was resisted by the Directors, and the question as to the right of the local governments to impose it, came before this court in the form of an appeal. During the few minutes that I spent here I heard some arguments, by the counsel for the State which had imposed the tax, in support of its right to do so. He argued that by the Federal compact the various States had relinquished in favour of the general government only the rights of levying importation and exportation duties, of making war and peace, and of coining money; but that they still retained and daily exercised the power of imposing internal taxes, and that there was nothing in the constitution of the United States' Bank which freed it from the operation of this right. I did not remain to hear the speakers on the opposite side, but the decision was ultimately given in favour of the bank.

In an adjoining room is at present exhibited Colonel Trumbull's painting of the Declaration of Independence. This is one of a series of historical paintings commemorative of the Revolution, which Congress has commissioned this artist to execute for the purpose of adorning the new Capitol.[11] In commemorating the event which gave birth to this great republic, the painter has placed before us most of the individuals who composed the general Congress, by which the Declaration of Independence was decreed and published; and the committee which was appointed to frame the document, in the act of presenting the draught at the table. I am no judge of such compositions, and may therefore be guilty of presumption in expressing any opinion, but I cannot help thinking that the painter might have selected a more interesting period of time in this great transaction. The picture indeed cannot be said to represent the *declaration of independence*, for though the instrument had been drawn up, it had not yet been adopted, much less made public. The great object has been to get together into one group the portraits of those self-devoted men, who were the principal actors in this event; but in effecting this the result is really calculated by its total want of epic grandeur to remind us somewhat of the Vicar of Wakefield's family picture. To the left of the canvass in the foreground is seated the President, John Hancock, immediately before him is the committee, consisting of Jefferson, Franklin, Adams, Livingstone, and Sherman, the last of whom is in the Quaker garb, and Jefferson is in the act of laying the scroll upon the table; to the right and in the back ground are the other members of Congress, most of them seated, and all as demure as if they had been assembled to attend a funeral. No opportunity was afforded in such a scene for the delineation of character, or the representation of animated action and intense emotion. The painter was not allowed to give scope to his imagination; for the event was too recent, the room in which it took place too plain, and too well known, and the meeting of a deliberative assembly altogether too commonplace a subject, for any considerable deviation from historical truth. The real value of the picture consists in the portraits, all of which are believed to be authentic; most of them Mr. Trumbull executed from life, for he began to collect the requisite materials many years ago, and the rest he copied from pictures believed to be accurate. Of the portraits of a small number of those who composed the Congress no trace could be discovered, and these are therefore not introduced. The size of the picture is eighteen feet by twelve.

As to the state of religion in Washington I can give you but little information; I have not happened to spend a Sabbath in it. There are two Episcopalian churches, one Presbyterian, one Associate Synod, two Baptist, two Methodist, one Quaker, and one Romish. The Popish chapel is dedicated to St. Patrick; it is a small building and somewhat paltry, but I saw in it a beautiful white marble font for *holy water* which has lately arrived from Italy. Standing within the basin is a figure of St. Patrick about twelve inches in height, wearing the mitre and sacerdotal vestments, and in the attitude of pronouncing a benediction on the water. The execution is beautiful, and we cannot but regret that one of the noblest of the fine arts should be so frequently pressed into the degrading service of this system of delusion.

Of society and manners here I know almost nothing, for both my visits have been very short. Respecting public characters I must be equally silent, for none have been pointed out to me except Commodores Decatur[12] and Rodgers.[13] They are both plain looking men, and were not in uniform when I met them. Commodore Rodgers' affair with the Little Belt, before the commencement of last war, has given us an idea that he is a man of more bluster than bravery; Americans however say that we are mistaken, and that during the war while commanding a fifty gun frigate, he actually hove to, and offered battle to a British seventy four gun ship, which she declined; I cannot help however doubting the accuracy of this story.[14]

"Punishment is 20 Dollars"

From *An Historical, Topographical, and Descriptive View of the United States of America, and of Upper and Lower Canada* (2nd Edition) by E. MacKenzie.

The industrious Eneas MacKenzie (1778-1832) was an English topographer, author and publisher. Born in Aberdeenshire, he would eventually settle in Newcastle-Upon-Tyne where after dabbling in several other pursuits he established himself as a printer and publisher. His other works include accounts of Newcastle-Upon-Tyne and County Palatine of Durham as well as contributions to a life of the Northumberland Piper James Allen. The firm of MacKenzie and Dent published works of history, travel, professional advice to farriers, and personal advice to young women.

Given MacKenzie's topographical approach, his descriptions of Washington, D.C. may be considered dry and statistical in nature, but he is clearly writing for a particular audience, those who may wish to invest in or emigrate to the United States. The financial details he provides, for example, are uncommon among the recorded observations of other authors. Regarding America writ large, he states in the Preface to his *Historical, Topographical, and Descriptive View* that "all those who are prepared to encounter the numerous privations and inconveniences of emigration, in order to enjoy the great and acknowledged advantages which America offers to adventurers, will find this work a FAITHFUL AND USEFUL GUIDE."

---

Columbia Territory.

*Situation and Extent.* The territory of Columbia, which formed a part of the states of Virginia and Maryland, became the permanent seat of government in the year 1801. This territory, extending on both .sides of the Patomak, contains a surface of ten miles square, of which the diagonals are north and south, and east and west, The south angle is at Fort Columbia, situated at Jones's point, at the mouth of Hunting creek, on the left bank of the Patomak.

*Natural Geography.* — The Patomak, which has already been described, traverses the territory of Columbia. From Washington to its mouth, in the Chesapeake bay, it is navigable for the largest frigate, a distance, in following its course, of about 200 miles. The tide water flows to the distance of three miles beyond Washington city, where the common tide rises to the height of four feet. By a survey of the Patomak, made in 1789, it was ascertained, that at the distance of 15 miles above the city of Washington, this river is 143 feet higher than at tide water; that from the mouth of Savage river, near the western limits of Maryland, to Fort Cumberland, a distance of 31 miles, the descent is 445 feet, or 14½ per mile; and from Fort Cumberland to tide water, a distance of 187 miles, the descent is 715 feet, or 3.82 per mile. By a survey, made in 1806, at the expence of the Patomak company, it was ascertained, that the Shenandoah river, from its mouth to Port Republic, has nearly the same breadth during all this distance of 200 miles, in which the descent is but 435 feet.

The Patomak company, by whom the navigation of the river has been opened, was incorporated for this purpose, by acts of the states of Maryland and Virginia, passed in the year 1784, which authorised the fund to be distributed in shares, and raised by subscription. The original capital, or stock, consisted of 701 shares, which at $444^{4/9}$ dollars, the value of each, amounted to 311,560 dollars. In 1807, the expences of the improvement of the Patomak amounted to 375,648 dollars; of the Shenandoah, to 65,000; and of the Conegocheague creek, to 500 dollars. The annual repairs, when the work shall have been completed, have been estimated at 20,000 dollars.

In a national point of view, this work will be of great advantage in accelerating the progress of agriculture, arts, and manufactures, diminishing the price of carriage, and facilitating the exchange of the productions and commodities of the countries watered by those rivers. The treasures of vast mountainous and woody tracts, hitherto unknown from the difficulty of communication, will be rendered accessible and inviting to every speculation, whether of a scientific or commercial nature.

The distance from Washington to the Upper or Matilda falls of the Patomak on the Virginia side, is about 14 miles. The perpendicular descent of the falls is 76 feet, but the rapids extend for several miles up the river. The scene is wild and magnificent. The romantic scenery of the Great falls, 59 miles from Washington, is seen most to advantage from the Virginia side, and is scarcely to be equalled. There is a stupendous projecting rock covered with cedar, where one may sit and gaze at the waters dashing with impetuosity over the rugged surface. At the close of winter, vast masses of ice, rolling over the rocks with a hideous crashing noise, present a scene truly sublime.

The surface of the district of Washington is beautifully irregular and diversified; in some parts level, in others undulating or hilly, and intersected by deep valleys. The soil is so various, that it is not easy to give an exact idea of its composition. On the level banks of the Patomak there is a deep alluvion formed by the depositions of this river, and containing fragments of primitive mountains, pyrites, gravel and sand, shells, and the remains of vegetable substances. The stone with which the basins of the Patomak canal are lined is a species of sandstone, similar to what is found in coal beds. The rock employed to form the foundation, or base, of the houses of Washington, is a species of gneiss, composed of felspar, quartz, and mica, of a leafy texture, owing to the abundance and disposition of the mica.

The fishes which inhabit the river Patomak, at and near Washington, are sturgeon, rock-fish, shad, gar, eel, carp, herring, pike, perch, mullet, smelt. In a distance of about 100 miles above and below Washington, 400,000 barrels of herrings are caught annually, of which a considerable quantity are cured and exported.[1] They are salted without being gutted, and the blood mixes with the brine, which in a few days is poured off, when the herrings are taken out, washed, and salted anew. The fisheries continue during the month of April. In 1768 an act was passed by the legislature, which, in 1798, became a permanent law, to prevent the destruction of young fish by wears or dams.

It is a prevailing opinion throughout the United States, that the climate of the district of Washington is unhealthy; but this opinion is not formed on good grounds, for it is certain, that in no season is it visited by habitual or endemical disease. The best proof of the salubrity of a place is the longevity of its inhabitants. During autumn bilious fever sometimes prevails; but, at this season, it is common to other parts of the United States.[2] In winter chronical diseases often occur, occasioned by the sudden changes of weather, which check perspiration; but these are not confined to this city. In July the heat is often oppressive; but it is believed, on good grounds, that the climate has been improved by the clearing of the country, and that the extremes both of heat and cold are now less violent than formerly. During the last ten years, the average depth of the snow has not exceeded eight or ten inched, though it was much greater in the memory of persons still living.

*Population.* — The population of the territory of Columbia in 1800 was 14,093; in 1810 it amounted to 24,023; that of the city was 8208; of Georgetown, 4948; of Alexandria, 7227; of Washington county, exclusive of towns, 2135; that of Alexandria county, 1325. In 1817 Georgetown and Washington were supposed to contain 20,000 inhabitants, and the whole district 30,000.[3]

## City of Washington.

The city of Washington is situated on the Patomak, at the confluence of this river with its eastern branch, which formerly bore the name of Annakostia, in lat. 38 deg. 55 min. north, and in long. 76 deg. 53 min. from Greenwich.

From Washington to Philadelphia the distance is 144 miles.

To Baltimore,   43

To Richmond,   132

To Annapolis,   40

The meridional line which passes through the capitol was drawn by Mr. Ellicot.[4] The longitude was calculated by Mr. Lambert.[5]

It is scarcely possible to imagine a situation more beautiful, healthy, and convenient, than that of Washington. The gently undulating surface produces a pleasing and varied effect. The rising hills on each side of the Patomak are truly picturesque; the river is seen broken and interrupted by the sinuosities of its course, and the sails of large vessels gliding through the majestic trees which adorn its banks, give additional beauty to the scenery.

The site of the city extends from north-west to south-east about four miles and a half, and from north-east to south-west about two miles and a half. The houses are thinly scattered over this space; the greatest number are in the Pennsylvania Avenue between the capitol arid the president's house, from the latter towards Georgetown, and near the barracks and navy yard on the eastern branch. The public buildings occupy the most elevated and convenient situations, to which the waters of the Tiber creek may be easily conducted, as well as to every other part of the city not already watered by springs. The streets run from north to south, and from east to west, crossing each other at right angles, with the exception of fifteen, named after the different states, and which run in an angular direction. The Pennsylvania street, or avenue, which stretches in a direct line from the president's house to the capital, is a mile in length, and 160 feet in breadth; the breadth of the narrowest streets is from 90 to 100 feet.

The plan of this city, of which we have given an engraving, is universally admired. The most eligible places have been selected for public squares and public building. The capitol is situated on a rising ground, which is elevated about 80 feet above the tide water of the Patomak, and 60 or 70 above the intermediate surface. This edifice will present a front of 650 feet, with a colonnade of 260 feet, and 16 Corinthian columns 31½ feet in height. The elevation of the dome is 150 feet; the basement story 20; the entablement 7; the parapet 6½; the centre of the building, from the east to the west portico, is 240 feet. The ceiling is vaulted, and the whole edifice is to be of solid masonry of hewn stone, which, in appearance, resembles that known by the name of the Portland stone. The centre, or great body of the building, is not vet commenced, but the two wings are nearly finished. The north wing, which contains the senate chamber, has the form of a segment, with a double-arched dome, and Ionic pillars. It is adorned with portraits of Louis XVI. and Mary Antoinette. Under the senate chamber are commodious rooms for the library, and the judiciary courts of the United States. The south wing, containing the hall of representatives, and rooms for transacting business by committees, is of a circular form, adorned with 24 Corinthian pillars, behind which are galleries and lobbies for the accommodation of those who listen to the debates.

The foundation was laid in 1794, the north wing was finished in 1801, the south wing in 1807. The interior was originally of wood, which soon decayed; and to substitute stone, it became necessary to change the whole arrangement. This magnificent edifice is the joint composition of several artists; Thornton, Latrobe, Hallet, and Hatfield.[6]

The post-office is a large brick building, situated at about equal distances from the president's house and the capitol. Under the same roof is the patent-office, and also the national library, for the use of members of congress. In the first of these departments are upwards of 900 specimens of native mechanical genius. This would appear to afford decisive proof, that Americans are not deficient in inventive talent. The library is small, consisting of but 3000 volumes; but it is select and well chosen, and includes various classes of literature, having been the property of Mr. Jefferson, for which he obtained from the United States 20,000 dollars. The former library, containing from 7000 to 8000, was destroyed by our *enlightened* countrymen. So great has been, at some periods, the depreciation of property in this city, that in 1802, what had originally cost 200,000 dollars, was sold for 25,000. This decay continued to go on, until the visit of general Ross, and the subsequent signature of peace: since that time it seems to have risen, like the phœnix from the flames, and is once more partially increasing in prosperity. There are now a number of two and three story brick buildings, none of which are uninhabited; and also some small wooden houses, though, according to the original plan, none were to be built less than three stories high, and all to have marble steps. But the childish folly of this scheme was soon subverted by the natural course of events; and though the existence of *"lower orders,"* even in the capital of the republic, may not accord with the vanity of its legislators, they ought to be told, that neither prosperity nor population can be possessed by any nation without a due admixture of the *natural classes* of society.

The president's house consists of two stories, and is 170 feet in length, and 85 in breadth. It resembles Leinster House, in Dublin, and is much admired.[7] Even the poet Moore styles it a "grand edifice," a "noble structure." The view from the windows fronting the river [looking southward] is extremely beautiful.

One of the objects embraced by the original plan was the establishment of a university, on an extensive scale, for the whole Union. A communication was made on this subject by the president to the congress in 1817.

The public offices, the treasury, department of state, and of war, are situated in a line with, and at the distance of 450 feet from, the president's house. These buildings, of two stories, have 120 feet in front, 60 in breadth, and 16 feet in height, and are ornamented with a white stone basement, which rises six or seven feet above the surface. It was originally proposed to form a communication between these offices and the house of the president, a plan which was afterwards abandoned.

The jail consists of two stories, and is 100 by 21 feet. The infirmary is a neat building. There are three commodious market-places, built at the expence of the corporation.

The public buildings at the navy-yard are the barracks, a work-shop, and three large brick buildings for the reception of naval stores. The barracks, constructed of brick, are 600 feet in length, 50 in breadth, and 20 in height. At the head of the barrack-yard is the colonel's house, which is neat and commodious. The work-shop, planned by Latrobe, is 900 feet in length.

The patent office, constructed according to the plan of J. Hoban, esq. (who gained the prize for that of the president's house), consists of three stories, and is 120 feet long, and 60 feet wide. It is ornamented with a pediment, and six Ionic pilasters. From the eminence on which it stands, the richly wooded hills rise on every side, and present a scene of unequalled beauty.

The inhabitants of the city form a body, politic and corporate, under the title of "Mayor and Council of Washington." The council, consisting of 12 members, not under 25 years of age, is elected annually by the free white male inhabitants aged 21 or upwards, who have paid taxes the year preceding the election, and is divided into two chambers, the first of which has seven, and the second five members. The fines, penalties, and forfeitures imposed by the council, if not exceeding 20 dollars, are recovered, like small debts, before a magistrate; and if greater than this sum, by an action of debt in the district-court of Columbia. In 1806, the corporation passed an act to establish an infirmary, for which the sum of 2000 dollars was appropriated, and trustees appointed for the superintendence of this establishment. In August, 1810, a sum not exceeding 1000 dollars was appropriated, for the support of the infirm and diseased; and the corporation have allotted certain squares (numbered 109 and 1026) for places of interment, which are situated at a proper distance from the populous part of the city. Two dollars are the price of a grave.

The canal, which runs through the centre of the city, commencing at the mouth of the Tiber creek, and connecting the Patomak with its eastern branch, is nearly completed. Mr. Law,[8] (brother to the late lord Ellenborough), the chief promoter of this undertaking, proposes to establish packet-boats, to run between the Tiber creek and the navy-yard, a conveyance which may be rendered more economical and comfortable than the hackney-coach. This canal is to be navigable for boats drawing three feet water. If the net profits exceed 15 per cent, on the sum expended, the excess is to be paid to the mayor and city council.

The Patomak bridge was built under the direction of a company, or board of commissioners, and the funds were raised by a subscription consisting of 2000 shares, at 100 dollars per share. The expences of the work amounted to 96,000 dollars, and consequently the real value of a share was 48. The bridge, which is covered with planks of white and yellow pine, is a mile in length, and is supported by strong piles, from 18 to 40 feet, according to the depth of the water. A neat railing separates the foot from the horse-way. By means of a simple crank and pulley, the draw-bridge, for the passage of vessels, is raised by the force of one individual.

The tolls are high: a four-horse carriage, 1½ dollar; a two horse carriage, 1 dollar; a four-horse waggon, 62½ cents; a two-horse waggon, 37½; a gig, 36½; a horse, 18½; a man, 6½. The toll of 1810 amounted to 9000 dollars. The interest of the stock has risen to eight per cent. After the lapse of 60 years, the corporation will be dissolved, and the bridge become the property of the United States.

It was an unfortunate circumstance, that, in planning this city, some provision was not made for preserving the fine trees which covered the soil, in those situations where they would have been useful or ornamental. The whole of the natural wood has been cut down, and its place is very poorly supplied by some few Lombardy poplars, which afford neither shade nor shelter. This is an error which nothing but time can repair.

The patent office is under the direction of Dr. Thornton, a native of the West Indies, now a citizen of the United States, who has a salary of 2000 dollars per annum. To obtain a patent for an art or machine, the inventor, if a citizen of the United States, declares upon oath, before a justice of the county where he resides, that he believes himself to be the true inventor; and he gives a description of this art or machine, and the use to which it is applied, accompanied, if necessary, with a drawing, in a letter addressed to the secretary of state of the United States; and this description is inserted in the patent, for which the sum of 30 dollars is paid to the treasury department. If the applicant is not a citizen of the United States, he must declare on oath, that he has resided therein more than two years. The copy-right of books, prints, maps, &c. is secured by depositing a copy thereof in the clerk's office of the district court, where the author or proprietor resides. This is recorded and published in one or more newspapers, during four weeks, commencing within two months of the date of the record. The right is thus secured, for the space of 14 years, to the citizens or residents of the United States; and by a renewal of those formalities, it is extended to their executors, administrators, and assigns, for another term of 14 years. The patents issued from the 1st of August, 1790, to the 1st of January, 1805, were 598; and the amount received at the treasury department for patents, from 1801 to 1809 inclusive, was upwards of 27,000 dollars.

Exclusive of the bank of the United States, there are seven banks in the district of Columbia. The Marine Insurance Company of Alexandria was incorporated in 1789, with the power of having a capital of 12,500 shares, at 20 dollars a share, or 250,000 dollars.

By an act of the city council, in December, 1804; the public schools of the city are placed under the direction of a board of thirteen trustees, seven of whom are elected annually by the joint ballot of the council, and six by individuals who contribute to the support of the schools. The net proceeds of taxes on slaves and dogs, of licences for carriages, and hacks for ordinaries and taverns, for selling wines and spirits, for billiard tables, for hawkers, and pedlars, for theatrical and other public amusements, are employed for the education of the poor of the city.

There are two academies in the city, under the direction of the corporation, which were established by the voluntary contributions of the inhabitants, and are supported by the corporation. In these two seminaries there are generally from 120 to 150 scholars, including those who pay for their tuition. The houses are large and commodious, and were intended to be the germ of a national university, in conformity to the plan described in the last will of general Washington. There are, besides, twelve or more schools in different parts of the city where the terms of tuition are under five dollars per quarter.

The Catholic college of Georgetown, which was erected, and is supported, by subscription, commenced in the year 1790, under the direction of the incorporated catholic clergy of the state of Maryland. It is a fine brick building, consisting of three stories, in length 153 feet, and 33 in breadth, and is fitted for the reception of 200 students. The terms of tuition are as follows: Students above twelve years of age pay 250 dollars; and under that age, 200; those who attend the classes pay 250, owing to extraordinary expences, and some particular indulgencies. The payments are made half-yearly in advance. To be admitted as a pensioner, the student must be a Roman Catholic. If a Protestant, he boards in a house convenient to the college, where he enjoys equal advantages with the Catholics, except as to admission to the instruction and exercises of the Roman religion. The students are instructed in the English, French, Latin, and Greek languages; in geography, arithmetic, algebra, geometry, and the different branches of classical education. Public examinations are holden four times a year.

A free school has been lately established by subscription, to be conducted according to the plan of Mr. Lancaster, who has engaged to send two masters from England for its superintendence and direction.

A public library has been lately established, by the subscription of 200 individuals, at twelve dollars each; and the directors of this association have obtained an act of incorporation, with powers suitable to the direction of the establishment, Mr. Boyle, a painter from Baltimore, collects objects of natural history, to form a museum.

There is no reading-room at Washington, which is perhaps owing to the profusion of newspapers received there by members of congress, from all parts of the Union. In 1817, seven newspapers were published in the district. In one of these, the *National Intelligencer*, the acts, and sometimes the opinions, of the government are first communicated to the public; and it is owing to this circumstance, that, in Europe, it is generally considered as the organ of the executive authority. This paper is published thrice a week. Other two are on the same scale; two appear weekly, and two daily.

Of societies there are, the Humane Society, the Washington Whig Society, two mason lodges, the Columbian Institute founded in 1817, and the Columbian Agricultural Society. This last consists of 200 members, who pay one dollar a year each, which is expended in premiums for the best cattle, cloth, flannels, stockings, carpets, &c. The American Society for Colonising Free People of Colour[9] was established in the end of 1816. Its object is to procure a situation on the western coast of

Africa, to which free people of colour may, with their own consent, be transported.

There are different sects, and a great variety of religious opinions, but no dissension The annual salary of a clergyman at Washington is about 1000 dollars, with a small mansion and lot of land, — a provision which is said to be inadequate to the support of a family; and it is probably owing to this circumstance, that two clergymen, the one a Presbyterian, and the other a Baptist, have clerkships in the treasury department. The laws of Virginia and Maryland, in relation to the clergy, admit of no external badge or distinction of their order in the ordinary intercourse of life, but only in the exercise of their sacred functions in their respective places of divine worship. Elsewhere, and at other times, it is as impossible to distinguish them from the crowd, as to recognize their places of worship, which are without steeple, cross, bell, or other distinctive sign of religious appropriation. By an act of December, 1792, for the suppression of vice, and punishing the disturbers of religious worship, persons offending in these respects are liable to fine and imprisonment, and to be bound over to good behaviour. For profane swearing and drunkenness, the penalty is 83 cents; and for labouring on Sunday, 1 dollar and 75 cents, applicable to all persons, and especially to apprentices, servants, and slaves. For adultery (of which there is scarcely an example) the punishment is 20 dollars; for fornication (which is too common) one half of this sum.

In 1815, there were in Washington nine physicians, and two apothecaries, who were also physicians; their fee in the city is a dollar a visit; in the country it is regulated by the distance.

*Georgetown* is finely situated on the north-east side of the Patomak river. It is divided from Washington by Rock creek, over which there are two bridges. The distance of Georgetown from Alexandria is ten miles; and there is a daily communication between these two places by means of a packet-boat.

In 1810, the population of Georgetown was upwards of 7000. Some trade has been carried on between this port and the West Indies. Mr. Scott, in his Geographical Dictionary, informs us, that the exports of 1794 amounted to 128,924 dollars. Flour and other articles are transported to Alexandria in vessels which do not draw more than nine feet water.

The houses of Georgetown, which are chiefly of brick, have a neat appearance. Several were built before the streets were formed, which gave rise to an observation from a French lady, that Georgetown had houses without streets, — Washington streets without houses.[10] The bank is a neat building. The churches, under the direction of trustees, are plain and without ornament.

*Alexandria* may be considered the port of Washington, from which it is distant only about seven miles. It was formerly named Belhaven, and is pleasantly situated on the Virginia, or west side of the river Patomak. The streets, like those of Philadelphia, run in straight lines, and intersect each other at right angles. The houses arc of a neat construction. Those erected at the expence of the public are, an episcopal church, an academy, court-house, bank, and jail. Alexandria has carried on a considerable commerce with New Orleans, and also with the East and West Indies, and some European ports. The warehouses and wharfs are very commodious. Vessels of 500 tons lie in the basins. Some have sailed from this port with 1200 hogsheads of tobacco on board.

There have been many failures among the principal merchants of this place, in consequence of losses abroad, or unfortunate speculations. Those who carry on business at present employ their capitals in a more cautious manner.

Manufactures are yet in their infancy. Two manufactories of cut nails have been lately established, and several of woollen and other cloths. House rent is cheap, for, except along the basins, it is not more than six per cent., and in some places not half that sum. By a census taken in 1817, the inhabitants were found to be, — whites, 5513; blacks, 2646, (of whom 1047 were free). Total, 8153. In this year a lottery was authorised by congress, to raise funds for building a penitentiary, a city-hall, and two Lancastrian schools.

There are already five churches, Protestant, Presbyterian, Catholic, Methodist, and Baptist. In the academy there are 40 scholars, 35 of whom learn Latin and classical literature, and 21 reading, writing, and arithmetic. There are nine or ten physicians, but there is no medical society. Any person may exercise this profession. In the town the usual fee is a dollar per visit; and five dollars to and within the distance of ten miles.

.... The ground of Washington was originally the property of private individuals, who, by an arrangement with the government, ceded one half to the public, in consideration of the enhanced price of the other, by virtue of this cession. Four thousand five hundred lots, each containing 6265 superficial feet, are the property of the nation, and have been estimated at 1,500,000 dollars. Some of these lots have been sold at 45 cents per foot, though the common price is from 8 to 15 cents, depending on the advantages of situation. Near the centre market several have been purchased at 25 cents. The original price of lots was from 200 to 800 dollars each, which shows that their value has considerably diminished. This has been owing to different causes, and particularly to the project of some eastern members of congress to transfer the seat of government to some other place. The value of this property has also suffered by litigation. In 1804, several purchasers refused to pay to the commissioners of the government the sums stipulated in the deed of sale, which were to be discharged, according to agreement, at certain fixed dates. In consequence of this refusal, the commissioners ordered the lots to be sold to the highest bidder, and they were repurchased by the former proprietors for one-tenth of the original cost; by which circumstance the government experienced a loss of 70,000 dollars. The supreme court, to whom the case was submitted, decided in favour of the proprietors, alleging, that, as a remedy had been sought in the sale of the lots, the government could not have recourse to another, and it also became responsible for the expences of the law-suit, amounting to 2000 dollars. The proprietors united in support of their mutual interests, which were defended by the ablest lawyers, except the attorney-general, who stood alone in the behalf of the government.

A house, consisting of three stories, 26 feet in front, and 40 feet deep, completely finished, costs from 4000 to 6000 dollars. A house of two stories, of the same length and breadth, is valued at from 3000 to 4000 dollars.

The rate of house-rent is proportioned to the expence of the materials of its construction, and the advantages of its situation. Bricks cost from $5¾$ to $6¾$ dollars per thousand. Their dimensions, as fixed by an act of the corporation, are $9⅛$, $4⅜$, $2⅝$ inches.

Calcareous stone, of a bluish colour, is brought from the neighbourhood of Georgetown, and purchased at a cheap rate. Un-slacked lime costs from 2 to $2¼$ dollars per barrel. Wood is cheap; pine and oak are brought from the eastern shore of the Chesapeake. A good bricklayer is paid at the rate of three dollars for every thousand bricks. Some of the houses are covered with slate, though generally with boards, called shingles, the use of which ought to be prohibited, on account of their combustible nature. Wood is chiefly employed for fuel, and oak and hickory are preferred, which are sold at the rate of four dollars per cord, except during an unusually severe winter, when the price has been from six to seven dollars. By an act of the corporation, a cord of wood must be eight feet in length, four in breadth, and "well stowed and packed." A good dray-horse can be purchased at Washington for 60, a saddle-horse for 130, and a milch-cow for 35 dollars.

The whole exports for the district of Columbia, for the year ending 30$^{th}$ September, 1817, were 1,768,658 dollars, of which 1,689,102 were domestic produce, and 79,556 foreign.

The inhabitants of Washington are social and hospitable. Respectable strangers, after the slightest introduction, are invited to dinner, tea, balls, and 'evening parties. Tea parties have become very expensive, as not only tea, but coffee, negus,[11] cakes, sweetmeats, iced creams, wines, and liquors, are often presented; and, in a sultry summer evening, are found too palatable to be refused. In winter, there is a succession of family balls, where all this species of luxury is exhibited.

Both sexes, whether on horseback or on foot, wear an umbrella in all seasons: in summer, to keep off the sunbeams; in winter, as a shelter from the rain and snow; in spring and autumn, to intercept the dews of the evening. Persons of all ranks canter their horses, which movement fatigues the animal, and has an ungraceful appearance. At dinner, and at tea parties, the ladies sit together, and seldom mix with the gentlemen, whose conversation naturally turns upon political subjects. In almost all houses toddy is offered to guests a few minutes before dinner. Gentlemen wear the hat in a carriage with a lady as in England. Any particular attention to a lady is readily construed into an intention of marriage. Boarders in boarding-houses, or in taverns, sometimes throw off the coat during the heat of summer; and in winter the shoes, for the purpose of warming the feet at the fire; customs which the climate only can excuse. In summer, invitation to tea parties is made verbally by a servant, the same day the party is given; in winter, the invitation is more ceremonious. The barber arrives on horseback to perform the operation of shaving; and here, as in Europe, he is the organ of all news and scandal.

.... In the summer of 1814, this metropolis was taken possession of by an English naval and land force, which set fire to the capitol, president's house, public offices, and navy-yard. The moveable property destroyed at the latter place has been estimated at 417,743 dollars; the loss sustained in buildings and fixtures at 91,425; the expences of rebuilding at 62,370; in all, 571,538 dollars. The loss sustained by the partial destruction of the capitol, president's house, and other public edifices, has been estimated at 460,000 dollars; in all, 1,031,538 dollars. The superintendent of the public buildings, in his report, dated the 29th of October, 1814, gave the following statement of their cost down to the date of their destruction: —

North wing of the capitol:[12]
$457,388
South wing of the capitol:
$329,774
President's house:
$334,334
Public offices:
$93,613
Total:
$1,215,109 dollars.

An English emigrant, in a letter to the editor, after reprobating in severe terms the Gothic barbarity of General Ross, exultingly observes, that the Englishmen employed in repairing the damages he effected were nearly as numerous as those that followed him.

"The Custom is to Shake Hands"

From *An Excursion Through the United States and Canada During the Years 1822-1823* by An English Gentleman.

William Newham Blane, Jr. (1800-1825) was the son of an English gentleman who was a Fellow of the Royal Society. Blane came to the United States perhaps burdened with some of the prejudices of earlier visitors among his countrymen and these prejudices were quickly realized upon his visit to Washington, D.C. Yet, he appears to have come away with a more favorable impression of the people of the United States; among them, President James Monroe. A subsequent printing of his *Excursion* (titled *Travels Through the United States*, etc.) carries this observation on the title page: "There is no subject upon which the people of England have been more completely misinformed, than that of the American character."
According to an obituary notice in *The Examiner* of London, the younger Blane died after suffering "a violent fever" during his subsequent travels in Egypt and Syria, ending the author's brief but promising career.

---

Before arriving at the Federal City, I passed through the little village of Bladensburgh, the spot where the action was fought (if action it can be called) which decided the fate of the capital in the last war. The only American troops that opposed General Ross[1] were a small body of marines, commanded by Major Miller,[2] and a few seamen, under Commodore Barney.[3] These brave fellows were all cut to pieces. The militia, although very numerous, ran away without firing a shot; and did not stop, until they had reached Montgomery, fifteen miles distant. On account of the cowardly conduct of the militia, this action is humourously called by the Americans, "the Bladensburgh Races."

I was much disappointed upon arriving at Washington. I had been told, indeed, that I should see a straggling city; but I had no idea that I should find the houses so very much scattered as they really are. An European, duly impressed with the idea of an ancient metropolis, might well be astonished at seeing the infant one of the United States.

It is situated in the district of Columbia, a tract of land ten miles square; which was ceded to the general government by the two States of Maryland and Virginia, and which is under the exclusive care and jurisdiction of the Congress. — This was done, to prevent any trouble that might arise from the acts or laws of any particular State.

The plan of the city is on a vast scale, and it will be many a long year before even one half of it will be completed. Instead of beginning from a centre or nucleus, from which it might gradually have expanded, the whole was laid out, and the lots sold, wherever individuals chose to select them. Owing to this, every one selected the spot, which he thought would be most desirable when the city should be finished; and consequently very few streets are as yet completed.

From its total want of commerce, Washington has not increased so rapidly as was expected; yet the census of 1820 makes the population of the city 13,247, and that of the whole district 33,039. Of course, if the United States continue to increase in wealth and population in the same proportion as they have hitherto done, the city must soon become considerable; and if, as seems probable, the canal which is to join the waters of the Ohio with the tide waters of the Potowmac is soon put in execution, Washington will at once become a place of great commerce.

But the city must expect nothing from the Government. Instead of fostering the infant metropolis, and taking a pride in ornamenting, embellishing, and increasing it, as one would naturally have supposed; the Congress has, on the contrary, been but a cold-hearted protector, and has acted the part of a step-father rather than of a parent. In fact, it has done little more than provide for its own convenience; for as the Capitol, the President's house, and the public offices, were necessary buildings, the city owes the Congress no thanks for them.

But the worst feature in the conduct of the government is, that the members, arriving from different parts of the Union, have very often shown a decided hostility to the place. Each member is warm in advocating any improvement by which his own State is to be immediately benefitted; but any canal, road, &c. merely intended for the general benefit of the Union, has almost always been treated with the most appalling indifference, and sometimes even with the most decided opposition. This was most strongly exemplified in the case of the great national road over the Alleghany Mountains.

Moreover, when in the first years of the Republic any establishment was in contemplation, each State endeavoured to have it in its own territory. Thus the different States struggled for the Mint, and the mother branch of the United States Bank, which were at last fixed in Philadelphia; and for the Military College, which was obtained by New York. Now had all these establishments been fixed at Washington, they would have been under the immediate eye of Government, and would have added to the importance and ornament of the metropolis. But one member says, "What is the city of Washington to

Pennsylvania?" and another, "How does the improvement of Washington benefit New York?" Of a truth we may assimilate this conduct to that of a parcel of importunate fellows pulling and tugging at the coat of a good-natured passive old gentleman; who, by the time one has torn off a skirt, and another a sleeve, remains very ill-provided with clothing.

The Capitol is a large and splendid mass of buildings, but though handsomely ornamented and embellished, has, at present, rather a heavy appearance, probably occasioned by its being perfectly isolated. It has cost a large sum, but is worthy of the nation, and does credit to their liberality.

The eminence on which it stands, rises gradually from the Potowmac, which it completely overlooks. Indeed the view from the western portico is one of the finest I ever saw. Immediately beneath is the most populous and best built part of the city. Pennsylvania Avenue, the principal street, commences at the Capitol, and terminates at another eminence, on which stands the large and handsome mansion of the President. This edifice and the Capitol appear, when viewed from a distance, to watch over the city below them; while in the left is seen the majestic Potowmac; and in the distance the small town of Alexandria, and the wooded hills of Virginia. In clear weather, the Blue Ridge, part of the Alleghanies, can be distinctly perceived, though distant forty miles.

The interior of the Capitol is ill arranged. There are, indeed, a few very splendid halls, but the passages are numerous, and, in general, very badly lighted. The lofty ceiling of the Hall of the Representatives is supported by very large polished columns, of a kind of American brescia,[4] of the most beautiful and variegated colours. Each member sits in a large massive and handsomely ornamented arm chair, partly resembling that of the Roman consuls. In front of these chairs there is a mahogany desk, on which are pens and paper, with a drawer below, in which the member locks up any papers he may want. These seats and desks are placed in rows, at small intervals, on the gradually sloping floor of the semicircle; while in front of them, and near the columns at the back part of the amphitheatre, is the elevated seat of the President of the Representatives. The *tout ensemble* of the Hall is very imposing. Indeed I never saw a finer room of the kind: for the Chamber of the Deputies at Paris is not to be compared to it, and our House of Commons does not pretend to any other merit than antiquity.

The Chamber of the Senate is built very much upon the same plan as the Hall of the Representatives, but in point of size, embellishment, and architectural beauty, is decidedly inferior.

The centre of the Capitol is occupied by a large and lofty rotunda, ninety-six feet in diameter, over which there is a dome. It is here, as I was informed, that the inauguration of the President will be solemnized.

In the centre should have been deposited, under a suitable monument, the bones of Washington; but they are still at Mount Vernon, in a miserable sepulchre, which Lieutenant Hall compares to an old ice-house. A Dutch gardener almost succeeded in stealing the precious relicks for the purpose of exhibiting them in some foreign country. The Congress did indeed once solicit Judge Washington,[5] the proprietor, to permit their removal, which was granted; but nothing has been done, nor is likely to be done for the present; so that the remains of this father of his country, this greatest of the moderns, lie without even a tombstone over them. — Such is national gratitude!

The Congress, in an unusual fit of liberality, ordered that the most striking events of the Revolution should be commemorated in four large pictures, for each of which they voted the sum of 8,000 dollars. A Mr. Trumbull,[6] the artist employed, has finished three of these pictures, which are at present in the Capitol. They are on a very large scale, the artist not having been at all sparing of his canvass. The first, the Signing of the Declaration of Independence, though a very heavy picture, is interesting from the number of portraits. The signers are for the most part dressed, not only in Quaker colours, but in Quaker style. I must of course except Jefferson, who forms a most marked and vivid contrast to the rest, being decorated with a bright red waistcoat. The second picture, the subject of which is the Surrender of General Burgoyne to General Gates, is much the best, some of the figures being very well executed. But the third picture, the Surrender of Lord Cornwallis, is the worst. In this the French officers, drawn up to allow the vanquished troops to pass through, are as stiff as Prussian sentries when they present arms: moreover, their heads are in a line of such accurate straightness, that they look like a set of figures drawn to illustrate the art of perspective.

The dome of the Capitol was not quite finished when I saw it, but this and part of the eastern front is all that is wanting to complete the vast edifice. The whole has been rebuilt since 1814, when, together with the President's house and the public offices, it was burnt by the British.

This was a most unjustifiable act; for, although undoubtedly the Americans, by the destruction of Newark, began the system of burning, which was pursued during the war, yet the British had already amply retaliated by laying waste most of the towns on the American frontier. Moreover, though the order given to the Secretary of War was somewhat equivocal, the Americans highly disapproved of the conduct of General M'Clure; and the Government accordingly removed him from his command. But even if Newark had been burnt intentionally, it would at any rate have been well for the British not to have emulated the Vandala and the Mahommedans in destroying the whole of the library of the Congress, containing a great number of old and valuable works. I may add that all the public records and documents also perished in the Capitol

— an irreparable loss to the Americans — but which was, therefore, perhaps a more agreeable triumph to their momentary conquerors. Instead of burning, it would have been much better to have levied a contribution on the city, as was done at Alexandria. This would have benefitted the victors without exposing them to the censure of posterity. Besides, nothing during the whole war tended so much to unite the Americans as the burning of the metropolis. Those who would not perhaps have opposed the British troops very heartily were now obliged to do so out of fear. "If," said the Baltimoreans, the Philadelphians, &c. &c. "these fellows come here, they will act as they did at Washington."

The City Hall, when finished, will be the handsomest building in the United States. It fronts the Potowmac and commands a very advantageous view of the city.

Few places could have been selected possessing greater natural beauties, and, at the same time, better adapted for the scite [sic] of a metropolis. I think, indeed, that Washington, in point of situation, ranks first among the American cities.

The Patent Office, to which strangers are freely admitted, contains a number of very interesting models. Among those of bridges, I particularly admired that of a straight bridge, constructed by means of timbers, connected diagonally over a span of 200 feet, at Fayetteville, in North Carolina. The model was placed across a division between two of the cases of the smaller models; and though it was apparently very slight, yet when a piece of wood was fastened to it by several small cords, it supported three or four of the visitors.

The entrance to the Navy-yard is through a very handsome, though simple, arched gateway of white stone. Immediately fronting this is a beautiful little rostrated column of white marble, surmounted by the American eagle. Round the column, and standing on a large and elevated pedestal of the same material, are some fine emblematical statues. This monument was erected by the officers of the American navy, to the memory of their comrades who fell at Tunis. It is one of the handsomest and most chaste little monuments that I have ever seen, and was made in Italy; indeed, I recognized it as a copy of the column of Duilius.[7] I observed that some of the figures surrounding it had been broken, evidently on purpose; and accordingly at the base of the column I found this inscription: "Mutilated by Britons, August 14, 1814." — But would not the English officers have punished any man detected in injuring it? Surely the damage must have been done by some ignorant and brutal soldier, when the Navy-yard was destroyed: for had it been otherwise, or had the British really intended to have injured the figures, they would not have stopped at breaking an arm or two. I should be glad to see this inscription effaced, as it tends to increase hostile feelings, which are contrary to the interest of both countries.

The chief curiosity in the Navy-yard is the ingenious and beautiful machinery, contrived by Commodore Rodgers,[8] for hauling up vessels of war out of the water; and thus obviating the necessity of dry docks, which, owing to the small rise and fall of the tide, could not be constructed without great difficulty. Large strong beams are run completely through the vessel, entering at the port-holes on one side and coming out at those on the opposite, while both the ends of the beams rest upon an inclined plane that slopes down to the water. Attached to each beam, just where it enters the port-hole, are two very strong chains, which are fastened to a large block of wood, made to fit the keel. These chains are tightened by wedges and screws — and, by this means, the ship is supported on its keel the same as when on the stocks. A large chain or two is put entirely round the vessel, from the bows to the stern, and to these a cable is attached, which is stretched forward to a windlass. The vessel is thus easily drawn up out of the water. Indeed, 150 men were able to draw up the Potowmac the largest frigate I ever saw, and which was on the plane when I was at Washington. Over the whole machine a very handsome roof has been built, which completely protects the vessel.

Besides the Potowmac, there was building, in the Navy-yard, a large frigate with an elliptical stern.

The Armoury is very prettily arranged, and kept in excellent order. I saw there several of the celebrated "repeating swivels." Each is composed of seven parallel barrels, fastened together with iron hoops, in the manner of Roman fasces, six forming the circle, with one in the centre. Each barrel is about four feet and a half long, and a quarter of an inch thick; and the whole engine turns on a pivot, much resembling that which is ordinarily used for a swivel, and is directed by means of a crooked iron handle. The lock that fires it is placed about eighteen inches from the muzzle. The chief secret is in the loading, which is difficult, and takes a long time. They are, therefore, sent ready loaded to the vessels and forts, where they are wanted, and after being once fired are sent home again. Their calibre is nearly the same as that of a musket, and they discharge altogether 350 balls, that is, seven at a time for fifty successive discharges, at half a second interval. These most formidable weapons appeared to be of a rough and cheap construction. A fort or vessel provided with a great number might keep up such a murderous fire, that advancing or boarding in the face of it would be almost impossible.

The Navy-yard is on what is called the eastern branch of the Potowmac. At a little distance off, on the main branch, is a straight wooden bridge, nine furlongs[9] in length, which presents a curious appearance.

The President's house, a noble mansion, or rather palace, built on an eminence fronting the Potowmac, was not quite finished when I was at Washington, but already formed a majestic object. The former mansion, with everything it contained, was burnt by the British.

Shortly after my arrival at Washington, as I was one day coming with a friend from visiting the public offices, he pointed out to me a well-dressed gentleman, walking by himself. "That," said he, "is the President of the United States." When this great personage met us, my friend introduced me to him. I took off my hat as a mark of respect; upon which the President did the same, and shook me by the hand, saying he was glad to see me. I went soon afterwards to pay my respects to him at his house, in company with the same friend. We were shown into a handsome room, where the President had been writing. When he came in, he shook us by the hand, requested us to sit down, and conversed upon a variety of topics. I may here observe, that whenever, in America, you are introduced to any one, the custom is to shake hands. I like this custom, as it is much more friendly, and puts you more at your ease, than the cold formal bow, with which, in England, and indeed in most of Europe, you are greeted at the performance of this ceremony. I was very much pleased with the unaffected urbanity and politeness of the President, so entirely different from what I should have met with on being introduced to a person of anything like the same importance in Europe. When going to pay my respects to a Duke of Tuscany, or even to a petty German prince, whose whole territory was not larger than a county in one of the United States, I have had to dress in a court uniform, and to pass by a whole file of soldiers, and then by half a dozen pages, officers, and chamberlains, with gold keys at their pockets, &c. But the President of the United States received me in my ordinary morning dress; and, though he is Commander-in-chief of the army and navy, has no need of sentinels at his door, being sufficiently protected by the love of his fellow citizens.

I can safely say that the manly simplicity of the President impressed me with much more respect, than the absurd mummery of European potentates. Yet surely if pride can be tolerated in any man, it must be in him, who (like President Monroe) has been placed at the head of the government of his native country, by the unanimous suffrage of eight millions of his fellow citizens. How much more has he to be proud of, than the petty distinction of birth or fortune! and what an immeasurable distance between him and a German *Princeling*! Yet, to judge by their manners and bearing, you would fancy the Prince was the greatest man on earth, and the President merely a private individual; whereas the one is a most unimportant personage, except in his own opinion, and the other is really a great man.

A short time before my arrival at Washington, there occurred a fine example of Republican simplicity. Jefferson, Madison, and Monroe, happened to meet together at the opening of a college at Charlottesville in Virginia. I suppose this is the only instance on record, of three men, two of whom *had been*, and one of whom actually *was*, at the head of the government of the self-same country, meeting by chance, and, in the most unceremonious and friendly way, passing the evening together. There were four Presidents alive when I was in the United States, — Adams, Jefferson, Madison, and Monroe.

The environs of Washington abound in picturesque scenery. From the hills, on the Virginia bank of the river, and also from those beyond the eastern branch, the city appears scattered over the plain below, and elevates itself here and there in some grand structure, such as the Capitol, the President's house, or the City Hall; while below rolls the mighty Potowmac, diversified with the numerous boats and vessels that are constantly moving over its surface.

"God Bless the American People"

From *Lafayette in America in 1824 and 1825* by Auguste Levasseur and John Davidson Godham.

Auguste Levasseur (1795-1878) is best known in America as private secretary to Gilbert du Mortier, Marquis de Lafayette (1757-1834) during the latter's farewell tour of the United States. Levasseur later served in the diplomatic corps as Consul in Haiti. John Davidson Godham (1794-1830) provided the English translation for the (Philadelphia) Carey and Lea edition.

Lafayette had been a hero of the American Revolution. Wounded during the Battle of Brandywine, he continued to command American troops and advocated for the American cause in his native France until the British were defeated at Yorktown. During subsequent revolutionary periods in France, Lafayette found himself variously arrested, exiled or imprisoned until he withdrew from public life in later years.

Approaching seventy upon his farewell tour of the United States, Lafayette was given a hero's welcome in every state he visited, and though he apparently visited them all, perhaps nowhere was his reception and farewell as emotional as in Washington, D.C.

After resting two days at Baltimore we set out for Washington city. General Lafayette wished to depart privately, and the citizens, always solicitous to satisfy his desires, contented themselves with calling in the evening employed several hours, and left in our hearts impressions of profound melancholy. We commenced our journey on the 1st of August, accompanied by two members of the Baltimore committee. A few miles from Washington we were met by an elegant carriage, which drew up near us, from which a young gentlemen alighted and inquired for General Lafayette. This was the eldest son[1] of the new president Mr. Adams, who was sent by his father to the nation's guest, to inform him that he had solicited and obtained from the citizens of the metropolis, permission to offer him the use of the president's house. The general accepted the invitation for himself and travelling companions, entered Mr. Adams's carriage, and we continued on our route. Our two members of the Baltimore committee had not anticipated such an occurrence, which threw them into considerable embarrassment. They had been zealous "Jackson men," and had declared themselves strongly against Mr. Adams, during the election; of this Mr. Adams was not ignorant, and on this occasion, it appeared difficult to them to present themselves under the auspices of General Lafayette, without exposing themselves to the chance of being thought willing to make the *amende honorable*. They determined to separate from our party, on entering the city, and took lodgings in a hotel.

During the canvass of the presidential election, I had frequently heard the adversaries of Mr. Adams accuse him of aristocratic habits, contracted, as they said, in the foreign courts at which he had passed many years.[2] This accusation appeared to me much opposed to what I had seen and have related of his conduct in the steam-boat going from Frenchtown to Baltimore; but, at length, in consequence of hearing the charge frequently repeated, I began to fear, that, with the exercise of power, he might fall into what we call in Europe the manners of a prince; my surprise was therefore the more agreeable, to find, on reaching Washington, that the president was not changed. It is true, we found Mr. Adams in the place of Mr. Monroe; but the public man was still the same. The plainness of the domestics, and facility of access to the house, appeared not to have undergone the least alteration, and in Mr. Adams's reception of us we experienced all the cordiality of his predecessor. He soon ascertained why our companions had not remained with us, and hastened to send them an invitation to dinner, which they accepted without embarrassment or hesitation, as men who understood the politeness intended them, but who did not consider themselves as being in any way pledged by accepting it.

The lodgings prepared for us in his own house by the president were plain, but commodious and in good taste. Anxious to enable General Lafayette to enjoy the repose he thought him to need after so many and such long voyages, and after numerous and profound emotions, he secluded himself with us in entire privacy. Aided by Mrs. Adams, her two sons, and two nieces, he made us taste, if I may so express myself, the sweets of domestic life. During the early portion of our stay, there rarely set down to table or around the hearth more than two or three persons at once, and usually these were some public officers who, after being occupied all day with the president in business, were detained by him to dinner and the familiar conversation of the evening. It was during this period which glided away so swiftly, that I could appreciate the character of Mr. Adams, whom I had previously known only by the eulogies of his friends or the attacks of opponents. I discovered that the first had but done him justice, and the last been misled by party spirit. It is difficult to find a more upright and better cultivated intellect than is possessed by the successor of Mr. Monroe. The beautiful reliefs of the capitol, to which he is not a stranger; his treatise on weights and measures, and the numerous diplomatic missions he has discharged with distinction, bear witness to his good taste in the arts, the correctness of his scientific judgment, and his skill in politics. As to the accusation of aristocracy, which some have preferred against him, it is sufficiently refuted by his manners, which remain unaltered by his elevation to the chief magistracy of the republic.[3]

.... On the 6th of September, the anniversary of Lafayette's birth, the president gave a grand dinner, to which all the public officers, and numerous distinguished persons then in Washington, were invited. The company had already assembled and were about to sit down to table, when the arrival of a deputation from the city of New York was announced, which came to present to General Lafayette, on behalf of the city council, a book containing an account of all the transactions and events occurring during his stay in that city. This magnificent volume, removed from its case, and exhibited to the company, excited general admiration. It is in fact a masterpiece that may be compared with the most beautiful and rich of those manuscripts which formed the glory and reputation of libraries before the discovery of printing: It contained fifty pages, each ornamented with vignettes designed and painted with the greatest skill; views and portraits perfectly executed, completed this work, of which the writing was done by Mr. Bragg, and the paintings by Messrs. Burton, Inman, and Cummings. The view of the Capitol at Washington, of the City Hall of New York, and the portraits of Washington, Lafayette, and Hamilton, left nothing to be desired; and in order that this beautiful work should be altogether national, it was upon American paper, and bound by Mr. Foster of New York with admirable richness and elegance.

General Lafayette gratefully accepted this fine present, to which the president and his cabinet gave additional value by placing their signatures in it. Although a large company partook of this dinner, and it was intended to celebrate Lafayette's birth-day, it was very serious, I may say, almost sad. We were all too much pre-occupied by the approaching journey to be joyous: we already felt, by anticipation, the sorrowfulness of separation. Towards the conclusion of the repast, the president, contrary to diplomatic custom, which forbids toasts at his table, arose and proposed the following: "To the 22$^{nd}$ of February and 6$^{th}$ of September, birthdays of Washington and Lafayette." Profoundly affected to find his name thus associated with Washington, the general expressed his thanks to the president, and gave this toast, "To the fourth of July, the birthday of liberty in both hemispheres."

At last the day which we ardently wished for, and whose approach, however, filled us with profound sadness, the day which would begin to convey us towards our country, but must, at the same time, separate us from a nation winch had so many claims to our admiration and affection, the day of our departure, the 7$^{th}$ of September, dawned radiantly. The workshops were deserted, the stores were left unopened, and the people crowded around the president's mansion, while the militia were drawn up in a line on the road the nation's guest was to move to the shore. The municipality collected about the general to offer him the last homage and regrets of their fellow citizens.

At eleven o'clock he left his apartment, slowly passed through the crowd which silently pressed after him, and entered the principal vestibule of the presidential dwelling, where the president, surrounded by his cabinet, various public officers, and principal citizens, had waited for him a few minutes. He took his place in the centre of the circle which was formed on his approach; the doors were open, in order that the people who were assembled with-Out might observe what took place, and the slight murmur of regrets which were heard at first among the crowd, was succeeded by a solemn and profound silence; the president, then visibly agitated by emotion, addressed him as follows, in the name of the American nation and government: —

"GENERAL LAFAYETTE — It has been the good fortune of many of my distinguished fellow-citizens, during the course of the year now elapsed, upon your arrival at their respective places of abode, to greet you with the welcome of the nation. The less pleasing task now devolves upon me, on bidding you, in the name of the nation, adieu.

"It were no longer seasonable, and would be superfluous, to recapitulate the remarkable incidents of your early life — incidents which associated your name, fortunes and reputation, in imperishable connection with the independence and history of the North American Union.

"The part which you performed at that important juncture was marked with characters so peculiar, that, realizing the fairest fable of antiquity, its parallel could scarcely be found in the *authentic* records of human history.

"You deliberately and perseveringly preferred toil, danger, the endurance of every hardship, and the privation of every comfort, in defence of a holy cause, to inglorious ease, and the allurements of rank, affluence, and unrestrained youth, at the most splendid and fascinating court of Europe.

"That this choice was not less wise than magnanimous, the sanction of half a century, and the gratulations of unnumbered voices, all unable to express the gratitude of the heart with which your visit to this hemisphere has been welcomed, afford ample demonstration.

"When the contest of freedom, to which you had repaired as a voluntary champion, had closed, by the complete triumph of her cause in this country of your adoption, you returned to fulfil the duties of the philanthropist and patriot in the land of your nativity. There, in a consistent and undeviating career of forty years, you have maintained, through every vicissitude of alternate success and disappointment, the same glorious cause to which the first years of your active life had been devoted, the improvement of the moral and political condition of man.

"Throughout that long succession of time, the people of the United States, for whom, and with whom you had fought the battles of liberty, have been living in the full possession of its fruits; one of the happiest among the family of nations, Spreading in population; enlarging in territory; acting and suffering according to the condition of their nature; and laying the foundations of the greatest, and, we humbly hope, the most beneficent power that ever regulated the concerns of man upon earth.

"In that lapse of forty years, the generation of men with whom you co-operated in the conflict of arms, has nearly passed away. Of the general officers of the American army in that war, you alone survive. Of the sages who guided our councils; of the warriors who met the foe in the field or upon the wave, with the exception of a few, to whom unusual length of days has been allotted by-heaven, all now sleep with their fathers. A succeeding, and even a third generation, have arisen to take their places; and their children's children, while rising up to call them blessed, have been taught by them, as well as admonished by their own constant enjoyment of freedom, to include in every benison upon their fathers, the name of him who came from afar, with them and in their cause to conquer or to fall.

"The universal prevalence of these sentiments was signally manifested by a resolution of congress, representing the whole people, and all the states of this Union, requesting the president of the United States to communicate to you the assurances of grateful and affectionate attachment of this government and people, and desiring that a national ship might be employed, at your convenience, for your passage to the borders of your country.

"The invitation was transmitted to you by my venerable predecessor; himself bound to you by the strongest ties of personal friendship, himself one of those whom the highest honours of his country had rewarded for blood early shed in her cause, and for a long life of devotion to her welfare. By him the services of a national ship were placed at your disposal. Your delicacy preferred a more private conveyance, and a full year has elapsed since you landed upon our shores. It were scarcely an exaggeration to say, that it has been, to the people of the Union, a year of uninterrupted festivity and enjoyment, inspired by your presence. You have traversed the twenty-four states of this great confederacy: You have been received with rapture by the survivors of your earliest companions in arms: You have been hailed as a long absent parent by their children, the men and women of the present age: And a rising generation, the hope of future time, in numbers surpassing the whole population of that day when you fought at the head and by the side of their forefathers, have vied with the scanty remnants of that hour of trial, in acclamations of joy at beholding the face of him whom they feel to be the common benefactor of all. You have heard the mingled voices of the past, the present, and the future age, joining in one universal chorus of delight at your approach; and the shouts of unbidden thousands, which greeted your landing on the soil of freedom, have followed every step of your way, and still resound, like the rushing of many waters, from every corner of our land.

"You are now about to return to the country of your birth, of your ancestors, of your posterity. The executive government of the Union, stimulated by the same feeling which had prompted the congress to the designation of a national ship for your accommodation in coming hither, has destined the first service of a frigate, recently launched at this metropolis, to the less welcome, but equally distinguished trust, of conveying you home. The name of the ship has added one more memorial to distant regions and to future ages, of a stream already memorable, at once in the story of your sufferings and of our independence.

"The ship is now prepared for your reception, and equipped for sea. From the moment of her departure, the prayers of millions will ascend to heaven that her passage may be prosperous, and your return to the bosom of your family as propitious to your happiness, as your visit to this scene of your youthful glory has been to that of the American people.

"Go, then, our beloved friend — return to the land of brilliant genius, of generous sentiment, of heroic valour; to that beautiful France, the nursing mother of the twelfth Louis, and the fourth Henry; to the native soil of Bayard and Coligni, of Turenne and Catinat, of Fenelon and D'Aguesseau. In that illustrious catalogue of names which she claims as of her children, and with honest pride holds up to the admiration of other nations, the name of Lafayette has already for centuries been enrolled. And it shall henceforth burnish into brighter fame; for if, in after days, a Frenchman shall be called to indicate the character of his nation by that of one individual, during the age in which we live, the blood of lofty patriotism shall mantle in his cheek, the fire of conscious virtue shall sparkle in his eye, and he shall pronounce the name of Lafayette. Yet we, too, and our children, in life and after death, shall claim you for our own. You are ours by that more than patriotic self-devotion with which you flew to the aid of our fathers at the crisis of their fate. Ours by that long series of years in which you have cherished us in your regard. Ours by that unshaken sentiment of gratitude for your services which is a precious portion of our inheritance. Ours by that tie of love, stronger than death, which has linked your name, for the endless ages of time, with the name of Washington.

"At the painful moment of parting from you, we take comfort in the thought, that wherever you may be, to the last pulsation of your heart, our country will be ever present to your affections; and a cheering consolation assures us, that we are not called to sorrow most of all, that we shall see your face no more. We shall indulge the pleasing anticipation of beholding our friend again. In the meantime, speaking in the name of the whole people of the United States, and at a loss only for language to give utterance to that feeling of attachment with which the heart of the nation beats, as the heart of one man — I bid you a reluctant and affectionate farewell."

An approving murmur drowned the last words of Mr. Adams, and proved how deeply the auditors sympathised with the noble sentiments he had expressed in favour of France, and her children whose whole life and recent triumph would add still more to his glory and exaltation. General Lafayette, deeply affected with what he heard, was obliged to pause a few moments before he was able to reply. At last, however, after having made an effort to regain his voice, he thus expressed himself:

"Amidst all my obligations to the general government, and particularly to you, sir, its respected chief magistrate, I have most thankfully to acknowledge the opportunity given me, at this solemn and painful moment, to present the people of the United States with a parting tribute of profound, inexpressible gratitude.

"To have been, in the infant and critical days of these states, adopted by them as a favourite son, to have participated in the toils and perils of our unspotted struggle for independence, freedom and equal rights, and in the foundation of the American era of a new social order, which has already pervaded this, and must, for the dignity and happiness of mankind, successively pervade every part of the other hemisphere, to have received at every stage of the revolution, and during forty years after that period, from the people of the United States, and their representatives at home and abroad, continual marks of their confidence and kindness, has been the pride, the encouragement, the support of a long and eventful life.

"But how could I find words to acknowledge that series of welcomes, those unbounded and universal displays of public affection, which have marked each step, each hour, of a twelve months' progress through the twenty-four states, and which, while they overwhelm my heart with grateful delight, have most satisfactorily evinced the concurrence of the people in the kind testimonies, in the immense favours bestowed on me by the several branches of their representatives, in every part and at the central seat of the confederacy?

"Yet, gratifications still higher await me; in the wonders of creation and improvement that have met my enchanted eye, in the unparalleled and self-felt happiness of the people, in their rapid prosperity and insured security, public and private, in a practice of good order, the appendage of true freedom, and a national good sense, the final arbiter of all difficulties, I have had proudly to recognise a result of the republican principles for which we have fought, and a glorious demonstration to the most timid and prejudiced minds, of the superiority, over degrading aristocracy or despotism, of popular institutions founded on the plain rights of man, and where the local rights of every section are preserved under a constitutional bond of union. The cherishing of that union between the states, as it has been the fare well entreaty of our great paternal Washington, and will ever have the dying prayer of every American patriot, so it has become the sacred pledge of the emancipation of the world, an object in which I am happy to observe that the American people, while they give the animating example of successful free institutions, in return for an evil entailed upon them by Europe, and of which a liberal and enlightened sense is everywhere more and more generally felt, show themselves every day more anxiously interested.

"And now, sir, how can I do justice to my deep and lively feelings for the assurances, most peculiarly valued, of your esteem and friendship, for your so very kind references to old times, to my beloved associates, to the vicissitudes of my life, for your affecting, picture of the blessings poured by the several generations of the American people on the remaining days of a delighted veteran, for your affectionate remarks on this sad hour of separation, on the country of my birth, full, I can say, of American sympathies, on the hope so necessary to me of my seeing again the country that has designed, near a half century ago, to call me hers? I shall content myself, refraining from superfluous repetitions, at once, before you, sir, and this respected circle, to proclaim my cordial confirmation of every one of the sentiments which I have had daily opportunities publicly to utter, from the time when your venerable predecessor, my old brother in arms and friend, transmitted to me the honourable invitation of congress, to this day, when you, my dear sir, whose friendly connection with me dates from your earliest youth, are going to consign me to the protection, across the Atlantic, of the heroic national flag, on board the splendid ship, the name of which has been not the least flattering and kind among the numberless favours conferred upon me.

"God bless you, sir, and all who surround us. God bless the American people, each of their states, and the federal government. Accept this patriotic farewell of an overflowing heart; such will be its last throb when it ceases to beat."

In pronouncing these last words, General Lafayette felt his emotion to be rapidly increasing, and threw himself into the arms of the president, who mingled his tears with those of the national guest, in repeating those heart-rending words, Adieu! Adieu! The spectators, overcome by the same feelings, also shed tears and surrounded their friend, once more to take him by the hand. To abridge this scene, which could not be suffered much longer, the general retired for a short time into his own apartment, where Mrs. Adams surrounded by her daughters and nieces came to express their wishes and regrets. On the evening before, this lady, whose cultivated mind and amenity of character had greatly contributed to the pleasure of our visit to the president's house, had presented him with a fine bust of her husband, and had added to this present a copy of verses in French, whose charm and elegance proved that this was not the first occasion in which her muse had spoken in our language.

Detained as if by a magic spell, General Lafayette could not make up his mind to leave his friends; a thousand pretexts seemed to retard the definitive moment of separation, but at last the first of the twenty-four guns, which announced his departure, having been heard, he again threw himself into Mr. Adams's arms, expressed to him his last good wishes for the American nation, and retired to his carriage. The president repeated the signal of adieu from the top of the steps, and at this sign the colours of the troops which were drawn up before the president's house were bowed to the earth.

"Nobody Would Inhabit Such a Town"

From *Personal Narrative of Travels in the United States and Canada in 1826* by Frederick Fitzgerald De Roos.

(John) Frederick Fitzgerald De Roos (1804-1861) entered the Royal Navy as a midshipman in 1818, just a few days after his fifteenth birthday. He was promoted to Lieutenant in 1825 and toured the United States and Canada the following year, by which time he was an experienced naval officer with service in the Mediterranean and off the South American continent. He achieved the rank of Commander in 1828.

Although De Roos is largely dismissive of the United States in general and of Washington, D.C. in particular, he does hold the young ladies of Georgetown in some regard "in point of dress, beauty, and conversational powers." In spite of his Saturday night observations, the good Lieutenant is to be found nevertheless in church on the following Sunday morning.

---

At length, to our great joy, we arrived at the capital of the United States, at twelve o'clock, having travelled 200 miles in forty-eight hours. On approaching Washington, the first object you encounter after passing a dreary common is the Capitol, — a magnificent building, which, from its vast size and extreme whiteness, is very striking in its appearance.

Its site is high, and finely commands the town. A noble avenue, three quarters of a mile in length, leads from it to that part of Washington which is completed. We drove through this, and proceeded to the principal inn of the town, called "The Indian Queen."[1]

Having got rid of the dust which had been intolerable throughout the journey, we went to the residence of Mr. Vaughan,[2] the English minister, to whom we had letters; and drove from thence to the Capitol. We entered the building by a magnificent portico, and saw the principal chamber of which the dome forms the roof. We were much struck with its immense size. The walls are destitute of ornament, if we except some pieces of sculpture representing various wars and treaties with the Indians. The artist might have selected subjects more creditable to his country. The senate-room and chamber of representatives occupy the two wings of the edifice; they are semicircular, lighted from the roof, and in their general appearance reminded me strongly of the Chamber of Deputies at Paris. There were desks and many other conveniences for the members, unknown to our Houses of Parliament. Being Saturday, the person whose business it usually is to show the building, was absent, and we were, consequently, disappointed of seeing the library, committee-rooms, and national pictures.

Our next visit was to the dock-yard, which is about a mile distant from the town, and conveniently situated on the eastern branch of the Potomac. We were admitted, without difficulty, by the sentry, who said, with much in difference, that "He *guessed* we were at liberty to see any part of it we pleased." Of this permission, of course, I was delighted to avail myself, as it was the first opportunity I had had enjoyed of comparing the American dock-yards with establishments of the same nature in England.

The area is about forty acres in extent, a considerable portion of which is unoccupied, although the gun-wharf and ordnance stores are contained within its bounds. The commissioner, or captain, has a small house near the entrance. I could observe no other residences belonging to officers. The workmen being absent, I was prevented from inspecting the store-houses. There were two frigates on the slips; one, in progress of building, was to be called the Susquehanna. She was constructed on the latest and most approved principles of the American builders, and was to mount 60 guns. Her timbers were close together, and her shape remarkable for very full bow, and a perfectly straight side. She had a round stern, but its rake and flatness, combined with the judicious construction of her quarter-galleries, gave it quite the appearance of being square.

The Potomac, another heavy and clumsy-looking 60 gun frigate, was hauled up on ways, in a cradle called Commodore Porter's inclined plane; an expedient, intended to save the expense and inconvenience of dry docks, for examining the bottoms of vessels where there is little tide. She was partly suspended by cables and partly by shores: the hauling up had been easily accomplished, but the ground having afterwards given way under her stern, the inclination of the plane had been altered, and I very much doubt whether she will ever be got down again. This, in the United States, where rigid economy is so much the order of the day, is likely to make the inclined plane very unpopular. I next went on board the Congress, of 38 guns; she had been newly coppered, and was lying along-side the yard, having been lately hove down there.

These were the only ships in or near Washington. In this place, they have a foundry of iron-tanks, for the supply of vessels not under the rank of frigates. They have likewise a machine, containing a partial application of steam to the making of blocks. The shell is formed of several pieces which are bolted together, and said to be stronger than those which are made by the famous engine, at Portsmouth. The operation is undoubtedly much less complicated. The sheds, or rather houses, under which they build their ships, are not of an approved construction. I visited the mast-house, and observed that the section of a made mast of their line of battle-ships does not differ materially from that of our own.

My expectations had been so much raised by the reputation which America bears in Europe with respect to maritime affairs that I left the yard with feelings of extreme disappointment. As I passed out of the gates, my attention was attracted by a monument which faces the entrance. It was erected to the memory of some officers, and bore an inscription declaring it to have been mutilated by Britons at the taking of Washington. At the capture of this city, many excesses were undoubtedly committed, but I have been assured that there are no grounds for this particular accusation. Let it however in justice be observed, that this is the only public inscription or memorial which I saw in the United States, of a nature calculated to wound the feelings of a stranger.

We extended our drive to the president's house and the different public offices, which are in general very handsome buildings, but look quite solitary in this wilderness of a town. In planning Washington, the Americans certainly reckoned without their host. A central piece of land was decreed by the States for the purpose of building an immense metropolis. The wood was cut down, the streets were marked out, and the public buildings erected; but it never occurred to the projectors that the situation presented no facilities for commerce, and that the circumjacent land was unfit for agriculture. Nobody would inhabit such a town by choice, those who are obliged by their avocations to make the capital their residence, inhabit a suburb called George's Town, which is more agreeably situated on the river Potomac. On our return to the inn, we found a gentleman, at whose house we had left a letter of introduction, who was kind enough not only to ask us to dinner, but offered to take us to a party at the French Minister's that evening.³

The prospect of seeing a little good company was quite refreshing, and we gladly accepted his offer. During dinner, the conversation chiefly turned upon the commission which was then employed in settling the price of the slaves taken by the English during the war, and we heard a very interesting account of that affair. It appears that the Americans founded their claim on a point of grammar in a clause which they had the cunning to insert in the last treaty of peace with England. The question was referred to the arbitration of the Russian cabinet, which decided in favour of America. We also heard an account of the debates and discussions in the last meeting of Congress.

During the session, a period of six months, three great questions were agitated: — The first, a question of legislature; the second, whether they should send deputies to the congress at Panama, to which a representative of each of the American Republics had been invited. The third, related to a proposed alteration in the constitution. The object of this latter was to vest the election of the president entirely in the people. By the present law, every man in the United States has a vote, but to obtain the presidency, the first candidate must have more voters than all the rest put together; in default of this, the election devolves upon the representatives. Thus, though General Jackson had a considerable majority of popular votes, he had not enough to outnumber all the other candidates, and the election going to the representatives, the weaker parties united their forces, and Adams was elected.

These three questions gave rise to endless discussions, each member thinking it necessary to deliver his own sentiments in detail. The questions were eventually referred to committees, Congress being unable, after all, to decide them. At the conclusion of the session, it was resolved that a commissioner or deputy, should be sent to the congress of

Republics at Panama; but it was too late, for the unhealthy season had commenced. Upon the other two questions, the committee stated, in their report, that no two individuals of their number were of the same opinion, and that it was impossible to come to any conclusion.

The construction and regulations of the American senate seem but ill adapted to the dispatch of public business. The conflicting interests of the different states which are represented — the anxiety of the members to deliver their sentiments, and the diffuseness of their long-winded orations, which wander into the most extraneous and irrelevant matter, frequently protract the discussion of unimportant subjects to debates of almost interminable duration. It must not, however, be supposed that the spirit of party, or disputes of local interest, have broken or impaired the great compact which binds them together. The slightest symptoms of danger to their "Union," whether arising from internal disaffection or foreign aggression, instantly tightens the social cord, and diffuses a high feeling of patriotism throughout the vast community. That the United States have more civil and religious liberty than ourselves, there can be no doubt; the power is more in the hands of the people, and their government approaches as near a commonwealth as any recorded in history.

The experiment of a democracy upon so great a scale was a bold conception, considering the fate which has hitherto invariably attended all systems of popular government — a conception worthy of a mighty mind, worthy of the philosophic statesman, who "eripuit cælo fulmen sceptrumque tyrannis."[4] How long this vast machine will continue to work, is a matter of interesting speculation. Hitherto, the Americans have enjoyed the advantage of occupying a country where the evils of an overflowing population have not been felt; where every man is either a farmer or a merchant; where there are no idlers; and, more than all, where there are no poor; for vile indeed must be the American who cannot in some capacity earn an ample maintenance. When, however, the means of carrying off a superfluous population begin to fail, which at some period must be the case; when the sated ambition of wealth gives place to the love of distinction and power; and when the struggle for superiority between the young and old States gives rise to disturbances, symptoms of which have already appeared, we may expect to see the disadvantages of a popular government. We have already observed how indecision and jealousy fetter the hands of the executive power. The violence and illiberality of the many; their inability to judge of most legislative acts, or to extend their views beyond the question of present advantage, are to be dreaded in disturbed times, as dangerous to the security of property and the stability of the state.

At eight in the evening, we went to our party in George's Town, which had all the agreeable characteristics of an European assembly. Singing, and finally dancing, were the amusements of the evening. Everybody complained of the insufferable heat, but danced on notwithstanding; the American young ladies holding a very respectable competition with their European entertainers, in point of dress, beauty, and conversational powers.

The next day (Sunday) a gentleman to whom we had been introduced, was so good as to call and take us to church; the building, which was small, was the only episcopal establishment in the city.[5] We saw the president of the United States, and Mr. Rush,[6] at their devotions. In manner and appearance, the clergyman bore a strong resemblance to Liston in the character of Mawworm.[7] The Americans have altered, and I think not improved, some parts of the Liturgy.

The sermon was worthy of the preacher; it treated of the oppression which the United States formerly endured while under the yoke of England, whose downfall, discomfiture, and damnation he confidently predicted. He referred to Young, whose poetry he quoted copiously, and then diverged into an impious allegory, which he fathered upon a Welsh curate. But as in no English church such allusions would be tolerated, I strongly suspect that the blasphemous absurdity was the produce of his own brain. I was sorry to learn that this man was considered much superior to American preachers in general.

We afterwards paid some visits; one to a Virginian family. The gentleman's daughter was considered a beauty and a great fortune, having nearly fifteen thousand dollars.

From New York to the southward, the women are in general pale, with slight figures. The higher ranks resemble in manner the middling classes in England. It is long before the ear is reconciled to the nasal twang of their pronunciation. Politics and travelling form the usual topics of conversation, in which the ladies take an active part. The events of the last war, and the capture of Washington in particular, I found to be a frequent topic of conversation. The attention of Europe was so completely engrossed by the mighty conflict, which decided its fate on the plains of Waterloo, that the Washington campaign was regarded with comparative in difference. At any other period, this brilliant enterprize, which placed in our hands the capital of America, and humbled her pride, would have filled the world with its renown, and raised the hero who executed it to the highest rank of military glory.

It was satisfactory to me, as a naval officer, to discover that the Americans are fully aware to whom the merit of planning this daring expedition belongs. They are fully aware that the conception of the undertaking originated in the brave admiral, whose skillful and effective co-operation so materially contributed to its success.

Having amused myself by taking a few rough sketches of the town, I dined with Mr. Vaughan, the English minister, and in the evening went to a tea-party, where I had another opportunity of observing the manners of American society. I here began to think the paleness of the ladies interesting, and the drawl of their speech became gradually less disagreeable.

In our way home, we called upon one of our fellow-travellers, and during the visit the Auditor for Foreign Affairs called. He gave us a very interesting account of three deputations of Indians that had come up with petitions to Congress, and had been encamped for the last two or three months near the capital. He dwelt much upon their eloquence, and the hardness of their fate. One "talk" which he had himself heard delivered by the orator of the deputation of the Seminole tribe, he recommended me to get from the newspapers, where it was well reported. The following brief extracts will give a general notion of the style of Indian eloquence.

After expressing to the Minister of War the desires of the Indians to have their territory extended to the Big Swamp, the Chief continued thus: — "You say our great father," (meaning the president of the United States), "does not wish to oppress his red children. We believe it, and that he will keep the treaty; and give us more land. Brother, you say that our great father owns a great country beyond the Big River,[8] towards the setting sun, and that he is willing to give us a part of it, if we will go there; and he advises us to send some of our chiefs with the Muscogees to look at it, and bring us back word what sort of country it is; but we have already said we did not intend to move again, and we will not go with them.

"We have no friends, and the people of that country are strangers to us. We will not involve ourselves in the troubles of the Muscogees. We are a separate people, and have nothing in common with them.

"Most of us were born in the land we now inhabit; and of that, we claim the undisturbed possession. In that land, our blood was first spilt; it has sunk deep into the earth, and made the country dear to us. We have heard that the Spaniards have sold the country to the American. This they had no right to do, the land was not theirs but belonged to the Seminole Indians.

"Brothers, we have come here to talk with our great father concerning this matter, and to have it finally arranged. We have not yet seen our great father. We have come many days' travel to see him, and do not wish to return without shaking hands with him."

After enumerating some more grievances, he went on to say: —

"Brother, you tell us that our great father wishes to place a school in our nation, to teach our children to read and write. We do not wish one at all. We do not believe that the Great Spirit intended that we should know how to read and write; for if he had intended this, he would have given us the knowledge as early as he gave it to the white people. Now it is too late; the white people have gained an advantage we can never recover, and it is better for us to remain as we are, red men, and live in our own way."

Here follows a curious tradition of the means by which the white people obtained this advantage, and he concluded in these words: —

"Brother, the business upon which we have come here is very important to our nation, and we wish to have it settled soon, that we may return to our homes, and make the hearts of our people glad by telling them what we have done."

"Do You Mean to Buy the Lad, Sir?"

From *Travels in North America, in the Years 1827 and 1828* by Captain Basil Hall.

Captain Basil Hall (1788-1844) joined the Royal Navy at thirteen years of age. He was promoted to Lieutenant at nineteen and made Captain before he turned thirty, by which time he had seen the world. An early work entitled *Extracts from a Journal Written on the Coasts of Chili, Peru, and Mexico* proved successful and was published in several editions. Shortly thereafter he left the navy, married, and sustained a prolific writing career.

Hall's *Travels in North America*, published in three volumes, went through as many editions and proved quite popular at home but was criticized in the United States for the author's stark depiction (and for a broader audience) of slavery in America. Hall devotes three chapters of his third volume of *Travels in North America* to his experiences in Washington, D.C., selections of which appear below.

---

From *Chapter One:*

We went from Baltimore to Washington, on the 29th of December, 1827. There was still daylight enough, when we arrived, to show this singular capital, which is so much scattered that scarcely any of the ordinary appearances of a city strike the eye. Here and there ranges of buildings are starting up, but by far the greater number of the houses are detached from one another. The streets, where streets there are, have been made so unusually wide, that the connexion is quite loose; and the whole affair, to use the quaint simile of a friend at Washington, looks as if some giant had scattered a box of his child's toys at random on the ground. On paper all this irregularity is reduced to wide formal avenues, a mile in length, running from the Capitol — a large stone building well placed on a high ground — to the President's house, and the public offices near it.

Washington stands on the left bank of the Potomac, in what is called the District of Columbia — a portion of territory distinct from all the States in the Union, and appropriated by common agreement as the site of the capital, and the residence of the General Government. This space contains one hundred square miles; and many persons in that country believe the time will come when their capital shall cover the whole area of this great square.

.... My chief object in arranging matters for visiting Washington at this period, was to attend to the proceedings of Congress,[1] of which I had everywhere heard so much. Connected with this purpose, was the desire of making acquaintance with the principal men of the country, assembled at head-quarters, expressly to devote themselves to public business. And I was well pleased to find these gentlemen had sufficient leisure to satisfy the enquiries of a stranger.

.... The most perfect decorum prevails at all times in the House — no coughing — no cheering — no hear! hear! — none of those indefinable, but significant sounds, which are so irresistibly efficacious in modifying the debates of the House of Commons. Every member of Congress is permitted to speak at any length he pleases, without interruption. I cannot say, however, that there is a correspondent degree of attention paid to what is said; for, independently of the reverberations of sound from the dome, or the waste of it in filling the intercolumniations, there are other sources of disturbance constantly going on, which drown a great part of what is said. Except when some remarkably good speaker has possession of the floor, the members, instead of attending to what is spoken, are busied in conversation — in writing letters — rapping the sand off the wet ink with their knuckles — rustling the countless multitude of newspapers which deluge the House — locking or unlocking their drawers — or moving up and down the avenues which divide the ranges of seats, and kicking before them, at every step, printed reports, letter covers, and other documents strewed on the floor. A couple of active little boys are always seen running to and fro with armfuls of papers, or carrying slips of writing from members to the chair, or from member to member. Whenever anyone rises to speak, who, there is reason to infer, from experience, or from internal evidence, will be lengthy, one of these little Mercuries flies off for a glass of water, which he places on the orator's desk.

A wide passage skirts the base of the columns, between each of which there stands a commodious sofa, on which the members, or such strangers as have the entre granted them by the Speaker, may lounge at their ease. Ladies are not allowed to come on the floor of the house, but only into the gallery. When, however, I chanced to go alone, I always found an excellent place behind the Speaker's chair, along with the Foreign Ambassadors and other strangers. The reporters for the newspapers had a place assigned to them in this quarter of the House.

…. On the 1st of January, 1828, the President held a levee, at which we attended. On the 4th of July — the grand anniversary of their independence — we were told, all the world attends; but on New Year's day there is some principle of exclusion exercised. How this matter is effected in practice I could never find out, but I can imagine the poor porter to have a delicate job of it; for, in a land of universal equality, the line of admission must often lie so close to that of exclusion, that to split the difference may require fine tools.

Be this as it may, we found the scene very interesting, as we not only saw and conversed with the President, but made acquaintance with several military and naval officers of distinction, and with many other persons we were anxious to meet. The suite of apartments thrown open consisted of two handsomely furnished drawing-rooms, leading to a well-proportioned ball-room, which, however, I was surprised to find entirely unfurnished and bare. Even the walls were left in their unpainted plaster. Here was a degree of republican simplicity beyond what I should have expected, as it seemed out of character with what I saw elsewhere. Upon enquiring into this matter, I learnt, that although one Congress had voted a sum of money, — twenty-five thousand dollars, or about five thousand guineas, — for the purpose of fitting up the President's house, the succeeding Congress, which, as usual, contained a large proportion of new members, fresh from the woods, asked what was the use of expending so much of the public money, when people could dance as well, or even better, in the empty room, than in one crowded with furniture. At all events, whatever be the cause, the fact bears testimony to a degree of economy, of which very few Americans that I conversed with did not complain, as being rather too parsimonious, and, all things considered, not a very dignified or discreet exposure, at the chief point of attraction for all foreigners.

I had read so much in the public papers of the discussions in Congress about the extravagance of the President, in the outfit of this house, especially respecting the monstrous fact of his having ordered a billiard-table as part of his furniture, that I looked sharply about for this dreadful engine of vice, which, innocent or insignificant as it may appear, was actually made to play a part in the great electioneering presidential question — which seemed to turn all men's heads. I myself heard this billiard-table spoken of in Congress more than once, with perfect seriousness, as a sort of charge against Mr. Adams, who was then President. I may add, that this was only one of a thousand petty darts which were levelled at the same person; and which, though insignificant, taken separately, were like those that subdued Gulliver, by no means to be despised when shot by multitudes.

.... But I am forgetting the Congress. — By the Constitution of the United States, as I have before mentioned, the President is not allowed to conclude treaties, or to fill up vacancies in official stations, without the concurrence of the Senate. He may negotiate the wisest possible treaty with a foreign nation, but he has no authority to ratify it without submitting it to the consideration of the Senate; — that is, to eight-and-forty persons, most of whom may not have had the smallest experience in that intricate branch of the science of government which has reference to foreign engagements. They may be able and public-spirited men, it is true; but mere talents and good intentions never did supply elsewhere, and never can supply anywhere, the place of that minute knowledge of what has gone before on the same subject, and of all the various interests and complicated relations which must be taken into consideration, before even a tolerable knowledge of the bearings of any treaty can be apprehended. Nevertheless, these public instruments require to pass through this popular ordeal before they can acquire a constitutional authority, or be binding on the nation. It is said, indeed, by some, that this leads to no evils in practice; but numerous instances of the contrary might easily be pointed out.

If the President, or the Secretaries of State, were to communicate personally with the Senate, which would then become a sort of Privy Council, the case might be in some degree different; though still, it may be supposed, there would be great difficulties in the way of transacting such delicate executive business with efficiency. But, when the whole matter submitted to the judgment of the Senate is reduced to writing, and their determination thereupon is likewise sent back to the Executive in the same form, it is easy to understand how essentially cramped, retarded, and confused, the public business must be; — for I presume it will hardly be denied, that in most negotiations with foreign powers, there may be circumstances of the greatest importance, the details of which it might be altogether inexpedient, with a due regard to the public interest, to communicate to so great a number of persons, many of whom are not likely to understand their value; and yet, without such knowledge, it may be impossible to see the bearing of the measures in progress.

In the earlier period of the government of America, General Washington, when President, used to come to the Senate to discuss such matters. But this practice, which, by the way, shows his opinion plainly enough, was soon discontinued, and would now be looked upon as highly unconstitutional. There can be no doubt, however, from this circumstance, corroborated by some of the best authorities of those days, that the Senate was intended to act the part of an executive council fully more than that of a legislative body. They have, unquestionably, legislative powers given them, but there seems no reason to believe, that the framers of the Constitution ever contemplated the large proportion in which the executive functions of the government have eventually come to be shared by the Senate.

On the contrary, there is abundant internal evidence, as well as some direct authority, for believing, that the statesmen who drew up the Constitution of America, foresaw the evils of uniting the Executive and Legislative power in the same hands, and sought to guard against this fatal rock — upon which so many antecedent republics have split — by a series of artificial checks, some of which look very well on paper, but few, in the opinion of most persons, have accomplished the purpose they were designed to serve.

.... The legislative and executive branches of the government are, in point of fact, absorbed by Congress. In England there is a well-known saying, that the King can do no wrong; in America, the maxim is nearly inverted, for it would seem as if the President could do no right. In England, the Monarch is exempted from all responsibility, while his ministers, being available persons, bear the whole burden, under whatever nominal or real authority their measures may have been carried on. In America, the power of the chief magistrate — the constitutional Executive of the country — has been gradually abridged, till his actual authority, either for good or for evil, has been almost annihilated. In that country, therefore, the Executive is deprived almost entirely of the power of action, but still he is held responsible. In England, the Executive virtually possesses great authority, but is nominally free from responsibility.

.... It will be recollected, that in America the President is elected for four years, and cannot be constitutionally removed, unless by impeachment, till the expiration of this period. In this respect, therefore, as has often been remarked, the Americans have actually much less power to change the persons who administer their government, than the English have. For though a minister may sometimes hold his place for a short time in England, in a minority, the occurrence is very rare. In point of fact, the people of England do indirectly, but substantially, elect their rulers — and, through the influence of their representatives, as unquestionably possess the power of changing them — a privilege which the Americans do not, and cannot constitutionally enjoy, as long as their President is elected for a certain period of years.

From *Chapter Two:*

Although the debates in the National Legislature formed the chief object of interest at Washington, many other incidental matters arose, from time to time, to vary the picture.

The following advertisement caught my eye, in one of the newspapers:—

Marshal's Sale.

By authority of a writ of fieri facias,[2] issued from the Clerk's Office of the Circuit Court, in this district, for the county of Washington, to me directed, I shall expose to sale, for cash, on Tuesday, the 15th instant, NEGRO GEORGE, a slave for life, and about sixteen years old. Seized and taken in execution of, as the goods and chattels of Zachariah Hazle, and will be sold to satisfy a debt due by him to William Smith.

Sale to be at the County Court-House Door, and to commence at 12 o'clock, M.

TENCH RINGGOLD,
Marshal District of Columbia.
Jan 10 — dts

I had often, in the course of my life, in the British West India possessions, and elsewhere, seen slavery in full operation; but as I had never happened to be actually present at the sale of a negro, I resolved to witness it for once, and in a place where, at first sight, such an incident might least of all have been looked for.

I repaired to the County Court-House, accordingly, at noon, on the 15th of January, 1827, and having found my way along an empty passage, I reached a door, from which people were departing and others entering, like bees crowding in and out of a hive. This was the Court of Justice. But the matters under discussion were either so completely technical, or my head was so full of the black boy, that I could not follow what was going on.

I came again into the passage, and walked along to the front door, which nearly faces the Capitol, distant about one-third of a mile. The flags were just hoisted on the top of the building, which intimate that the Senate and the House of Representatives had assembled to discuss the affairs of this free nation[3] — slavery amongst the rest.

The only man I could see in the passage, was a great heavy-looking black fellow, who appeared so much downcast and miserable, that I settled within myself that this must needs be no other than Negro George, placed there for inspection. But the Deputy-marshal, who entered at this moment, holding in one hand the advertisement copied above, and in the other the writ of fieri facias alluded to therein, undeceived me, by saying that the man I pointed to was a slave indeed, though not for sale, but that I should see the other immediately.

It was soon buzzed about, I suspect, amongst the purchasers, that a suspicious-looking stranger was making enquiries respecting the boy; for a tall man, wrapped in a cloak, whom I had observed for some time cutting large junks of tobacco from a lump which he drew from his waistcoat pocket, and thrusting them into his mouth, evidently in a fidget, now came up to me, and said, with an air of affected carelessness, "Do you mean to buy the lad, sir?"

"I? Oh, no!" I exclaimed.

The tall man drew a satisfied breath on hearing this, and said, in a more natural tone, "I am glad of it, sir — for I do; and am very anxious to succeed, because I know the chap well, and have become interested in him, and he himself — ah ! there he stands — wishes to become my property."

"How is that?"

"Why," said he, "you must know that his owner was indebted to me fifty dollars, and would not or could not pay me, so I had a lien upon this boy, and the Court allowed me to have him latterly, pending the litigations. There have been three or four law-suits about him, and he has been knocking about from hand to hand ever since March, 1822 — five years — and he is now to be sold to satisfy this debt."

"What says the boy to all this?" I asked.

"Come here, George," he called, and the lad joined us. "Don't be scared, my boy," said the gentleman, "there is no one going to hurt you."

"Oh, I am not scared," answered the boy, though he trembled all the while. He looked very ill at ease, I thought, and I soon found out the cause, in his apprehension of being purchased by a person, of whom, I suppose, he had some previous knowledge, and whose looks certainly were as little inviting as anything could well be. He was a short, lean man, with a face deeply wrinkled, not so much with age or care, as with the deep seams of intemperance. His two little eyes were placed so far back in his head, that you could not see them in profile, and when viewed in front through a pair of enormous spectacles sparkled in a very ominous manner; while his straight, scanty, and disordered hair, formed an appropriate sky-line to the picture. I began to take considerable interest in the little fellow's fate, and whispered to my tall companion, that I hoped he would get the boy.

After various delays, the slave was put up to auction, at the end of the passage, near which four or five persons had by this time collected. There was a good deal of laughing and talking amongst the buyers, and several jests were sported on the occasion, of which their little victim took no more notice, than if he had been a horse or a dog. In fact, he was not a chubby shining little negro, with a flat nose, thick lips, and woolly hair, but a slender, delicate-looking youth, more yellow than black, with an expression every way suitable, I thought, with the forlorn situation in which he was placed — for both his parents, and all his brothers and sisters, he told me, had been long ago sold into slavery, and sent to the Southern States — Florida or Alabama — he knew not where!

"Well, gentlemen," cried the Deputy-marshal, "will you give us a bid? Look at him — as smart a fellow as ever you saw — works like a tiger!"

One of the spectators called out, "Come, I'll say 25 dollars;" another said 35 — another said 40 — and at last 100 dollars were bid for him.

From the spot where I was standing, in the corner, behind the rest of the party, I could see all that was passing. I felt my pulse accelerating at each successive offer, and my cheek getting flushed — for the scene was so very new that I almost fancied I was dreaming.

The interest, after a time, took a different character, to which, however, I by no means wished to give utterance, or in any shape to betray; but at this moment, the Deputy-marshal, finding the price to hang at 100 dollars, looked over to me, and said, "Do give us a bid, sir — won't you?"

My indignation was just beginning to boil over at this juncture, and I cried out, in answer to this appeal, with more asperity than good sense or good breeding, — "No! no! I thank God we don't do such things in my country!"

"And I wish, with all my heart," said the auctioneer, in a tone that made me sorry for having spoken so hastily — "I wish we did not do such things here."

"Amen!" said several voices.

The sale went on.

"We can't help it, however," observed the Marshal; "we must do our duty. 100 dollars are bid, gentlemen! One — hundred — dollars !"

The ominous personage with the deep-set eyes now called out, to my horror, and that of the poor boy, "120!"

Just at this moment a farmer, who had come from the country, and seemed pleased with the looks of the youth, nodded to the auctioneer, and said, "130."

My tall friend now said, "140," which was echoed by the new comer with, "142!"

Upon which these two bidders having exchanged looks, walked apart for a couple of minutes, whispering something, which I did not hear. I observed the farmer nod several times, as if assenting to some compromise. They now returned, and the tall gentleman said, "I will give 143 dollars for him," while the other, though more than once appealed to by the auctioneer, spoke no more.

"143 dollars are bid for this lad! One hundred and forty-three dollars — once! twice! — Are you all done, gentlemen? — Thrice! — The lad is yours, sir, — a slave for life!"

I patted the boy on the head, wished his new master, my tall friend, all joy of his bargain, and ran off as fast as I could down one of the avenues, hoping, by change of place, to get rid of the entanglement of many unpleasant thoughts which crowded upon me during the sale; and perhaps willing, by a good scamper over the ground, to satisfy myself of the identity of my own freedom.

I asked a gentleman afterwards, whether such things were common in that part of the country. Instead of answering my question, he picked up a newspaper at random, and pointed out the following advertisement.

Marshal's Sale.

By authority of a writ of fieri facias, issued from the Clerk's Office of the Circuit Court of this district, for the county of Washington, to me directed, I shall expose to public sale, for cash, on Monday, 31st instant, the following slaves, viz.: — Charity, Fanny, Sandy, Jerry, Nace, Harry, Jem, Bill, Anne, Lucy; Nancy and her five children, George, Penn, Mary, Francis, and Henry; Flora and her seven children, Robert, Joseph, Fanny, Mary, Jane, Patty, and Betsy; Harry; and also four mules, four carts, one carriage and harness. Seized and taken in execution, as the goods and chattels of John Threlkeld, and will be sold to satisfy a debt due by him to the Bank of the United States, use of the United States, and the Bank of the United States.

Sale to be at the dwelling of Alexander Burrows, and commence at 11 o'clock a. m.

TENCH RINGGOLD,
Marshal of the district of Columbia.
Dec 24 — dts

I should be doing the inhabitants of the district of Columbia great injustice, and also leave a needless degree of pain on the minds of others, were I not to mention the sincere desire which is felt, and perhaps, as far as possible, acted upon, in that quarter, to remedy, if not altogether to remove, an evil apparently so inconsistent with the principles applied to everything else in America.

From *Chapter Three:*

On the 8th of January, 1828, on going to the House of Representatives, I found the members presenting resolutions of a great variety of kinds, touching everything and anything. I have before observed, that there is neither discipline nor organization in this body, as to the conduct of business. Consequently, any member brings forward the subject which is uppermost in his own thoughts, or which he has reason to know will be agreeable to his constituents, whose express agent he is. This indiscriminate and desultory mode of proceeding, without concert amongst themselves, leads to the repetition of innumerable proposals already before the house, or which have been discussed over and over again in preceding Congresses. Such topics, it might be thought, should have been put to rest long ago. But, alas! nothing is allowed to settle in that busy and much agitated country.

The motion which interested me most was brought forward by a member for one of the Southern States, who, in disregard of the usual habit, came soon to his point, and spoke well upon it. The object was to direct one of the committees of the house, I forget which, to take measures for placing in a vacant niche, or compartment, in the rotunda or great hall of the Capitol, a painting of the battle of New Orleans, gained by General Jackson over the English.

The motion seemed appropriate to the day, 8th of January, the anniversary of that victory; and there is no saying how far such a proposal might have been received, had it been left purely to its own merits. But this was not the course of any American debate which it was my fortune to hear.

A gentleman who was standing by me asked what I thought of the suggestion; to which I answered, that there could be nothing more reasonable, and begged to ask in my turn, if he thought there could be any objection started in the house.

"Wait a little while," said he, "and you'll see; for," he continued, "you know the whole depends upon the presidential politics of the house?"

I said I did not know.

"Surely," he replied, "you are aware that General Jackson is a candidate for the Presidency; — now, if this motion succeeds, it will be what is called 'a sign of the times,' and, so far as the opinion of Congress goes, will help on one side the grand object of all men's thoughts at this moment. But you will see ere long, that the Adams party will, in some way or other, entangle this question, and prevent its getting through the house. They are in a minority, it is true; but you are aware how much torment the weaker party can always give the stronger, if they set about it systematically. Indeed," he observed, "I should not be surprised if this little matter, which the good sense of the house, if it were fairly taken, would discuss and settle in ten minutes, may not, under the fiery influence of party spirit, last as many days; for there is no knowing beforehand whether a debate with us is to last a day, or a week, or even a month. So I beg you to watch the progress of this one."

The proposer of the measure concluded his speech by saying, that as there could be no doubt of its adoption, he begged to propose Mr. Washington Alston,[4] of Boston, as the artist who ought to execute the work, not only from his being the most skillful painter in the country, but from his being a native of the same State with General Jackson, namely, Tennessee.

I had no notion that the debate would run off upon this point, because the gentleman named was, beyond all question, the best artist in America. Besides which, there was some address, I was told, in having pointed out an artist residing in the North, to perform the service; a degree of consideration which it was thought would conciliate the members from that quarter, who were mostly in favour of Mr. Adams.

These small shot, however, failed to hit their mark, as will be seen by the following observations of a gentleman from one of the Eastern States, which I extract from the debate, as given in the National Intelligencer,[5] chiefly to show their rambling style of discussion.

"He said he should not have risen, had not the resolution moved by the honourable gentleman from South Carolina designated the name of the artist to be employed. When it was recollected that Mr. Trumbull, the gentleman who had executed the paintings now in the Rotundo, was a native of the State which he represented on that floor, he trusted his honourable friend would excuse him if he ventured to suggest, that no course ought to be pursued, in this stage of the business, which went to exclude the employment of that venerable and patriotic individual in executing any paintings that might be ordered. If the artist to whom the gentleman had alluded, was a native of the same State with the hero of our second war, the artist he himself had named had been an actor in his own person in the war of the Revolution. He had been a prisoner, and had suffered severely in that contest; and he must be permitted to say, that great injustice had been done him, from the manner in which his paintings had at first been displayed. They were placed in a small and obscure room, beneath our feet, and the artist had the mortification to know, that the most unkind and most unfeeling strictures had there been passed upon them, in consequence of this their disadvantageous location. His fame had suffered, his feelings had suffered, and all his friends who knew the circumstances, had suffered with him. It was with pride and pleasure, he said, that he had witnessed their removal to a situation more worthy of their excellence, and he had witnessed the tears of joy glistening in his venerable eyes, under the consciousness that, at last, justice had been done him. He admitted, very willingly, the high merit of Mr. Alston; but, if Congress should conclude, in this matter, to depart from the class of our revolutionary worthies, there were other native artists, besides Mr. Alston, who would desire not to be precluded from a chance of employment. He therefore moved the following amendment, — to strike out the name of 'Washington Alston' and to insert the words, 'some suitable artist.'"

The debate for some time turned on the merits of this amendment, though it wandered every now and then into the presidential question, and its innumerable ramifications, many of which were nearly unintelligible to a stranger. At length another Eastern State member rose, and cast amongst the disputants a new apple of discord, or rather a new sort of mystification and discursive eloquence. He said, "that while he did not refuse to do homage to the great and acknowledged merit of Mr. Alston, he wished to suggest a further amendment of the resolution, which was, — 'that it might be made to embrace the battles of Bunker's Hill, Monmouth, Prince Town, and the attack on Quebec.'"

This proposal, whether it were seriously intended for the consideration of the House or not, was followed by one obviously meant as a bitter jest against one of the parties in the House. In the State for which the member who spoke last was the representative, it appears there had been, during the late war with England, a disposition expressed by some persons for opening pacific negotiations with the enemy, or in some way thwarting the measures of Government. A meeting, known by the name of the Hartford Convention, was accordingly assembled, at the very moment of the battle of New Orleans. The gentleman who now rose, therefore, proposed to amend the amended amendment, by moving, that "another painting be placed alongside that of the victory of New Orleans, representing this meeting, which was in full session at the same time."

Several members now made speeches, and most of them so entirely wide of the mark, that, I venture to say, any one coming into the House, and listening for half an hour, would not have been able to form a probable conjecture as to the real nature of the topic under discussion.

"It Reminded Me Much of a Russian City"

From *Transatlantic Sketches: Comprising Visits to the Most Interesting Scenes in North and South America, and the West Indies* by Captain J. E. Alexander.

Sir James Edward Alexander (1803-1885) was a Scot and proudly identified himself upon the title page of his *Transatlantic Sketches* upon its publication in 1833 as a member of the 42nd Royal Highlanders. Trained at the Royal Military College at Sandhurst, Alexander was a lifelong soldier and peripatetic traveler. He served in the British Army during the Russo-Turkish War and the Crimean War, among other conflicts. Alexander recorded both his travel and military experiences in a number of popular works published during a long and successful career.

Although the recounting of his experiences in Washington, D.C. is somewhat cursory, Alexander acknowledges a soldierly regard for then President Andrew Jackson, and his military bearing does on occasion yield long enough to appreciate some of the ladies he encounters.

As is the case with many British travelers who visited Washington, D.C. during the early 19th century, it seems all roads to the capital city lead through Bladensburg, Maryland.

We next passed through the village of Bladensburgh, consisting of two rows of indifferent wooden houses; crossed the small stream by the bridge, where considerable loss was sustained by our troops from the American artillery; ascended the hill on which the enemy's lines were drawn up, which fired with little effect by platoons on our light infantry in extended order; saw where our lads rushed to the charge, and the scattered cypress trees, beautifully dispersed over the gently ascending eminence, where the slain fell, and beside which they lie buried; snow-wreaths here and there lay in the hollows, and the scene was one of quiet beauty.

The road continued through some dark woods and an uncultivated country; and, after passing a single bullock-cart, on lifting up my eyes, I saw before me, on a bare plain, the great dome and the massive pile of the capitol at Washington, with a few inferior houses round it, and hardly a living object moving on the silent scene — a strange approach to the metropolis of "a fine, free, and flourishing country."

I found the principal hotel (Gadsby's)[1] full of Members of Congress, who were well lodged and entertained in this very superior establishment, built as a hollow square of four stories, with covered galleries round the interior, and a fountain in the centre of the court.

In walking through Washington, it reminded me much of a Russian city; the streets of great length and breadth, the houses inconveniently scattered over an open and treeless plain, and no bustle of commerce. There were many good stores, and numerous lottery-offices; but in one material point the Americans were greatly inferior to my old friends the Muscovites — in the heating of their houses. The snow lay on the ground some inches in thickness —

"The wind whistled cold,
And the stars glimmer'd red;"

... yet, in some of the best mansions, it was impossible to sit still, so great was the cold within doors from the houses being badly finished, and the grates with the anthracite coals being quite inadequate to the purpose for which they were intended.

The Inspector General[2] was so kind as to accompany me to the President's house, a handsome building of the Ionic order, of two stories and a basement, overlooking the Potomac and an extensive landscape from its elevated site. We entered an iron gate before the edifice, drove round a grass-plat enclosed with posts and chains, and alighted at a lofty portico of four columns. On knocking at the entrance-door, at which there were neither guards nor liveried retainers, after a considerable delay, one of the leaves was opened by a little man in a fur cap and grey short coat, who said he would ask if General Jackson could be seen; he then left us in an empty hall. It was bitterly cold, and General Wool piloted me upstairs to an anteroom, in which there was a fire, sundry chairs without backs, book shelves without books, and, in plain frames, four coloured scriptural prints indifferently executed.

The President's nephew and adopted son, Mr. Jackson, a tall young man, recently married (as almost all American young gentlemen *fortunately* are), came and conversed with us for some time, and then conducted us into a handsome drawing-room with yellow furniture, where we found the ladies of the family dressed *à la Parisienne*, and all of them extremely affable and agreeable; they consisted of young Mrs. Jackson, Mrs. Donaldson, Miss Eason and Miss Farquhar.[3]

After sitting some time with the ladies, we conducted them to their carriage, and then were shown into a room where the President was seated at a table covered with newspapers, and before a huge fire. He rose at our entrance, and, shaking hands, inquired after our health with the formal politeness of the old school. The General is about six feet high, of a spare make and upright carriage, dressed in black, with a black stock, wears his white hair combed back from his face, which is long, and his nose of corresponding dimensions. In face and figure he reminded me of the late Lieutenant-Governor of the Royal Military College, General Butler.[4]

Behind the President there was a full-length portrait of Bolivar,[5] similar to one I saw in the possession of Sir Robert Wilson; and round the room were models of agricultural implements.

The party in opposition to the re-election of General Jackson to the presidential chair had spread a report that he was seriously ill, and could not live; and it was with a peculiar expression that he replied to General Wool's interrogatory regarding his health, that he had not been so well for ten years. A tooth had annoyed him, and an unskillful dentist, in removing it, had also drawn with it a part of the jaw; the accident had confined him to the house for some days, but now he had got over the annoyance.

We remained with the President a quarter of an hour, during which time he made inquiries regarding my progress through the States, asked my opinion of what I had seen, and then spoke at some length on the engrossing question of reform, trusted that there would be no revolution in England, and that the constitution would still be preserved in its purity. It would be very improper for me to repeat the General's words during this very interesting; interview, as it would be a betrayal of confidence, of which former travellers in the States have sometimes been accused; let it suffice to say, that I retired much pleased with my reception by the chief magistrate of the United States, who politely invited me to take a family-dinner with him in a few days.

General Jackson commenced life without the advantages of a liberal education — his energy of character alone brought him forward; first on service in the revolutionary contest, then distinguished in Indian warfare on the western frontier, he was the terror of the red men from the Mississippi to the Rocky Mountains; he likewise engaged in political life, and acted in a judicial capacity. As a General of the Militia of Tennessee, he was selected to repel the British invasion of New Orleans in 1814: his success on that occasion was of incalculable benefit to the States, and occasioned his promotion to the high office which he has filled with excellent judgment for three years, and has given general satisfaction both to the citizens and to foreigners.

We next inspected the four public offices, two on each side of the President's house, appropriated to the treasury, state, navy, and war departments; in the latter, I had the honour of making the acquaintance of Governor Cass, secretary-at-war, and of General Macomb, commander of the army.

We proceeded along the Pennsylvania Avenue, a mile long, (the upper end ornamented with double rows of poplars), and ascended the eminence on which the great pile of the capitol is built, by broad stairs. In the middle of the ascent was a marble monument, consisting of an eagle-surmounted column on a square base, on which were also allegorical figures representing History, Fame, Commerce, and America, This monument, erected in memory of the naval officers who fell in the Tripolitan war, formerly stood in the navy yard, but lately was removed to a better site.

We entered the circular Rotunda in the centre of the capitol, excellently paved, and with the great and echoing circumference of the dome overhead. In four niches round the walls were sculptured representations of the fight between Boon (one of the first pioneers of the West) and an Indian chief — the landing at Plymouth of the Pilgrim Fathers fleeing from England for conscience sake — the treaty between Penn and two Indian chiefs on the Delaware — and the last, the escape of Captain John Smith in 1606, from the uplifted war club of King Powhatan, on the intercession of his daughter Pocahontas. Four large oil paintings, by Col. Trumbull, represented the Declaration of Independence, General Washington resigning his commission, and the surrender of Cornwallis and Burgoyne at Yorktown and Saratoga. Connected with these two last, I beg to subjoin an anecdote highly creditable to the American character, and also to show that a regard for the feelings of others is confined to no particular country.

A British officer on a visit to Washington made the acquaintance, at a hotel, of two officers of the United States artillery; they showed him whatever was worthy of notice in or about the city, but they dissuaded him from entering the capitol, as they said it was in an unfinished state, and contained nothing that could interest him. However, one day he went alone to the capitol, and found that the cause of the dissuasions of his friends was the pictures above mentioned. They thought it would vex him to see these memorials of British defeat.

In the National Library, also in the capitol, I found a large collection of choice works, and the librarian kindly afforded me every facility in consulting them on several occasions. The hall of the senate was a neat semicircular chamber, but the hall of representatives is the great attraction in the capitol. I was introduced to it by General Aaron Ward,[6] on the day that the President's message was read. The Speaker's chair, or rather curtained throne, was placed in front of a row of lofty windows, with crimson drapery; the seats and desks of the members of Congress were placed in semicircular and ascending rows. Corinthian pillars of great size, with polished shafts of variegated pudding stone, in which blue predominated, and crowned with marble capitals, were disposed round the walls, and opposite to the Speaker was a capacious gallery. The members wore their hats, as in St. Stephen's, and one or two I remarked in fur caps and white great coats, probably from the far west. Well may the Americans vaunt of their country, when representatives salute each other in Congress after journeys over two thousand miles of United States territory.

There is silence in the great hall; a door opens and a voice announces, "The Message of the President." Instead of a procession, a single individual in a cloak, enters with a bundle of papers in his hand, tied with red tape, and advancing up the centre passage, presents it to the Speaker; he unties it, and reads aloud the important document.

THE MESSAGE. — The President congratulated his fellow citizens of the Senate and House of Representatives on the continued and increasing prosperity of their beloved country, and gave a satisfactory view of the agriculture, manufactures, and internal improvements in the United States. He then alluded to the state of the navigation and trade, and had much satisfaction in noticing the late arrangements with Great Britain relating to Colonial trade, productive of mutual good feeling and amicable relations between the two countries, which he hoped would not be interrupted. He next mentions his desire that an early settlement of the boundaries should take place between Canada, New Brunswick, and the States. Then spake of the claims (for indemnity) on France, Spain, and Denmark, the two Sicilies, Portugal, &c. for irregularities committed on American vessels, and for the redress of injuries. Commercial treaties with Russia and Austria, Prussia and the Porte, it was anticipated, would open a vast field for the enterprize of American merchants. Increased facilities attended the commerce to China and the East Indies, and satisfaction was to be required by an armed force, for piratical outrages committed in Sumatra on American merchantmen.

The nature of the connection with the independent States of South and Central America, was next in order, and it was hoped that trade would increase with them on the subsiding of civil commotions. A revisal of the Consular laws was recommended. The removal of the Indian tribes to the west bank of the Mississippi was noticed, and the President trusted that the States *would not be long embarrassed with an Indian population,* though experiments might be made to reclaim the red-men from barbarism, and to teach them the habits and enjoyments of civilized life.

The state of public finance, as shown by the Secretary of the Treasury, was very gratifying; the revenue of 1831 amounted to twenty-seven millions seven hundred thousand dollars, and the expenditure for all objects (other than the public debt) did not exceed fourteen millions seven hundred thousand. The payment on account of the principal and interest of the debt during the year was sixteen millions and a half of dollars, and it was anticipated that within four years of the President's administration, the whole of the public debt would be extinguished — a remarkable case in the history of nations.

A modification of the tariff which shall produce a reduction of revenue to the wants of the Government, and an adjustment of the duties on imports, with a view to equal justice in relation to all national interests, and to the counteraction of foreign policy, so far as it may not be injurious to these interests, was deemed one of the principal objects which demanded the consideration of Congress, and arrangements should also be made to relieve the people from unnecessary taxation after the extinction of the national debt.

The insolvent debtors (to the United States) should be relieved; the complicated system of public accounts should be improved; the laws of the District of Columbia (round Washington) should be revised: and the extension of the judiciary system in the States of Indiana, Illinois, Missouri, Alabama, Mississippi, and Louisiana, which have not the benefits of a circuit, but only of a district court.

Leaving to the investigation of an enlightened people and their representatives the present organization of the bank of the United States, with a view to its improvement, the President's message concluded in these words: "Permit me to invoke that Power which superintends all governments, to infuse into your deliberations at this important crisis of our history a spirit of mutual forbearance and conciliation; in that spirit was our Union formed, and in that spirit must it be preserved."

Among other distinguished persons to whom I had letters from Mr. Washington Irving,[7] was General Jackson's political opponent, Henry Clay, Esq. a Senator of the United States. I waited on him at his hotel, and found him to be a tall and spare-made man, about fifty-five years of age, in black, with a high forehead, thin brown hair, fresh complexion, straight nose, and front teeth rather prominent. His demeanour was quiet, though he is a Kentuckian; he wore a smile on his countenance in speaking, and was slow and distinct in his articulation; yet his appearance and manner evidently implied that

"He plunges into the sea who seeks for pearls,
And he who seeks greatness has watchful nights."

With him sat a nephew of the great Washington, a tall and robust man, with a florid complexion, and the sedate manner of his celebrated relative.[8]

I inspected the arsenal, across the Tiber and at some distance from the city, by invitation from Lieutenant Lymington, and found it, though small, in the most perfect order.[9] I visited the (indifferent) Washington Theatre, and had my money returned; for the gas would not burn, and there was no performance. I attended a Presbyterian church on Sunday,[10] where I heard an admirable discourse from a Mr. Post on the "signs of the times," on which we should not shut our eyes and ears, but be up and doing. Education was the distinctive mark of the present age, in which peace prevailed, and in which the comforts of the poor were attended to, and the security of the rich.

At the table of our excellent Chargé d'affaires, Mr. Bankhead,[11] I met the Members of the Corps Diplomatique, two English travellers of fortune, Messrs. Davidson and Gibb, and a daughter of the Emperor Iturbide,[12] a charming young lady, rather *petite*, with black sparkling eyes and raven tresses. She had been educated at the convent near Washington, a very interesting establishment of sixty nuns, descendants from rich Catholic families; they instruct one hundred boarders, and their day charity-school consists of two hundred pupils, for which they deserve great praise.

The day before I left Washington, I dined *en famille* with the President, and considered my being asked in this kind and friendly manner as a compliment to the service to which I belonged. The General had not begun to give dinners that season, and my stay being short; owing to my anxiety to return to England, from the stirring times that were anticipated, if I had not been invited to a family-dinner, I could not have partaken of the hospitality of the chief magistrate at all.

To a small and comfortable drawing-room, with mirrors and a chandelier, and in which there was a full-length portrait of Washington, I was introduced by Mr. Baird (the butler) to General Jackson, who was seated in a high-backed arm chair, round which were the members of the family, the ladies composing one quarter of the semicircle, and the gentlemen the other. My excellent friend General Wool, and his lady, were the only strangers besides myself.

After another discourse on English Reform, we handed the ladies into the blue dining-room, where a well-cooked dinner and choice wines refreshed the senses. The services of plate and crystal were in excellent taste. Two brown domestics assisted Mr. Baird, who gave his opinion on the dishes and liquors as he helped them, and seemed to be the factotum of the establishment. After some lively conversation regarding ages of wine and ages of individuals, remarks on the changes in the face of the country, the increase of fields and the decrease of the forest, the General drank "Our absent Friends," and we all rose, and handed the ladies back to the drawing-room, where they were arranged as before, till coffee was served, when two of the young demoiselles went to the piano, sang and played Scotch airs; the General regaled himself with a long pipe in his easy chair, à la Parr,[13] and retired to bed at nine. Thus ended the party at the President's.

"The Spitting was Incessant"

From *Domestic Manners of the Americans* by Mrs. Trollope.

When Frances Milton Trollope (1779-1863) first set sail for America in November, 1827, her family was in difficult financial circumstances and she was in search of a solution. Over the course of her three year visit, she dabbled in the promise of utopian societies and speculated on a possible business venture, a bazaar to be established in Cincinnati, Ohio, its success wishfully envisioned by her mostly absent husband. But Mrs. Trollope's prospects failed to improve and she returned to England in even more dire circumstances. Now in the throes of middle age and her husband's health failing, yet determined to resolve her difficulties and care for her children, she took to writing. Her first work, *Domestic Manners of the Americans*, proved highly successful in England and set her on a course toward a prolific and successful writing career.

As was often the case with English authors of the period, Mrs. Trollope's *Domestic Manners of the Americans* painted an unflattering portrait of the United States, where the author was criticized for her well-sharpened quill. Nevertheless, it remains one of the most enduring and oft-cited social commentaries on America in her early years.

By far the shortest route to Washington, both as to distance and time, is by land; but I much wished to see the celebrated Chesapeake bay, and it was therefore decided that we should take our passage in the steam-boat. It is indeed a beautiful little voyage, and well worth the time it costs; but as to the beauty of the bay, it must, I think, be felt only by sailors. It is, I doubt not, a fine shelter for ships, from the storms of the Atlantic, but its very vastness prevents its striking the eye as beautiful: it is, in fact, only a fine sea view. But the entrance from it into the Potomac river is very noble, and is one of the points at which one feels conscious of the gigantic proportions of the country, without having recourse to a graduated pencil-case.

The passage up this river to Washington is interesting, from many objects that it passes, but beyond all else, by the view it affords of Mount Vernon, the seat of General Washington. It is there that this truly great man passed the last years of his virtuous life, and it is there that he lies buried: it was easy to distinguish, as we passed, the cypress that waves over his grave.

The latter part of the voyage shews some fine river scenery; but I did not discover this till some months afterwards, for we now arrived late at night.

Our first object the next morning was to get a sight of the capitol, and our impatience sent us forth before breakfast. The mists of morning still hung around this magnificent building when first it broke upon our view, and I am not sure that the effect produced was not the greater for this circumstance. At all events, we were struck with admiration and surprise. None of us, I believe, expected to see so imposing a structure on that side the Atlantic. I am ill at describing buildings. but the beauty and majesty of the American capitol might defy an abler pen than mine to do it justice. It stands so finely too, high, and alone.

The magnificent western facade is approached from the city by terraces and steps of bolder proportions than I ever before saw. The elegant eastern front, to which many persons give the preference, is on a level with a newly-planted but exceedingly handsome inclosure, which, in a few years, will offer the shade of all the most splendid trees which flourish in the Union, to cool the browns and refresh the spirits of the members. The view from the capitol commands the city and many miles around, and it is itself an object of imposing beauty to the whole country adjoining.

We were again fortunate enough to find a very agreeable family to board with; and soon after breakfast left our comfortless hotel near the water, for very pleasant apartments in F. street.[1]

I was delighted with the whole aspect of Washington; light, cheerful, and airy, it reminded me of our fashionable watering-places. It has been laughed at by foreigners, and even by natives, because the original plan of the city was upon an enormous scale, and but a very small part of it has been as yet executed. But I confess I see nothing in the least degree ridiculous about it; the original design, which was as beautiful as it was extensive, has been in no way departed from, and all that has been done has been done well. From the base of the hill on which the capitol stands extends a street of most magnificent width, planted on each side with trees, and ornamented by many splendid shops. This street, which is called Pennsylvania Avenue, is above a mile in length, and at the end of it is the handsome mansion of the President; conveniently near to his residence are the various public offices, all handsome, simple, and commodious; ample areas are left round each, where grass and shrubs refresh the eye. In another of the principal streets is the general post-office, and not far from it a very noble town-hall. Towards the quarter of the President's house are several handsome dwellings, which are chiefly occupied by the foreign ministers. The houses in the other parts of the city are scattered, but without ever losing sight of the regularity of the original plan; and to a person who has been travelling much through the country, and marked the immense quantity of new manufactories, new canals, new rail-roads, new towns, and new cities, which are springing, as it were, from the earth in every part of it, the appearance of the metropolis rising gradually into life and splendour, is a spectacle of high historic interest. Commerce had already produced large and handsome cities in America before she had attained to an individual political existence, and Washington may be scorned as a metropolis, where such cities as Philadelphia and New York exist; but I considered it as the growing metropolis of the growing population of the Union, and it already possesses features noble enough to sustain its dignity as such.

The residence of the foreign legations and their families gives a tone to the society of this city which distinguishes it greatly from all others. It is also, for a great part of the year, the residence of the senators and representatives, who must be presumed to be the elite of the entire body of citizens, both in respect to talent and education. This cannot fail to make Washington a more agreeable abode than any other city in the Union. The total absence of all sights, sounds, or smells of commerce, adds greatly to the charm. Instead of drays you see handsome carriages; and instead of the busy bustling hustle of men, shuffling on to a sale of "dry goods" or "prime broad stuffs," you see very well-dressed personages lounging leisurely up and down Pennsylvania Avenue.

Mr. Pishey Thompson, the English bookseller, with his pretty collection of all sorts of pretty literature, fresh from London, and Mr. Somebody,[2] the jeweller, with his brilliant shop full of trinkets, are the principal points of attraction and business. What a contrast to all other American cities! The members, who pass several months every year in this lounging easy way, with no labour but a little talking, and with the douceur of eight dollars a day to pay them for it, must feel the change sadly when their term of public service is over.

There is another circumstance which renders the evening parties at Washington extremely unlike those of other places in the Union -, this is the great majority of gentlemen. The expense, the trouble, or the necessity of a ruling eye at home, one or all of these reasons, prevents the members' ladies from accompanying them to Washington; at least, I heard of very few who had their wives with them. The female society is chiefly to be found among the families of the foreign ministers, those of the officers of state, and of the few members, the wealthiest and most aristocratic of the land, who bring their families with them. Some few independent persons reside in or near the city, but this is a class so thinly scattered that they can hardly be accounted a part of the population.

But, strange to say, even here a theatre cannot be supported for more than a few weeks at a time. I was told that gambling is the favourite recreation of the gentlemen, and that it is carried to a very considerable extent; but here, as elsewhere within the country, it is kept extremely well out of sight. I do not think I was present with a pack of cards a dozen times during more than three years that I remained in the country. Billiards are much played, though in most places the amusement is illegal. It often appeared to me that the old women of a state made the laws, and the young men broke them.

Notwithstanding the diminutive size of the city, we found much to see, and to amuse us.

The patent office is a curious record of the fertility of the mind of man when left to its own resources; but it gives ample proof also that it is not under such circumstances it is most usefully employed. This patent office contains models of all the mechanical inventions that have been produced in the Union, and the number is enormous. I asked the man who shewed these, what proportion of them had been brought into use, he said about one in a thousand; he told me also, that they chiefly proceeded from mechanics and agriculturists settled in remote parts of the country, who had begun by endeavouring to hit upon some contrivance to enable them to get along without sending some thousand and odd miles for the thing they wanted. If the contrivance succeeded, they generally became so fond of this offspring of their ingenuity, that they brought it to Washington for a patent.

At the secretary of state's office we were shewn autographs of all the potentates with whom the Union were in alliance; which, I believe, pretty well includes all. To the parchments bearing these royal signs manual were appended, of course, the official seals of each, enclosed in gold or silver boxes of handsome workmanship: I was amused by the manner in which one of their own, just prepared for the court of Russia, was displayed to us, and the superiority of their decorations pointed out. They were superior, and in much better taste than the rest; and I only wish that the feeling that induced this display would spread to every corner of the Union, and mix itself with every act and with every sentiment. Let America give a fair portion of her attention to the arts and the graces that embellish life, and I will make her another visit, and write another book as unlike this as possible.

Among the royal signatures, the only ones which much interested me were two from the hand of Napoleon. The earliest of these, when he was first consul, was a most illegible scrawl, and, as the tradition went, was written on horseback; but his writing improved greatly after he became an emperor, the subsequent signature being firmly and clearly written. — I longed to steal both.

The purity of the American character, formed and founded on the purity of the American government, was made evident to our senses by the display of all the offerings of esteem and regard which had been presented by various sovereigns to the different American ministers who had been sent to their courts. The object of the law which exacted this deposit from every individual so honoured, was, they told us, to prevent the possibility of bribery being used to corrupt any envoy of the Republic. I should think it would be a better way to select for the office such men as they felt could not be seduced by a sword or a snuff-box. But they, doubtless, know their own business best.

The bureau for Indian affairs contains a room of great interest: the walls are entirely covered with original portraits of all the chiefs who, from time to time, have come to negotiate with their great father, as they call the President. These portraits are by Mr. King,[3] and, it cannot be doubted, are excellent likenesses, as are all the portraits I have ever seen from the hands of that gentleman. The countenances are full of expression, but the expression in most of them is extremely similar; or rather, I should say that they have but two sorts of expression; the one is that of very noble and warlike daring, the other of a gentle and naive simplicity, that has no mixture of folly in it, but which is inexpressibly engaging, and the more touching, perhaps, because at the moment we were looking at them, those very hearts which lent the eyes such meek and friendly softness, were wrung by a base, cruel, and most oppressive act of their great father.

We were at Washington at the time that the measure for chasing the last of several tribes of Indians from their forest homes, was canvassed in congress, and finally decided upon by the fiat of the President. If the American character may be judged by their conduct in this matter, they are most lamentably deficient in every feeling of honour and integrity. It is among themselves, and from themselves, that I have heard the statements which represent them as treacherous and false almost beyond belief in their intercourse with the unhappy Indians. Had I, during my residence in the United States, observed any single feature in their national character that could justify their eternal boast of liberality and the love of freedom, I might have respected them, however much my taste might have been offended by what was peculiar in their manners and customs. But it is impossible for any mind of common honesty not to be revolted by the contradictions in their principles and practice. They inveigh against the governments of Europe, because, as they say, they favour the powerful and oppress the weak. You may hear this declaimed upon in Congress, roared out in taverns, discussed in every drawing-room, satirized upon the stage, nay, even anathematized from the pulpit: listen to it, and then look at them at home; you will see them with one hand hoisting the cap of liberty, and with the other flogging their slaves. You will see them one hour lecturing their mob on the indefeasible rights of man, and the next driving from their homes the children of the soil, whom they have bound themselves to protect by the most solemn treaties.

In justice to those who approve not this treacherous policy, I will quote a paragraph from a New York paper, which shews that there are some among them who look with detestation on the bold bad measure decided upon at Washington in the year 1830.

"We know of no subject, at the present moment, of more importance to the character of our country for justice and integrity than that which relates to the Indian tribes in Georgia and Alabama, and particularly the Cherokees in the former state. The Act passed by Congress, just at the end of the session, co-operating with the tyrannical and iniquitous statute of Georgia, strikes a formidable blow at the reputation of the United States, in respect to their faith, pledged in almost innumerable instances, in the most solemn treaties and compacts."

There were many objects of much interest shewn us at this Indian bureau; but, from the peculiar circumstances of this most unhappy and ill-used people, it was a very painful interest.

The dresses worn by the chiefs when their portraits were taken, are many of them splendid, from the embroidery of beads and other ornaments; and the room contains many specimens of their ingenuity, and even of their taste. There is a glass case in the room, wherein are arranged specimens of worked muslin, and other needle-work, some very excellent hand-writing, and many other little productions of male and female Indians, all proving clearly that they are perfectly capable of civilization. Indeed, the circumstance which renders their expulsion from their own, their native lands, so peculiarly lamentable, is, that they were yielding rapidly to the force of example; their lives were no longer those of wandering hunters, but they were becoming agriculturists, and the tyrannical arm of brutal power has not now driven them, as formerly, only from their hunting grounds, their favourite springs, and the sacred bones of their fathers, but it has chased them from the dwellings their advancing knowledge had taught them to make comfortable; from the newly-ploughed fields of their pride; and from the crops their sweat had watered. And for what? To add some thousand acres of territory to the half-peopled wilderness which borders them.

The Potomac, on arriving at Washington, makes a beautiful sweep, which forms a sort of bay, round which the city is built. Just where it makes the turn, a wooden bridge is thrown across, connecting the shores of Maryland and Virginia. This bridge is a mile and a quarter in length, and is ugly enough.[4] The navy-yard, and arsenal, are just above it, on the Maryland side, and make a handsome appearance on the edge of the river, following the sweep above mentioned. Near the arsenal (much too near) is the penitentiary, which, as it was just finished, and not inhabited, we examined in every part. It is built for the purpose of solitary confinement for life. A gallows is a much less nerve-shaking spectacle than one of these awful cells, and assuredly, when imprisonment therein for life is substituted for death, it is no mercy to the criminal; but if it be a greater terror to the citizen, it may answer the purpose better. I do not conceive, that out of a hundred human beings who had been thus confined for a year, one would be found at the end of it who would continue to linger on there, *certain it was forever*, if the alternative of being hanged were offered to them. I had written a description of these horrible cells, but Captain Hall's picture of a similar building is so accurate, and so clear, that it is needless to insert it.

Still following the sweep of the river, at the distance of two miles from Washington, is George Town, formerly a place of considerable commercial importance, and likely, I think, to become so again, when the Ohio and Chesapeake canals, which there mouths into the Potomac, shall be in full action. It is a very pretty town, commanding a lovely view, of which the noble Potomac and the almost nobler capitol, are the great features. The country rises into a beautiful line of hills behind Washington, which form a sort of undulating terrace on to George Town; this terrace is almost entirely occupied by a succession of gentlemen's seats.[5] At George Town the Potomac suddenly contracts itself, and begins to assume that rapid, rocky, and irregular character which marks it afterwards, and renders its course, till it meets the Shenandoah at Harper's Ferry, a series of the most wild and romantic views that are to be found in America.

Attending the debates in Congress was, of course, one of our great objects; and, as an English woman, I was perhaps the more eager to avail myself of the privilege allowed. It was repeatedly observed to me that, at least in this instance, I must acknowledge the superior gallantry of the

Americans, and that they herein give a decided proof of surpassing the English in a wish to honour the ladies, as they have a gallery in the House of Representatives erected expressly for them, while in England they are rigorously excluded from every part of the House of Commons.

But the inference I draw from this is precisely the reverse of that suggested. It is well known that the reason why the House of Commons was closed against ladies was, that their presence was found too attractive, and that so many members were tempted to neglect the business before the House, that they might enjoy the pleasure of conversing with the fair critics in the galleries, that it became a matter of national importance to banish them — and they were banished. It will be long ere the American legislature will find it necessary to pass the same law for the same reason. A lady of Washington, however, told me an anecdote which went far to shew that a more intellectual turn in the women, would produce a change in the manners of the men. She told me, that when the Miss Wrights were in Washington, with General Lafayette, they very frequently attended the debates, and that the most distinguished members were always crowding round them. For this unwonted gallantry they apologized to their beautiful countrywomen by saying, that if they took equal interest in the debates, the galleries would be always thronged by the members.

The privilege of attending these debates would be more valuable could the speakers be better heard from the gallery; but, with the most earnest attention, I could only follow one or two of the orators, whose voices were peculiarly loud and clear. This made it really a labour to listen; but the extreme beauty of the chamber was of itself a reason for going again and again. It was, however, really mortifying to see this splendid hall, fitted up ill so stately and sumptuous a manner, filled with men, sitting in the most unseemly attitudes, a large majority with their hats on, and nearly a]l, spitting to an excess that decency forbids me to describe.

Among the crowd, who must be included in this description, a few were distinguished by not wearing their hats, and by sitting on their chairs like other human beings, without throwing their legs above their heads. Whenever I enquired the name of one of these exceptions, I was told that it was Mr. This, or Mr. That, *of Virginia*.

One day we were fortunate enough to get placed on the sofas between the pillars, on the floor of the House; the galleries being shut up, for the purpose of making some alterations, which it was hoped might improve the hearing in that part of the House occupied by the members, and which is universally complained of, as being very defective.[6] But in our places on the sofas we found we heard very much better than upstairs, and well enough to be extremely amused by the rude eloquence of a thorough horse and alligator orator from Kentucky, who entreated the house repeatedly to "go the whole hog."

If I mistake not, every debate I listened to in the American Congress was upon one and the same subject, namely, the entire independence of each individual state, with regard to the federal government. The jealousy on this point appeared to me to be the very strangest political feeling that ever got possession of the mind of man. I do not pretend to judge the merits of this question. I speak solely of the very singular effect of seeing man after man start eagerly to his feet, to declare that the greatest injury, the basest injustice, the most obnoxious tyranny that could be practised against the state of which he was a member, would be a vote of a few million dollars for the purpose of making their roads or canals; or for drainage; or, in short, for any purpose of improvement whatsoever.

During the month we were at Washington, I heard a great deal of conversation respecting a recent exclusion from Congress of a gentleman, who, by every account, was one of the most esteemed men in the house, and, I think, the father of it.⁷ The crime for which this gentleman was out-voted by his own particular friends and admirers was, that he had given his vote for a grant of public money for the purpose of draining a most lamentable and unhealthy district, called *"the dismal swamp."*⁸

One great boast of the country is, that they have no national debt, or that they shall have none in two years. This seems not very wonderful, considering their productive tariff, and that the income paid to their president is £6,000 *per annum*;⁹ other government salaries being in proportion, and all internal improvements, at the expense of the government treasury, being voted unconstitutional.

The Senate-chamber is, like the Hall of Congress, a semicircle, but of very much smaller dimensions. It is most elegantly fitted up, and what is better still, the senators, generally speaking, look like gentlemen. They do not wear their hats, and the activity of youth being happily past, they do not toss their heels above their heads. I would I could add they do not spit; but, alas! "I have an oath in heaven," and may not write an untruth.

A very handsome room, opening on a noble stone balcony is fitted up as a library for the members. The collection, as far as a very cursory view could enable me to judge, was very like that of a private English gentleman, but with less Latin, Greek, and Italian. This room also is elegantly furnished; rich Brussels carpet; library tables, with portfolios of engravings; abundance of sofas, and so on. The view from it is glorious, and it looks like the abode of luxury and taste.

I can by no means attempt to describe all the apartments of this immense building, but the magnificent rotunda in the centre must not be left unnoticed. It is, indeed, a noble hall, a hundred feet in diameter, and of an imposing loftiness, lighted by an ample dome.

Almost any pictures (excepting the cartoons) would look paltry in this room, from the immense height of the walls; but the subjects of the four pictures which are placed there, are of such high historic interest that they should certainly have a place somewhere, as national records. One represents the signing of the declaration of independence; another the resignation of the presidency by the great Washington; another the celebrated victory of General Gates at Saratoga; and the fourth.... I do not well remember, but I think it is some other martial scene, commemorating a victory; I rather think that of York Town.

One other object in the capitol must be mentioned, though it occurs in so obscure a part of the building, that one or two members to whom I mentioned it, were not aware of its existence. The lower part of the edifice, a story below the rotunda, &c., has a variety of committee rooms, courts, and other places of business. In a hall leading to some of these rooms, the ceiling is supported by pillars, the capitals of which struck me as peculiarly beautiful. They are composed of the ears and leaves of the Indian corn, beautifully arranged, and forming as graceful an outline as the acanthus itself. This was the only instance I saw, in which America has ventured to attempt national originality; the success is perfect. A sense of fitness always enhances the effect of beauty. I will not attempt a long essay on the subject, but if America, in her vastness, her immense natural resources, and her remote grandeur, would be less imitative, she would be infinitely more picturesque and interesting.

The President has regular evening parties, every other Wednesday, which are called his levees; the last syllable is pronounced by everyone as long as possible, being exactly the reverse of the French and English manner of pronouncing the same word. The effect of this, from the very frequent repetition of the word in all companies, is very droll, and for a long time I thought people were quizzing these public days. The reception rooms are handsome, particularly the grand saloon, which is elegantly, nay, splendidly furnished; this has been done since the visit of Captain Hall, whose remarks upon the former state of this room may have hastened its decoration; but there are a few anomalies in some parts of the entertainment, which are not very courtly. The company are about as select as that of an Easter-day ball at the Mansion-house.

The churches at Washington are not superb; but the Episcopalian and Catholic were filled with elegantly dressed women. I observed a greater proportion of gentlemen at church at Washington than anywhere else.

The Presbyterian ladies go to church three times in the day, but the general appearance of Washington on a Sunday is much less puritanical than that of most other American towns; the people walk about, and there are no chains in the streets, as at Philadelphia, to prevent their riding or driving, if they like it.

The ladies dress well, but not so splendidly as at Baltimore. I remarked that it was not very unusual at Washington for a lady to take the arm of a gentleman, who was neither her husband, her father, nor her brother. This remarkable relaxation of American decorum has been probably introduced by the foreign legations.

At about a mile from the town, on the high terrace ground above described, is a very pretty place, to which the proprietor has given the name of Kaleirama.[10] It is not large, or in any way magnificent, but the view from it is charming; and it has a little wood behind, covering about two hundred acres of broken ground, that slopes down to a dark cold little river, so closely shut in by rocks and evergreens, that it might serve as a noon-day bath for Diana and her nymphs. The whole of this wood is filled with wild flowers, but such as we cherish fondly in our gardens.

A ferry at George Town crosses the Potomac, and about two miles from it, on the Virginian side, is Arlington,[11] the seat of Mr. Custis, who is the grandson of General Washington's wife. It is a noble looking place, having a portico of stately white columns, which, as the mansion stands high, with a back ground of dark woods, forms a beautiful object in the landscape. At George Town is a nunnery, where many young ladies are educated, and at a little distance from it, a college of Jesuits for the education of young men, where, as their advertisements state, "the humanities are taught."

We attended mass at the chapel of the nunnery, where the female voices that performed the chant were very pleasing. The shadowy form of the veiled abbess in her little sacred parlour, seen through a grating and a black curtain, but rendered clearly visible by the light of a Gothic window behind her, drew a good deal of our attention; every act of genuflection, even the telling her beads, was discernible, but so mistily that it gave her, indeed, the appearance of a being who had already quitted this life, and was hovering on the confines of the world of shadows.

The convent has a considerable inclosure attached to it, where I frequently saw fi'om the heights above it, dark figures in awfully thick black veils, walking solemnly up and down.

The American lady, who was the subject of one of Prince Hohenlohe's celebrated miracles, was pointed out to us at Washington. All the world declare that her recovery was marvellous.

There appeared to be a great many foreigners at Washington, particularly French. In Paris I have often observed that it was a sort of fashion to speak of America as a new Utopia, especially among the young liberals, who, before the happy accession of Philip, fancied that a country without a king, was the land of promise; but I sometimes thought that, like many other fine things, it lost part of its brilliance when examined too nearly; I overheard the following question and answer pass between two young Frenchmen, who appeared to have met for the first time.

"Eh bien, Monsieur, comment trouvez-vous la liberté et l'égalité mises en action?"

"Mais, Monsieur, je vous avoue que le beau idéal que nous autres, nous avons conçu de tout cela à Paris, avait quelque chose de plus poétique que ce que nous trouvons ici!"

On another occasion I was excessively amused by the tone in which one of these young men replied to a question put to him by another Frenchman. A pretty looking woman, but exceedingly deficient in *tournure*, was standing alone at a little distance from them, and close at their elbows stood a very awkward looking gentleman. "Qui est cette dame?" said the enquirer. "Monsieur," said my young *fat* with an indescribable grimace, "c'est la femelle de ce male," indicating his neighbour by an expressive curl of his upper lip.

The theatre was not open while we were in Washington, but we afterwards took advantage of our vicinity to the city, to visit it. The house is very small, and most astonishingly dirty and void of decoration, considering that it is the only place of public amusement that the city affords. I have before mentioned the want of decorum at the Cincinnati theatre, but certainly that of the capital at least rivalled it in the freedom of action and attitude; a freedom which seems to disdain the restraints of civilized manners. One man in the pit was seized with a violent fit of vomiting, which appeared not in the least to annoy or surprise his neighbours; and the happy coincidence of a physician being at that moment personated on the stage, was hailed by many of the audience as an excellent joke, of which the actor took advantage, and elicited shouts of applause by saying, "I expect my services are wanted elsewhere."

The spitting was incessant; and not one in ten of the male part of the illustrious legislative audience sat according to the usual custom of human beings; the legs were thrown sometimes over the front of the box, sometimes over the side of it; here and there a senator stretched his entire length along a bench, and in many instances the front rail was preferred as a seat.

I remarked one young man, whose handsome person, and most elaborate toilet, led me to conclude he was a first-rate personage, and so I doubt not he was; nevertheless, I saw him take from the pocket of his silk waistcoat a lump of tobacco, and daintily deposit it within his cheek.

I am inclined to think this most vile and universal habit of chewing tobacco is the cause of a remarkable peculiarity in the male physiognomy of Americans; their lips are almost uniformly thin and compressed. At first I accounted for this upon Lavater's[12] theory, and attributed it to the arid temperament of the people; but it is too universal to be so explained; whereas the habit above mentioned, which pervades all classes (excepting the literary) well accounts for it, as the act of expressing the juices of this loathsome herb, enforces exactly that position of the lips, which gives this remarkable peculiarity to the American countenance.

A member of Congress died while we were at Washington, and I was surprised by the ceremony and dignity of his funeral. It seems that whenever a senator or member of Congress dies during the session, he is buried at the expense of the government, (this ceremony not coming under the head of internal improvement), and the arrangements for the funeral are not interfered with by his friends, but become matters of State. I transcribed the order of the procession as being rather grand and stately.

Chaplains of both Houses.
Physicians who attended the deceased.
Committee of arrangement.
THE BODY,
(Pall borne by six members.)
The Relations of the deceased,
with the Senators and Representatives
of the State to which he belonged, as Mourners.
Sergeant at arms of the House of Representatives.
The House of Representatives,
Their Speaker and Clerk preceding.
The Senate of the United States.
The Vice-president and Secretary preceding,
The President.

The procession was of considerable extent, but not on foot, and the majority of the carriages were hired for the occasion. The body was interred in an open "grave yard" near the city. I did not see the monument erected on this occasion, but I presume it was in the same style as several others I had remarked in the same burying-ground, inscribed to the memory of members who had died at Washington. These were square blocks of masonry without any pretension to splendour.

"To Dazzle with False Glitter"

From *Men and Manners in America* by Thomas Hamilton.

Thomas Hamilton (1789-1842) dedicated his *Men and Manners* to William Wolryche-Whitmore, then a Member of Parliament. In his dedication, in defending his motivation for writing the book, Hamilton makes the following observation:

"... when I found the institutions and experience of the United States deliberately quoted in the reformed Parliament, as affording safe precedent for British legislation, and learned that the drivellers who uttered such nonsense, instead of encountering merited derision, were listened to with patience and approbation, by men as ignorant as themselves, I certainly did feel that another work on America was yet wanted, and at once determined to undertake a task which inferior considerations would probably have induced me to decline."

In the selections that follow, Hamilton contrasts the style and character among some men who speak in Congress, where laws are made, with those who speak in the Supreme Court, where laws are interpreted. Both institutions at that time were meeting in the same building.

---

I have already said that the speaking in the Senate is very superior to that in the other House; an opinion which I early took up, and subsequently felt no temptation to change. Yet the faults of both bodies differ rather in degree than in character. There is the same loose, desultory, and inconclusive mode of discussion in both; but in the Senate there is less talking for the mere purpose of display, and less of that tawdry emptiness and vehement imbecility which prevails in the Representatives. Though the members of the Senate be absolutely and entirely dependent on the people, they are dependent in a larger sense; dependent not on the petty clubs and coteries of a particular neighbourhood, but on great masses and numbers of men, embracing every interest and pursuit, and covering a wide extent of country. Then, from the comparative paucity of their numbers, there is less jostling and scrambling in debate, more statesmanlike argument, and less schoolboy declamation; in short, considerably less outcry, and a great deal more wool.

The Senate contains men who would do honour to any legislative assembly in the world. Those who left the most vivid impression on my memory are Mr. Livingstone,[1] now Secretary of State, and Mr. Webster,[2] whose power, both as a lawyer and a debater, are without rival in the United States. Of these eminent individuals, and others, whose intercourse I enjoyed during my stay in Washington, I shall hereafter have occasion to speak. There were other members of the Senate, however, to whose speeches I always listened with pleasure. Among these were General Hayne,[3] from South Carolina, — who, as Governor of that State, has since put the Union in imminent peril of mutilation, — and Mr. Tazewell,[4] of Virginia, a speaker of great logical acuteness, clear, forcible, and direct in his arguments. General Smith, of Maryland,[5] and Mr. Forsyth,[6] of Georgia, both struck me as being particularly free from the sins that do most easily beset their countrymen. When either of these gentlemen addressed the House, I always felt secure, not only that they had something to say, but that they had something worth saying; an assurance of which they only who have gone through a course of Congressional debates can appreciate the full value.

But whatever advantages the speeches of the Senate may possess over those of the Representatives, certainly brevity is not of the number. Every subject is overlaid; there is a continual sparring about trifles, and, it struck me, even a stronger display of sectional jealousies than in the other House. This latter quality probably arises from the senators being the representatives of an entire community, with separate laws, interests, and prejudices, and constituting one of the sovereign members of the confederation. When a member declares his opinions on any question, he is understood to speak the sentiments of a State, and he is naturally jealous of the degree of respect with which so important a revelation may be received. Then there are state antipathies, and state affinities, a predisposition to offence in one quarter, and to lend support in another; and there is the *odium in longum jaciens* between the Northern and Southern States, shedding its venom in every debate, and influencing the whole tenor of legislation.

One of the great evils arising, in truth, out of the very nature of the Union, is the sectional spirit apparent in all the proceedings of Congress. A representative from one State by no means considers himself bound to watch over the interests of another; and each being desirous to secure such local objects as may be conducive to the advantage of his own district, every species of trickery and cabal is put in requisition by which these objects may be obtained. There can be no doubt that the prevalence of such feelings is quite inconsistent with sound and wholesome legislation. Measures are estimated, not by their own merits, and their tendency to benefit the whole Union, but by the degree in which they can be made to subserve particular interests. One portion of the States is banded against another; there is no feeling of community of interests; jealousies deepen into hostilities; the mine is laid, a spark at length falls, and the grand federal Constitution is blown into a thousand fragments.

Many evils arise from the circumstance of the Government, both in its executive and legislative branches, being purely elective. The members of the latter, being abjectly dependent on the people, are compelled to adopt both the principles and the policy dictated by their constituents. To attempt to stem the torrent of popular passion and clamour, by a policy at once firm and enlightened, must belong to representatives somewhat more firmly seated than any which are to be found in Congress. Public men in other countries *may* be the parasites of the people, but in America they are necessarily so. Independence is impossible. They are slaves, and feel themselves to be so. They must act, speak, and vote according to the will of their master. Let these men hide their chains as they will, still they are on their limbs, galling their flesh, and impeding their motions; and it is, perhaps, the worst and most demoralizing result of this detestable system, that every man, ambitious of popular favour, — and in America who is not so? — is compelled to adopt a system of reservation. He keeps a set of exoteric dogmas, which may be changed or modified to suit the taste or fashion of the moment. But there are esoteric opinions, very different from anything to be found in State documents, or speeches in Congress, or 4th of July orations, which embody the convictions of the man, and which are not to be surrendered up at the bidding of a mob.

I speak now of minds of the higher order. The majority of Congress are fitted for nothing better than what they are. God meant them to be tools, and they are so. But there are men among them qualified to shine in a higher sphere; who stand prominently out among the meaner spirits by whom they are surrounded, and would be distinguished in any country by vigour, activity, and comprehension of thought.

These men must feel, that to devote their great powers to support and illustrate the prejudices of the ignorant and vulgar, is to divert their application from those lofty purposes for which they were intended. It cannot he without a sense of degradation that they are habitually compelled to bear part in the petty squabbles of Congress; to enter keenly into the miserable contests for candles-ends and cheeseparings; to become the cats' paws of sectional cupidity; to dole out prescribed opinions; to dazzle with false glitter, and convince with false reasoning; to flatter the ignorant, and truckle to the base; to have no object of ambition but the offices of a powerless executive; to find no field for the exercise of their higher faculties; to know they are distrusted, and, judging from the men with whom they mingle, to feel they ought to be so.

... In the basement story of one of the wings of the Capitol is the hall of the Supreme Court of the United States. It is by no means a large or handsome apartment; and the lowness of the ceiling, and the circumstance of its being underground, give it a certain cellar-like aspect, which is not pleasant. This is perhaps unfortunate, because it tends to create in the spectator the impression of justice being done in a corner; and, that while the business of legislation is carried on with all the pride, pomp, and circumstance of glorious debate, in halls adorned with all the skill of the architect, the administration of men's rights is considered an affair of secondary importance. Though the American law courts are no longer contaminated by wigs, yet the partiality for robes would appear not yet to be wholly extinct. The judges of the Supreme Court wear black Geneva gowns;[7] and the proceedings of this tribunal are conducted with a degree of propriety, both judicial and forensic, which leaves nothing to be desired. I certainly witnessed none of those violations of public decency, which in the State Courts are matters of ordinary occurrence. There was no lounging either at the bar or on the bench; nor was it, apparently, considered necessary to sink the gentleman in the lawyer, and assume a deportment in the discharge of professional duty which would not be tolerated in private society.

The Supreme Court consists of seven judges, removable only by impeachment, and possesses a federal jurisdiction over the whole Union. It sits annually in Washington for about two months, and is alone competent to decide on questions connected with the constitution or laws of the United States. Though possessing original jurisdiction in a few cases, its chief duties consist in the exercise of an appellate jurisdiction from the Circuit Courts, which are held twice a-year in the different States.

It would be tedious to enumerate the various cases in which the Federal Courts, in their three gradations of Supreme, Circuit, and District, exercise an exclusive or concurrent jurisdiction. It is enough that it should be generally understood that the Supreme Court is the sole expounder of the written constitution; and when we consider how open this important instrument has been proved to diversity of interpretation, what opposite meanings have been put upon its simplest clauses, and, in short, that the Constitution is precisely whatever four judges of this court may choose to make it, it will be seen how vitally important is the power with which it has been intrusted, and how difficult must be its exercise.

But the difficulties of the Supreme Court do not end here. Its jurisdiction extends not over a homogeneous population, but a variety of distinct communities, born under different laws, and adopting different forms in their administration.

Causes before the State Courts, in which the laws of the United States are even collaterally involved, are removable by writ of error to the Supreme Federal Court, and the decision of the State Court may be affirmed or reversed. In the latter case, a mandate is issued directing the State Court to conform its judgment to that of the Supreme Court. But the State tribunal is at perfect liberty to disregard the mandate, should it think proper; for the principle is established, that no one court can command another, but in virtue of an authority resting on express stipulation, and it is the duty of each judicature to decide how far this authority has been constitutionally exercised.

Then the legislatures of different States have found it occasionally convenient to pass laws for the purpose of defrauding their foreign creditors, while, in the case of Great Britain at least, the federal government is bound by express treaty that no lawful impediment shall be interposed to the recovery of the debts due by American citizens to British subjects. Under such circumstances, the Federal Court, backed by the whole honest portion of the people, certainly succeeded in putting a stop to the organized system of State swindling adopted by Kentucky after the late war; but awkward circumstances occurred, and the question may yet be considered practically undecided, whether the State legislatures possess a controlling power over the execution of a judgment of the Supreme Court.

Should a case occur, as is far from improbable, in which the federal legislature and judiciary are at variance, it would, no doubt, be the duty of the latter to declare every unconstitutional act of the former null and void. But under any circumstances, the Court has no power of enforcing its decrees. For instance, let us take the Indian question, and suppose, that in defiance of treaties, Georgia should persist in declaring the Creek and Cherokee Indians subject to the State laws, in order to force them to migrate beyond the Mississippi. The Indians appeal to the Supreme Court, and demand protection from unprincipled violence. The Court recognises their rights, and issues its mandate, which is just so much waste paper, unless the Government choose to send a military force along with it, which neither the present Congress nor executive would be inclined to do.

With all its sources of weakness, however, the United States Court is a wise institution. It is truly the sheet-anchor of the Union; and the degree of respect in which its decrees are held, may be considered as an exact index of the moral strength of the compact by which the discordant elements of the federal commonwealth are held together.

The most distinguished lawyers of the Union practise in the Supreme Court, and I had there an opportunity of hearing many of the more eminent members of Congress. During my stay there was no Jury trial, and the proceedings of the Court consisted chiefly in delivering judgments, and in listening to legal arguments from the bar. The tone of the speeches was certainly very different from anything I had heard in Congress. The lawyers seemed to keep their declamation for the House of Representatives, and in the Supreme Court spoke clearly, logically, and to the point. Indeed, I was more than once astonished to hear men whose speeches in Congress were rambling and desultory, in an extreme degree, display, in their forensic addresses, great legal acuteness, and resources of argument and illustration of the first order. In addressing the bench, they seemed to cast the slough of their vicious peculiarities, and spoke, not like schoolboys contending for a prize, but like men of high intellectual powers, solicitous not to dazzle but to convince.

"The Road to Washington"

From *Journal of a Residence and Tour in the United States of North America: From April, 1833, to October, 1834* by E. S. Abdy.

Edward Strutt Abdy (1791-1846) was, at the time of his visit to the United States, a Fellow of Jesus College, Cambridge and an abolitionist in his native England. He came to the United States in the company of two other Englishmen, one of whom (William Crawford) had been sent by the British Government "to inspect the prisons of the United States." Subsequent to Crawford's work, Abdy decided to continue his tour in the United States for the unambiguous purpose of serving "the cause of humanity" in providing "a full and faithful picture" of slavery in the country.

In a prescient observation, Abdy writes in the Introduction to his work that the British have "a closer and a deeper interest in the question of American slavery; for, if the Southern portion of the Union should endeavor to prevent its discussion, and resist or separate from the other, a civil or a servile war would ensue...."

---

In the afternoon I left Baltimore by the stage, for Washington (thirty-eight miles). The coach was filled with young men, who seemed to pay more attention to their rings and brooches and gold watches, than to the cleanliness of their hands, or the purity of their language. It rained in torrents, and the road was in a wretched state. About seven in the evening we entered the capital of the greatest slave-holding nation on the face of the globe; I speak of commercial, not of feudal, slavery: — of a system *forced* upon society, not springing naturally from its progress: — a disease engendered by the vices of its maturity, not an infirmity incidental to its infancy.

I put up at Gadsby's hotel — an establishment upon an immense scale: — between three and four hundred persons having been at one time accommodated there. At Baltimore, the bedroom doors were locked, at the hotel; and the guests requested to leave their keys at the bar of the house. Here, on the contrary, I was informed that no precaution of the kind was necessary. As the servants at the one were white, and at the other black, I was curious to learn the cause of this difference. I asked, therefore, one of the waiters at the breakfast table how many servants there were; and whether they were free. " Sir," replied the man, "there are seventy or eighty of us; and not one freeman." My heart sunk within me at this unexpected piece of intelligence. I felt shocked beyond description at the idea of being surrounded by slaves. "Do you belong to the master of the house?" I inquired. "No," was his reply: "my owner lives at Alexandria: — I am let out, as many others are, to the landlord: — there are many here who do not know each other, even by name." The man spoke in a dejected voice, but his language was good — much better than what I had heard the day before in the stage. I conversed with him some time; — as long, indeed, as I remained the only white in the room; — and felt deeply convinced, by what he told me, that his fellow bondsmen, as well as himself, were unhappy and discontented.

If slaves are all thieves, why does Gadsby allow his doors to be left unlocked, and so much valuable property exposed? Is the whip a better preventive of crime than the penitentiary? Or is he who is compelled to labor more honest than the man who is hired? Gadsby's treatment of those under his care is, I was told, mild and considerate, — this is the more to his credit — for he is an Englishman, long resident in the country; and it is generally observed that the English slave-owners are more cruel masters than the Americans; and of the latter, the southerners are less severe than those from the north. It is well known that those habits, which are most repugnant to our nature, are, when once they have obtained the mastery, the least easily subdued; while they are more severely condemned, from their supposed indication of innate depravity.

The rain continued to pour down as abundantly as the preceding day; and rendered it impossible to explore the topography of this infant metropolis. There was nothing going on in the Halls of Congress particularly interesting to a stranger. I went, however, to the Capitol, which is situated on a commanding eminence, and has a very imposing appearance, from the form of the edifice and the material of which it is built. The latter is white free-stone; add the approach is by three or four flights of steps. As the decorations are of the Corinthian order, the whole, though perhaps somewhat too splendid for republican simplicity, is calculated to produce a strong impression on the mind of the spectator.

The rotunda, which occupies the centre of the capitol, and is placed between the two chambers, where the Senate and the House of Representatives hold their sessions, is composed of marble, and lighted from the dome above. It is a noble room. Its various ornaments, whether in painting or in sculpture, are illustrative of those historical events which are most interesting to the country. Near each is placed a small sketch in outline, with the names of the figures introduced in the original. As it is drawn on paper, and intended for the hand, a stranger is saved the trouble of asking for a guide, and the still greater trouble of listening to his mechanical explanation of the different objects before him. In front of the paintings were various wooden boxes, that attracted my attention; and it was sometime before I could make out what they were. They contained some vegetable production, like mustard and cress. Upon a closer inspection, I discovered they were placed there for the accommodation of those who are addicted to tobacco in its various forms; and who, "cum pituita molesta est,"[1] might, for want of such conveniences, forget the sanctity of the place, and the respect due to the departed worthies whose images are around them. It would be as well, I thought, if Chantrey's beautiful statue of Washington, in the State House at Boston, had some protection against a beastly practice, which had so disfigured and debased the pedestal, that, were the artist to see it, "by Jove 'twou'd make him mad." The whole has since been railed in, and is now out of the reach of the spitters. To attempt a description of the disgusting habits here alluded to, would be to sin against that delicacy which they outrage. The very remembrance of what I have seen is inexpressibly disgusting.

The Chamber of the Representatives is semi-circular in its form, and rather gaudily furnished. The gallery, appropriated to the public, commands a full view of "the House;" above which it is sufficiently elevated to separate the members from the audience, and afford the latter an opportunity of seeing as well as of hearing what is going on below. Each member had his chair and desk; and most of them were busily employed in writing or reading, while one of them, who was presenting a petition, was dilating upon its contents; — they were of a local nature, and of no general interest. The appearance of the members was much the same as that which our House of Commons would present. It seemed to me, however, that there were not so many young men among them as are to be seen in the latter. Twenty-five is the minimum age allowed by the constitution.

From the House of Representatives I proceeded to the Senate. The room in which the latter sits is of similar form, but smaller and more plainly furnished. The galleries were very full; and, as I could not get a seat, I staid [*sic*] but a short time, during which some matters of form were going on.

While waiting to see one of the members of Congress, for whom I had a letter, I was accosted by a man to whom I had been introduced the preceding summer. He was one of the representatives from that part of New York State where I had been staying. Having informed him of my object, he very civilly offered his services; and, going into the chamber, returned in the course of five or ten minutes with the person I wanted, — Mr. Edward Everett.[2] The introduction was followed by a reception the coldest and most constrained I ever experienced in any country. The letter I put into his hand was from a friend in London, with whom he had had, I believe, some correspondence on the subject of the Cherokees. I gave him my address, and told him I should be happy to take back to England any answer he might wish to send to his correspondent, who, I knew, was particularly anxious to obtain from him some information relative to the Indians. I neither heard nor saw any more of Mr. Edward Everett.

Finding that some chiefs of the Cherokee tribe were in the city, I called at their hotel, and had along interview with two or three of them. They were all dressed in the same style as the whites. They had the manners and language of well-educated men. One of them had no mark of the Indian about him; and all were of mixed blood. The former had been imprisoned by the Georgians for a violation of their despotic laws. Upon my asking him whether the tribe did not hold slaves, he replied that they did so; but that they considered and treated them rather as free laborers.[3] He was himself, he said, a friend to universal liberty, and would always use what influence he had in its favor. He had lately bought a slave, to whom he was giving wages, on condition that he should return his master the purchase-money as soon as he could earn enough for that purpose. The negro was willing to perform his part of the bargain; but the whites in the neighborhood were much displeased at the arrangement, and tried to get the man away from him. It will be seen from this anecdote, as well as from the nature of existing circumstances, that the Indians who are settled in the slave States could not employ the blacks as hired laborers, however much they might prefer free to forced work. The whites would not probably condescend to be employed by them.

The Cherokee told me that his people raised a good deal of corn, and had plenty of cattle. Some of them were wealthy; and most, if not all, were sufficiently civilized to form a quiet and respectable society. Had it not been for the discovery of the gold mines on their lands, they would probably have been allowed to remain a longer time in the State.[4]

They were all strongly opposed to the scheme of removing beyond the Mississippi; as they could have no security against the recurrence of that injustice from which former treaties had been unable to protect them. There was no rancor or resentment perceptible in their language. It was evident, however, from what they said, that they had little hope of receiving, at the white man's hand, an equitable adjudication of their claims.

.... Frequent petitions have been presented to congress, praying for the abolition of slavery in the district of Columbia: — nothing however has been done; and the memorials are no more respected than the subject or the signers. There is no part of the Union, from which the road to Washington leads through the temple of Liberty.

I was led, from seeing a great many advertisements in the papers, offering rewards for runaway slaves, more particularly in the case of a woman and three children, to infer, that with such facilities of escape, this species of property must be of a very precarious and evanescent nature. Upon inquiry, however, I found I had judged very erroneously of the vigilance exercised in its protection. Many of those, I was assured, for whose apprehension these rewards are offered, have already been sold by their owners; who have recourse to this expedient, either to escape public censure, or, as is more probable, to conceal the distress which has compelled them to part with a sort of property that is not easily replaced. Nearly all menial services are engrossed by this portion of the population, more especially in the hotels, where the free blacks are not likely to seek or to find employment. The latter are obliged to register their names at the proper offices in the district, and to give security for good behavior to the amount of 500 dollars. The fee for registration is one dollar and a quarter — about five shillings. Electors with us pay a shilling for this form. Personal liberty under a republic is thus five times as dear as political liberty under a limited monarchy.

Slaves on the farms are allowed a peck of Indian corn per week each, with the addition of a daily herring — a luxury which is far from being universal. Tavern-keepers and others who hire them of their masters, pay a certain sum per month, and feed them; the latter finding their clothing. One day I went to see the "slaves' pen" — a wretched hovel, "right against" the Capitol, from which it is distant about half a mile, with no house intervening. The outside alone is accessible to the eye of a visitor; what passes within being reserved for the exclusive observation of its owner, (a man of the name of Robey), and his unfortunate victims. It is surrounded by a wooden paling fourteen or fifteen feet in height, with the posts outside to prevent escape, and separated from the building by a space too narrow to admit of a free circulation of air. At a small window above, which was unglazed and exposed alike to the heat of summer and the cold of winter, so trying to the constitution, two or three sable faces appeared, looking out wistfully to while away the time and catch a refreshing breeze; the weather being extremely hot. In this wretched hovel, all colors, except white — the only guilty one — both sexes, and all ages, are confined, exposed indiscriminately to all the contamination which may be expected in such society and under such seclusion. The inmates of the gaol, of this class I mean, are even worse treated; some of them, if my informants are to be believed, having been actually frozen to death, during the inclement winters which often prevail in the country. While I was in the city, Robey had got possession of a woman, whose term of slavery was limited to six years. It was expected that she would be sold before the expiration of that period, and sent away to a distance, where the assertion of her claim would subject her to ill-usage. Cases of this kind are very common.

"Ladies of America are Uncommonly Frank"

From *Impressions of America: During the Years 1833, 1834, and 1835* by Tyrone Power.

The life of Irish actor Tyrone Power (1797-1841) was cut short when he and all other passengers and crew were lost at sea aboard the *SS President*, then bound from New York to Liverpool, in March, 1841. Power had begun a successful career as a stage actor and comedian in his native Ireland and while he often portrayed Irish characters in productions with Irish themes, he avoided playing typical stock characters based on his countrymen, characters he considered altogether clichéd.

Like many 19th British and Continental actors, Power toured the United States in hopes of establishing himself among audiences there, a feat he was well on his way to accomplishing when he boarded the *SS President* on its fateful voyage. Writing early in the 20th century, American theatre historian Montrose Jonas Moses praised Power's *Impressions of America* for its "unprejudiced, lucid view of the state of this country...." Among Tyrone Power's descendants who pursued the arts is the late Hollywood film actor Tyrone Edmund Power, III (1914-1958).

*Washington*

On arriving at Baltimore, I found that so woeful was the condition of the road between this city and the capital, that, although the distance is but thirty-seven miles, and that there remained full three hours of daylight, still no regular stage would encounter, until morning, the perils of the road.

I thereon made an agreement with two gentlemen, — one of whom was an excellent and learned judge, on some State business; and the other a Philadelphia merchant, escorting his daughter, and a pretty young lady her friend, on a visit of pleasure to Washington, — that we would together engage an extra coach for our party; and, instead of starting, at the monstrous hour of five in the morning, set out at half-past eight, when, with the advantage of a light load and good horses, we might reasonably hope to reach our destination before dark.

This was done accordingly: an extra or exclusive carriage, to hold six inside, was contracted for with the proper authorities, and chartered to Washington city, to start between eight and nine next morning, for the sum of twenty-five dollars, or about six pounds sterling.

With the punctuality for which these people are distinguished throughout the States, our carriage drove up to Barnum's door at a few minutes after eight; and, breakfast being despatched, our party was seated fairly, with all the luggage built upon the permanent platform which graces the rear of these machines, within the time appointed: a very creditable event, when it is considered there were two young ladies of the party.

The air was mild as in May, and there being a goodly promise of sunshine, I resigned my share of the inside to my servant Sam, — the very pink of brown gentleman in appearance, besides being a pattern of good-breeding; and seeing something unusually knowing in the look of our wagonner, mounted the box by his side, uneasy though it was; for never was any thing worse contrived for comfort than the outside of a Yankee stage-coach, — except, perhaps, the inside of an English mail.

Mr. Tolly, whose acquaintance I now made, let me record, was the only driver I ever met in America who took up his leather, and packed his cattle together, with that artist-like air, the perfection of which is only to be seen in England.

The coachmen are not here, as with us, a distinct class, distinguished by peculiar costume, and by characteristics the result of careful education and exclusive habits; but might be taken for porters, drovers, or anything else indeed, — being men who have followed, and are ready again to follow, a dozen other vocations, as circumstances might require: they are nevertheless, generally, good drivers, and uniformly, sober steady fellows.

Mr. Tolly, however, one might see at a glance — despite the disadvantages of his toggery,[1] plant, and all his other appointments — was born to look over four pair of lively ears; and had Fortune only dropped him in any stable-loft between London and York, there would not have been a cooler hand or a neater whip on the North road.

About a mile from the city we came upon the country turnpike; and of this, as I now viewed it for the first time, any comprehensible description is out of the question, since I am possessed of no means of illustrating its condition to English senses, — a Cumberland fell, ploughed-up at the end of a very wet November, would be the Bath road compared with this, the only turnpike leading from one of the chief seaboard cities to the capital of the Union.

I looked along the river of mud with despair. Mr. Tolly will pronounce this impracticable after the night's rain, thinks I; but I was mightily mistaken in my man: without pausing to pick or choose, he cheered his leaders, planted his feet firmly, and charged gallantly into it.

The team was a capital one, and stuck to their dirty work like terriers. Some of the holes we scrambled safely by would, I seriously think, have swallowed coach and all up: the wheels were frequently buried up to the centre; and more than once we had three of our cattle down together all of-a-heap, but with whip and voice Mr. Tolly always managed to pick them out and put them on "their legs again; indeed," as he said, if he could only see his leaders' heads well up, he felt "pretty certain the coach must come through, slick as soap."

Mr. Tolly and myself very soon grew exceedingly intimate; a false reading of his having at starting inspired him with a high opinion of my judgment, and stirred his blood and mettle, both of which were decidedly game.

Whilst smoking my cigar, and holding on by his side with as unconcerned an air as I could assume, I, in one of our pauses for breath, after a series of unusually heavy lurches, chanced to observe, by way of expressing my admiration, "This is a real *varmint* team you've got hold on, Mr. Tolly."

"How did you find that out, sir?" cries Tolly, biting off about a couple of ounces of 'baccy.[2]

"Why, it's not hard to tell so much, after taking a good look at them, I guess," replied I.

"Well, that's rum, anyhow! but, I guess, you're not far out for once," answers Mr. Tolly, with a knowing grin of satisfaction: "sure enough, they are all from Varmont,[3] and I am Varmont myself as holds 'em — all mountain boys, horses and driver — real Yankee flesh and blood; and they can't better them, I know, neither one nor t'other, this side the Potomac."[4]

I found my *hirgo*[5] was thrown away, but did not attempt an explanation, and became in a little time satisfied that this odd interpretation of my compliment had answered an excellent purpose; for my companion became exceedingly communicative, and most indefatigable in his exertions.

More plucky or more judicious coachmanship, or better material under leather, I never came across in all my journeyings. About half way we bade adieu to my Varmont friend, to my great regret.

Wearied with my rough seat, which the companionship of Mr. Tolly had alone rendered endurable so long, I now got inside; the Philadelphia gentleman succeeding to the vacancy on the box.

I did my best to draw my fair companions into a little chat, but found my *vis-à-vis* — the daughter of my successor outside — most impracticable; a monosyllable was the extent of her exertion; whilst her companion, who was a lively, intelligent-looking girl, and very pretty withal, was necessarily chilled by the taciturnity of her senior. I note this as being an unusual case, since, when once properly introduced, the ladies of America are uncommonly frank and chatty, and evince an evident desire to please and be amiable; which is creditable to themselves, and to strangers is both flattering and agreeable.

In the good old judge, whom I had the honour of meeting often after, I found one of the most amusing and intelligent companions a man could desire to rumble over a villanous road with, and for a couple of hours we made time light, when our day's journey had well-nigh terminated in an adventure that might have been attended with ugly consequences.

Although the road for this stage was something less bad, our driver was not a Tolly; in avoiding some Charybdis[6] or other, he let his leaders slip down a bank about eight feet deep, whither, but for the good temper and steady backing of the wheel-horses, we should have followed: as it was, we managed to pick out our cattle, and got off with a couple of broken traces. These being duly cobbled, away we scrambled again, I resuming my seat on the box; the last occupant having become most heartily sick of his elevation.

About the end of nine hours' hard driving, the high dome of the Capitol showed near; and the city toll-gate, situated about a mile from this magnificent building, was opened. The prospect was, notwithstanding, yet sufficiently uncheery; a steep hill lay in front, having a road that looked like a river of black mud meandering about one side of it — the other side was seamed with various tracks made by the vehicles of bold explorers, who, like ourselves, had been doubtful about facing the regular road — the counsel of a well mounted countryman, who reported that he had just passed the wrecks of two coaches on the turnpike, decided us to eschew it, and boldly try across country.

We all alighted, except the ladies; and acting as pioneers, pushed up the hill, breasting it stoutly. It was very well we took this route; for, having at last safely crowned it, we beheld on our right the two coaches that left Baltimore three hours before us, hopelessly pounded in the highway, regularly swamped within sight of port; for the Capitol was not over three or four hundred yards from them.

The passengers were all out, most of them assisting to unharness and unload, that, by combining both teams, they might extricate their vehicles one at a time.

Here, within the shadow of the Capitol, I was struck with the gloomy and unimproved condition of the surrounding country. Except our caravan, not a living thing moved within sight — all was desert, silent, and solitary as the prairies of Arkansas.

The great avenue once entered upon, the scene changed, and we rattled along briskly over a well Macadamized road. The judge we set down at the top of the Capitolinean hill, where his honourable brothers held their headquarters; my other companions had rooms secured at Gadsby's, where we next halted; but to my inquiries here, I was answered "All quite full."

They advised me, at the same time, to try Fuller,[7] which I thought waggish enough: however, after driving about a mile farther down the avenue, I found at Mr. Fuller's hotel rooms taken for me by a considerate friend, and had to congratulate myself now and henceforward on being the best-lodged errant homo in the capital of the United States.

The windows of my sitting-room, I perceived, commanded a view the whole extent of the avenue; but, for the present, I limited my speculation to the dinner that was soon placed before me, and which a fast of eleven hours had rendered a particularly desirable prospect.

*Theatre, Washington*

I made my *début* professionally in the capital upon the 12<sup>th</sup> of February. The theatre[8] here was a most miserable-looking place, the worst I met with in the country, ill-situated, and difficult of access; but it was filled nightly by a very delightful audience; and nothing could be more pleasant than to witness the perfect *abandon* with which the gravest of the senate laughed over the diplomacy of the "Irish Ambassador." They found allusions and adopted sayings applicable to a crisis when party feelings were carried to extremity. The elaborate display of eloquence with which Sir Patrick seeks to *bother* the Spanish envoy was quoted as the very model of a speech for a non-committal orator, and recommended for the study of several gentlemen who were considered as aiming at this convenient position, very much to their amusement.

The pieces were ill-mounted, and the company unworthy the capital, with the exception of two very pretty and very clever native actresses, Mesdames Willis and Chapman. The latter I had the satisfaction of seeing soon after transferred to New York, in which city she became a monstrous favourite, both in tragedy and comedy: a very great triumph for Mrs. Chapman — for she succeeded Miss

F. Kemble in some of her best parts, and an excellent comic actress, a Mrs. Sharpe — acting on the same night Julia in "The Hunchback," and the Queen of Hearts in "High, Low, Jack, and Game," with a cleverness which rarely accompanies such versatility.

I have much pleasure in offering this just tribute to a very amiable person, who has, since my departure from the States, quitted the stage, on which, had she been fortunately situated, she would have had very few superiors.

I wonder there are not many more native actresses? since, I am sure, there is a great deal of latent talent in society here both for opera and the drama: the girls, too, are generally well educated; are pretty, have much expression, a naturally easy carriage, and great imitative powers. The latter talent is singularly common amongst them; and I have met, not one, but many young women, who would imitate the peculiarities of any actress or actor just then before the public with an accuracy and humour quite remarkable.

I acted here seven nights on this occasion, and visited the city again in May, when I passed three or four weeks most agreeably. I had the pleasure, too, during this last visit, of seeing the plans for a theatre worthy the audience,[9] and which, I trust, has by this time been happily erected, as the greatest part of the fund needed was readily subscribed for; and the attempt can hardly fail amongst a people so decidedly theatrical, and who are, besides, really in absolute want of public amusements for the number of stray men turned loose here during the session, many of whom are without other home than the bar-room of an inn, or better means of keeping off *ennui* than ginsling or the gaming-table.

I shall now throw together in this place the result of my " Impressions " as received during my separate visits.

The scenery in the neighbourhood is naturally as beautiful and varied as woods, rocks, and rivers, in all their most charming features, can combinedly render it. One of the finest of many noble prospects is, in my mind, that from the heights just over George Town. From this point the vast amphitheatre of city, valley, and river may be embraced at a glance, or followed out in detail, as time or inclination prompts.

Following the windings of the majestic Potomac below the bridge, — which, viewed from this elevation, looks like a couple of cables drawn across its channel, — the town of Alexandria is clearly seen: away, on the other side. Fort Washington may be made out; and, opposite to this, the ever-hallowed, Mount Vernon is visible; a glimpse in itself worthy a pilgrimage to every lover of that rare combination — virtue and true patriotism!

Turning from this direction, and setting your face towards the Capitol, you perceive extended in dotted lines, the thinly-furnished streets of the city: viewed from here, the meager supply of buildings in proportion to its extent is made obvious; each separate house may be traced out; and, in their irregular and detached appearance, all design becomes confounded. It seemed to me as though some frolicsome fairy architect, whilst taking a flight with a sieveful of pretty houses, had suddenly betaken her to riddling them over this attractive site as she circled over the valley in her airy car....

## *Impressions of Washington Society, Public and Private*

I attended several large assemblies at Washington, and must here, after a second visit, and so much experience as my opportunities afforded, enter my protest against the sweeping ridicule it has pleased some writers to cast upon these doings here; since I saw none of those outrageously unpresentable women, or coarsely habited and ungainly men, so amusingly arrayed by some of my more observant predecessors. I can only account for it by referring to the rapid changes ever taking place here, and to which I have alluded in my introduction to these "Impressions."

The ordinary observances of good society are, I should say, fully understood and fully practised at these public gatherings, and not more of the ridiculous presented than might be observed at any similar assemblage in England, if half so much; since here I have commonly found that persons who have no other claims to advance save money or a seat in the legislature, very wisely avoid *reunions*, where they could neither look to receive nor bestow pleasure.

It is quite true that many of these members, all of whom are by rank eligible to society, maybe met with, who are more rusty of bearing than most of those within St. Stephen's; but I will answer for this latter assembly outfacing them in samples of rudeness, ill-breeding, and true vulgarity: for it is a striking characteristic of the American, that, if not conventionally polished perhaps, you will rarely find him either rude or discourteous; whilst amongst those who, in the nature of the government, are elevated from a comparatively obscure condition to place and power, although refinement cannot be inserted as an addendum to the official diploma, the aspirant usually adopts with his appointment a quiet formal strain of ceremony, which protects himself, and can never give offence to any.

In the absence of that ease and self-possession which can only be acquired by long habitual intercourse with well-bred persons, this surely is the wisest course that could be adopted, and a hundred degrees above that fidgety, jackdaw-like assumption of *nonchalance* with which the ill-bred amongst ourselves seek to cover their innate vulgarity.

At all these assemblies, as elsewhere, great real attention is paid to women; and I vow I have, in this respect, seen more ill-breeding, and selfish rudeness, at a fashionable rout in England, than could be met with, at any decent crush, from Natchetoches to Marble-head. Beyond these points within the States I speak not, since without them the land is strange to me.

No levee of the President's has occurred during my sojourn here; but I learn that in the true spirit of democracy, the doors on these occasions are open to every citizen without distinction of rank or costume; consequently the assemblage at such times may be oddly compounded enough.

As for private society in Washington, although limited, it can in no place be conducted in a manner more agreeable, or extended to the stranger with more unostentatious freedom. Once presented to a family, and the house is thenceforward open to you. From twelve o'clock until two, the inmates either visit or receive visitors: between these hours, the question, "Are the ladies at home?" being answered in the affirmative, you walk into the drawing-room without farther form; and, joining the circle, or enjoying a *tête-à-tête*, as it may happen, remain just so long as you receive or can impart amusement.

Again, after six, if you are so disposed, you sally forth to visit. If the family you seek beat home, you find its members forming a little group or groups, according to the number present, each after their age and inclination; and politics, dress, or scandal are discussed: or, if the night be serene, — and what lovely nights have I witnessed here, even at this early season! — (May) — you make a little party to the covered stoup, or balcony, extended along the back-front of most houses; and here a song, a romp, a waltz, or a quiet still talk, while away hours of life, unheeded until passed, but never to be recalled without pleasure. About eleven the guests generally depart, and by midnight the great avenue of this city is hardly disturbed by a foot-fall; not a sound comes on the ear except the short, fierce wrangle of packs of vagrant curs crossing each other's hunting-ground, which they are as tenacious of as the Indians are of their prairies.

At this hour I used often, after returning from a party, such as is described above, to put on my morning-gown and slippers, and light my pipe, then sallying forth, have strolled from Fuller's to the Capitol; and climbing its bold hill, have looked down along the sleeping city, speculating upon its possible destinies until my fancies waxed threadbare, and then quietly returned, making a distance of nearly three miles, without encountering an individual or hearing the sound of a human voice.

At set balls even, the first hour of morning generally sees ample space on the, till then, crowded floor; and the most ardent pleasure-lovers rarely overleap the second by many minutes.

The consequence of this excellent plan is, that, although the ladies are weak in numbers, they are always, to use an expressive sporting phrase, ready to come again; rising, the morning after a dance, unwearied and elastic in mind and body. I hope, for the sake of my American friends, it will be very long before these healthful hours are changed to those which custom has made fashionable in England; hours that soon fade the roses even on their most genial soil, the cheeks of the fair girls of Britain, blighting the healthful and the young, and withering the aged and the weak.

Much of the population of Washington is migratory; and, during a long session, samples may be found here of all classes, from every part of the Union, whether represented or not. There are, however, generally resident a few old Southern families, who, together with the foreign ministers and their suites, form the nucleus of a permanent society, where the polish of Europe is grafted upon the simple and frank courtesy of the best of America. Were it not in violation of a rule I have imposed upon myself as imperative, I could name families here whose simple yet refined manners would do honour to any community, and from an intercourse with whom the most fastidious conventionalist would return satisfied.

---

"The Bottom of an Old Lake"

From *Travels in North America During the Years 1834, 1835 & 1836* by Sir Charles Augustus Murray.

Topographical observations aside, Sir Charles Augustus Murray (1806-1895), born the son of a peer of the Realm and educated at Oxford, spent long enough in America to become smitten with young Elizabeth Wadsworth, daughter of the wealthy and influential New Yorker James Wadsworth. Their romance proved tragic. Wadsworth did not approve of his daughter's relationship with Murray, who subsequently returned to England to serve in Queen Victoria's household. After Wadsworth died in 1844, Elizabeth and Charles were reunited. They married in 1850. Elizabeth would die in childbirth the following year, though their son Charles James Murray would survive. By this time, Murray had established a career in diplomacy, serving in various posts including Egypt and Persia.

 Although Murray is almost uniformly dismissive of all things Washington, he does find something of substance in the debates in Congress, especially in the eloquence of Henry Clay's checked thunder.

---

My first object of curiosity and interest was naturally the Congress, and I accordingly drove to the Capitol; an edifice in the appearance of which a stranger, who judges from the relations of British travellers, will be agreeably surprised. It certainly cannot claim the merit of simplicity or uniformity of character, neither are its proportions or decorations in strict accordance with the rules of Grecian architecture; but the effect is altogether grand and imposing; and well will it be for America, if the moral materials composing its congressional assembly prove as well-proportioned and durable as the building in which they hold their sittings. The circular hall, or saloon, in which are four entrances, to the vestibule, the library, the Senate, and the Hall of Representatives, is spacious, and well lighted by a dome. It seems a favourite lounging-place for idlers of all classes, and contains four pictures by Colonel Trumbull, representing scenes connected with the revolutionary history. On this account they may be interesting to Americans, but to a lover of the fine arts they offer no attraction whatever. The Hall of Representatives is a spacious semicircular apartment, containing galleries for reporters and the public, and having its floor furnished with an elbow-chair and a table for each member.

It happened, when I arrived, that the question before the house was not one of much importance: and the scene, for the time, resembled rather a large club or cafe than a deliberative assembly; for certainly three-fourths of the members were writing their private letters, reading newspapers, and chatting as comfortably as if they had been in the front room of Brooke's or White's.[1] This hall, from its dimensions and decorations, possesses every requisite for the purpose to which it is appropriated, except one, and that one is the most vital: it is scarcely possible to hear two words in five, uttered by a speaker of ordinary lungs. I have been told, that Mr. Clay, when he was in that house, and some few others, could make themselves understood; but I think I never saw an apartment of the same magnitude in which the voice was so completely lost; and even breathless silence will not avail much, as there is an echo which so mingles the present with the preceding tones, as to render distinctness altogether impossible, except by means of the very slowest enunciation; a method quite incompatible with the vehement and redundant declamation, which is one of the leading features of American oratory.

The Senate is of much smaller size, and in every way better adapted for argumentative debate; it is also furnished with galleries for reporters and the public, and round the exterior curve of the semi-circle, on the floor, is one for ladies, and for those who have leave of admission from senators; while in the base of the semicircle, behind the President's chair, is a large recess open to members of the other house and to foreign ministers.

As I had obtained the favour of the entree to the lower, or ladies' gallery, I entered there and found every seat occupied by a fair politician. There was, moreover, a considerable number of gentlemen standing to hear the discussion. I had not stood there more than five minutes, when one of the door-keepers was sent in with a chair for my convenience. I was, I confess, struck by this polite attention to a stranger: whether I was indebted to the Vice-President or to some other senator for it, I regretted much that I had not an opportunity of thanking him for a civility which I have much pleasure in recording.

The discussion being upon local and unimportant subjects, I did not remain long on this occasion, but returned a few days afterwards, to hear the debate upon the relations with France. The circumstances connected with this question are well known. The President, in his message, demanded from Congress provisional authority for making reprisals upon French property, in the contingency of the (continued) non-payment by France of the indemnity promised by her in the treaty of 1831 to the United States. In order fully to understand the management of this important question in the Senate, it must be remembered, that in that body the opposition had a majority, while in the House of Representatives they were in a minority. The debate was opened by Mr. Clay, the framer of the resolutions adopted by the committee on foreign relations, the last of which formed the ground-work of the present motion, "that it was inexpedient, at the present time, to grant the provisional authority requested by the President."

It is well known that Mr. Clay[2] is one of the most vehement and eloquent opponents of the President's government; and here certainly was a magnificent opportunity for displaying those peculiar powers which distinguish his oratory, inasmuch as the word "reprisals" was so much calculated to wound the pride and dignity of France, and to give that nation a plea for breaking off all further negotiation upon the subject. All the property and intelligence of America were naturally averse to a war with France; the inevitable consequence of which, even if successful, must be an expense of money threefold greater than the indemnity demanded; and Mr. Clay had a fine occasion, and one which none could have improved better than himself, of uttering a philippic against the government for giving France so fair an excuse for transferring the question from her diplomatists to her admirals: but he took a wiser and more statesman-like course; and in a speech at once able, temperate, and eloquent, argued the expediency of deferring any legislative measure in regard to the relations with France he deprecated all national division and dissension on this question, and expressed his willingness to modify his motion, so as to secure a unanimous vote upon the occasion.

The speeches of most of those who took part in the debate adopted a similar tone; and a resolution, proposed by Mr. Webster,[3] and slightly altered by Mr. Clay's original motion, was carried unanimously.

The whole debate was highly creditable both to the temper and ability of the house, and that not so much from what was said, as from what was not said, on a question touching national vanity, and perhaps almost national honour, and when it was so difficult to avoid expressions irritating to the feelings of the respective parties to the treaty. The original sentence in the President's message which caused the debate, has been much censured for its imprudence whether justly or not, is a matter of doubt. In all such inquiries the object in view must be first clearly ascertained. If that object was to maintain peace with France by every means compatible with the honour of the United States, the paragraph in question was imprudent; but the President was probably influenced by other views. No man, much less a stranger, has a right to impute motives; but they are to any observer a fair and open field for conjecture; and it is possible, that the President was not very averse to a little quarrel with France, seeing that his revenue was unburthened, and that such a national cause was calculated to cement that union between the States, which various conflicting accidents and interests had occasionally threatened to weaken, since the last war.

To return to Mr. Clay: his manner and voice are both admirably adapted for a leader in a popular assembly; the former is earnest and energetic (though perhaps deficient in that grace and dignity which characterize the oratory of Earl Grey);[4] the latter is full and manly; and though its tones cannot be pronounced musical, still they are modulated to the subject-matter, and produce upon the hearer that most powerful of all effects a conviction that, if provoked, the lion could roar yet more terribly. As an illustration of this last-mentioned principle, the Miltonian reader may remember with what mighty force that great master has applied it, when, after describing the power, and strength, and terror, with which the Son drove upon, and overthrew the rebellious host of angels, he concludes

"Yet half his strength he put not forth, but checked His thunder in mid-volley."

Mr. Webster spoke a few words upon this question, but they were delivered with that grave impressive manner, resulting from conscious power. In a cause where the result was dependent upon logical argument and profound knowledge of constitutional law, I should imagine that Mr. Webster would find few equals, and no superior, on either side of the Atlantic; but, in directing the impulse and exciting the passions of a popular assembly, he is, probably, less successful than Mr. Clay.

About this time a member of Congress[5] died suddenly, in consequence of which the houses adjourned for two days. The respective members wore a crape on the arm, and the greater part attended his funeral. It may not be irrelevant here to remark, that the death of a citizen in one of the Atlantic cities of the United States produces a greater sensation, and is accompanied with more demonstration of respect, than a similar event in any other country which I have seen. If a member of Congress dies, the houses adjourn, as above-mentioned; if a wealthy and influential merchant dies, as was lately the case in Baltimore, his funeral is attended by great numbers of his fellow-citizens, independently of his relatives; and even the flags of the shipping in harbour are hoisted half-mast high. Similar instances might be adduced in other walks of life.

At the public funeral of the member of congress above-mentioned, an attempt was made upon the life of the President,[6] the failure of which can only be attributed to a Providential interference, such as the sceptic may deny, or the thoughtless worldling may ridicule, but which is at the same time more consonant with religion and reason than a belief in the wonderful coincidence of fortuitous circumstances, necessary to produce the same result. The wretch who attempted this murder (and who appears to labour under that dangerous kind of insanity which just trembles upon the verge of responsibility), stood only a few feet from the President, under the portico of the Capitol. He deliberately snapped a pistol at him, which missed fire, and before his arm could be arrested, he drew another from his pocket, snapped it, and it also missed fire, when he was knocked down and secured. On examination it was found, that both pistols were new, both carefully loaded with ball and good powder; yet both the detonating caps exploded without igniting the charge. I had this account from several gentlemen, who were close to the President at the time; and on the trial which followed, it was established and recorded by legal process. Let the "Doctrinaires" of chance account for it as they can.

The old General showed his ancient and undoubted courage upon the occasion. When the first pistol was snapped at him, he looked straight at, and went straight towards the wretch who held it; and when the second was presented, he never swerved, but attacked his opponent with a stout stick, which he usually carries. Had not a blow from some other hand anticipated his intention, he would probably have spared the law the trouble of investigating the matter.

It is singular how little noise or feeling the occurrence seems to have excited, except in the shameless and villainous instance of one or two scribblers in the government newspapers, who wished to attribute the attempt at assassination to the effect produced by the speeches of Mr. Calhoun.[7] The character of that gentleman needs no defence or refutation of such calumnies. He is indeed one of the most distinguished men in the Union. His name is familiar to Europe as the great champion of the Southern States, and the pillar of that nullification question which threatened at one time to dismember the confederation. His manner is lofty and commanding; his eye, searching, keen, and deeply set under a considerate brow. He is an acute reasoner, and the analytic power of his mind is most remarkable. Some there are who consider him as a more eminent statesman than either Clay or Webster: this is a question that I do not feel able or called upon to decide. That they are all three men of whom America has just reason to be proud, is a truth to which I have much pleasure in here recording my testimony.

... The month of March had now arrived; and as the rivers had become navigable, and the roads were supposed to be passable, I began to meditate an excursion to Richmond and other parts of Virginia. The Congress had broken up on the 4$^{th}$, and with it the bustle and gaiety of Washington society. Every day announced new departures; and the scattered village, denominated a city, began to assume the silent and melancholy appearance which is natural to its construction, and which is only partially cheered by the stirring season of congress. In truth it is impossible to imagine a more comfortless situation for a town, or a town more foolishly and uncomfortably laid out. The houses are small, and their walls thin; the streets are so broad as to render the insignificant appearance of the buildings more remarkable; and the dust in dry weather is only to be equalled in annoyance by the filth and mud after rain. The principal street is the Pennsylvania Avenue, which is above a mile long, and is the best piece of macadamized road in the United States; but they appear never to scrape off the dust; and I have been more nearly blinded and choked there, after three days of dry weather in March, than ever I have been in Rotten Row on a Sunday in June; though in the former case the dust was raised by one solitary hackney-coach, and the latter was the joint production of horses and carriages to be counted by thousands.

Many streets are in embryo, many only in prescience, or rather imagination, where their existence will probably terminate as it began. Paradise-row must be content to be "represented" by one small brick shop or store Pleasant-place, by two groceries and a livery stable while Prospect-place may, with its two or three separate and humble tenements, continue to look over the damp swampy flat extending from the town to the Potomac.

The greater part of the site of Washington is probably the bottom of an old lake, of which the Capitol Hill formed one of the borders; and though the preceding names are jestingly adduced, the joke is not very far from the truth. The inhabitants seem to have persisted, in defiance equally of experience and common sense, in believing that their city was one day to become the centre of wealth and commerce, as it is of legislature; overlooking apparently the trifling impediments that the soil of all the neighbouring country is wretchedly poor, that the channel of the Potomac is so shallow that neither merchant-ship nor frigate, nor any craft of five hundred tons' burthen, can come up to their harbour of Georgetown; and that, moreover, they must compete with the neighbouring wealthy and flourishing town of Baltimore.

In pursuance of their commercial dreams, they have carried on a canal, parallel for many miles with the stream of the Potomac, upon borrowed Dutch capital; the interest of which they are unable to pay without a yearly begging petition to Congress, who will in the end be obliged also to pay the principal.[8]

The funds for defraying the ordinary municipal expenses, such as constables, street-paving, lighting, &c. are raised by assessment on the inhabitants, imposed by the corporation, and amounting upon an average to three-quarters of one per cent, on the property of each individual. This method is very commonly practised in America, and appears, in political phrase, to "work very well."

What renders this tax peculiarly heavy in Washington is, that the city is laid out in lots, four-fifths of which are unoccupied and totally profitless. These are valued, rated, and assessed by the corporation, as if they were built upon and paid a rent. The only appeal from their assessment is to themselves, in another form of sitting; the redress to be obtained, and the equity observed, may be estimated by those who knew the working of the old burgh system in Scotland. In fact, the town of Washington was overwhelmed by debt, and the greater part of it mortgaged to different banks, before they subscribed the million dollars to the great canal. Consequently, the few who possessed any property free of debt voted against that subscription, knowing that the weight of it must fall upon them; but the majority, whose property was already mortgaged, and who had nothing, were of course "liberal" and "patriotic" subscribers on the occasion. In fact, it may be safely affirmed, that unless Congress pays the debt, the whole city of Washington (with the exception of the Capitol Hill and other lots belonging to the public) must soon be for sale, and be the property of the Dutch bankers.

"The President Offered Me Bonbons"

From *Retrospect of Western Travel* by Harriet Martineau.

By the time she visited the United States in 1835, Harriet Martineau (1802-1876) was already an established and successful author in her native England, writing on social issues including political economy, poor laws and taxation. A two-year tour of the U.S. produced the popular but controversial *Society in America*, which was criticized there for its portrayals of slavery and her observations on the "political non-existence of women."

Martineau's *Retrospect of Western Travel* appeared shortly thereafter and was conceived as a more popular work, yet it draws on the same experiences as *Society in America*. It was written, as Martineau states in her Preface, with the goal of supplying to the English "what the Americans do not want — a picture of the aspect of the country, and of its men and manners." Ms. Martineau did not fail.

---

Washington is no place for persons of domestic tastes. Persons who love dissipation, persons who love to watch the game of politics, and those who make a study of strong minds under strong excitements, like a season at Washington; but it is dreary to those whose pursuits and affections are domestic. I spent five weeks there, and was heartily glad when they were over. I felt the satisfaction all the time of doing something that was highly useful; of getting knowledge that was necessary to me, and could not be otherwise obtained; but the quiet delights of my Philadelphia home (though there half our time was spent in visiting) had spoiled me for such a life as everyone leads at the metropolis. I have always looked back upon the five weeks at Washington as one of the most profitable, but by far the least agreeable, of my residences in the United States.

Yet we were remarkably fortunate in our domestic arrangements there. We[1] joined a party of highly esteemed and kind friends: a member of the House of Representatives from Massachusetts, his wife and sister-in-law, and a Senator from Maine. We... had a drawing-room to ourselves and a separate table at Mrs. Peyton's boarding-house; so that we formed a quiet family group enough, if only we had had any quiet in which to enjoy the privilege.

We arrived at Washington on the 13th of January, 1835, the year of the short session of Congress which closes on the 4th of March, so that we continued to see the proceedings of Congress at its busiest and most interesting time.

The approach to the city is striking to all strangers from its oddness. I saw the dome of the Capitol from a considerable distance at the end of a straight road; but, though I was prepared by the descriptions of preceding travellers, I was taken by surprise on finding myself beneath the splendid building, so sordid are the enclosures and houses on its very verge. We wound round its base, and entered Pennsylvania Avenue, the only one of the grand avenues intended to centre in the Capitol which has been built up with any completeness. Our boarding-house was admirably situated, being some little way down this avenue, a few minutes' walk only from the Capitol, and a mile in a straight line from the White House, the residences of the heads of departments and the British legation.

In Philadelphia I had found perpetual difficulty in remembering that I was in a foreign country. The pronunciation of a few words by our host and hostess, the dinner table, and the inquiries of visiters [sic] were almost all that occurred to remind me that I was not in a brother's house. At Washington it was very different. The city itself is unlike any other that ever was seen, straggling out hither and thither, with a small house or two a quarter of a mile from any other; so that, in making calls "in the city," we had to cross ditches and stiles, and walk alternately on grass and pavements, and strike across a field to reach a street. Then the weather was so strange; sometimes so cold that the only way I could get any comfort was by stretching on the sola drawn before the fire up to the very fender (on which days every person who went in and out of the house was sure to leave the front door wide open); then the next morning, perhaps, if we went out muffled in furs, we had to turn back and exchange our wraps for a light shawl. Then we were waited upon by a slave appointed for the exclusive service of our party during our stay. Then there were canvass-back ducks, and all manner of other ducks on the table, in greater profusion than any single article of food, except turkeys, that I ever saw. Then there was the society, singularly compounded from the largest variety of elements; foreign ambassadors, the American government, members of Congress, from Clay and Webster down to Davy Crockett, Benton from Missouri, and Cuthbert, with the freshest Irish brogue, from Georgia; flippant young belles, "pious" wives dutifully attending their husbands, and groaning over the frivolities of the place; grave judges, saucy travellers, pert newspaper reporters, melancholy Indian chiefs, and timid New-England ladies, trembling on the verge of the vortex; all this was wholly unlike anything that is to be seen in any other city in the world; for all these are mixed up together in daily intercourse, like the higher circle of a little village, and there is nothing else. You have this or nothing; you pass your days among these people, or you spend them alone. It is in Washington that varieties of manners are conspicuous. There the Southerners appear to the most advantage, and the New-Englander to the least; the ease and frank courtesy of the gentry of the South (with an occasional touch of arrogance, however) contrasting favourably with the cautious, somewhat *gauche*, and too deferential air of the members from the North. One fancies one can tell a New-England member in the open air by his deprecatory walk. He seems to bear in mind perpetually that he cannot fight a duel, while other people can. The odd mortals that wander in from the western border cannot be described as class, for no one is like anybody else. One has a neck like a crane, making an interval of inches between stock and chin. Another wears no cravat, apparently because there is no room for one. A third has his lank black hair parted accurately down the middle, and disposed in bands in front, so that he is taken for a woman when only the head is seen in a crowd. A fourth puts an arm round the neck of a neighbour on either side as he stands, seeming afraid of his tall wire-hung frame dropping to pieces if he tries to stand alone; a fifth makes something between a bow and a courtesy to everybody who comes near, and proses with a knowing air: all having shrewd faces, and being probably very fit for the business they come upon.

Our way of life was so diversified that it is difficult to give an account of our day; the only way in which one day resembled another being that none had any privacy. We breakfasted about nine, surrounded by the heaps of newspapers, documents, and letters which the post and newsman brought to the parliamentary members of our party. We amused ourselves with the different versions given by the Globe and Intelligencer — the administration and opposition papers — to speeches and proceedings at which we had been present the day before; and were kindly made by our representative friend with the nature of much of his business, the petitions he had to present, the dilemmas in which he was placed by his constituents of different parties, and his hopes and fears about favourite measures in progress. These senator happened, from a peculiar set of circumstances, to be an idle man just now. He taught me many things, and rallied me on my asking him so few questions, while, in fact, my head was already so much too full with what was flowing in upon me from all sides, that I longed for nothing so much as to go to sleep for a week. This gentleman's peculiar and not very agreeable position arose out of the troublesome question of Instructions to Representatives. Senators are chosen for a term of six years, one third of the body going out every two years; the term being made thus long in order to ensure some stability of policy in the Senate, if the government of the state from which the senator is sent changes its politics during his term, he may be annoyed by instructions to vote contrary to his principles, and if he refuses, by a call to resign, on the ground or his representing the opinions of the minority. This had been the predicament of our companion; and the question of resigning or not under such circumstances had become generally a very important and interesting one, but one which there was no means of settling. Each member in such a scrape must act as his own judgment and conscience dictate under the circumstances of the particular case. Our companion made a mistake. When the attempt to instruct him was made, he said he appealed from the new legislature of his state to the people who chose him. He did appeal by standing candidate for the office of governor of his state, and was defeated. No course then remained but resigning; which he did immediately, when his senatorial term was within half a session of its close. He had withdrawn from the Senate Chamber, and was winding up his political affairs at the time when we joined his party.

At a little before eleven we usually set out for the Capitol, and passed the morning either in the Senate Chamber or the Supreme Court, unless it was necessary to make calls, or to sit to the artist who was painting my portrait, or to join a party on some excursion in the neighbourhood. We avoided spending the morning at home when we could, as it was sure to be entirely consumed with callers, and we became too much exhausted before the fatigues of the evening began. Much amusement was picked up in the artist's apartment in the Capitol; members and strangers dropped in, and the news of the hour circulated; but the Senate Chamber was our favourite resort. We returned home to dinner sometime between four and six, and the cloth was seldom removed before visiters entered. The stream continued to flow in during the whole evening, unless we were all going out together. We disappeared, one by one, to dress for some ball, rout, levee, or masquerade, and went out, more or less willingly, according as we left behind us visiters more or less pleasant. The half hour round our drawing-room fire after our return was the pleasantest time of the day, weary as we were. Then our foreigners' perplexities were explained for us; we compared impressions, and made common property of what had amused us individually; and, in some sort, set our overcharged minds in order before we retired to rest.

Our pleasantest evenings were some spent at home in a society of the highest order. Ladies, literary, fashionable, or domestic, would spend an hour with us on their way from a dinner to a ball. Members of Congress would repose themselves by our fireside. Mr. Clay, sitting upright on the sofa, with his snuff-box ever in his hand, would discourse for many an hour in his even, soft, deliberate tone, on any one of the great subjects of American policy which we might happen to start, always amazing us with the moderation of estimate and speech which so impetuous a nature has been able to attain. Mr. Webster, leaning back at his ease, telling stories, cracking jokes, shaking the sola with burst after burst of laughter, or smoothly discoursing to the perfect felicity of the logical part of one's constitution, would illuminate an evening now and then. Mr. Calhoun, the cast-iron man, who looks as if he had never been born and never could be extinguished, would come in sometimes to keep our understandings upon a painful stretch for a short while, and leave us to take to pieces his close, rapid, theoretical, illustrated talk, and see what we could make of it. We found it usually more worth retaining as a curiosity than as either very just or useful. His speech abounds in figures, truly illustrative, if that which they illustrate were but true also. But his theories of government (almost the only subject on which his thoughts are employed), the squarest and compactest that ever were made, are composed out of limited elements, and are not therefore, likely to stand service very well. It is at first extremely interesting to hear Mr. Calhoun talk; and there is a never-failing evidence of power in all he says and does which commands intellectual reverence; but the admiration is too soon turned into regret, into absolute melancholy. It is impossible to resist the conviction that all this force can be at best but useless, and is but too likely to be very mischievous. His mind has long lost all power of communicating with any other. I know of no man who lives in such utter intellectual solitude. He meets men, and harangues the fireside as in the Senate; he is wrought like a piece of machinery, set a going vehemently by a weight, and stops while you answer; he either passes by what you say, or twists it into a suitability with what is in his head, and begins lo lecture again. Of course, a mind like this can have little influence in the Senate, except by virtue, perpetually wearing out, of what it did in its less eccentric days; but its influence at home is to be dreaded. There is no hope that an intellect so cast in narrow theories will accommodate itself to varying circumstances; and there is every danger that it will break up all that it can, in order to remould the materials in its own way. Mr. Calhoun is as full as ever of his nullification doctrines; and those who know the force that is in him, and his utter incapacity of modification by other minds (after having gone through as remarkable a revolution of political opinion as perhaps any man ever experienced), will no more expect repose and self-retention from him than from a volcano in full force. Relaxation is no longer in the power of his will. I never saw any one who so completely gave me the idea of possession. Half an hour's conversation with him is enough to make a necessarian of anybody. Accordingly, he is more complained of than blamed by his enemies. His moments of softness in his family, and when recurring to old College days, are hailed by all as a relief to the vehement working of the intellectual machine; a relief equally to himself and others. Those moments are as touching to the observer as tears on the face of a soldier.

One incident befell during my stay which moved everybody. A representative from South Carolina[2] was ill, a friend of Mr. Calhoun's; and Mr. Calhoun parted from us one day, on leaving the Capitol, to visit this sick gentleman. The physician told Mr. Calhoun on his entrance that his friend was dying, and could not live more than a very few hours. A visiter, not knowing this, asked the sick man how he was. "To judge by own feelings," said he "much better; but by the countenances of my friends, not." And he begged to he told the truth. On hearing it, he instantly beckoned Mr. Calhoun to him, and said, "I hear they are giving you rough treatment in the Senate. Let a dying friend implore yow to guard your looks and words so as that no undue, warmth may make you appear unworthy your principles." "This was friendship, strong friendship," said Mr. Calhoun to me and to many others; and it had its due effect upon him. A few days after, Colonel Benton, a fantastic senator from Missouri, interrupted Mr. Calhoun in a speech, for the purpose of making an attack upon him which would have been insufferable if it had not been too absurdly worded to be easily made anything of. He was called to order; this was objected to; the Senate divided upon the point of order, being dissatisfied with the decision of the chair; in short Mr. Calhoun sat for full two hours hearing his veracity talked about before his speech could proceed. He sat in stern patience, scarcely moving a muscle the whole time; and, when it was all settled in his favour, merely observed that his friends need not fear his being disturbed by an attack of this nature from such a quarter, and resumed his speech at the precise point where his argument had been broken off. It was great, and would have satisfied the "strong friendship" of his departed comrade if he could have been there to see it.

Our active-minded genial friend. Judge Story,[3] found time to visit us frequently, though he is one of the busiest men in the world; writing half a dozen great law-books every year; having his full share of the business of the Supreme Court upon his hands; his professorship to attend to; the District Courts at home in Massachusetts, and a correspondence which spreads half over the world. His talk would gush out for hours, and there was never too much of it for us; it is so heartfelt, so lively, so various; and his face all the while, notwithstanding his gray hair, showing all the mobility and ingenuousness of a child's. There is no tolerable portrait of Judge Story, and there never will be. I should like to bring him face to face with a person who entertains the common English idea of how an American looks and behaves. I should like to see what such a one would make of the quick smiles, the glistening eye, the gleeful tone, with passing touches of sentiment; the innocent self-complacency, the Confiding, devoted affections of the great American lawyer; The preconception would be totally at fault.

With Judge Story sometimes came the man to whom he looked up with feelings little short of adoration — the aged Chief-justice Marshall.[4] There was almost too much mutual respect in our first meeting; we knew something of his individual merits and services; and he maintained through life, and carried to his grave, a reverence for woman as rare in its kind as in its degree. It had all the theoretical fervour and magnificence of Uncle Toby's,[5] with the advantage of being grounded upon an extensive knowledge of the sex. He was the father and the grandfather of women; and out of this experience he brought, not only the love and pity which their offices and position command, and the awe of purity which they excite in the minds of the pure, but a steady conviction of their intellectual equality with men; and, with this, a deep sense of their social injuries. Throughout life he so invariably sustained their cause, that no indulgent libertine dared to flatter and humour; no skeptic, secure in the possession of power, dared to scoff at the claims of woman in the presence of Marshall, who, made clearsighted by his purity, knew the sex far better than either.

How delighted we were to see Judge Story bring in the tall majestic, bright-eyed old man! old by chronology, by the lines on his composed face, and by his services to the republic; but so dignified, so fresh, so present to the time, that no feeling of compassionate consideration for age dared to mix with the contemplation of him. The first evening he asked me much about English politics, and especially whether the people were not fast ripening for the abolition of our religious establishment; an institution which after a long study of it, he considered so monstrous in principle, and so injurious to true religion in practice, that he could not imagine that it could be upheld for anything but political purposes. There was no prejudice here on account of American modes being different; for he observed that the clergy were there, as elsewhere, far from being in the van of society, and lamented the existence of much fanaticism in the United States; but he saw the evils of an establishment the more clearly, not the less, from being aware of the faults in the administration of religion at home. The most animated moment of our conversation was when I told him I was going to visit Mr. Madison on leaving Washington. He instantly sat upright in his chair, and with beaming eyes began to praise Mr. Madison. Madison received the mention of Marshall's name in just the same manner; yet these men were strongly opposed in politics, and their magnanimous appreciation of each other underwent no slight or brief trial.

Judge Porter sometimes came, a hearty friend, and much like a fellow-countryman, though he was a senator of the United States, and had previously been, for fourteen years, Judge of the Supreme Court of Louisiana. He was Irish by birth. His father was vindictively executed, with cruel haste, under martial law, in the Irish rebellion; and the sons were sent by their noble-minded mother to America, where Alexander, the eldest, has thus raised himself into a station of high honour. Judge Porter's warmth, sincerity, generosity, knowledge, and wit are the pride of his constituents, and very ornamental lo the Senate. What their charm is by the fireside may be imagined.

Such are only a few among a multitude whose conversation filled up the few evenings we spent at home. Among the pleasantest visits we paid were dinners at the president's, at the houses of heads of departments, at the British legation, and at the Southern members' congressional mess. We highly enjoyed our dinings at the British legation, where we felt ourselves at home among our countrymen. Once, indeed, we were invited to help to do the honours as English ladies to the seven Judges of the Supreme Court, and seven great lawyers besides, when we had the merriest day that could well be. Mr. Webster fell chiefly to my share, and there is no merrier man than he; and Judge Story would enliven a dinner table at Pekin. One laughable peculiarity at the British legation was the confusion of tongues among the servants, who ask you to take fish, flesh and fowl in Spanish Italian, German, Dutch, Irish, or French. The foreign ambassadors are terribly plagued about servants. No American will wear livery, and there is no reason why any American should. But the British ambassador must have livery servants. He makes what compromise he can, allowing his people to appear without livery out of doors except on state occasions; but yet he is obliged to pick up his domestics from among foreigners Who are in want of a subsistence for a short time, and are sure to go away as soon as they can find any employment in which the wearing a livery is not requisite. The woes of this state of things, however, were the portion of the host, not of guests; and the hearty hospitality with which we were ever greeted by the minister and his attaches, combined with the attractions of the society they brought together, made our visits to them some of the pleasantest hours we passed in Washington.

Slight incidents were perpetually showing, in an amusing way, the village-like character of some of the arrangements at Washington. I remember that some of our party went one day to dine at Mr. Secretary Cass's, and the rest of us at Mr. Secretary Woodburys'. The next morning a lady of the Cass party asked me whether we had candied oranges at the Woodbury's. "No." "Then," said she, "they had candied oranges at the attorney-general's." "How do you know?" "Oh, as we were on the way, saw a dish carried; and as we had none at the Cass's I knew they must either be for the Woodbury's or the attorney-general." There were candied oranges at the attorney-general's.

When we became intimate some time afterward with some Southern friends, with whom we now dined at their congressional mess, they gave us an amusing account of the preparations for our dinner. They boarded (from a really self-denying kindness) at a house where the arrangements were of a very inferior kind. Two sessions previous to our being there they had invited a large party of eminent persons to dinner, and had committed the ordering of the arrangements to a gentleman of their mess, advising him to engage a French cook in order to ensure a good dinner. The gentleman engaged a Frenchman, concluding he must be a cook, which, however, he was not; and the dinner turned out so unfortunately, that the mess determined to ask no more dinner-company while they remained in that house. When we arrived, however, it was thought necessary to ask us to dinner. There was little hope that all would go rightly; and the two senators of the mess were laughingly requested, in case of any blunder, to talk nullification as fast as possible to us ladies. This was done so efficaciously, that, when dinner was over, I could not have told a single dish that was on the table, except that a ham stood before me, which we were too full of nullification to attack. Our hosts informed us, long afterward, that it was a bad dinner badly served; but it was no matter. At the president's I met a very large party, among whom there was more stiffness than I saw in any other society in America. It was not the fault of the president or his family, but of the way in which the company was unavoidably brought together. With the exception of my party, the name of everybody present began with J, K, or L; that is to say, it consisted of members of Congress, who are invited alphabetically, to ensure none being left out. This principle of selection is not perhaps, the best for the promotion of ease and sociability; and well as I liked the day, I doubt whether many others could say they enjoyed it. When we went in the president was standing in the middle of the room to receive his guests. After speaking a few words with me, he gave me into the charge of Major Donelson, his secretary, who seated me, and brought up for introduction each guest as he parsed from before the president. A congressional friend of mine (whose name began with a J) stationed himself behind my chair, and gave me an account of each gentleman who was introduced to me; where he came from, what his politics were, and how, if at all, he distinguished himself. All this was highly amusing. At dinner the president was quite disposed for conversation. Indeed, he did nothing but talk. His health is poor, and his diet of the sparest. We both talked freely of the governments of England and France; I, novice in American politics as I was, entirely forgetting that the great French question was pending, and that the president and the King of the French were then bandying very hard words. I was most struck and surprised with the president's complaints of the American Senate, in which there was at that time a small majority against the administration. He told me that I must not judge of the body by what I saw it then, and that after the 4$^{th}$ of March I should behold a Senate more worthy of the country. After the 4$^{th}$ of March there was, if I remember rightly, a majority of two in favour of the government. The ground of his complaint was, that the senators had sacrificed their dignity by disregarding the wishes of their constituents. The other side of the question is, that the dignity of the Senate is best consulted by its members following their own convictions, declining instructions for the term for which they are elected. It is a serious difficulty, originating in the very construction of the body, and not to be settled by dispute.

The president offered me bonbons for a child belonging to our party at home, and told me how many children (of his nephew's and his adopted son's) he had about him, with a mildness and kindliness which contrasted well with his tone upon some public occasions. He did the honours of his house with gentleness and politeness to myself, and, as far as I saw, to everyone else. About an hour after dinner he rose, and we led the way into the drawing room, where the whole company, gentlemen as well as ladies, followed to take collide; after which everyone departed, some homeward, some to make evening calls, and others, among whom were ourselves, to a splendid ball at the other extremity of the city.

General Jackson is extremely tall and thin, with a slight stoop, betokening more weakness than naturally belongs to his years. He has a profusion of stiff gray hair, which gives to his appearance whatever there is of formidable in it. His countenance bears commonly an expression of melancholy gravity; though, when roused, the fire of passion flashes from his eyes, and his whole person looks then formidable enough. His mode of speech is slow and quiet, and his phraseology sufficiently betokens that his time has not been passed among books. When I was at Washington albums were the fashion and the plague of the day. I scarcely ever came home but I found an album on my table or requests for autographs; but some ladies went much further than petitioning a foreigner who might be supposed to have leisure. I have actually seen them stand at the door of the Senate Chamber, and send the doorkeeper with an album, and a request to write in it, to Mr. Webster, and other eminent, members. I have seen them do worse; stand at the door of the Supreme Court, and send in their albums to Chief-justice Marshall while he was on the bench hearing pleadings. The poor president was terribly persecuted; and to him it was a real nuisance, as he had no poetical resource but Watt's hymns. I have seen verses and stanzas of a most ominous purport from Watts, in the president's very conspicuous handwriting, standing in the midst of the crowquill compliments and translucent charades which are the staple of albums. Nothing was done to repress this atrocious impertinence of the ladies. I always declined writing more than name and date; But senators, judges, and statesmen submitted to write gallant nonsense at the request of any woman who would stoop to desire it.

Colonel Johnson,[6] now Vice-president of the United States, sat opposite to me at the President's dinner table. This is the gentleman once believed to have killed Tecumseh, and to have written the Report on Sunday Mails, which has been the admiration of society ever since it appeared; but I believe Colonel Johnson is no longer supposed to be the author of either of these deeds. General Mason spoke of him to me at New York with much friendship, and with strong hope of his becoming president. I heard the idea so ridiculed by members of the federal party afterward, that I concluded General Mason to be in the same case with hundreds more who believe their intimate friends sure of being president. But Colonel Johnson is actually Vice-president, and the hope seems reasonable; though the slavery question will probably be the point on which the next election will turn, which may again be to the disadvantage of the colonel. If he should become president, he will be as strange-looking a potentate as ever ruled. His countenance is wild, though with much cleverness in it; his hair wanders all abroad, and he wears no cravat. But there is no telling how he might look if dressed like other people.

I was fortunate enough once to catch a glimpse of the invisible Amos Kendall,[7] one of the most remarkable men in America. He is supposed to be the moving spring of the whole administration; the thinker, planner, and doer; but it is all in the dark. Documents are issued of an excellence which prevents their being attributed to persons who take the responsibility of them; a correspondence is kept up all over the country for which no one seems to be answerable; work is done, of goblin extent and with goblin speed, which makes men look about them with a superstitious wonder; and the invisible Amos Kendall has the credit of it all. President Jackson's Letters to his Cabinet are said to be Kendall's; the Report on Sunday Mails is attributed to Kendall; the letters sent from Washington to appear in remote country newspapers, whence they are collected and published in the Globe as demonstrations of public opinion, are pronounced to be written by Kendall. Every mysterious paragraph in opposition newspapers relates to Kendall; and it is some relief to the timid that his having now the office of postmaster general affords opportunity for open attacks upon this twilight personage; who is proved, by the faults in the post office administration, not to be able to do quite everything well. But he is undoubtedly a great genius. He unites with his "great talent for silence" a splendid audacity. One proof of this I have given elsewhere, in the account of the bold stroke by which he obtained the sanction of the Senate to his appointment as postmaster-general.[8]

It is clear that he could not do the work he does (incredible enough in amount anyway) if he went into society like other men. He did, however, one evening; I think it was at the attorney-general's. The moment I went in, intimations reached me from all quarters, amid nods and winks, "Kendall is here:" "That is he." I saw at once that his plea for seclusion (bad health) is no false one. The extreme sallowness of his complexion, and hair of such perfect whiteness as is rarely seen in a man of middle age, testified to disease. His countenance does not help the superstitious to throw off their dread of him. He probably does not desire this superstition to melt away; for there is no calculating how much influence was given to Jackson's administration by the universal belief that there was a concealed eye and hand behind the machinery of government, by which everything could be foreseen, and the hardest deeds done. A member of Congress told me this night that he had watched through four sessions for a sight of Kendall, and had never obtained it till now. Kendall was leaning on a chair, with head bent down, and eye glancing up at a member of Congress with whom he was in earnest conversation, and in a few minutes he was gone.

Neither Mr. Clay nor any of his family ever spoke a word to me of Kendall except in his public capacity; but I heard elsewhere and repeatedly the well-known story of the connexion of the two men early in Kendall's life. Tidings reached Mr. and Mrs. Clay one evening, many years ago, at their house in the neighbourhood of Lexington, Kentucky, that a young man, solitary and poor, lay ill of a fever in the noisy hotel in the town. Mrs. Clay went down in the carriage without delay, and brought the sufferer home to her house, where she nursed him with her own hands till he recovered. Mr. Clay was struck with the talents and knowledge of the young man (Kendall), and retained him as tutor to his sons, heaping benefits upon him with characteristic bounty. Thus lar is notorious fact. As to the causes of their separation and enmity, I have not heard Kendall's side of the question, and therefore say nothing; but go on to the other notorious facts, that Amos Kendall left Mr. Clay's political party sometime after Adams had been, by Mr. Clay's influence, seated in the presidential chair, and went over to Jackson; since which time he has never ceased his persecutions of Mr. Clay through the newspapers. It was extensively believed, on Mr. Van Buren's accession, that Kendall would be dismissed from office altogether: and there was much speculation about how the administration' would get on without him. But he appears to be still there. Whether he goes or stays, it will probably be soon apparent how much of the conduct of Jackson's government is attributable to Kendall's influence over the mind of the late president, as he is hardly likely to stand in the same relation to the present.

I was more vividly impressed with the past and present state of Ireland while I was in America than ever I was at home. Besides being frequently questioned as to what was likely to be done for the relief of her suffering millions — suffering to a degree that it is inconceivable to Americans that freeborn whites should ever be — I met from time to time with refugee Irish gentry, still burning with the injuries they or their fathers sustained in the time of the rebellion. The subject first came up with Judge Potter; and I soon afterward saw, at a country-house where I was calling, the widow of Theobald Wolfe Tone. The poor lady is still full of feelings which amazed me by their bitterness and strength, but which have, indeed, nothing surprising in them to those who know the whole truth of the story of Ireland in those dreadful days. The descendants of "the rebels" cannot be comforted with tidings of anything to be done for their country. Naturally believing that nothing good can come out of England — nothing good for Ireland they passionately ask that their country shall be left to govern herself. With tears and scornful laughter they beg that nothing may be "done for her" by hands that have ravaged her with gibbet, fire, and sword, but that she may be left to whatever hopefulness may yet be smouldering under the ashes of her despair. Such is the representation of Ireland to American minds. It may be imagined what a monument of idiocy the forcible maintenance of the Church of England in Ireland must appear to American statesmen. "I do not understand this Lord John Russel of yours," said one of the most sagacious of them. "Is he serious in supposing that he can allow a penny of the revenues, a plait of the lawn-sleeves of that Irish Church to be touched, and keep the whole from coming down, in Ireland first, and in England afterward?" We fully agree in the difficulty of supposing Lord John Russell serious. The comparison of various, but, I believe, pretty extensive American opinions about the Church of England yields rather a curious result. No one dreams of the establishment being necessary or being designed for the maintenance of religion; it Is seen by Chief-justice Marshall and a host of others to be an institution turned to political purposes. Mr. Van Buren, among many, considers that the church has supported the state for many years. Mr. Clay, and a multitude with him, anticipates the speedy fall of the establishment. The result yielded by all this is a persuasion not very favourable (to use the American phrase) "to the permanence of our institutions."

Among our casual visitors at Washington was a gentleman who little thought, as he sat by our fireside, what an adventure was awaiting him among the Virginia woods. If there could have been any anticipation of it, I should have taken more notice of him than I did; as it is, I have a very slight recollection of him. He came from Maine, and intended before his return to visit the springs of Virginia, which he did the next summer. It seems that he talked in the stages rashly, and somewhat in a bragging style — in a style, at least, which he was not prepared to support by a harder testimony about abolitionism. He declared that abolitionism was not so dangerous as people thought; that he avowed it without any fear: that he had frequently attended abolition meetings in the North, and was none the worse for it in the slave states, &c. He finished his visits at the Springs prosperously enough; but, on his return, when he and a companion were in the stage in the midst of the forest, they met at a crossroad — Judge Lynch; that is, a mob with hints of cowhide and tar and feathers. The mob stopped the stage, and asked for the gentleman by name. It was useless to deny his name, but he denied everything else. He denied his being an abolitionist; he denied his having ever attended abolition meetings, and harangued against abolitionism from the door of the stage with so much effect, that the mob allowed the steps to be put up, and the vehicle to drive off, which it did at full speed. It was not long before the mob became again persuaded that this gentleman was a fit object of vengeance, and pursued him; but he was gone as fast as horses could carry him. He did not relax his speed even when out of danger, but fled all the way into Maine. It was not on the shrinking at the moment that one would animadvert so much as on the previous bragging. I have seen and felt enough of what peril from popular hatred is, in this martyr age of the United States, to find ii easier to venerate those who can endure than to despise those who flinch from the ultimate trial of their principles; but every instance of the infliction of Lynch punishment should be a lesson to the sincerest and securest to profess no more than they are ready to perform.

One of our mornings was devoted to an examination of the library and curiosities of the State Department, which we found extremely interesting. Our imaginations were whirled over the globe at an extraordinary rate. There were many volumes of original letters of Washington's and other revolutionary leaders bound up, and ordered to be printed, for security, lest these materials of history should be destroyed by fire or other accident. There were British parliamentary documents. There was a series of the Moniteur[9] complete, wherein we found the black list of executions during the reign of terror growing longer every day; also the first mention of Napoleon; the tidings of his escape from Elba; the misty days immediately succeeding, when no telegraphic communication could be made; his arrival at Lyons, and the subsequent silence till the announcement became necessary that the king and princes had departed during the night, and that his majesty the emperor had arrived at his palace at the Tuileries at eight o'clock the next evening. Next we turned to Algerine (French) gazettes, publishing that Mustaphas and such people were made colonels and adjutants. Then we lighted upon the journals of Arnold during the Revolutionary war, and read the postscript of his last letter previous to the accomplishment of his treason, in which he asks for hard cash, on pretence that the French had suffered so much by paper money that he was unwilling to offer them anymore. Then we viewed the signatures of treaties, and decreed Metternich's to be the best; Don Pedro's the worst for flourish, and Napoleon's for illegibility. The extraordinary fact was then and there communicated to us that the Americans are fond of Miguel from their dislike of Pedro, but that they hope to "get along" very well with the Queen of Portugal. The treaties with oriental potentates are very magnificent, shining, and unintelligible to the eyes of novices. The presents from potentates to American ambassadors are laid up here; gold snuffboxes set in diamonds, and a glittering array of swords and cimeters. There was one fine Damascus blade, but it seemed too blunt to do any harm. Then we lost ourselves in a large collection of medals and coins — Roman gold coins, with fat old Vespasian and others — from which we were recalled to find ourselves in the extremely modern and democratic United States! It was a very interesting morning.

We took advantage of a mild day to ascend to the skylight of the dome of the Capitol, in order to obtain a view of the surrounding country. The ascent was rather fatiguing, but perfectly safe. The residents at Washington declare the environs to be beautiful in all seasons but early winter, the meadows being gay with a profusion of wild flowers; even as early as February with several kinds of heart's-ease. It was a particularly cold season when I was there; but on the day of my departure, in the middle of February, the streets were one sheet of ice, and I remember we made a long slide from the steps of our boarding house to those of the stage. But I believe that that winter was no rule for others. From the summit of the Capitol we saw plainly marked out the basin in which Washington stands, surrounded by hills except where the Potomac spreads its waters. The city was intended to occupy the whole of this basin, and its seven theoretical avenues may be traced; but all except Pennsylvania Avenue are bare and forlorn. A few mean houses dotted about, the sheds of a navy-yard on one bank of the Potomac, and three or four villas on the other, are all the objects that relieve the eye in this space intended to be so busy and magnificent. The city is a grand mistake. Its only attraction is its being the seat of government, and it is thought that it will not long continue to be so. The far western states begin to demand a more central seat for Congress, and the Cincinnati people are already speculating upon which of their hills or tablelands is to be the site of the new Capitol. Whenever this change takes place all will be over with Washington; "thorns shall come up in her palaces, and the owl and the raven shall dwell in it," while her sister cities of the east will be still spreading as fast as hands can be found to build them.

"A Subject of Grave Reflection"

From *A Diary in America* by Captain Marryat.

The prolific English author and veteran of Her Majesty's Royal Navy Captain Frederick Marryat (1792-1848), best-known today as a writer of adventuresome sea tales, was basking in the recent success of his novel of the Napoleonic Wars *Mr. Midshipman Easy* when he visited the United States in 1837-1838. According to an early biographer, in the fall of 1837, Marryat was "in good humor with America," and the country was "well pleased with him." Unfortunately, these feelings did not last.

Tensions between upper and lower Canada during these years spilled over into Marryat's American visit. Marryat gave a speech in Toronto in which he praised a certain upper Canadian loyalist, Lieutenant Drew, for his role in "cutting out" (capturing at anchor or in harbor) the ship *Caroline*, which *sans* crew the loyalists sent to her destruction over Niagara Falls. The Americans were "then in a particularly thin-skinned state," and Marryat's otherwise fair welcome turned fowl. For his praise of Lieutenant Drew, Marryat (in effigy) and his books were burned back in the states.

---

Washington. — Here are assembled from every State in the Union, what ought to be the collected talent, intelligence, and high principle of a free and enlightened nation. Of talent and intelligence there is a very fair supply, but principle is not so much in demand; and in everything, and everywhere, by the demand the supply is always regulated.

Everybody knows that Washington has a Capitol; but the misfortune is that the Capitol wants a city. There it stands, reminding you of a general without an army, only surrounded and followed by a parcel of ragged little dirty boys; for such is the appearance of the dirty, straggling, ill-built houses which lie at the foot of it.

Washington, notwithstanding, is an agreeable city, full of pleasant clever people, who come there to amuse and be amused; and you observe in the company (although you occasionally meet some very queer importations from the Western settlements) much more *usage du monde* and continental ease than in any other parts of the State. A large portion of those who come up for the meeting of Congress, as well as of the residents, having travelled, and thereby gained more respect for other nations, are consequently not so conceited about their own country as are the majority of the Americans.

If anything were required to make Washington a more agreeable place than it is at all times, the arrival and subsequent conduct of Mr. Fox[1] as British ambassador would be sufficient. His marked attention to all the Americans of respectability; his *empressement* in returning the calls of English gentlemen who may happen to arrive; his open house; his munificent allowance, dedicated wholly to the giving of fêtes and dinner parties as his Sovereign's representative; and, above all, his excessive urbanity, can never be forgotten by those who have ever visited the Capitol.

The Chamber of the House of Representatives is a fine room, and taking the average of the orations delivered there, it possesses this one great merit — *you cannot hear in it*.[2] Were I to make a comparison between the members of our House of Commons and those of the House of Representatives, I should say that the latter have certainly great advantages. In the first place, the members of the American Senate and House of Representatives are paid, not only their travelling expenses to and fro, but eight dollars a day during the sitting of Congress. Out of these allowances many save money, and those who do not, are at all events enabled to bring their families up to Washington for a little amusement. In the next place, they are so comfortably accommodated in the house, every man having his own well-stuffed arm-chair, and before him his desk, with his papers and notes! Then they are supplied with everything, even to penknives with their names engraved on them — each knife having two pen-blades, one whittling blade, and a fourth to clean their nails with, showing, on the part of the government, a paternal regard for their cleanliness as well as convenience. Moreover, they never work at night, and do very little during the day.

It is astonishing how little work they get through in a session at Washington: this is owing to every member thinking himself obliged to make two or three speeches, not for the good of the nation, but for the benefit of his constituents. These speeches are printed and sent to them, to prove that their member makes some noise in the house. The subject upon which he speaks is of little consequence, compared to the sentiments expressed.

It must be full of eagles, star-spangled banners, sovereign people, claptrap, flattery, and humbug. 1 have said that very little business is done in these houses; but this is caused not only by their long-winded speeches about nothing, but by the fact that both parties (in this respect laudably following the example of the old country) are chiefly occupied, the one with the paramount and vital consideration of keeping in, and the other with that of getting in — thus allowing the business of the nation, (which after all is not very important, unless such a trump as the Treasury Bill turns up), to become a very secondary consideration.

And yet there are principle and patriotism among the members of the legislature, and the more to be appreciated from their rarity, Like the seeds of beautiful flowers, which, when cast upon a manure-heap, spring up in greater luxuriance and beauty, and yield a sweeter perfume from the rankness which surrounds them, so do these virtues shew with more grace and attractiveness from the hot-bed of corruption in which they have been engendered. But there has been a sad falling-off in America since the last war, which brought in the democratic party with General Jackson. America, if she would wish her present institutions to continue, must avoid war; the best security for her present form of government existing another half century, is a state of tranquility and peace; but of that hereafter. As for the party at present in power, all I can say in its favour is, that there are three clever gentlemen in it — Mr. Van Buren, Mr. Poinsett, and Mr. Forsyth.[3] There may be more, but I know so little of them, that I must be excused if I do not name them, which otherwise I should have had great pleasure in doing.

Mr. Van Buren is a very gentleman-like, intelligent man; very proud of talking over his visit to England, and the English with whom he was acquainted. It is remarkable, that although at the head of the democratic party, Mr. Van Buren has taken a step striking at the very roots of their boasted equality, and one on which General Jackson did not venture — *i. e.* he has prevented the monocracy from intruding themselves at his levees. The police are now stationed at the door, to prevent the intrusion of any improper person. A few years ago, a fellow would drive his cart, or hackney coach, up to the door; walk into the saloon in all his dirt, and force his way to the president, that he might shake him by the one hand, whilst he flourished his whip in the other. The revolting scenes which took place when refreshments were handed round, the injury done to the furniture, and the disgust of the ladies, may be well imagined. Mr. Van Buren deserves great credit for this step, for it was a bold one; but I must not praise him too much, or he may lose his next election.[4]

The best lounge at Washington is the library of the Capitol, but the books are certainly not very well treated. I saw a copy of Audubon's Ornithology, and many other valuable works, in a very dilapidated state; but this must be the case when the library is open to all, and there are so many juvenile visitors. Still it is much better than locking it up, for only the bindings to be looked at. It is not a library for show, but for use, and is a great comfort and amusement.

There are three things in great request amongst Americans of all classes — male, I mean — to wit, oysters, spirits, and tobacco. The first and third are not prohibited by Act of Congress, and may be sold in the Capitol, but spirituous liquors may not. I wondered how the members could get on without them, but upon this point I was soon enlightened. Below the basement of the building is an oyster-shop and refectory. The refectory has been permitted by Congress upon the express stipulation that no spirituous liquors should be sold there, but law-makers are too often law-breakers all over the world. You go there and ask for pale sherry, and they hand you gin; brown sherry, and it is brandy; madeira, whiskey; and thus do these potent, grave, and reverend signors evade their own laws, beneath the very hall wherein they were passed in solemn conclave.

It appears that tobacco is considered very properly as an article of fashion. At a store, close to the hotel, the board outside informs you that among fashionable requisites to be found there, are gentlemen's shirts, collars, gloves, silk handkerchiefs, and the best chewing tobacco. But not only at Washington, but at other large towns, I have seen at silk-mercers and hosiers this notice stuck up in the window —

"*Dulcissimus* chewing tobacco." — So prevalent is the habit of chewing, and so little, from long custom, do the ladies care about it, that I have been told that many young ladies in the south carry, in their work-boxes, &c., pig-tail, nicely ornamented with gold and coloured papers; and when their swains are at fault, administer to their wants, thus meriting their affections by such endearing solicitude.

I was rather amused in the Senate at hearing the claims of parties who had suffered during the last war, and had hitherto not received any redress, discussed for adjudication. One man's claim, for instance, was for a cow, value thirty dollars, eaten up, of course, by the Britishers. It would naturally be supposed that such claims were unworthy the attention of such a body as the senate, or when brought forward, would have been allowed without comment: but it was not so. The member who saves the public money always finds favour in the eyes of the people, and therefore every member tries to save as much as he can, except when he is himself a party concerned. And there was as much arguing and objecting, and discussion of the merits of this man's claim, as there would be in the English House of Commons at passing the Navy Estimates. Eventually he lost it. The claims of the Fulton family were also brought forward, when I was present, in the House of Representatives. Fulton[5] was certainly the father of steam-navigation in America, and to his exertions and intelligence, America may consider herself in a great degree indebted for her present prosperity. It once required six or seven months to ascend the Mississippi, a passage which is now performed in fifteen days. Had it not been for Fulton's genius, the west would still have remained a wild desert, and the now flourishing cotton growing States would not yet have yielded the crops which are the staple of the Union. The claim of his surviving relatives was a mere nothing, in comparison with the debt of gratitude owing to that great man; yet member after member rose to oppose it with all the ingenuity of argument. One asserted that the merit of the invention did not belong to Fulton; another, that even if it did, his relatives certainly could found no claim upon it; a third rose and declared that ho would prove that, so far from the government owing money to Fulton. Fulton was in debt to the government. And thus did they go on, showing to their constituents how great was their consideration for the public money, and to the world (if another proof were required) how little gratitude is to be found in a democracy. The bill was thrown out, and the race of Fultons left to the chance of starving, for anything that the American nation seemed to care to the contrary. Whitney,[6] the inventor of the gin for clearing the cotton of its seeds (perhaps the next greatest boon ever given to America), was treated in the same way. And yet, on talking over the question, there were few of the members who did not individually acknowledge the justice of their claims, and the duly of the state to attend to them; but the *majority* would not have permitted it, and when they went back to their constituents to be re-elected, it would have been urged against them that they had voted away the public money, and they would have had the difficult task of proving that the interests of the *majority*, and of the majority alone, had regulated their conduct in congress.

There was one event of exciting interest which occurred during my short stay at Washington, and which engrossed the minds of every individual; the fatal duel between Mr. Graves and Mr. Cilley.[7] Not only the duel itself, but what took place after it, was to me, as a stranger, a subject for grave reflection. Notice of Mr. Cilley's decease having been formally given to the House, it adjourned for a day or two, as a mark of respect, and a day was appointed for the funeral.

The coffin containing the body was brought into the House of Representatives, and there lay in state, as it were. The members of Senate and the Supreme Court were summoned to attend, whilst an eulogium was passed on the merits and virtues of the deceased by the surviving representative of the State of Maine: the funeral sermon was delivered by one clergyman, and an exhortation by another, after which the coffin was carried out to be placed in the hearse. The following printed order of the procession was distributed, that it might be rigidly attended to by the members of the two Houses and the Supreme Court: —

Order of Arrangements<br>
for the Funeral of<br>
The Hon. JONATHAN CILLEY,<br>
Late a Representative in Congress,<br>
from the State of Maine.

The Committee of Arrangement, Pall bearers, and Mourners, will attend at the late residence of the deceased, at Mr. Birth's, in Third-street, at 11 o'clock a. m., Tuesday, February 27th; at which time the remains will be removed, in charge of the Committee of Arrangements, attended by the Serjeant-at-Arms of the House of Representatives, to the hall of the House. At 12 o'clock, meridian, funeral service will be performed in the hall of the House of Representatives, and immediately after the procession will move to the place of interment in the following order: —

The Chaplains of both Houses.<br>
Committee of Arrangement, <i>viz.</i></p>

Mr. Evans, of Maine.

Mr. Atherton. of N. H.<br>
Mr. Coles, of Va.<br>
Mr. Connor, of N.C.<br>
Mr. Johnson, of La.<br>
Mr. Whittlesey, of Ohio.

Mr. Fillmore, of N. Y.

Pall-bearers, *viz.*

Mr. Thomas, of Maryland.
Mr. Campbell, of S. C.
Mr. Williams, of N. H.
Mr. Ogle, of Pennsylvania.
Mr. White, of Indiana.
Mr. Martin, of Ala.

The Family and Friends of the deceased.
The Members of the House of Representatives,
and Senators from Maine, as Mourners.
The Serjeant-at-Arms of the House of Representatives.
The House of Representatives,
preceded by their Speaker and Clerk.
The Serjeant-at-Arms of the Senate.
The Senate of the United States,
preceded by the Vice President and their Secretary.
The President of the United States.
The Heads of the Departments.
Judges of the Supreme Court, and its Officers.
Foreign Ministers.
Citizens and Strangers.

*February 26th*, 1838.

The burial-ground being at some distance, carriages were provided for the whole of the company, and the procession even then was more than half a mile long. I walked there to witness the whole proceeding; but when the body had been deposited in the vault I found, on my return, a vacant seat in one of the carriages, in which were two Americans, who went under the head of "Citizens." They were very much inclined to be communicative. One of them observed of the clergyman, who, in his exhortation, had expressed himself very forcibly against the practice of duelling: —

"Well, I reckon that chaplain won't be 'lected next year, and sarve [sic] him right too; he did pitch it in rather too strong for the members; that last flourish of his was enough to raise all their danders."

To the other, who was a more staid sort of personage, I put the question, how long did he think this tragical event, and the severe observations on duelling, would stop the practice.

"Well, I reckon three days, or thereabouts," replied the man.

I am afraid that the man was not far out in his calculation. Virginia, Mississippi, Louisiana, and now Congress, as respects the district of Columbia, in which Washington is built, have all passed severe laws against the practice of duelling, which is universal; but they are no more than dead letters. The spirit of their institutions is adverse to such laws; and duelling always has been, and always will be, one of the evils of democracy. I have, I believe, before observed, that in many points a young nation is, in all its faults, very like to a young individual; and this is one in which the comparison holds good. But there are other causes for, and other incentives to this practice, besides the false idea that it is a proof of courage. Slander and detraction are the inseparable evils of a democracy; and as neither public nor private characters are spared, and the law is impotent to protect them, men have no other resource than to defend their reputations with their lives, or to deter the defamer by the risk which he must incur.

And where political animosities are carried to such a length as they are in this exciting climate, there is no time given for coolness and reflection. Indeed, for one American who would attempt to prevent a duel, there are ten who would urge the parties on to the conflict. I recollect a gentleman introducing me to the son of another gentleman who was present. The lad, who was about fourteen, I should think, shortly after left the room; and then the gentleman told me, before the boy's father, that the lad was one of the right sort, having already fought, and wounded his man; and the father smiled complacently at this tribute to the character of his son. The majority of the editors of the newspapers in America are constantly practising with the pistol, that they may be ready when called upon, and are most of them very good shots. In fact, they could not well refuse to fight, being all of them colonels, majors, or generals, — "*tam Marte quam Mercurio.*"[8] But the worst feature in the American system of duelling is, that they do not go out, as we do in this country, to satisfy honour, but with the determination to kill. Independently of general practice, immediately after a challenge has been given and received, each party practises as much as he can.

And now let us examine into the particulars of this duel between Mr. Graves and Mr. Cilley. It was well known that Mr. Graves had hardly ever fired a rifle in his life. Mr. Cilley, on the contrary, was an excellent rifle-shot, constantly in practice: it was well known, also, that he intended to fix a quarrel upon one of the southern members, as he had publicly said he would. He brought his rifle down to Washington with him; he practised with it almost every day, and more regularly so after he had sent the challenge, and it had been accepted. It so happened that, contrary to the expectation of all parties, Mr. Cilley, instead of Mr. Graves, was the party who fell: but surely, if ever there was a man who *premeditated murder*, it was Mr. Cilley. I state this, not with the wish to assail Mr. Cilley's character, as I believe that almost any other American would have done the same thing; for whatever license society will give, that will every man take, — and moreover, from habit, will not consider it as wrong.

But my reason for pointing out all this is to show that society must be in a very loose state, and the standard of morality must be indeed low in a nation, when a man who has fallen in such a manner, — a man who, had he killed Mr. Graves, would, according to the laws of our country, have been condemned and executed for murder, (inasmuch as, from his practising after the challenge was given, it would have proved *malice prepense*, on his part) should now, because he falls in the attempt, have *honours paid to his remains*, much *greater* than we paid to those of *Nelson*, when he fell so nobly in his country's cause. The chief magistrate of England, which is the king, did not follow Nelson to the grave; while the chief magistrate of the United States (attended by the Supreme Court and judges, the Senate, the representatives), does honour to the remains of one who, if Providence had not checked him in his career, would have been considered as a cold-blooded murderer. And yet the Americans are continually dinning into my ears — "Captain Marryat, we are a very moral people!" Again, I repeat, the Americans are the happiest people in the world in their own delusions. If they wish to be a moral people, the government must show them some better example than that of paying those honours to vice and immorality which are only due to honour and to virtue.

## "Just One Month"

From *Souvenirs of a Diplomat* by Adolphe Fourier de Bacourt.

The French diplomat Adolphe Fourier de Bacourt (1801-1865) began his career at twenty-one years of age in Turin and would be involved in diplomacy at the highest levels for the rest of his life. His *Souvenirs* (*Private Letters*) were translated for publication by his niece, whose mother was an executrix of Talleyrand (Charles-Maurice de Talleyrand-Périgord) and in part responsible for the eventual publication of his papers years after his death.

The author served only briefly as Minister to the United States, perhaps due to the failure of Martin Van Buren to secure a second terms as President. The brevity and urgency of his *Souvenirs* seems altogether appropriate in describing the situation in Washington, D.C. during the era of the 10th President of the United States, William Henry Harrison.

---

Washington, November 2, 1840.

We are now in the exciting week preceding the election, and will know in eight days who will be President of the United States. You cannot imagine what a fever everyone is in: it is political excitement, boiling over with rage! The day before yesterday in Philadelphia the Van Buren party demolished the house which was the headquarters of the opposite party. There is no organized civil force in the United States, so the populace can go to any imaginable excess without fear of repression; time will probably make them feel the need of an armed force, and the day when this armed force shall have the preponderance in the country will be the end of the present Constitution. So I think if they are right in saying that kings will eventually be done away with, they will be able to say the same thing of republics in America. I console myself better with the one than the other.

Washington, November 10, 1840.

My friend Van Buren is beaten and General Harrison is victorious. The election will not, however, be decided for fifteen days yet, and the new President will not enter upon his duties until March 4, 1841. I am sorry on my own account at the result, which, besides, will be prejudicial to the country. The Democratic Party, which is in power now, has been directed by Mr. Van Buren and his friends with moderation and wisdom, but when it becomes the Opposition party it will put no bounds to its violence. The Whig Party (which is called that of the aristocracy — my God, what aristocracy!) will split as soon as they come into power, and the governmental machine will find itself opposed by a furious democracy. To give you an idea of the American Constitution, this is what is to take place after the new election. From this time to the 4th of March next Mr. Van Buren will hold the office of President, which puts him in a very ridiculous position in face of those who have taken the power away from him. Congress, in which he has a majority, will meet in December. Of course nothing will be done to aid the coming Administration, who in coming into power on March 4 will find, in the first place, the

Treasury empty, and be able to do nothing until the following December, for Congress is irrevocably dissolved on the 4th of March, and they cannot call a new one until December, because new members must be elected during the interval. It seems to me that the old maxim, "The King is dead: long live the King," is better than these intervals, which open the door so wide to all sorts of disorder. Such a Constitution is vicious in its consequences as in its principle, in spite of the theories, more or less specious, of M. de Tocqueville.

Mr. Van Buren bears his defeat with dignity, and as they say here, with *fortitude*. General Harrison was born in the State of Virginia, which is thought the model State as regards pure republican principles, joined with good education and good manners. It is, in one word, the birthplace of *gentlemen*. Take notice, I beg of you, that I am only the reporter of public opinion, and that I do not guarantee the quality of these so-called *gentlemen*. Mr. Harrison left Virginia very early, as all these poor devils in that State do, to seek his fortune in the West. He settled in Ohio, and later entered the army, and was distinguished enough to be made a General, which does not signify much in America. He served without success from 1812 to 1814 against the English; afterward against the Indians, and his great exploit was a victory he gained over them at a place called Tippecanoe. He lost one hundred and fifty men, and killed three hundred of the enemy. And for that this conqueror has received the brilliant title of "The Hero of Tippecanoe;" and it is the refrain of all the songs,[1] of all the pieces of prose and of poetry, in his honor, which have been plentiful during this past year. General Jackson, the predecessor of Mr. Van Buren, sent General Harrison back to his home, where, a new Cincinnatus,[2] he has conducted his plough; he has also been notary in his village. The party opposed to Mr. Van Buren not daring to bring forward their most distinguished men, who are more brilliant than the

Democrats, brought General Harrison from his obscurity to make him a candidate for the Presidency, and from that time he has become a great personage, and his sayings and doings are looked upon as important — *Americanly* speaking.

Thus he said that he preferred his log-cabin — a house built with trunks of trees — to the palace of a king; and his *log-cabin* has become an emblem of the party: it is painted on all their flags; it serves as their banner everywhere; they have built one in the middle of Washington. And there, for the last six months, the partisans of the new President have met and yelled speeches and songs. He also said that he drank nothing but hard cider, and not the foreign wines of the aristocrats. Since then it is not the proper thing to get drunk on anything but *hard cider*, and they have vaunted this drink in prose and in verse. He also said that his log-cabin had no lock, and that all good Democrats could come in and be welcome at any time; then Harrisonian hospitality became proverbial! To tell you all the stupidities that have been inspired by these poor sayings I have cited, during the last year, would be impossible. I have seen nothing, heard nothing, read nothing, in which the log-cabin or hard cider did not appear. The newest style in dress is called Tippecanoe, and the American women in everything they wear seek to do honor to the illustrious conqueror. Thanks to all these truly ridiculous proceedings, this General, not heard of yesterday, is elected to-day; and solely on account of his mediocrity, which they judge inoffensive, he is to occupy the first position, and govern the country during the next four years. Opinions are divided on the course he will follow. Some say that, like Sixtus V.,[3] he will throw away his crutches, and putting aside those who have brought him into power, will rule with an ability that will astonish the universe. But most persons say that he is a vain man, without mind or talent, who will be a puppet in the hands of flatterers, and those who wish to control him will ruin the country while quarrelling amongst themselves. However, they say he is an amiable man, rather vulgar, and having the mania of quoting the Greeks and Romans, whom he knows nothing about, but thinks it good taste to appear to know.

We are buried in snow: in the same degree of latitude as Lisbon, we have the temperature of Sweden in winter and of the tropics in summer.

Washington, April 2, 1841.

Our new President is sick, and is so much worse to-day that his life is in danger. No President has ever died whilst in power; the post of Vice-President has always been looked upon as insignificant, and the man who occupies this supposed sinecure was only nominated after the refusal of several others. Now he will find himself President for the next four years, as ordained by the Constitution; and this unlooked-for change causes great excitement in the country. It will have no influence on our relations, and will not prevent the extra session of Congress. The Vice-President is Mr. Tyler of Virginia, where the Administration of General Harrison has met with opposition, but the general opinion is that Mr. Tyler's tendencies are more Harrisonian than Virginian.

Washington, April 5, 1841.

General Harrison died yesterday. He commenced his term on the 4$^{th}$ of March. His reign has lasted just one month, and the poor old man has had nothing but cares and worries during this month of responsibility. His death unsettles all that had been decided upon by the leaders of the victorious party and the conquered, Mr. Van Buren's party, will begin to agitate again. The funeral takes place on the day after to-morrow, and of course the Diplomatic Corps are invited.

Washington, April 12, 1841.

The funeral took place on the 7th. The procession started from the President's house, and proceeded on a walk four miles to the cemetery. The ceremonies and the funeral oration passed off in the most proper manner, which is to be noticed in this country, where everything else is very strange. The obsequies lasted altogether about five hours.

Mr. John Tyler is a widower, but has a son who is married, and his wife will do the honors of the Presidency.[4] This young woman was formerly an actress, and has played in the theatre in Washington under the name of Miss Cooper; I had the imprudence to say that she would represent[5] very well. The next day it was repeated to her. What a singular country, where a woman can pass from the boards of a theatre to a kind of scaffolding which serves as a republican throne!

I paid a visit to Mr. Southard,[6] Vice-President of the Senate, who, according to the Constitution of the United States, will replace Mr. Tyler in case of his death; he is a man of middle age, whose manners are better than those of the present generation.

Washington, April 25, 1841.

All the Diplomatic Corps went to present their respects to the President for the first time. In the absence of Mr. Fox, who was sick, Mr. Bodisco[7] made the address. Mr. Tyler made a very appropriate reply, then came forward, and gave a shake hand to each of us, accompanied with a short speech. What he said to me I will repeat in as near his own words as possible: "I am delighted to make the acquaintance of the French Minister, who comes from a country to which we owe much, and to which we are united by the bonds of gratitude. I shall endeavor to establish intimate and friendly relations with you, sir, who have had the advantage of living in intimate relations with the most distinguished diplomat in the whole world and of all time. King Louis Philippe and Prince Talleyrand while living here obtained the right of citizenship, and America is proud to count them amongst her citizens."

I give you the exact words of the President, and I hope that you will be satisfied. As to me, I am always happy to find myself under the protection of a name and a souvenir that I cherish and respect. Mr. Tyler conducted himself during this audience in a manner to satisfy everyone; without being a man of genius, he is thought to be greatly superior to General Harrison.

"Magnificent ... Magnificent"

From *American Notes for General Circulation* by Charles Dickens.

Charles Dickens (1812-1870), accompanied by his wife Katherine Thompson Dickens, née Hogarth (1815-1879) departed England bound for America aboard the Cunard steamer *Britannia* on January 3rd, 1842. The celebrated English novelist was just shy of thirty years of age and had already authored *The Pickwick Papers, Oliver Twist* and *Nicholas Nickleby*. His *American Notes* would be published before year's end with the following Dedication:

> *I dedicate this book to those friends of mine in America, who, giving me a welcome I must ever gratefully and proudly remember, left my judgment free; and who, loving their country, can bear the truth, when it is told good humouredly, and in a kind spirit.*

Dickens may have been given the celebrity treatment during his visit to the United States, but he chose not to focus on such things in reminiscing about his journey. While in the final pages of his book, he does express his feelings about the American people as being "frank, brave, cordial, hospitable and affectionate," readers will perhaps agree that Charles Dickens often found Washington, D.C. most *Dickensian*.

We left Philadelphia by steamboat at six o'clock one very cold morning, and turned our faces towards Washington.

In the course of this day's journey, as on subsequent occasions, we encountered some Englishmen (small farmers, perhaps, or country publicans at home) who were settled in America, and were travelling on their own affairs. Of all grades and kinds of men that jostle one in the public conveyances of the States, these are often the most intolerable and the most insufferable companions. United to every disagreeable characteristic that the worst kind of American travellers possess, these countrymen of ours display an amount of insolent conceit and cool assumption of superiority quite monstrous to behold. In the coarse familiarity of their approach, and the effrontery of their inquisitiveness (which they are in great haste to assert, as if they panted to revenge themselves upon the decent old restraints of home), they surpass any native specimens that came within my range of observation; and I often grew so patriotic, when I saw and heard them, that I would cheerfully have submitted to a reasonable fine, if I could have given any other country in the whole world the honor of claiming them for its children.

As Washington may be called the headquarters of tobacco-tinctured saliva, the time is come when I must confess, without any disguise, that the prevalence of those two odious practices of chewing and expectorating began about this time to be anything but agreeable, and soon became most offensive and sickening. In all the public places of America this filthy custom is recognized. In the courts of law the judge has his spittoon, the crier his, the witness his, and the prisoner his; while the jurymen and spectators are provided for, as so many men who in the course of nature must desire to spit incessantly. In the hospitals the students of medicine are requested, by notices upon the wall, to eject their tobacco juice into the boxes provided for that purpose, and not to discolor the stairs. In public buildings, visitors are implored, through the same agency, to squirt the essence of their quids, or "plugs," as I have heard them called by gentlemen learned in this kind of sweetmeat, into the national spittoons, and not about the bases of the marble columns. But in some parts this custom is inseparably mixed up with every meal and morning call, and with all the transactions of social life. The stranger who follows in the track I took myself will find it in its full bloom and glory, luxuriant in all its alarming recklessness, at Washington. And let him not persuade himself (as I once did, to my shame), that previous tourists have exaggerated its extent. The thing itself is an exaggeration of nastiness which cannot be outdone.

On board this steamboat there were two young gentlemen, with shirt-collars reversed as usual, and armed with very big walking sticks, who planted two seats in the middle of the deck, at a distance of some four paces apart, took out their tobacco-boxes, and sat down opposite each other to chew. In less than a quarter of an hour's time, these hopeful youths had shed about them on the clean boards a copious shower of yellow rain; clearing, by that means, a kind of magic circle, within whose limits no intruders dared to come, and which they never failed to refresh and re-refresh before a spot was dry. This, being before breakfast, rather disposed me, I confess, to nausea; but looking attentively at one of the expectorators, I plainly saw that he was young in chewing, and felt inwardly uneasy himself A glow of delight came over me at this discovery; and as I marked his face turn paler and paler, and saw the ball of tobacco in his left cheek quiver with his suppressed agony, while yet he spat and chewed and spat again, in emulation of his older friend, I could have fallen on his neck and implored him to go on for hours.

We all sat down to a comfortable breakfast in the cabin below, where there was no more hurry or confusion than at such a meal in England, and where there was certainly greater politeness exhibited than at most of our stage-coach banquets. At about nine o'clock we arrived at the railroad station, and went on by the cars. At noon we turned out again to cross a wide river in another steamboat; landed at a continuation of the railroad on the opposite shore, and went on by other cars; in which, in the course of the next hour or so, we crossed by wooden bridges, each a mile in length, two creeks called respectively Great and Little Gunpowder. The water in both was blackened with flights of canvas-backed ducks, which are most delicious eating, and abound hereabouts at that season of the year.

These bridges are of wood, have no parapet, and are only just wide enough for the passage of the trains; which, in the event of the smallest accident, would inevitably be plunged into the river. They are startling contrivances, and are most agreeable when passed.

We stopped to dine at Baltimore, and, being now in Maryland, were waited on for the first time by slaves. The sensation of exacting any service from human creatures who are bought and sold, and being, for the time, a party as it were to their condition, is not an enviable one. The institution exists, perhaps, in its least repulsive and most mitigated form in such a town as this; but it *is* slavery; and though I was, with respect to it, an innocent man, its presence filled me with a sense of shame and self-reproach.

After dinner, we went down to the railroad again, and took our seats in the cars for Washington. Being rather early, those men and boys who happened to have nothing particular to do, and were curious in foreigners, came (according to custom) round the carriage in which I sat; let down all the windows; thrust in their heads and shoulders; hooked themselves on conveniently by their elbows; and fell to comparing notes on the subject of my personal appearance, with as much indifference as if I were a stuffed figure. I never gained so much uncompromising information with reference to my own nose and eyes, the various impressions wrought by my mouth and chin on different minds, and how my head looks when it is viewed from behind, as on these occasions. Some gentlemen were only satisfied by exercising their sense of touch; and the boys (who are surprisingly precocious in America) were seldom satisfied, even by that, but would return to the charge over and over again. Many a budding President has walked into my room, with his cap on his head and his hands in his pockets, and stared at me for two whole hours; occasionally refreshing himself with a tweak at his nose, or a draught from the water-jug; or by walking to the windows and inviting other boys in the street below to come up and do likewise; crying, "Here he is!" "Come on!" "Bring all your brothers!" with other hospitable entreaties of that nature.

We reached Washington at about half past six that evening, and had upon the way a beautiful view of the Capitol, which is a fine building of the Corinthian order, placed upon a noble and commanding eminence. Arrived at the hotel, I saw no more of the place that night, being very tired, and glad to get to bed.

Breakfast over next morning, I walk about the streets for an hour or two, and, coming home, throw up the window in the front and back, and look out. Here is Washington, fresh in my mind and under my eye.

Take the worst parts of the City Road and Pentonville,[1] or the straggling outskirts of Paris, where the houses are smallest, preserving all their oddities, but especially the small shops and dwellings, occupied in Pentonville (but not in Washington) by furniture-brokers, keepers of poor eating-houses, and fanciers of birds. Burn the whole down; build it up again in wood and plaster; widen it a little; throw in part of St. John's Wood; put green blinds outside all the private houses, with a red curtain and a white one in every window; plough up all the roads; plant a great deal of coarse turf in every place where it ought *not* to be; erect three handsome buildings in stone and marble anywhere, but the more entirely out of everybody's way the better; call one the Post Office, one the Patent Office, and one the Treasury; make it scorching hot in the morning, and freezing cold in the afternoon, with an occasional tornado of wind and dust; leave a brick-field without the bricks, in all central places where a street may naturally be expected; and that's Washington.

The hotel in which we live[2] is a long row of small houses fronting on the street, and opening at the back upon a common yard, in which hangs a great triangle. Whenever a servant is wanted, somebody beats on this triangle from one stroke up to seven, according to the number of the house in which his presence is required; and as all the servants are always being wanted, and none of them ever come, this enlivening engine is in full performance the whole day through. Clothes are drying in this same yard, female slaves, with cotton handkerchiefs twisted round their heads, are running to and fro on the hotel business; black waiters cross and re-cross with dishes in their hands; two great dogs are playing upon a mound of loose bricks in the centre of the little square; a pig is turning up his stomach to the sun, and grunting, "That's comfortable!" and neither the men nor the women nor the dogs nor the pig nor any created creature takes the smallest notice of the triangle, which is tingling madly all the time.

I walk to the front window, and look across the road upon a long, straggling row of houses, one story high, terminating nearly opposite, but a little to the left, m a melancholy piece of waste ground with frowzy grass, which looks like a small piece of country that has taken to drinking, and has quite lost itself. Standing anyhow and all wrong, upon this open space, like something meteoric that has fallen down from the moon, is an odd, lop-sided, one-eyed kind of wooden building, that looks like a church, with a flagstaff as long as itself sticking out of a steeple something larger than a tea-chest. Under the window is a small stand of coaches, whose slave-drivers are sunning themselves on the steps of our door, and talking idly together. The three most obtrusive houses near at hand are the three meanest. On one — a shop, which never has anything in the window, and never has the door open — is painted, in large characters, "THE CITY LUNCH." At another, which looks like the back way to somewhere else, but is an independent building in itself, oysters are procurable in every style. At the third, which is a very, very little tailor's shop, pants are fixed to order; or, in other words, pantaloons are made to measure. And that is our street in Washington.

It is sometimes called the City of Magnificent Distances,[3] but it might with greater propriety be termed the City of Magnificent Intentions; for it is only on taking a bird's-eye view of it from the top of the Capitol, that one can at all comprehend the vast designs of its projector, an aspiring Frenchman. Spacious avenues, that begin in nothing and lead nowhere; streets, mile long, that only want houses, roads, and inhabitants; public buildings that need but a public to be complete; and ornaments of great thoroughfares, which only lack great thoroughfares to ornament, — are its leading features. One might fancy the season over, and most of the houses gone out of town forever with their masters. To the admirers of cities it is a Barmecide Feast; a pleasant field for the imagination to rove in; a monument raised to a deceased project, with not even a legible inscription to record its departed greatness.

Such as it is it is likely to remain. It was originally chosen for the seat of government as a means of averting the conflicting jealousies and interests of the different States; and very probably, too, as being remote from mobs, — consideration not to be slighted, even in America. It has no trade or commerce of its own; having little or no population beyond the President and his establishment, the members of the legislature who reside there during the session, the government clerks and officers employed in the various departments, the keepers of the hotels and boarding-houses, and the tradesmen who supply their tables. It is very unhealthy. Few people would live in Washington, I take it, who were not obliged to reside there; and the tides of emigration and speculation, those rapid and regardless currents, are little likely to flow at any time towards such dull and sluggish water.

The principal features of the Capitol are, of course, the two Houses of Assembly. But there is, besides, in the centre of the building, .a fine rotunda, ninety-six feet in diameter, and ninety-six high, whose circular wall is divided into compartments, ornamented by historical pictures. Four of these have for their subjects prominent events in the Revolutionary struggle. They were painted by Colonel Trumbull, himself a member of Washington's staff at the time of their occurrence; from which circumstance they derive a peculiar interest of their own. In this same hall Mr. Greenough's large statue of Washington has been lately placed. It has great merits, of course, but it struck me as being rather strained and violent for its subject. I could wish, however, to have seen it in a better light than it can ever be viewed in where it stands.

There is a very pleasant and commodious library in the Capitol; and from a balcony in front the bird's-eye view of which I have just spoken may be had, together with a beautiful prospect of the adjacent country. In one of the ornamented portions of the building[4] there is a figure of Justice; whereunto, the Guide Book[5] says, "the artist at first contemplated giving more of nudity, but he was warned that the public sentiment in this country would not admit of it, and in his caution he has gone, perhaps, into the opposite extreme." Poor Justice! she has been made to wear much stranger garments in America than those she pines in, in the Capitol. Let us hope that she has changed her dress-maker since they were fashioned, and that the public sentiment of the country did not cut out the clothes she hides her lovely figure in just now.

The House of Representatives is a beautiful and spacious hall of semicircular shape, supported by handsome pillars. One part of the gallery is appropriated to the ladies, and there they sit in front rows, and come in and go out. as at a play or concert. The chair is canopied, and raised considerably above the floor of the house;, and every member has an easy-chair and a writing-desk to himself; which is denounced by some people out of doors as a most unfortunate and injudicious arrangement, tending to long sittings and prosaic speeches. It is an elegant chamber to look at, but a singularly bad one for all purposes of hearing. The Senate, which is smaller, is free from this objection, and is exceedingly well adapted to the uses for which it is designed. The sittings, I need hardly add, take place in the day; and the parliamentary forms are modelled on those of the old country.

I was sometimes asked, in my progress through other places, whether I had not been very much impressed by the *heads* of the lawmakers at Washington; meaning not their chiefs and leaders, but literally their individual and personal heads, whereon their hair grew, and whereby the phrenological character of each legislator was expressed; and I almost as often struck my questioner dumb with indignant consternation by answering, "No, that I didn't remember being at all overcome." As I must, at whatever hazard, repeat the avowal here, I will follow it up by relating my impressions on this subject in as few words as possible.

In the first place — it may be from some imperfect development of my organ of veneration — I do not remember having ever fainted away, or having even been moved to tears of joyful pride, at sight of any legislative body. I have borne the House of Commons like a man, and have yielded to no weakness but slumber in the House of Lords. I have seen elections for borough and county, and have never been impelled (no matter which party won) to damage my hat by throwing it up into the air in triumph, or to crack my voice by shouting forth any reference to our Glorious Constitution, to the noble purity of our independent voters, or the unimpeachable integrity of our independent members. Having withstood such strong attacks upon my fortitude, it is possible that I may be of a cold and insensible temperament, amounting to iciness, in such matters; and therefore my impressions of the live pillars of the Capitol at Washington must be received with such grains of allowance as this free confession may seem to demand.

Did I see in this public body an assemblage of men bound together in the sacred names of Liberty and Freedom, and so asserting the chaste dignity of those twin goddesses, in all their discussions, as to exalt at once the Eternal Principles to which their names are given, and their own character, and the character of their countrymen, in the admiring eyes of the whole world?

It was but a week since an aged, gray-haired man, a lasting honor to the land that gave him birth, who has done good service to his country, as his forefathers did, and who will be remembered scores upon scores of years after the worms bred in its corruption are but so many grains of dust, — it was but a week since this old man had stood for days upon his trial before this very body, charged with having dared to assert the infamy of that traffic which has for its accursed merchandise men and women and their unborn children. Yes. And publicly exhibited in the same city all the while, gilded, framed, and glazed, hung up for general admiration, shown to strangers not with shame, but pride, its face not turned towards the wall, itself not taken down and burned, is the Unanimous Declaration of The Thirteen United States of America, which solemnly declares that All

Men are created Equal, and are endowed by their Creator with the Inalienable Rights of Life, Liberty, and the Pursuit of Happiness!

It was not a month since this same body had sat calmly by, and heard a man, one of themselves, with oaths which beggars in their drink reject, threaten to cut another's throat from ear to ear. There he sat among them; not crushed by the general feeling of the assembly, but as good a man as any.

There was but a week to come, and another of that body, for doing his duty to those who sent him there; for claiming in a Republic the Liberty and Freedom of expressing their sentiments, and making known their prayer; would be tried, found guilty, and have strong censure passed upon him by the rest. His was a grave offence indeed; for, years before, he had risen up and said, "A gang of male and female slaves for sale, warranted to breed like cattle, linked to each other by iron fetters, are passing now along the open street beneath the windows of your Temple of Equality! Look!" But there are many kinds of hunters engaged in the Pursuit of Happiness, and they go variously armed. It is the Inalienable Right of some among them, to take the field after their Happiness, equipped with cat and cart-whip, stocks and iron collar, and to shout their view halloa! (always in praise of Liberty) to the music of clanking chains and bloody stripes.

Where sat the many legislators of coarse threats, of words and blows such as coal-heavers deal upon each other, when they forget their breeding? On every side. Every session had its anecdotes of that kind, and the actors were all there.

Did I recognize in this assembly a body of men who, applying themselves in a new world to correct some of the falsehoods and vices of the old, purified the avenues to Public Life, paved the dirty ways to Place and Power, debated and made laws for the Common Good, and had no party but their Country?

I saw in them the wheels that move the meanest perversion of virtuous Political Machinery that the worst tools ever wrought. Despicable trickery at elections; underhanded tamperings with public officers; cowardly attacks upon opponents, with scurrilous newspapers for shields, and hired pens for daggers; shameful trucklings to mercenary knaves, whose claim to be considered is, that every day and week they sow new crops of ruin with their venal types, which are the dragon's teeth of yore, in everything but sharpness; aidings and abettings of every bad inclination in the popular mind, and artful suppressions of all its good influences: such things as these, and, in a word, Dishonest Faction in its most depraved and most unblushing form, stared out from every corner of the crowded hall.

Did I see among them the intelligence and refinement, the true, honest, patriotic heart, of America? Here and there were drops of its blood and life, but they scarcely colored the stream of desperate adventurers which sets that way for profit and for pay. It is the game of these men, and of their profligate organs, to make the strife of politics so fierce and brutal, and so destructive of all self-respect in worthy men, that sensitive and delicate-minded persons shall be kept aloof, and they, and such as they, be left to battle out their selfish views unchecked. And thus this lowest of all scrambling fights goes on, and they who in other countries would, from their intelligence and station, most aspire to make the laws, do here recoil the furthest from that degradation.

That there are among the representatives of the people in both Houses, and among all parties, some men of high character and great abilities, I need not say. The foremost among those politicians who are known in Europe have been already described, and I see no reason to depart from the rule I have laid down for my guidance, of abstaining from all mention of individuals. It will be sufficient to add, that to the most favorable accounts that have been written of them I more than fully and most heartily subscribe; and that personal intercourse and free communication have bred within me, not the result predicted in the very doubtful proverb, but increased admiration and respect. They are striking men to look at, hard to deceive, prompt to act, lions in energy, Crichtons[6] in varied accomplishment, Indians in fire of eye and gesture, Americans in strong and generous impulse, and they as well represent the honor and wisdom of their country at home as the distinguished gentleman who is now its minister at the British Court sustains its highest character abroad.

    I visited both houses nearly every day during my stay in Washington. On my initiatory visit to the House of Representatives, they divided against a decision of the chair; but the chair won. The second time I went, the member who was speaking, being interrupted by a laugh, mimicked it, as one child would in quarrelling with another, and added, "that he would make honorable gentlemen opposite sing out a little more on the other side of their mouths presently." But interruptions are rare; the speaker being usually heard in silence. There are more quarrels than with us, and more threatenings than gentlemen are accustomed to exchange in any civilized society of which we have record; but farm-yard imitations have not as yet been imported from the Parliament of the United Kingdom. The feature in oratory which appears to be the most practised and most relished is the constant repetition of the same idea or shadow of an idea in fresh words; and the inquiry out of doors is not, "What did he say?" but, "How long did he speak?" These, however, are but enlargements of a principle which prevails elsewhere.

    The Senate is a dignified and decorous body, and its proceedings are conducted with much gravity and order.

Both houses are handsomely carpeted; but the state to which these carpets are reduced by the universal disregard of the spittoon with which every honorable member is accommodated, and the extraordinary improvements on the pattern which are squirted and dabbled upon it in every direction, do not admit of being described. I will merely observe, that I strongly recommend all strangers not to look at the floor; and if they happen to drop anything, though it be their purse, not to pick it up with an ungloved hand on any account.

It is somewhat remarkable too, at first, to say the least, to see so many honorable members with swelled faces; and it is scarcely less remarkable to discover that this appearance is caused by the quantity of tobacco they contrive to stow within the hollow of the cheek. It is strange enough, too, to see an honorable gentleman leaning back in his tilted chair, with his legs on the desk before him, shaping a convenient "plug " with his penknife, and when it is quite ready for use, shooting the old one from his mouth, as from a popgun, and clapping the new one in its place.

I was surprised to observe that even steady old chewers of great experience are not always good marksmen, which has rather inclined me to doubt that general proficiency with the rifle of which we have heard so much in England. Several gentlemen called upon me who, in the course of conversation, frequently missed the spittoon at five paces, and one (but he was certainly short-sighted) mistook the closed sash for the open window, at three. On another occasion, when I dined out, and was sitting with two ladies and some gentlemen round a fire before dinner, one of the company fell short of the fireplace, six distinct times. I am disposed to think, however, that this was occasioned by his not aiming at that object, as there was a white marble hearth before the fender, which was more convenient, and may have suited his purpose better.

The Patent Office at Washington furnishes an extraordinary example of American enterprise and ingenuity: for the immense number of models it contains are the accumulated inventions of only five years, the whole of the previous collection having been destroyed by fire. The elegant structure in which they are arranged is one of design rather than execution, for there is but one side erected out of four, though the works are stopped. The Post Office is a very compact and very beautiful building. In one of the departments, among a collection of rare and curious articles, are deposited the presents which have been made from time to time to the American ambassadors at foreign courts by the various potentates to whom they were the accredited agents of the Republic, — gifts which by the law they are not permitted to retain. I confess that I looked upon this as a very painful exhibition, and one by no means flattering to the national standard of honesty and honor. That can scarcely be a high state of moral feeling which imagines a gentleman of repute and station likely to be corrupted, in the discharge of his duty, by the present of a snuff-box, or a richly mounted sword, or an Eastern shawl; and surely the Nation who reposes confidence in her appointed servants is likely to be better served than she who makes them the subject of such very mean and paltry suspicions.

At Georgetown, in the suburbs, there is a Jesuit College,[7] delightfully situated, and, so far as I had an opportunity of seeing, well managed. Many persons who are not members of the Romish Church avail themselves, I believe, of these institutions, and of the advantageous opportunities they afford for the education of their children. The heights in this neighborhood, above the Potomac River, are very picturesque, and are free, I should conceive, from some of the insalubrities of Washington. The air, at that elevation, was quite cool and refreshing, when in the city it was burning hot.

The President's mansion is more like an English clubhouse, both within and without, than any other kind of establishment with which I can compare it. The ornamental ground about it has been laid out in garden walks. They are pretty, and agreeable to the eye, though they have that uncomfortable air of having been made yesterday which is far from favorable to the display of such beauties.

My first visit to this house was on the morning after my arrival, when I was carried thither by an official gentleman, who was so kind as to charge himself with my presentation to the President.

We entered a large hall, and, having twice or thrice rung a bell which nobody answered, walked without further ceremony through the rooms on the ground-floor, as divers other gentlemen (mostly with their hats on, and their hands in their pockets) were doing very leisurely. Some of these had ladies with them, to whom they were showing the premises; others were lounging on the chairs and sofas; others, in a perfect state of exhaustion from listlessness, were yawning drearily. The greater portion of this assemblage were rather asserting their supremacy than doing anything else, as they had no particular business there that anybody knew of. A few were closely eying the movables, as if to make quite sure that the President (who was far from popular) had not made away with any of the furniture, or sold the fixtures for his private benefit.

After glancing at these loungers, who were scattered over a pretty drawing-room, opening upon a terrace which commanded a beautiful prospect of the river and the adjacent country, and who were sauntering too about a larger state-room called the Eastern Drawing-room, we went upstairs into another chamber, where were certain visitors waiting for audiences. At sight of my conductor, a black, in plain clothes and yellow slippers, who was gliding noiselessly about, and whispering messages in the ears of the more impatient, made a sign of recognition, and glided off to announce him.

We had previously looked into another chamber fitted all round with a great bare wooden desk or counter, whereon lay files of newspapers, to which sundry gentlemen were referring. But there were no such means of beguiling the time in this apartment, which was as unpromising and tiresome as any waiting-room in one of our public establishments, or any physician's dining-room during his hours of consultation at home.

There were some fifteen or twenty persons in the room. One, a tall, wiry, muscular old man from the West, sunburnt and swarthy, with a brown-white hat on his knees and a giant umbrella resting between his legs, who sat bolt upright in his chair, frowning steadily at the carpet, and twitching the hard lines about his mouth, as if he had made up his mind "to fix" the President on what he had to say, and wouldn't bate him a grain. Another, a Kentucky farmer, six feet six in height, with his hat on, and his hands under his coat-tails, who leaned against the wall and kicked the floor with his heel, as though he had Time's head under his shoe, and were literally "killing" him. A third, an oval-faced, bilious-looking man, with sleek black hair cropped close, and whiskers and beard shaved down to blue dots, who sucked the head of a thick stick, and from time to time took it out of his mouth to see how it was getting on. A fourth did nothing but whistle. A fifth did nothing but spit. And indeed all these gentlemen were so very persevering and energetic in this latter particular, and bestowed their favors so abundantly upon the carpet, that I take it for granted the Presidential housemaids have high wages, or, to speak more genteelly, an ample amount of "compensation," which is the American word for salary, in the case of all public servants.

We had not waited in this room many minutes before the black messenger returned, and conducted us into another of smaller dimensions, where, at a business-like table covered with papers, sat the President himself. lie looked somewhat worn and anxious, and well he might, being at war with everybody; but the expression of his face was mild and pleasant, and his manner was remarkably unaffected, gentlemanly, and agreeable. I thought that in his whole carriage and demeanor he became his station singularly well.

Being advised that the sensible etiquette of the republican court admitted of a traveller like myself declining, without any impropriety, an invitation to dinner, which did not reach me until I had concluded my arrangements for leaving Washington some days before that to which it referred, I only returned to this house once. It was on the occasion of one of those general assemblies which are held on certain nights between the hours of nine and twelve o'clock, and are called, rather oddly, Levees.

I went with my wife at about ten. There was a pretty dense crowd of carriages and people in the court-yard, and, so far as I could make out, there were no very clear regulations for the taking up or setting down of company. There were certainly no policemen to soothe startled horses, either by sawing at their bridles or flourishing truncheons in their eyes; and I am ready to make oath that no inoffensive persons were knocked violently on the head, or poked acutely in their backs or stomachs, or brought to a stand-still by any such gentle means, and then taken into custody for not moving on. But there was no confusion or disorder. Our carriage reached the porch in its turn, without any blustering, swearing, shouting, backing, or other disturbance, and we dismounted with as much ease and comfort as though we had been escorted by the whole Metropolitan Force from A to Z inclusive.

The suite of rooms on the ground-floor were lighted up, and a military band[8] was playing in the hall. In the smaller drawing-room, the centre of a circle of company, were the

President and his daughter-in-law,[9] who acted as the lady of the mansion; and a very interesting, graceful, and accomplished lady too. One gentleman who stood among this group appeared to take upon himself the functions of a master of the ceremonies. I saw no other officers or attendants, and none were needed.

The great drawing-room, which I have already mentioned, and the other chambers on the ground-floor, were crowded to excess. The company was not, in our sense of the term, select, for it comprehended persons of very many grades and classes; nor was there any great display of costly attire; indeed some of the costumes may have been, for aught I know, grotesque enough. But the decorum and propriety of behavior which prevailed were unbroken by any rude or disagreeable incident; and every man, even among the miscellaneous crowd in the hall who were admitted, without any orders or tickets, to look on, appeared to feel that he was a part of the Institution, and was responsible for its preserving a becoming character, and appearing to the best advantage.

That these visitors, too, whatever their station, were not without some refinement of taste and appreciation of intellectual gifts, and gratitude to those men who by the peaceful exercise of great abilities shed new charms and associations upon the homes of their countrymen, and elevate their character in other lands, was most earnestly testified by their reception of Washington Irving,[10] my dear friend, who had recently been appointed Minister at the court of Spain, and who was among them that night, in his new character, for the first and last time before going abroad. I sincerely believe that, in all the madness of American politics, few public men would have been so earnestly, devotedly, and affectionately caressed as this most charming writer; and I have seldom respected a public assembly more than I did this eager throng, when I saw them turning with one mind from noisy orators and officers of state, and flocking with a generous and honest impulse round the man of quiet pursuits; proud in his promotion, as reflecting back upon their country, and grateful to him with their whole hearts for the store of graceful fancies he had poured out among them. Long may he dispense such treasures with unsparing hand; and long may they remember him as worthily!

---

"Every Species of Alcoholic Beverage"

From *The Western World, Or, Travels in the United States in 1846-47* by Alexander MacKay.

Alexander MacKay (1808-1852) visited the United States, on behalf of *The Morning Chronicle*, a London newspaper, with the stated intention of writing a new book about the ever-evolving character of American life in order to accommodate the ever-enduring curiosity of an English audience. Distinguishing himself from some early English writers, without mentioning names, he also committed to spending sufficient time in the country, more than, say, a mere six months, in order to better understand it. As MacKay states in his Introduction, "it is absolutely essential that a man should step aside from the hotel, the railway and the steamer, and live *with* the people, instead of living, as the mere traveller does, *beside* them."

MacKay's writing reflects the sense of urgency and attention to detail of a seasoned newspaperman. He spent several months of his American trip in Washington, D.C., and his work suggests he did indeed live *with* Washington society for a period of time, though he *rarely* mentions names.

---

To convey to the mind of the reader anything like an adequate idea of Washington, is no easy task. It so violates one's preconceived notions of a capital, and is, in its general features, so much at variance with the estimate which one forms of the metropolitan proprieties, that it is difficult, in dealing with it as a capital, to avoid caricaturing a respectable country town. It is as unique in its physical character as it is in its political position, answering all its purposes, yet at the same time falling far short of its expectations.

Washington presents itself in two distinct aspects, one comprising that which it is, and the other that which it was to be. The difference between the intention and the reality is great indeed, and can only be appreciated by viewing the city from some point, from which both design and execution can be estimated together. The point in every way most favourable in this respect, is the dome of the Capitol; and, with the reader's consent, we will ascend it together, and take a bird's-eye view of Washington.

The view from this elevated point is extensive, and in some respects pleasantly varied. The whole of the district of Columbia is within the range of your vision, with a considerable expanse of the circumjacent States of Maryland and Virginia. You have water, town, and field at your feet, with long stretches of forest beyond, and hazy wooded slopes in the distance.

Both the site and the plan of Washington are beneath you, as if delineated on a gigantic map. The ground upon which the city is laid out is on the north bank of the Potomac, at the head of tidewater, and about 120 miles from Chesapeake Bay. On the noble estuary of that river the southern side of the city rests, being flanked on the eastern side by a broad and deep creek, called the East Branch. In a northern or western direction, there are no particular marks to designate its limits. If the design of its founders was too grand for realization, it was because of its being incommensurate with the wants of the locality. In a commercial point of view it is a superfluity, and politically and socially speaking, it is not that powerful magnet which, like the centralizing capitals of the old world, can draw to itself the wealth and fashion of the country. In that on which they chiefly relied for its future greatness, its projectors committed a capital blunder. There are too many social and political centres in the United States for the presence of the federal government to command at Washington a monopoly of the wealth, the talent, and the fashion of the country; too many foci of commercial action around it, to admit of the forced growth of a large community, in a country where such communities can only as it were spontaneously arise.

The Capitol was very appropriately selected as the centre of the whole plan. From it was to radiate magnificent avenues, of indefinite length in some directions, and of an almost fabulous width in all. Having secured this great frame-work, it was easy to fill up the rest of the diagram. In these avenues all the side streets were to begin and terminate; the whole being conceived pretty much on the plan of an out-door spider's web, with its beautiful radiations and intervening parallels. Some of these avenues are laid out and can be traced, from a variety of marks, by the eye, others having, as yet, no definite existence but in the intellect of the surveyor. The avenues, being designed as the great thoroughfares, were to be called after the different States of the Union, — a very appropriate starting point for the nomenclature of the capital, — the same idea being carried out in the navy, the different States giving their names to the ships of the line. From the direction of the East Branch to Georgetown, one avenue was laid out, extending for about three miles, broken only in two places by the grounds of the Capitol and those of the President's house. This is in the main line of the town, and nearly one-half of it is covered with grass.

Such being the plan of Washington, what has been the execution? The main body of the town lies to the west of the Capitol, on low ground, completely overlooked by the elevated plateau, on the slope of which that pile is built. The basis of this part of the town is Pennsylvania Avenue, running almost from your feet, a broad straight course for a full mile, until it terminates in the grounds of the President's house, built upon a similar though a less elevation than the Capitol, On the north this. avenue is flanked by a low ridge, which the city completely covers, streets running along it parallel to the avenue, and others intersecting them at right angles. In this direction, and in this only, has the city anything like a town look about it. In every other direction, you have nothing but incipient country villages, with here and there a few scattered houses of wood or brick, as the case may be, and ever and anon a street just begun and then stopped, as if it were afraid to proceed any further into the wilderness. Taking a rapid glance at the whole, plan and execution considered, it reminds one of an unfinished piece of lady's needlework, with a patch here and there resting upon the canvass, the whole enabling one to form an idea, and no more, of the general design. Let us now descend, and take a short stroll through the town.

We emerge from the grounds of the Capitol upon Pennsylvania Avenue, which originally consisted of two rows of houses and four rows of trees. The latter are now reduced to two, which, when the trees have attained their growth, will throw a grateful shade upon the thoroughfare. The first feature about the avenue that strikes you, is its amazing width. The houses visible on the opposite side, are three hundred feet distant from you, enough to destroy all community of interest and feeling between them, if houses had either one or the other. There seems, in fact, to be little or no bond of union between them; and instead of looking like the two sides of one and the same street, they seem as if they were each a side of two different streets. The mistake of this prodigality of surface was discovered too late to be remedied. In the first place, it destroys the symmetry of the street; for, to be well-proportioned, the houses on either side should rise to a height of twenty stories at least, whereas they are, generally speaking, only three. In the next place, the cost of keeping it in order is ruinous; and as Pennsylvania Avenue is the Broadway of Washington, all the other streets are beggared for the sake of the pet. To pave it was like attempting to pave a field — a circumstance to which is attributable the fact, that the rest of the streets, with the exception of their broad ample brick footways, are left unpaved. In wet weather, to cross any of them, even Pennsylvania Avenue, is a hazardous matter. Nobody ever crosses them for pleasure. It requires serious business to drag you from one side to the other.

Turning from the Avenue to the right, we have at the top of the street, which we thus enter, a large unfinished brick building, with the holes occasioned by the scaffolding yet in the walls, and with a liberty pole rising to the very clouds in front of it. This is the City Hall, the funds for building which were raised by lottery; but someone decamping with a portion of them, the building, which was founded in chance, runs a chance of never being completed. Continuing almost in the same line to the westward, we come to the General Post Office, the choicest architectural *bijou* in Washington, being a neat classic structure built of white marble, and about the size of Trinity House.[1] Its beauties are, however, almost lost from defect of site, the fate of so many of our own finest public edifices. Immediately to the north of the Post Office is the Patent Office, an imposing pile, with a massive Doric portico in the centre, approached by a broad and lofty flight of stairs. But one quarter of it is, as yet, built; the design consisting of four similar fronts, which will enclose a hollow square. Farther west, and at the end of the nearest parallel street to Pennsylvania Avenue, is the Treasury,[2] a handsome building, the front of which presents one of the finest, as it is certainly one of the longest colonnades in the world. But this brings us to the Executive mansion and its adjuncts.

In the midst of a large open square, on a piece of high ground overlooking the Potomac, though about a quarter of a mile back from it, is the President's House, or the "White House," as it is more generally called. It is a spacious and elegant mansion, surrounded by soft sloping lawns, shaded by lofty trees, and dotted with shrubbery. Within this square, and forming, as it were, its four angles, are the four departments of State, those of the Treasury, of State, of War, and of the Navy, each of which is approached by the public from one of the four streets which encompass the Executive grounds. To each a private path also leads from the President's house, the chief magistrate sitting, as it were, like a spider, in the centre of his web, from which he constantly overlooks the occurrences at its extremities. With the exception of the Treasury, which is new, the departments are plain brick buildings, painted in singular taste, of a son of diluted sky-blue colour.

With the exception of the Capitol, to which I shall presently advert, this list comprises the only architectural features worthy of notice in the general view of Washington. Separated, as they are, at great distances from each other, their effect is entirely lost. On my once suggesting to a resident, that it would have been much better had they all been placed together, so as to have formed a noble square, which, viewed as a centre, would have imparted a unity to one's idea of the town; he told me that they all now deeply regretted that this had not been the case, the only reason assigned for scattering them being to prevent the different heads of departments from being constantly disturbed by the intrusion of members of Congress. As they are, Washington has no visible centre — no one point upon which converge the ideas of its inhabitants. But let us back again to the Capitol.

It is a thousand pities that its front is not turned upon Pennsylvania Avenue. The city being intended to grow the other way, the front of the Capitol was turned to the east; but the town having taken the contrary direction, the legislative palace has the appearance of turning its back upon it. But notwithstanding this, it has a most imposing effect, rising, as it does, in classic elegance from its lofty site, over the greensward and rich embowering foliage of the low grounds at its base. As seen at one end of the Avenue, from the grounds of the President's house at the other, there are few buildings in the world that can look to better advantage. I have seen it when its milk-white walls were swathed in moonlight, and when, as viewed from amid the fountains and shrubbery which encircle it, it looked more like a creation of fairy-land than a substantial reality. Passing to the high ground, on its eastern side, we have its principal front, the chief feature of which is a deep Corinthian portico, approached by a double flight of steps, and from which seems to spring the lofty dome, which crowns the building, and gives solidity to the whole, by uniting it, as it were, in one compact mass. This elevation is well seen from the spacious esplanade in front, and from the ornamental grounds immediately beyond. The stairs leading to the portico are flanked by pedestals, designed for groups of statuary, one of which only is as yet occupied, by a marble group, representing Columbus holding a globe in his extended right hand, with an aboriginal native of the new world, a female figure, crouching beside him in mingled fear and admiration. The execution of this group is much better than its design, which is ridiculously theatric. Ascending the steps, you have, beneath the portico, in a niche on either side of the door leading into the body of the building, a marble figure of Peace and War. Passing through this door, you are ushered at once into the rotunda, surmounted by, and lighted from the dome. It extends the whole width of the main building, the perpendicular part of its walls being divided into large panels, designed for the reception of historic paintings. Most of these are already filled, chiefly with incidents of the revolutionary struggle; whilst those still empty will, no doubt, soon be occupied by representations of some of the more prominent events of the Mexican war. Turning to the left, on entering the rotunda, you pass through a door which leads to the House of Representatives, an enormous semicircular chamber, with a lofty vaulted roof, resembling on the whole, the bisection of a dome. A row of massive and lofty pillars, composed of a kind of "pudding stone," which takes a polish equal to that of marble, spring from the floor, and form an inner arc to the outer one formed by the circular wall of the chamber. Between the pillars and this wall is the strangers' gallery. The speaker's chair occupies, as it were, the centre of the chord of the arc, being immediately in front of a screen of smaller pillars, supporting another gallery, occupying a deep recess in the wall, and which is set apart for such private friends as members choose to introduce into it. The seats of members radiate from the chair back to the great pillars, leaving an open semicircular space immediately in front of the clerk's table. The hall looks well, but is ill-adapted for its purpose, it being far too large to speak in with comfort, in addition to which, its acoustic arrangements are anything but perfect.

To get to the senate chamber you have to cross the rotunda. Its general outline is, in most respects, similar to that of the House of Representatives, differing from it in this, that it is not above one-third the size. It is lighter, neater, and much better in its effect than its rival chamber in the other wing of the Capitol; and is, in every way, admirably adapted for public speaking, it is also provided with galleries for the public, seats being raised around the body of the chamber for the diplomatic corps, the judges, and such members of the government as choose to be witnesses of the deliberations of the Senate.

Ascending one day to the gallery, I witnessed a sight which brought into painful contrast some of the lights and shadows of American life. Crouched at the top of the dark staircase was an object, the precise form and character of which I did not at first comprehend; nor was it until my eye had adjusted itself to the imperfect light, that I discovered it to be an aged negro, his hair partially whitened with years, and his fingers crooked with toil. Near him was the door leading into the gallery. It was slightly ajar. The ceiling of the chamber was visible to him, and the voices of the speakers came audibly from within. Someone was then addressing the house. I listened and recognised the tones of one of the representatives of Virginia, the great breeder of slaves, dogmatizing upon abstract rights and constitutional privileges. What a commentary was that poor wretch upon his language! To think that such words should fall upon such ears; the freeman speaking, the slave listening, and all within the very sanctuary of the constitution. I entered the chamber, and could not help, during all the time that I remained there, seeing in fancy that decrepit old slave kneeling at the foot of the chair in impotent supplication for justice.

Immediately after the house had risen, I perceived him busy with others cleaning out the chamber. Indeed, during the session, the whole Capitol is daily swept by negroes; the black man cleaning what the white man defiles. Who will erase the moral stain that casts such a shadow over the republic? Will the white man have the magnanimity to do it; or will the black man have to purify the constitution for himself, as he now sweeps the dust of his oppressors from the steps of the Capitol?

... From the district of Columbia, as from an elevated point of sight, there are some respects in which the whole confederation may be advantageously viewed. To the federal capital, whilst Congress is in session, converge as to a focus the diversified peculiarities and conflicting interests of the Union. Elsewhere you come in contact with but its *disjecta membra*; whilst here, although some features may be but faintly traced, the republic is to be seen in its entire outline. Here the east and the west, the north and the south; the free interest and the slave interest; the commerce, the manufactures, and the agriculture of America, meet face to face, discern their relative positions, and measure each other's strength. This is the arena common to all parties; the spot where great material interests clash and are reconciled again; where national policies are built up and are overthrown; where faction develops its strategy, and moral forces exhaust themselves in periodic conflict with each other. Here also is to be seen in constant whirl the balance-wheel, such as it is, of the most complicated political machine on earth; and here may be best appreciated the working and the value of the constitution.

Contemplated from the capital, however, the republic is better understood in its political than in its social character. It is quite true that the different phases of American society are to be met with in Washington. But to form a correct estimate of social life in America, it must be carefully considered beyond the bounds of the capital. Its development in Washington is peculiar, owing to the heterogeneous elements which are there thrown together, and considered alone would afford but an inadequate idea of the social system of the continent. In the singular moral agglomeration which Washington presents, whatever may be disagreeable in American society comes strongly out. A more extended survey leaves a better impression. But before taking this survey, it may be as well to initiate the reader into some of the peculiarities of Washington life.

The first thing that strikes the stranger is the unsettled aspect which society there presents. Long before he has analyzed it, and searched into its peculiarities, he discerns the traces of instability which are deeply imprinted upon it.

He scarcely perceives a feature about it that is permanent — a characteristic that is durable. It affords no tokens to him of constant and undeviating progression; but, on the contrary, all the evidences of froward and fitful life. It seems to have had no past, whilst it is difficult to divine what its future will be — to have been formed today, and not designed to last beyond tomorrow. It appears, in short, to be a mere temporary arrangement, to give time for the organization of something better.

Nor is all this difficult to account for. It is the natural consequence of the fluctuating materials of which it is composed, and of the frequently irreconcilable qualities of its component parts. It is like a fabric of coarse texture, hastily woven of ill-assorted materials, speedily dissolved only to be woven again anew. No sooner does it assume a shape than its outlines disappear again, to be once more brought into form, which it is destined again to lose. It is this succession of semi-formation and semi-dissolution — this periodicity in its construction and disintegration — that makes the chronic condition of society in Washington present the same phenomena to the stranger, as other social systems have exhibited when in a state of violent transition.

The better to understand this, let me here present the reader with a general idea of the capital. At best, Washington is but a small town, a fourth-rate community as to extent, even in America. When Congress is not sitting, it is dull and insipid to a degree, its periodical excitements disappearing with the bulk of its population. It is, in fact, a town of boarding-houses and hotels; the principal occupation of those left behind, after the rising of Congress, appearing to be, to keep the empty town well aired for the next legislative session and the next influx of population. During the recess, the population consists of the *corps diplomatique*, the chief and subordinate officials of the government and their families, idle-shopkeepers, boarding-house keepers, and slaves. Sometimes the diplomatic body and the higher civil functionaries of the republic, withdraw altogether for the sickly months of August and September. A more forlorn and lifeless appearance can scarcely be conceived than is then worn by the American capital. It is like a body without animation, a social *cadaver*, a moral Dead Sea.

From this state of torpidity it is annually roused about the beginning of December, the first Monday of which is the day fixed by the constitution for the assemblage of Congress. For some weeks previously to this, the note of preparation is sounded; the hotels are re-opened, whole streets of boarding-houses are put in order for the winter, shopkeepers replenish their stocks, and the deserted village once more assumes the aspect of a tolerably bustling town. But it is not till about the beginning of the year that the tide of population may be regarded as at its full. And what a motley heterogeneous assemblage does Washington then contain! Within a narrow compass you have the semi-savage "Far Westerner," the burly backwoodsman, the enterprising New-Englander, the genuine Sam Slick, the polished Bostonian, the adventurous New Yorker, the staid and prim Philadelphian, the princely merchant from the sea-board, the wealthy manufacturer, the energetic farmer and the languid but uncertain planter. Were Washington a large town, with a permanent and settled society, this influx of incongruous elements might periodically merge in without sensibly affecting it. But this is not the case, and it is from the different pursuits, the diversified habits, the opposite views, the conflicting sentiments, the unadjusted sympathies and incompatible tastes of this motley concurrence of legislators, placemen, place-hunters, partisans and idlers, that the characteristics of Washington society annually arise. It is impossible for such materials to combine into a structure, either harmonious or ornamental. Let me not be understood, however, to say that there are no exceptions to this unflattering picture: for amongst the permanent, as well as the occasional residents of Washington, are many who would do honour to any society; but they are not sufficiently numerous to impart a character to Washington life. They have, generally, their own coteries, to which they confine themselves. They withdraw from that which is foreign to their tastes, and thus the better features of Washington life are concealed beneath the surface. They can neither resist the tide, nor guide the current; so they modestly dip their heads, and let it pass over them. It is the rough incongruous crowd that gives society its tone and colouring: and what renders the thing all the more hopeless is, that whilst the general characteristics of the crowd remain, the individuals are constantly changing. Those present today are gone tomorrow, their places being occupied by others of the same stamp with themselves. You might as well attempt to construct a city of the ever-shifting sands of the desert, as to organize anything like a permanent social fabric out of the incoherent and evanescent materials which are to be found in Washington.

To reduce the moral chaos, thus annually presented, to something like shape and order, the most powerful influences are required, and some of the best of these are wanting. In no part of the republic is the social sway of woman so limited as it is in the capital. This does not arise from any inferiority in the Washington ladies, but from the absolute paucity of their numbers. The great majority of those who crowd into the city during the session, either leave their families behind them or have none to accompany them. It is quite true, that most of the members of the Senate, and several of the Lower House, are accompanied by their wives and children; but these, with the flying visiters, male and female, who constantly come and go, are exceptions to the rule. To the great bulk of the merely sessional residents, the stay of a few months in Washington is regarded more in the light of a protracted "spree" than as anything else. They may, to be sure, have their legislative and other duties to attend to, but these merely constitute a part of the round of excitements to which they give themselves up. A walk into the streets, a visit to one of the hotels, the very complexion of the boarding-houses, will suffice to show the dearth in Washington society of the more softening influences. When neither House of Congress is sitting, groups of male idlers are constantly to be seen loitering in the streets, or smoking and chewing in crowds in front of the hotels, where they ogle with little delicacy the few women that pass; or noisily congregated in the bar-room, treating themselves liberally to gin slings, sherry cobblers, and mint juleps. The more quietly disposed of the members of Congress take up their quarters in the boarding-houses more convenient to the capital, where they are accommodated in messes, sometimes twenty of them living together under the same roof, and daily meeting at the same table. These "Congress messes" are imitated elsewhere, and for one boarding-house with mixed company, there are ten in which no female but the landlady is to be met with. It is obvious that such a development of social life can give rise to but little variety of mental occupation. Parties, generally speaking, with no very extensive range of intellectual acquirement, thus kept constantly together, under almost the same circumstances, have but few topics of conversation, but these unfortunately are prolific of wrangling and excitement. Politics and party questions occupy nine-tenths of their time, in discussing which their minds are kept, as it were, in a continual state of fever heat. The habit of disputation which this engenders, and the state of normal antagonism into which it casts their minds, are by no means favourable to the cultivation of the social amenities. Their constant intercourse with each other is as that of partisans or political opponents. The tie of friendship is subservient to considerations of party and self-interest, and it is seldom that they find those ameliorating influences intervening between them, which, in other portions of the world, partly separate only to keep men in kindlier contact with each other. The Sabine women interfered between their kinsmen and their husbands, and made friends of those who had been mortal enemies. It is a thousand pities that the genial presence of similar arbitrators does not interfere to sooth the asperities of political disputation in the American capital.

From all this may be readily conceived how coarse and unattractive a surface Washington society presents to the world. On most persons who come in contact with it is its effect speedily discernible. In the case of some it tarnishes the lustre of pre-contracted refinements; in that of others, as colours are fixed by fire, it aggravates the rougher and more repulsive features of their character. Many sink to the condition of moral bears — demeaning themselves as if they had never known a social restraint, and as if the more graceful conventionalities of civilization were essentially alien to their nature. In their mutual intercourse, but little courtesy of manner or suavity of disposition is displayed. They are manly without being gentlemanly. When they do approach a lady, their demeanour is more that of elaborate awkwardness than of ease and self-possession. Their politeness partakes largely of the characteristics of their daily life; it is bustling, obtrusive, and sometimes offensive. Time and again have I seen ladies blush at the awkward ambiguity of their compliments. But how can it be otherwise with those, who generally exchange the duties of the day only for the grosser amusements? In the way of the higher amusements, Washington is very ill provided. Were music cultivated, or did the drama flourish in it, or were there other sources of intellectual pastime to which the jaded politician could resort, the aspect of things might be changed. But as it is, the approach of a third rate vocalist, of a peripatetic juggler, or a strolling equestrian company, creates a sensation in Washington equal to that of an English village under the same lofty excitements. I once witnessed the performance of an equestrian company there, when the whole population seemed to have gathered under the tent, including the diplomatic corps, and the functionaries of government, with the exception of the President. This want of intellectual amusement, combined with the inadequacy of female society, throws many into a course of habitual, but still temperate dissipation. From morning till night the bar-rooms of the hotels are full; the bar, indeed, being the chief source of the hotel-keepers' revenue. Amongst those who frequent them is generally to be found a large sprinkling of members of Congress. Some of these gentlemen, for want of other occupation, raised a subscription two or three years ago, for the purpose of presenting a testimonial to one of the bar-keepers of the National Hotel, whose fame as a compounder of gin sling and mint julep was almost co-extensive with the bounds of the republic. Amongst the ornaments of the bar was a portrait of this functionary, exhibiting his adroit manipulations in the more critical operations of his calling. The testimonial consisted of two silver cups, similar to those used by him in compounding his mixtures, the inscription on one of them testifying that they were a token of the admiration of the donors, for his "eminent services at the Washington bar." I do not mean to say that this was a national tribute to the worthy in question, but it speaks volumes, that its principal promoters were members of the federal legislature.

Few as are the virtues of social life which sparkle on the surface of Washington society, it was some time ere I was made aware of the extent to which its vices were covertly practised. Walking home one morning, about two o'clock, with a friend, he asked me, whilst passing down Pennsylvania Avenue, to accompany him to a place where he would show me a feature of Washington life to which I was yet a stranger. We thereupon entered an open lobby, and passed upstairs, when, on opening the first door we came to, I beheld, as thick and as busy as bees in a hive, a set of men in crowds around several tables, engaged in the hazards, and plunged in all the excitements of gambling — the game being faro,[3] and the stakes by no means contemptible.

I remained for some time contemplating a scene, singularly diversified, as respects character and the display of passion. The company was of a very mixed character, comprising artisans, tradesmen, shop-keepers, a few professional men, and many idlers. Noisiest and busiest of all, was one of the members for Alabama; and it was not long ere I heard exclamations, alternating between satisfaction and disappointment, breaking from lips which I had heard discourse most eloquently in the Capitol on the aristocratic vices of England. The night was hot, the atmosphere of the room was stifling, and most of those present were in their shirt-sleeves. In a back room, the door of which stood invitingly open, was a table amply set out with a gratuitous provision of edibles, and every species of alcoholic beverage. On entering we were invited to partake, but declined. The less experienced hands vainly endeavoured to drown their excitements by frequent potations — the more knowing kept aloof from the bottle.

On quitting this scene, we entered three other houses close by, only to witness, in each, a similar exhibition.

"I am surprised," said I to my friend, on our finally emerging into the open air, "to find so small a community as that of Washington so largely impregnated with some of the worst vices of the wealthier and more luxurious capitals of Europe."

"Many of those whom you have just seen," said he, "are driven to the gambling-table merely to while away their time."

"But could they not," inquired I, "accomplish the same object by seeking other occupations?"

"The worst of it is," rejoined he, "that their opportunities in that respect are limited. Such of them as have a taste for society soon exhaust the round of their acquaintances, and having no other sources of legitimate pastime within reach, must elect between *ennui* and questionable devices to avoid it. Such, on the other hand, as have no taste for social intercourse, resort perhaps naturally enough, to equivocal practices. Add to this, that some of the members, who receive eight dollars a-day and live perhaps on three, have spare cash in hand, which they look upon as so much money found, and which they are willing to risk, on the ground that, if they lose it they will be none the poorer. This calls annually to Washington a number of professional gamblers, who generally manage to fleece a few of the people's representatives, although they sometimes get plucked themselves."

As already intimated, the foregoing description is not universally applicable to Washington society. It is its portraiture, as it strikes the stranger who stands aside an impartial observer of its general development. Such as I have shown it to be, is it in the main, — the ungainly product of unsympathetic elements, — the rough fabric, woven of intractable materials. Its softer and more attractive features have to be sought to be observed: they do not, however, enter into the general picture, being more like ornaments upon the frame. Notwithstanding its general roughness, there are pleasant by-ways in Washington life. Its turbulent current is flanked by many quiet eddies, where refinement prevails, and whence the social graces are not banished.

The better portion of Washington society is confined to a very narrow circle. It has a fixed and, at the same time, a flitting aspect, a nucleus and a coma. Its permanent centre is composed of the families of the resident officials; its varying adjuncts consist of such families as are only sessionally resident, and such flying visiters as are eligible to its circle. Amongst the members of the resident families is to be found a degree of refinement and elegance, which would do no discredit to the best society in the most fashionable capitals. Their mutual intercourse is easy and graceful, and pleasantly contrasts with the general boorishness which surrounds them-. Nor are they deficient in spirit, humour, vivacity, or intellectual acquirements — the young ladies being well disciplined both in the essentials and the accomplishments of education, and well trained to all the conventional elegancies of life. Amongst the resident families may be comprised the different members of the diplomatic corps, embracing the representatives of all the great powers, with the single exception of Austria. Forming a large proportion of the circle in which they move, their influence upon its general character is permanent as it is obvious. Superadded to these are the families of such members of Congress as choose to come thus accompanied to the capital during the legislative session. These again comprise two classes; such as fuse into the more select society of the town, and such as combine to form a circle of their own. The latter generally consists of New Englanders, who are more staid of habit, more sedate in their social deportment, and more severe in their moral and intellectual discipline, than the more mercurial Southerner, with whom they are placed in temporary juxtaposition. It was my good fortune to know several families from Massachusetts and the neighbouring States, who were thus banded together, having monopolized several contiguous boarding-houses, and holding but little intercourse with any beyond the pale of their own circle. But the great majority of these temporary residents merge at once into the society of the capital. Composed, as it thus is, of different but not unharmonious materials, the better order of society in Washington exhibits a mixed but very pleasing aspect, presenting a happy combination of European urbanity and American accessibility. It is thus characterized by a politeness which disowns frigidity, and a cordiality which discards affectation.

It is unnecessary here to enter into further particulars concerning it, partaking, as it largely does, of the characteristic features of American society; of which a general view will be taken in the following chapter. It may be as well, however, to make a passing allusion to its accessible quality — not that it throws its doors open to every stranger who knocks for admittance, but that it is readily satisfied with a good recommendation and a gentlemanly deportment. The following may serve as an illustration of the ease which marks its general intercourse, and the perfect confidence which its different members have in each other. The first time I went to the President's house was without any formal invitation. I was visiting one evening a family which honoured me with its friendship and intimacy, when an invitation came from Mrs. Polk, inviting its members to the Executive mansion, which was hard by. The attendance of a professional vocalist had suddenly been procured, and the invitation was to a private concert, in one of the family drawing-rooms. The young ladies declined, on the ground of having visitors; an answer was immediately returned, inviting them to bring their friends. We accordingly went; and thus my first presentation to the President and his lady was of a more agreeable character than had it been attended with all the formalities of a state occasion. It is very common for the families of such members as live in the hotels, to give weekly "hops," as they are called, which are neither more nor less than dancing parties, divested of some of the usual ceremonies of such assemblages. To one of these, occurring on the same evening at the National hotel, my friends were invited, as was I, to come under their auspices. The amusements of the evening were thus pleasantly varied between music and the dance; the demeanour of all whom I met at both places being such as bespoke a refinement at once easy and unexceptionable. The true source of this rather attractive feature of American life will be subsequently considered.

The life of such of the residents as move in this circle is one of constant excitement during the session, and of comparative repose during the recess. I once remarked to a lady, that Washington must be very dull when Congress was not sitting. She assured me that it was quiet, but not dull. It was true, she said, that, for the sickly months, it was deserted by all who could afford to leave it; but it appears that, for some time after the rising of Congress, the resident society enjoys many a pleasant reunion, without the presence of strangers, or of the excitements which mark the period of the year when they are drawn to the town. The *élite* of Washington then meet each other almost as friends who had been separated for some time; when their intercourse is of the most easy, friendly, and informal description.

During the season, the time of the fashionables is pretty well occupied with balls, public and private, soirées, concerts, and other entertainments. In addition to the part which they take in the "west-end" doings of Washington, the *corps diplomatique* keep up a distinctive circle of their own; forming, as it were, a less world within a very little one. Prominent in that circle is the sexagenarian envoy of Russia, with his young and lovely American wife: between whom and the bachelor plenipotentiary of England a friendly emulation seems to exist, as to who can give the best dinner-party. In the summer-time, when the grounds around the White House are clothed in verdure, and the still more beautiful precincts of the capital are shrouded in foliage, and enamelled with flowers, a military band performs for some hours twice a week, in each alternately, when Washington presents a scene as gay as Kensington Gardens sometimes exhibit, under similar circumstances; the population turning out in their best attire, and promenading in groups to the sound of music, over the soft grass, amongst trees, shrubs, and flowers, and amid refreshing fountains, whose marble basins are filled with gold and silver fish.

The Rotunda of the Capitol and the Library of Congress are two favourite places of lounging during the day, at least between twelve and three, whilst both Houses are sitting. The latter particularly seems to have been consecrated to the purposes of flirtation. It is a large and handsome room, occupying the whole breadth of the back wing of the Capitol, well filled with books, which are seldom read, however, during these hours. It is flanked by a spacious colonnade balcony, which commands a noble prospect, comprising the basin of the Potomac, and a considerable portion of the State of Virginia, the principal part of the town, and long successive sweeps of the fertile plains of Maryland. On this balcony, in the room, and in the different "chapters" or recesses into which it is divided on either side, may daily be encountered during the session a fair representation of the beauty and accomplishment of America. Here are to be found the exquisitely formed and vivacious Creole from New Orleans; the languid but interesting daughters of Georgia and the Carolinas; the high-spirited Virginia belle, gushing with life, and light of heart; the elegant and springy forms of the Maryland and Philadelphia maidens, and the clear and high-complexioned beauties of New England. They are surrounded by their male friends, aged and young, the *attachés* of the different embassies enjoying a mustachioed conspicuity in the scene, and pass the hours in frivolous chit-chat, laughing and merry all the while. Now and then a busy politician enters from either house, with bustling gait and pensive brow, refers to some political volume, and disappears, leaving the room once more in the possession of the idler, the flirt, and the coxcomb.

The conversation of one of the groups of idlers chanced one day to take a literary turn, when a discussion arose as to the authorship of the passage, "Music hath charms, &c." Being unable to solve the difficulty, two or three of the ladies bounded towards a sofa, on which reclined the veteran ex-President, John Quincy Adams,[4] jaded with political warfare and panting with the heat, which was excessive. He had just come from the House of Representatives, where he had been listening to a fierce debate, involving the character of one of the first statesmen of the Union, and one of the greatest ornaments of his country. Without ceremony, they presented their difficulty to him, and begged him to solve it; but the "best read man in America," as he was styled, was discomfited, and had to own himself so, after being convinced of his error in hinting that the passage might be found in the "Merchant of Venice." The incident is trifling in itself, but it is nevertheless characteristic.

But one of the most interesting of all the features of Washington life is the society of its leading politicians. The ability and grasp of thought of some of these men are only equalled by their suavity and courtesy. It must be confessed, however, that this description applies to but few in number — the real statesmen of the country — not the crowd of brawling and obstreperous political adventurers who unfortunately play too conspicuous a part in the social drama of the capital. Foremost of those who do honour to their country by the pre-eminence of their talents, the purity of their intentions, and the lustre of their social qualities, is John C. Calhoun,[5] one of the senators for South Carolina. It was my privilege frequently to enjoy the society of this gifted and distinguished personage, who, by the charms of his conversation, as well as by his affable demeanour, excites the admiration of all who approach him, whether old or young, friend or adversary.

The foregoing sketch may suffice as an outline of social life in the American capital. If, in its main features, it is not as attractive as are the conventional phenomena of more polished communities, it will be seen that it is not deficient in traits which relieve the rudeness of its general character, or in veins of sterling ore beneath, which, to some extent, atone for its superficial asperities.

"A Fit Act of Hero Worship"

From *A Second Visit to North America* by Sir Charles Lyell.

Sir Charles Lyell (1797-1875) was a Scottish geologist, a Fellow of the Royal Society in London, and author of *Principles of Geology*, then a pioneering work on the subject. Lyell traveled twice to the United States during the 1840s and wrote books about each visit. The record of his first visit in 1841-1842 focused primarily on subjects particular to his profession. His second visit in 1845-1846 produced a more expansive account in which the eminent geologist recorded broader impressions of the United States.

During his visit to Washington, D.C., Lyell would set aside topics such as the coal fields of Alabama, fossilized footprints therein, the falls of Niagara and the drifting of icebergs for more human subjects, including the varieties in eloquence among members of Congress, the costume of Supreme Court judges, and slavery in the District of Columbia.

---

Dec. 13 [1845]. *Washington.* — Went into the House of Representatives; the front seats in the gallery are reserved for ladies. We found the member for Connecticut, Mr. Rockwell,[1] on his legs, delivering what seemed to me an admirable speech against the annexation of Texas, especially that part of its new constitution which prohibited the Legislature from taking steps towards the future abolition of slavery. Some of the representatives were talking, others writing, none listening. The question was evidently treated as one gone by — mere matter of history, which the course of events had consigned to the vault of all the Capulets. Nevertheless, a feeling of irritation and deep disgust is pervading the minds of the anti-slavery party at this sudden accession of new territory, open to a slave population. A powerful reaction has begun to display itself, so that the incorporation of Texas into the Union may eventually be attended with consequences most favourable to the good cause, rousing the whole North to make a stand against the future extension of slavery. Mr. Winthrop[2] has hailed this more hopeful prospect in the happiest strain of eloquence, addressing "the lone star of Texas," as it was called, in the words of Milton: —

"Fairest of stars, *last in the train of night*,
If rather thou belong'st not to the dawn."

Crossing the Rotunda, we passed into the Senate, and heard General Cass,[3] of Michigan, delivering a set speech on the Oregon question.[4] The recent acquisition of Texas, which we had heard condemned in the other House as a foul blot on their national policy, was boasted of by him as a glorious triumph of freedom. He drew an animated picture of the aggrandising spirit of Great Britain with her 150 millions of subjects, spoke of her arrogance and pride, the certainty of a war, if they wished to maintain their just rights, and the necessity of an immediate armament.

"Great Britain," he said, "might be willing to submit the Oregon question to arbitration, but the crowned heads, whom she would propose as arbiters, would not be impartial, for they would cherish anti-republican feelings."

I thought the style of this oration better than its spirit, and it was listened to with attention; but in spite of the stirring nature of the theme, none of the senators betrayed any emotion.

When he sat down, others followed, some of whom read extracts from the recently delivered speeches of Sir Robert Peel and Lord John Russell[5] on the Oregon affair, commenting freely and fairly upon them, and pointing out that there was nothing in the tone of the British Government, nor in the nature of their demands, which closed the door against an amicable adjustment. I came away from this debate much struck with the singular posture of affairs; for the executive and its functionaries seem to be doing their worst to inflame popular passions, while the Legislature, chosen by universal suffrage, is comparatively calm, and exhibits that sense of a dangerous responsibility, which a president and his cabinet might rather have been expected to display.

In reference to one of the arguments in General Cass's speech, Mr. Winthrop soon afterwards moved in the House of Representatives (Dec. 19. 1845), "That arbitration does not necessarily involve a reference to crowned heads; and if a jealousy of such a reference is entertained in any quarter, a commission of able and dispassionate citizens, either from the two countries concerned, or from the world at large, offers itself as an obvious and unobjectionable alternative."

A similar proposition emanated simultaneously, and without concert, from the English Cabinet, showing that they were regardless of precedents, and relied on the justice of their cause. Although it was declined, the mere fact of a great nation having waived all punctilious etiquette, and offered to settle a point at issue by referring the question to private citizens of high character and learned in international law, proves that the world is advancing in civilisation, and that higher principles of morality are beginning to gain ground in the intercourse between nations. "All who ought to govern," said a member of Congress to me, "are of one mind as to Lord Aberdeen's overture;[6] but they who do govern here, will never submit to arbitration."

The senate consists at present of fifty-nine members, and will soon be augmented by two from Texas and two from Iowa, the Union consisting now of twenty-seven states, with a population of about twenty millions.

The appearance of the members of the House of Representatives is gentlemanlike, although I doubt not that the scenes of violence and want of decorum described by many travellers, are correct pictures of what they witnessed. In this nation of readers they are so sensitive to foreign criticism, that amendment may be confidently looked for. At this moment, the papers, by way of retaliation, are amusing their readers, with extracts from a debate in the Canada House of Assembly. The following may serve as an example: — "Our Canadian friends occasionally read us a lecture on courtesy and order, we therefore cite from a report of their legislative proceedings, what we presume they intend as a model for our imitation. Mr. De B. appealed to the chair to stop the member for Quebec, and threatened, if he was not called to order, that he must go over and pull his nose; at which Mr. A. rejoined, 'Come and do it, you scoundrel!'" Another example of recrimination that I have lately seen, consisted in placing in two parallel columns, first an extract from the leading article of the London Times, rating the Americans in good set terms for their rudeness to each other in debate, and coarse abuse of England; and, secondly, an account given by the same journal of a disorderly discussion in the House of Commons on an Irish question, in which, among other incidents, a young member of the aristocracy (intoxicated let us hope) rose in the midst of the hubbub, and imitated the crowing of a cock.

A member of Congress, who frequented, when in London, the gallery of the House of Commons, tells me he was struck with what seemed an affectation of rusticity, members lolling in lounging attitudes on the benches with their hats on, speaking with their hands thrust into their breeches pockets, and other acts, as if in defiance of restraint. The English method of coughing down a troublesome member is often alluded to here, and has, on one occasion, been gravely recommended for adoption, as a parliamentary usage which might advantageously be imitated, rather than the limitation of each speaker to one hour, a rule now in force, which has too often the effect of making each orator think it due to himself to occupy the House for his full term.

It would be impossible to burlesque or caricature the ambitious style of certain members of Congress, especially some who have risen from humble stations, arid whose schooling has been in the back-woods. A grave report, drawn up in the present session by the member for Illinois,[7] as chairman of a Post-Office Committee, may serve as an example. After speaking of the American republic as "the infant Hercules," and the extension of their imperial dominion over the "northern continent and oriental seas," he exclaims,

> "the destiny of our nation has now become revealed, and great events, quickening in the womb of time, reflect their clearly defined shadows into our very eye-balls.
>
> Oh, why does a cold generation frigidly repel ambrosial gifts like these, or sacrilegiously hesitate to embrace their glowing and resplendent fate?
>
> Must this backward pull of the government never cease, and the nation tug forever beneath a dead weight, which trips its heels at every stride?"

From the Senate House, we went to another part of the Capitol to hear Mr. Webster[8] plead a cause before the Judges of the Supreme Court. These judges wear black gowns, and are, I believe, the only ones in the United States who have a costume. The point at issue was most clearly stated, namely, whether the city of New York had a legal right to levy a tax of one dollar on every passenger entering that port, who had never before visited any port of the Union. The number of emigrants being great, no less than 100,000 dollars had been annually raised by this impost, the money being applied chiefly as an hospital fund. It was contended that the Federal Government alone had the right of imposing duties on commerce, in which light this passenger tribute ought to be viewed. The Court, however, ruled otherwise.

It was pointed out to me, as a remarkable proof of the ascendancy of the democratic party in the Federal Government for many years past, that only one of all the judges now on the bench had been nominated by the Whigs.[9]

One day, as we were walking down Pennsylvania Avenue with Mr. Winthrop, we met a young negro woman, who came up to him with a countenance full of pleasure, saying it was several years since she had seen him, and greeting him with such an affectionate warmth of expression, that I began to contrast the stiffness and coldness of the Anglo-Saxon manners with the genial flow of feeling of this southern race. My companion explained to me, that she was a very intelligent girl, and was grateful to him for an act of kindness he had once had an opportunity of showing her. I afterwards learnt, from some other friends to whom I told this anecdote, that three years before, Mr. Winthrop and a brother member of Congress from the North had been lodging in the house of this girl's mistress, and hearing that she was sentenced to be whipped for some offence, had both of them protested they would instantly quit the house if the mistress persevered. She had yielded, and at length confessed that she had been giving way to a momentary fit of temper.

Washington is situated in the district of Columbia, comprising an area of 100 square miles, borrowed from the neighbouring states[10] to form an independent jurisdiction by itself. Several attempts have been made to declare it free, but hitherto in vain, thanks to the union of the northern democrats and southern slave-owners, aided by the impracticable schemes of the abolitionists.

The view of the city and the river Potomac from the hill on which the Capitol stands is fine; but, in spite of some new public edifices built in a handsome style of Greek architecture, we are struck with the small progress made in three years since we were last here. The vacant spaces are not filling up with private houses, according to the original plan, so that the would-be metropolis wears still the air of some projector's scheme which has failed. The principal hotels, however, have improved, and we were not annoyed, as when last here, by the odours left in the room by the coloured domestics, who had no beds, but slept anywhere about the stairs or passages, without changing their clothes. With similar habits, in a hot climate, no servants of any race, whether free or slave, African or European, would be endurable.

In the public museum at the Patent Office I was glad to see a fine collection of objects of natural history brought here by the late Exploring Expedition, commanded by Captain Wilkes.[11] Among other treasures is a splendid series of recent corals, a good description of which, illustrated by plates, will soon be published by Mr. Dana,[12] at the expense of Government. These zoophytes are accompanied by masses of solid limestone, occasionally including shells, recently formed in coral reefs, like those mentioned by Mr. Darwin[13] as occurring in the South Seas, some as hard as marble, others consisting of conglomerates of pebbles and calcareous sand. In several of the specimens I saw the imbedded zoophytes and shells projecting from the weathered surface, as do the petrifactions in many an ancient limestone where they have resisted disintegration more than the matrix. Other fragments were as white and soft as chalk; one in particular, a cubic foot in bulk, brought from one of the Sandwich Islands, might have been mistaken for a piece of Shakspeare's [sic] Cliff, near Dover. It reminded me that an English friend, a professor of political economy, met me about fifteen years ago on the beach at Dover, after he had just read my *Principles of Geology*, and exclaimed, "Show me masses of pure white rock, like the substance of these cliffs, in the act of growing in the ocean over areas as large as France or England, and I will believe all your theory of modern causes." Since that time we have obtained data for inferring that the growth of corals, and the deposition of chalk-like calcareous mud, is actually going on over much wider areas than the whole of Europe, so that I am now entitled to claim my incredulous friend as a proselyte.

In one of the glass cases of the Museum I saw the huge skull of the *Megatherium*,[14] with the remains of other extinct fossil animals found in Georgia, — a splendid donation presented by Mr. Hamilton Couper.[15] In another part of the room were objects of antiquarian interest, and among the rest some sculptured stones from the ruins of Palenque,[16] inscribed with the hieroglyphic or picture-writing of the Aborigines, with which Stephens's lively work on Central America, and the admirable illustrations of Catherwood, had made us familiar.[17] The camp-chest of General Washington, his sword, the uniform worn by him when he resigned his commission, and even his stick, have been treasured up as relics in this national repository. If the proposition lately made in the public journals, to purchase Washington's country residence and negro-houses, at Mount Vernon, and to keep them forever in the state in which he left them, should be carried into effect, it would not only be a fit act of hero-worship, but in the course of, time this farm would become a curious antiquarian monument, showing to after-generations the state of agriculture at the period when the Republic was founded, and how the old Virginian planters and their slaves lived in the eighteenth century.

Before leaving Washington we called, with Mr. Winthrop, at the White House, the residence of the President. A coloured servant in livery came to the door, and conducted us to the reception-room, which is well proportioned and well furnished, not in sumptuous style, but without any affectation of republican plainness. We were politely received by Mrs. Polk,[18] her husband being engaged on public business. I was afterwards introduced to General Scott,[19] to Captain Wilkes, recently returned from his expedition to the South Seas, to Mr. Bancroft,[20] Secretary of the Navy, and called on our minister, Mr. Pakenham,[21] and our old friends, M. and Madame de Gerolt, the Prussian minister and his wife.[22] I also examined a fine collection of fossils, belonging to Mr. Markoe,[23] who has taken an active part in founding an institution here for the promotion of science and natural history. The day before our departure I had a long and agreeable conversation with our ex-minister, Mr. Fox,[24] whose sudden and unexpected death happened a few months later. I told him that some English travellers wondered that I should set out on a long tour when the English and American papers were descanting on the probability of a war. He said, that "when Macleod[25] was detained prisoner in 1841, there was really some risk, because he might have been hanged any day by the New Yorkers, in spite of the desire of the Federal Government to save him; but now there is no war party in England, and all reasonable men here, including the principal officers of the army, and navy, are against it. Some of the Western people may be warlike, for there are many patriots who believe that it is their destiny to rise on the ruins of the British empire; but when the President, according to treaty, shall have given notice of a partition of Oregon, there will be time for negotiation. If one of two disputants threatens to knock the other down eighteen months hence, would you apprehend immediate mischief?" "They are not arming," said I. "No augury can be drawn from that fact," he replied; "the people are against large peace establishments, knowing that there is no fear of hostile attacks from without unless they provoke them, and satisfied that their wealth and population are annually increasing. They are full of courage, and would develop extraordinary resources in a war, however much they would suffer at the first onset."

We then conversed freely on the future prospects of civilisation in the North American continent. He had formed far less sanguine expectations than I had, but confessed, that though he had resided so many years in the country, he knew little or nothing of the Northern States, especially of New England. When I dwelt on the progress I had witnessed, even in four years, in the schools and educational institutions, the increase of readers and of good books, and the preparations making for future scientific achievements, he frankly admitted that he had habitually contemplated the Union from a somewhat unfavourable point of view. I observed to him that Washington was not a metropolis, like London, nor even like Edinburgh or Dublin, but a town which had not thriven in spite of government patronage. The members of Congress did not bring their families to it, because it would often take them away from larger cities, where they were enjoying more refined and intellectual society. It was as if the Legislature of the British empire, representing not only England, Scotland, and Ireland, but Canada, Newfoundland, the West Indies, Australia, the Cape, and all the other dependencies of the British crown, were to meet in some third-rate town. Nor even then would the Comparison be a fair one, because if there be one characteristic more than another which advantageously distinguishes three-fourths of the American population, it is the high social, intellectual, and political condition, relatively speaking, of the working classes. The foreign diplomatist residing in Washington lives within the borders of the slave territory, where the labourers are more degraded, and perhaps less progressive, than in any European state. Besides, the foreign ambassador, in his official and political capacity, too often sees exposed the weak side of the constitution of the Union, and has to deplore the powerlessness of the federal executive to carry out its own views, and to control the will of thirty independent States, or as many *imperia in imperio*.[26] Just when he may have come to an understanding with the leading statesmen on points of international law, so that his negotiations in any other metropolis would have been brought to a successful issue, he finds that the real difficulties are only beginning. It still remains to be seen whether the government is strong enough to contend with the people, or has the will so to act, or whether it will court popularity by yielding to their prejudices, or even exciting their passions. Such is at this moment the position of affairs, and of our minister at Washington.

"We are the Same People"

From *Travels in the United States, etc., During 1849 and 1850* by Lady Emmeline Stuart-Wortley.

Lady Emmeline Charlotte Elizabeth Stuart-Wortley, née Manners (1806-1855) was a prolific Victorian-era editor and writer of poetry, plays, prose and travelogues. The daughter of the 5th Duke of Rutland, she spent her youth at the 11th century Castle Belvoir and became a widow of independent means upon the death of her husband in 1844.

Lady Stuart-Wortley referred to her book on the United States as "the gossip of travel." As such, she on occasion refers to people in her acquaintance by their initials or by nicknames. Among them, Madame C. de la B — and V — may be identified with some confidence. Others, such as that fine judge of hogs she calls Stentor, well, who knows?

One of Lady Stuart-Wortley's later journeys proved tragic. She would succumb to dysentery while traveling in the Ottoman Empire with V — in 1855.

---

Washington would be a beautiful city if it were built; but as it is not I cannot say much about it. There is the Capitol, however, standing like the sun, from which are to radiate majestic beams of streets and avenues of enormous breadth and astonishing length; but at present the execution limps and lingers sadly after the design.

This noble metropolitan myth hovers over the north bank of the Potomac (this Indian name means, I believe, the wild swan, or the river of the wild swan), about one hundred and twenty miles from Chesapeake bay and at the head of tide water. Pennsylvania Avenue is splendid: it is about three hundred feet broad; but the houses are not colossal enough to be in keeping with the immense space appropriated to the thoroughfare. They should be at least as high as the highest of old Edinburgh houses, instead of like those of London, which some one compared to the Paris ones making a profound curtsey. Now these Pennsylvania Avenue habitations seem making a very distant curtsey indeed to their opposite non-neighbours; and it made us think of people at an immensely wide dining-table, separated as "far as the poles asunder" by way of a pleasing rencontre and social intercourse. However, that is merely fancy; you do not want to talk across the streets; and this appearance would vanish if the houses were taller and larger.

Washington is called the "City of Magnificent Distances:"[1] it reminds one a little of a vast plantation with the houses purposely kept far apart to give them room to grow and spread: the "sidewalks" of Pennsylvania Avenue are twenty-six feet wide.

My unseen friend, Stentor,[2] was in the same railroad car with us from Baltimore to this place, and the gentleman who was hard of hearing as well at least I can hardly think there can be two sets of lungs of such marvellous power in the same country. Still, the theme of his discourse was very different; one subject occupied him all the way, — it was hogs. The car was full, I was at some distance from him, but no other voice was heard — how could it be? Poor Stentor! he was lamenting with a most lachrymose roar, the abduction of some magnificent swine: their size was something prodigious, unparalleled (*maestoso*), their fat (in a melting tone) unheard of, — they were Stentor's! The howl with which this dreadful fact was enunciated made one start.

But this was not all. Some friends, possessors of almost equally enchanting animals, had lost theirs too. "One wonderfully splendid creature of enormous dimensions (emphatically expressed in a perfect hurrah), and promising to grow much huger, was found killed (this in a lackadaisical bellow of grief and ire), supposed to be with a spiteful motive, but the wretches will suffer for it, (a nine-times-nine, and-one-cheer-more sort of a tone)! It was the most magnificent hog quite, that ever;" — and here, wonderful to relate, the noise of the railroad, together perhaps with his own emotions, overpowered the narrator. There was that terrible din that they make sometimes in the States when another train is expected. Very quickly, however, this was over, and there was Stentor shouting as loud as ever, or rather louder, as if indignant at the interruption.

"The lovely interesting widow was much afflicted," continued he. "What," thought I, "can he mean, the widow of the pig!" I found soon she was the proprietress of the fat animal he was grieving for. He thundered on in the same way, and on the same subject, till we arrived; and if he did not leave his poor friend much more deaf than he found him, it is matter of surprise. What an invaluable "muezzin"[3] he would make!

I have had the great pleasure since I came here of making acquaintance with Madame C. de la B, — the Spanish *ministress* here, the authoress of a most charming and entertaining work on Mexico, published some years ago. It made one long to go to Mexico, and I find it is not at all impracticable, from Madame C — 's account. I have a great mind to try it.[4]

We went to see the Capitol soon after our arrival. There is a fine colossal statue by Greenhough, of Washington, placed in front of it. The Capitol itself is a very noble-looking and imposing structure, though I think disadvantageously situated with regard to the city, as it seems rather to present the appearance of running away from it, while, like the flight of Louis Philippe in the memorable days of February, there is nothing running after it. However, it is an exceedingly striking and handsome building, and is otherwise very finely situated.

It is built on an elevation that is about seventy-two feet above tide water. It is of the Corinthian order of architecture, and is built of freestone; and the front, including the wings, is three hundred and fifty-two feet long, and the depth of the wings is one hundred and twenty-one feet. The projection in the main front, which looks to the East (hardly complimentary to the West, in this world of the West), is decorated by a handsome portico of twenty-two lofty Corinthian columns. The broad steps leading to the portico are adorned by pedestals, on one of which is a group in marble, representing Columbus, with a globe in his outstretched hand, and an Aboriginal American of that New World he discovered, a female figure, in a lovely, half-crouching, attitude of veneration and wonder, beside him.[5] The remaining pedestals will, in process of time, no doubt, be ornamented by groups of statuary. To the highest top of the dome the height of the building is one hundred and twenty feet. The rotunda, which is under the dome, is ninety-five feet in diameter, and the same in height. In this rotunda there are some celebrated pictures by Trumbull representing historical subjects.

The hall of the House of Representatives is in the second story of the south wing. Its form is semicircular; it is ninety-six feet long and sixty feet high, and has a dome supported by twenty-four columns of native variegated marble, whose capitals are of Italian marble. The chair of the Speaker occupies, so to say, the centre of the chord of the arc, the members' seats radiate back from the chair to the massive pillars. Congress is not sitting now. The Senate chamber is in the second story of the north wing, semicircular like the other, but of smaller dimensions, being seventy-eight feet long and forty-five feet high. The library is a fine room, containing thirty thou sand volumes.

After seeing the Capitol, we went to have a glimpse of the Navy Yard. There we beheld two mountainous-looking ship-houses, a man-of-war steamer, the *Alleghany*, lately dismantled, &c. Keeping guard on board the Alleghany, was an old Irish marine, with his face tied up for the toothache, — a most lugubrious-looking sentinel.

We saw a sadder sight after that, a large number of slaves, who seemed to be forging their own chains, but they were making chains, anchors, &c., for the United States navy. I hope and think slavery will be done away with soon in the district of Columbia, where it seems indeed strikingly out of place.[6]

Madame C. de la B — kindly took us to Georgetown a day or two ago in her carriage. It is on the left bank of the Potomac river, two miles to the west of Washington, from which it is separated by Rock creek, over which are two bridges. I think the situation of Georgetown delightful: it commands a fine view of the Potomac, of Washington, and the circumjacent country. Here you observe a number of handsome buildings and pleasant-looking country seats, and here, I believe, many of the *corps diplomatique* reside.

Dr. Heap,[7] American consul at Tunis (whom we made acquaintance with there), called on me lately. I was glad to see him, but very sorry to learn that he had had more than one melancholy loss lately. His charming daughter, Mrs. Ferrier, was in a very delicate, indeed alarming, state of health while we were there: she has since died, and she left her husband suffering from the same complaint — consumption.

Dr. Heap told me how well the Bey[8] had behaved on the occasion of the death of my poor much-esteemed friend, Sir Thomas Reade.[9] He sent two thousand troops to attend the funeral, and offered the Abdellia[10] to Lady Reade for her life, if she would like to live there. I was so much reminded of Tunis by the way in which Dr. Heap shook the forefinger of the right hand before his chin, whenever he wished to say "No." This negative sign is constantly used there; and I remember little dear Peter Reade, at five years old, gravely shaking his little finger backwards and forwards before his innocent childish countenance, when asked anything from which he dissented, as solemnly as the oldest Moor in the Regency.

The General Post-Office here is a handsome, white marble building, classical and simple. The Patent Office is to the north of it, and is a very noble structure. The Treasury is splendid, and has a colonnade of extraordinarily great length and beauty. The President's mansion, usually called the "White House," is of ample size, and of simple architecture; it has altogether a noble effect: quiet lawns surround it, and some fine trees are grouped near: it is said to be not at all in a healthy situation.

We have just paid a visit by appointment to the hero-President.[11] Madame C — kindly took us there. I was much pleased at being allowed to take V — :[12] she may never have another opportunity of being presented to a President of the United States. She was delighted at going.

General Taylor[13] received us most kindly. He had had two councils to preside over that morning, and when we first arrived at the White House, he was actually engaged in an extra Session of Council — in short, overwhelmed with business, which rendered it doubly kind and amiable of him to receive us. Mrs. Bliss,[14] the charming daughter of the President, was in the drawing-room when we first went in. Mrs. Taylor has delicate health, and does not do the honours of the Presidential mansion. Mrs. Bliss received us most cordially and courteously, saying her father would come as soon as his presence could be dispensed with. Presently after, the President made his appearance: his manners are winningly frank, simple, and kind, and though characteristically distinguished by much straightforwardness, there is not the slightest roughness in his address. There was a quick, keen, eagle-like expression in the eye which reminded me a little of the Duke of Wellington's.

He commenced an animated conversation with Madame C. de la B — and us: amongst other things, speaking of the routes, he recommended me to follow, steam navigation, Mexico, and the Rio Grande, &c.

He was so exceedingly good-natured as to talk a great deal to my little girl about roses and lilies, as if he had been quite a botanist all his life. This species of the slight, childish daffydowndilly[15] talk was so particularly and amiably considerate and kind to her, that it overcame her shyness at once, and the dread she had entertained of not understanding what he might say to her.

I was quite sorry when the time came for us to leave the White House. General Taylor strongly advised me not to leave America without seeing St. Louis: he said he considered it altogether perhaps the most interesting town in the United States: he said he recollected the greater part of it a deep dense forest. He spoke very kindly of England, and adverting to the approaching acceleration and extension of steam communication between her and America (the contemplated competition about to be established by "Collin's line"[16]) he exclaimed, "The voyage will be made shorter and shorter, and I expect England and America will soon be quite alongside of each other, ma am."

"The sooner the better, sir," I most heartily responded, at which he bowed and smiled.

"We are the same people," he continued, "and it is good for both to see more of each other."

"Yes," I replied, "and thus all detestable old prejudices will die away."

"I hope so," he said: "it will be for the advantage of both."

He continued in this strain and spoke [so nobly of England, that it made one's heart bound to hear him. And he evidently felt what he said; indeed, I am sure that honest, high hearted, true-as-steel, old hero could not say anything he did not feel or think.

A little while before we took leave he said, "I hope you will visit my farm near Natchez: Cypress Grove is the name — a sad name," he said, with a smile, "but I think you will find it interesting." I thanked him, and promised so to do. A short time previously, after talking about the beauties of Nature in the South, General Taylor had said to V — , that belonged to return to that farm, and to his quiet home near the banks of the Mississippi, and added, that he was sorely tired of public life, and the harassing responsibilities of his high office. The President insisted most courteously on conducting us to our carriage, and bareheaded he handed us in, standing on the steps till we drove off, and cordially reiterating many kind and friendly wishes for our prosperous journey, and health, and safety.

We afterwards went to Madame C — 's, and stayed some time in her pleasant house. She kindly wishes me to go to a party at her house to night, but the sudden hot weather has given me a headache, and I fear I shall not be able. It is the Indian Summer here, now, which answers to the French "Eté de St. Martin,"[17] only it is twenty times as hot. The spacious high rooms in the White House felt quite oppressively warm, and here we are suffocated with heat, though the drawing-room is a large apartment. I think it is like a July in England, when our summer has *not* "set in with its usual severity." Fans and parasols are plentiful; and there are no fires except the apparently indispensable ones which are lit, it would almost seem, for the benefit of the very numerous fire-companies here and elsewhere in the Union. ———

"No! No! ... No! No!"

From *The Homes of the New World: Impressions of America* by Fredrika Bremer.

By the time the Swedish feminist and political reformer Fredrika Bremer (1801-1865) made her lengthy visit to the United States in 1849-1851, she was already an established author and well-known in the English speaking world for her *Sketches of Everyday Life*, published in London and New York during the 1840s.

In her note "To The Reader," Bremer confesses to a degree of "egotism" in this work, making clear that her impressions of America are presented as letters to her sister, "to whom even the innermost might be revealed." The candor she suggests her work to possess is fluently wrought by the English author and editor Mary Howitt, who also translated her *Sketches* in the 1840s.

Bremer's description of the debate over the Compromise Bill, perhaps the most contentious issue in America during her visit, is a vivid portrayal of the high drama that increasingly played out in the nation's capital during the run up to the American Civil War.

---

I have visited every day the Senate and the Assembly of Representatives, though generally the former, because I hear well there, and because as a parliamentary assembly it seems, in every case, to stand above the other.

In the House of Representatives no speaker may occupy more than an hour of time. As soon as the hour is at an end, and a little bell rings, another speaker has a right to interrupt him, even should it be in the very midst of his most profound argument, or in the highest flight of his genius, and demand general attention for *his* speech, which may occupy another hour, after which he again must give place to someone else, and as the speakers in a general way speak with great ease, and have a deal to say, they are anxious to make good use their power, and that I suppose is the reason for the headlong speed with which the speech is hurled forth, like an avalanche, into the house, at least, it has been so every time I have been there. A certain kind of hurry-hurry seems to prevail in this house, which contrasts strongly with the decorum of the Senate. There, each Senator may speak as long as he will, nay even, through the whole of the session if he chose, without any one having a right to interrupt him, except to make an observation or with his consent.

During this talking however, whether in the Senate or the House of the Representatives, I am often enough minded of Mr. Poinsett's[1] words, when I praised the American talent for talking. "It is a great misfortune!" but is it better as regards this misfortune in other countries assemblies where people make speeches? And if I do sigh now and then as I listen to a speech, yet I am interested by many on account of their straightforwardness, on account of the subjects upon which they touch, or on count of the speakers themselves. I like both to see and to hear parliamentary assemblies. Human nature seems to me great, when it stands forth and does battle for some high purpose or principle, and if it be possessed power or of genius, it wins great victories; and I love see human nature great and important, to see it from its private little world, its isolated point, labour for — the whole World. And even without genius, human nature represents, as a moral power, an interesting sight, merely by its "*yes*" or "*no*." Such an assembly is in its operation a grand dramatic scene, and there sometimes occur in it scenes and episodes of much more vital effect, than many a one which we witness on the stage.

Some such, at which I have been present here, I will mention to you. But first a word about the scene itself, that is to say, the Senate, because it has an especial interest for me, inasmuch as all the senators represent States, and the characteristic and poetic features of these present themselves to my imagination, in picturesque groups, in the men who represent them. Each State in the Union sends two senators to Congress. These stand up in the Senate and are addressed not as Mr. this or that, but as the Senator of Kentucky, or Massachusetts, or Mississippi, or Louisiana, and so on; and I then immediately see before me an image of Kentucky, or Massachusetts, or Mississippi, or Louisiana, according to what I know of the life and temperament of the States, as well in spirit as in natural scenery, even though the human representative may not answer to it; and the whole fashion and form of this hemisphere stands before me like a great drama, in which Massachusetts and Louisiana, Carolina and Pennsylvania, Ohio and Alabama, and many others, are acting powers with definite individuality. Individuality is again supplied by the surname, which chance, or the humour of the people, have given to some of the States, and according to which it would be easy to christen all. Thus I behold here the Emperor-State (New York), the Granite State (New Hampshire); the Key-stone State (Pennsylvania); the Wolverines (Michigan); and many other tilt and combat with the Giant State (Kentucky); with the Palmetto State (Carolina); the French State (Louisiana), and so on. And the warfare that goes on about the Gold State called also the Pacific State (California), calls forth all those marked features and circumstances which distinguish and separate the Northern and the Southern States, and which set them in opposition one to the other. I will now tell you what the great apple of contention oks like, which has been here fought for during the last seven months. Behold! —

## THE COMPROMISE BILL.

*The admission of California as a State into the Union, the arrangement of Territorial Administration for Utah* (the Mormon State) *and New Mexico, as well the project for determining the western and north-western boundary of Texas.*

And now a word in explanation: in order that a State can have a right to be admitted as such into the Union is necessary for it to have a population of, at least, 55,000 souls. Until then every separate portion of the United States' land is called territory and is governed, during the period of its development and minority, more immediately by the Federal Administration which appoints a governor and other officials, and furnishes troops to defend the inhabitants against the Indians or other enemies whatever they may be, of whom the population of the Territory may complain. Every State in the Union has right to form its own laws, on condition that they do it encroach upon the enactments of the other Federal States, as well as that the form of government be republican. The Territory again has not the privileges of the State, and people are not yet agreed as to how far its privileges of self-government ought to extend. Well now; California, the population of which became suddenly augmented to above 150,000 souls, principally by emigration from the free North-Eastern States, desires to be admitted into the Union as a Free State. New Mexico, which in consequence of the Mexican law, is free from slavery, and Utah which calls its young population. "Latter-Day Saints," desire also, as Territory, resolutely to oppose the introduction of slavery.

But as these three States, — that which has attained its majority as well as those which yet remain in their minority — are situated below a geographical line, called the Missouri line, which accordingly to ancient agreement is to constitute the line of separation between the Free States and the Slave States, so that all the States north of this line shall have a right to be free from slaves, and all States lying to the south of it have a right to slaves and slave-labour; and as three new States would disturb the balance of political power between the North and the South and give the preponderance to the North and the Free States, therefore do all the men of the South — yet not all!— cry "No! No!" to this; and the ultras amongst them add, "rather will we break with the North and form ourselves into a separate Union— the Southern States' Union! We will declare war against the North!"

The Southerners insist upon it that both California and New Mexico shall be open to receive their slave-institutions, and beyond this they insist that Congress shall pass a law forbidding the Free States to give harbourage and protection to fugitive slaves, and that it shall give to them, the Southerners, the right to demand and obtain the aid of the legislative power in the Free States, for the recovery, of their human property.

To this the men of the North shout "No! No!" with all their might. And the ultras of their party, add, "Rather, bloody war! We will never consent to Slavery! Away with Slavery! We will remain a free people! Congress shall pass a law to forbid slavery in every new State."

Many of the Southerners admit in the meantime the right of California to enter the Union as a free State, but deny to the Territories any right to legislate for themselves on the question of Slavery. The Southerners in general maintain that they do not contend for the cause of slavery, but for States' rights and the cause of the Constitution. Many are right in this assertion, but with many others, it is easy to see that the interests of slavery colour their opposition.

Other questions of contention belong to the same category, as for instance, whether Columbia, the district which Washington stands, shall continue to hold slaves or not. There is at the present time, within sight of the Capitol, a gloomy, grey building, half-buried in trees, as if ashamed of itself, that is a Slave-pen, where slaves are brought up or kept for sale. Washington is situated in the Slave State of Maryland. One portion of the Southerners are anxious to maintain, even here, their beloved domestic institutions, as the phrase is. Another point of contention is the question about the boundaries between Texas and Mexico, and about a strip of land between the Slave-State and the yet free territory, or which shall have, and which shall give up, this piece; and freedom and Slavery get to fighting anew on this ground about this piece of land.

Such is the aspect which this great apple of discord presents, an actual gordian knot which seems to demand the sword of an Alexander to sever.

Henry Clay's[2] scheme of compromise says, California shall be introduced into the Union as a free state, according to her wishes; because her population of nearly 200,000 have a right to determine their measures. New Mexico shall wait for the determination of the law, until le is possessed of a population large enough to constitute state. She shall, in the meantime, continue to be a Territory without slaves. And the same with regard to Utah.

On the contrary, the Slave States shall possess the right to demand the restoration of their fugitive slaves, and, if it be necessary, to regain them by the aid of law, as the constitution has decreed.

Columbia[3] shall be a free district, from which slaver shall be banished.

These, I believe, are the principal points of Clay's scheme to bring about peace between the North and South. Both North and South, however, demand greater concession, each on his own side, and exclaim "No! No!" to the Compromise Bill.

This bill, which has many clauses introduced under the same head, all of which Clay wishes to have carried at the same time, has thence obtained the name of "the Omnibus Bill," and is contested under this appellation. Many Senators, who go with Clay on certain points, have separated from him on others; and it seems as if the Omnibus Bill, as such, had nearly the whole Senate against it, although some special questions seem likely to be decided according to Clay's views, among which is the principal one of California's admission into the Union as a free state but even they who are agreed on important points may fall out with each other about trifles; and the other day I heard Mississippi sharply taken to task by Mississippi for his "dis-union tendency," on which the other half of Mississippi cried "Shame on dis-unionists!"

But now for a little about the *dramatis personæ,* or such of them as appear to me most remarkable.

Henry Clay has his seat against the wall, to the right of the entrance, is always there, attentive, lively, following the discussion, throwing in now and then a word, and not unfrequently taking himself the lead in it. His cheek and eye have a feverish glow, his voice and words art always energetic, urged on by the impulsiveness of the soul, and compel attention; his arguments are to the purpose, striking, and seeming to me to bear the stamp of strong conviction, ought to produce conviction in others and when his strong resounding voice thunders the battle-cry *"California"* (the last syllable of which he sounds in a peculiar manner) through the Senate, amid the fight for the freedom of California, then they feel that the old warrior leads them forth to victory. Although born in a slave state, Kentucky, and its representative, and though a slave-holder himself. Clay's sympathies are evidently wholly and entirely in favour of the system of freedom; and at the opening of this session he frankly declared that he never would allow the introduction of slavery into any new state. And herein I recognise the great statesman and the free son of the New World. On a former occasion also, he proposed a plan by which to free his native land from slavery, and which does not seem to be an. impracticable one. It is this: that all children born of slaves, after a certain year, I believe that it was this present year of 1850, should be declared free, and should be brought up in a humane manner in schools, and should be taught mechanical arts and handicraft trades. This project so noble in its intention, so practical, and which in so rational a manner opens the way for a twofold emancipation, has nevertheless been rejected. The ultras, on both sides, in the Anti-Slavery and Pro-Slavery camps will not hear of it. I believe that the concession which Clay, whilst he is combating for the freedom of California and the neutrality of Mexico, makes to the Southern States, in yielding to their demands with regard to the restoration of their fugitive slaves, is a measure rendered imperative by the necessity of the moment. Since I have been in the Slave States, and seen and heard the bitterness which exists there, in particular in South Carolina, against the conduct and interference of the Northerners in the question of slavery, — since I have often heard the wish expressed for separation from the North, which ferments there, and which even makes itself seen in the Senate, I consider this concession to be necessary for the prevention of civil war at the present moment; whilst the feelings of the South are afresh irritated by the probable accession to the North, of California, and eve of New Mexico, and Utah into its group of States. The concession has its legal ground, inasmuch as conformable with the constitution of the United States, the States are bound to respect each other's laws, and according to the laws of the Slave States, the slaves constitute a portion of the slave-holder's lawful property.

I perfectly understand the bitterness which the supporters of Anti-Slavery principles must feel at the thought that their free soil may not be an asylum for the unfortunate slave, and that the slave-catcher may there have a free career, and demand the assistance of the officials of the free states. I know that I myself would rather suffer death than give up an unfortunate slave who had taken refuge with me; but is there, at this moment, an alternative between this concession and civil war? Clay seems to consider that there is not, and Daniel Webster[4] seems to coincide with him, though he has not, as yet, expressed himself openly on Clay's Compromise Bill.

I believe that Clay makes this concession reluctantly, and that he would not have proposed it, if he had regarded it as anything more than temporary, if his own large heart and his statesman's eye had not convinced him that the time is not far distant when the noble hearts' impulse of the South will impel them voluntarily to a nobler, humaner legislation as regards the slave-question; and that urged on necessarily by the liberal movement of humanity, as well in Europe, as in America, the New World will rid itself of this its greatest lie.

And this I also believe, thanks to the noble minds with which I became acquainted in the South, — thanks to the free South, which grows and extends itself in the bosom of the Slave States; and who can feel the movement of the spirit over the whole of this vast world's formation without feeling that the spirit of God floats over the deep, and will divide light from darkness by his almighty — "Be thou light!" The crimson of dawn is already on the hills, and tinging the tops of the forest-trees. He who will see it, may! I do not dread the darkness conquering here.

Near Clay, and before him in the row of seats, you see the representative of the Granite State, Mr. Hale,[5] from

New Hampshire, with a head not unlike that of Napoleon, and a body and bearing like a great fat boy; a healthy strong Highland character, immovable in his principles as the granite mountains, and with a mind as fresh as the wind which blows around them. A strong anti-slavery supporter, and inflexible towards any concession on this question, he frequently puts the whole house into the best of tempers by his humour and his witty and sarcastic sallies. I like the man very much. Near to him I see the senator from Texas (the first president of that republican Texas), General Houston,[6] who required a month to travel from his State to Washington. People listen willingly to the magnificent old general, for the sake of the picturesque and fresh descriptions which he introduces in his speeches. His expression is good-tempered and manly, with a touch of military chivalry. He has the peculiarity of cutting little bits of wood with his penknife during all the discussions in the Senate. I also see the senator from Pennsylvania, a man of Quaker-like simplicity, and with a pure and handsome countenance, among the Anti-Slavery leaders. The two senators from Ohio, Corwin and Chase,[7] are here; the former you are already acquainted with. I see him in the Senate, sitting silent and tranquil; he has already delivered his sentiments on the important subject, and now merely makes occasionally a short observation on some speech of a Southerner. Chase has a remarkably noble and handsome exterior; I have seldom seen amore noble or prouder figure. Such a man in private life must be a dominant spirit, and awaken love or hate. In public he expresses himself firmly, but in few words, for the principle of freedom.

The senator from New York, Mr. Seward,[8] is a little man, not at all handsome, and with that nasal twang which not unfrequently belongs to the sons of Boston. Seward is from that city. Yet, nevertheless, that voice has uttered, during the present session, some of the greatest and noblest thoughts. He is a stout Anti-Slavery man, and is against any compromise.

"I will labour," said he, lately, at the close of a speech, "for the support of the Union, not by concessions to slavery, but by the advancement of those laws and institutions which make her a benefactor to the whole human race." Good and great!

If I now advance from the point where I began, and on the side of the principal entrance, I find, not far from Clay, a Southerner and a champion of slavery, the senator from Georgia, Judge Berrion,[9] a man of talent and wit, and also a kind and god-fearing man, a man of refinement and high breeding, whom it grieved me to see advocating the dark side of the South, on the plea that he must maintain its rights. He stands now in opposition to Clay on the question of California's right to freedom, and the personal hostility between them has gone so far, that Clay gave up his place at our *table d'hôte*. (Clay has resumed his seat, and Berrion sits at the table).

In the middle of this camp sits the colossus Daniel Webster, in his arm-chair, with his sallow cheek and brow, and seems to be oppressed with thought, or with the heat, perhaps with both. I call him a colossus, not because I see in him an overpowering intellectual greatness, but on account of his magnificent head and massive appearance, although he is not a large figure. and because his influence is felt as something colossal. He has been extremely handsome, possessed of a natural, kingly, dignity, and is described as having, by his mere presence, exercised an almost magical power over human masses. He is now above sixty, and is still a handsome, powerful man, although years and thought seem to weigh upon him. Clay, though more than seventy, is in appearance a youth in comparison with Webster. Clay is always ready to fire off; Webster seems to deliberate carefully as to the charging of his piece before he applies the match.

The senators of Illinois, General Shield and Judge Douglas,[10] are both small men, but men of talent and even of genius. In the deep, beautiful eyes of Douglas, glows a dark fire which it is said burns with ambitious desires for the office of President; but the same desires influence Clay, Webster, Seward, and many others. He speaks but little, at least in company, but his presence is felt. He looks like an ardent, clever, and determined, little man. General Shield, fair, blue-eyed, and with an honest glance, is of a more frank character. He distinguished himself, and was severely wounded, in the war with Mexico. I love to talk with him and to hear him talk. He is an active-minded and warm American, and seems to me to understand the peculiar aspect and vocation of his country.

Let us now cast a glance into the other camp. The hawk from Missouri, Colonel Benton,[11] sits there in the midst of his own people, as well as the lion from Kentucky in the other camp, and just opposite to him. He is one of the oldest senators in Congress, and highly esteemed for his learning, his firmness, and his courage. He has fought a duel,[12] and in cold blood slowly taken aim, and in cold blood shot his man, and he looks as if he could shoot his man in cold blood still. This duel, or more correctly speaking, his behaviour in it, has cast a shadow upon his character in the eyes of many. He belongs to the population of "the Borderers," in America, to that class which springs up on the outskirts of the wilderness, and among a half-savage people, he has evidently accustomed himself to club-law; has accustomed himself to go with pistol and bowie-knife (a kind of crooked knife universal as a weapon in the Slave States, and called after its inventor), and which is carried, as our gentlemen carry a penknife and pencil, in the breast pocket. And Colonel Benton is a suitable representative of a Slave State, where the wild Missouri pours its turbid waters along its perilous course, forming the western boundaries of the savage mountain-land of the

Indian tribes, and extending eastward to the gigantic Mississippi, where heathenism still contends for dominion with Christian law, — of that yet only half-civilised Missouri may a cold-blooded duellist like Colonel Benton very well be regarded as a worthy representative, where he can, by his resolute will and his determined behaviour, make himself both esteemed and feared as a political character. In exterior he is a strong-built, powerful, broad-shouldered, broad-chested man; the forehead is lofty, and the somewhat grey hair rises thin and slightly curled above it; below gleam out a pair of lively, but cold, grey eyes, and between them shoots forth an aquiline nose; the lower part of the countenance is strong, and shows a strong will and strong animal propensities. The figure and expression are powerful, but somewhat heavy, and are deficient in nobility. He has advocated in the Senate the freedom of California, but has opposed Mr. Clay's "Omnibus Bill." In society I have found him candid, extremely polite, and kind; nevertheless there was a something within me which felt a repulsion to that cool, blood-stained hand. If it were not for this, I should like to see more of the man. His unreserved acknowledgment in the Senate that, although the representative of a Slave State, a native of a Slave State, and himself a slave-holder, *he yet regarded slavery as an evil*, and should regard it as a *crime* to aid in the extension of the *curse* to territory which had hitherto been free; this manly, candid declaration, from a man in his position, deserves all esteem, and his vivid description of nature and the circumstances of life in the Western lands, shows both knowledge and talent.

Near to the senator from Missouri, and most striking in the camp of the Southerners, stands forth Soulé,[13] the senator of Louisiana, and forming a strong contrast to the former. The hawk of Missouri is a proper representative of the State, with the wild river and the richly metallic mountains, the boundary of the Indians. The land where the orange glows, where the sugar-cane flourishes, and where French civilisation and French manners have been naturalised ever since they fled thither from France at the period of its extremest refinement; that flowery, beautiful Louisiana could not have sent to Congress a more worthy representative than the French Consul Soulé. Possessed of that beauty peculiar to the South, with its delicate features, eyes and hair of that rich dark colour which distinguish the Spaniards, and also the handsomest portion of the French population, Soulé has that grace of manner and expression which is found among the men of these nations, and which is not met with among the Anglo-Saxons and Northmen, however good and handsome they may be. Soulé has come forward in the Senate on the Californian question, to advocate "the rights of the South," but always as a man of genius and tact; and on the occasion of a resolution which was opposed to the interests of Louisiana as a Slave State; he also declared himself for the preservation of the Union. His great speech produced a great effect, and I have heard it praised by many. I have read it, and find nothing in it to admire as of a superior character. The rights of the South are the highest object for which he contends, and his highest impulse is a chivalric sense of honour as regards — his own honour. "The South must not yield because the South is the weaker combatant. If the South shall be conquered, no blush of shame must tinge her cheek."

Soulé is a French knight, but not of the highest order, not a Bayard nor a Turenne.

Mr. Dickinson,[14] a cold-blooded senator from Alabama, a man of an acute and stern aspect, highly esteemed for integrity of character in the camp of the Southerners, sits near the inflammable Mississippi, that is to say, the younger of the senators from that State, a young man of handsome person and inflammable temperament, who talks violently for "Southern rights."[15] The other, and elder senator of Mississippi, Mr. Foote,[16] is a little, thin, and also fiery man, whom I believe to be a really warm patriot. He stands for the Union, and his most brilliant moments are when he hurls himself into a violent dithyrambic against all and each who threaten it. The explosions of his indignant feelings almost lift him up from the earth, as the whole of his slender but sinewy frame responds in vehement agitation to the apostrophes of the spirit. These are sometimes so keen and full of rebuke that I wonder at the coolness with which the Senate, and certain senators in particular, listen to them: but it seems to me as if they listened with that sort of feeling with which a connoisseur regards the clever work of an artist. For the rest, Mr. Foote is always on the alert, quick to interrupt, to make observations, and sometimes calls forth by his mercurial temperament a universal smile, but of a good-natured kind, as at the bottom is Mr. Foote himself

Near the combustible Mississippi I see a young man, also handsome, and with features bearing a remarkable resemblance to those of the Indian. That is the senator from Virginia — his name has escaped my memory — and he is said to be a descendant of Pocahontas, the Indian heroine of Virginia. For my part, this is the most remarkable thing about him. [17]

But now, my child, you must have had enough for to-day of politics and political gentlemen. I shall write more when I have seen more.

Two deputies from the Mormonites may also be seen in the Senate, (yet not within the Senate, but in the outer court) who present to Congress the request from the Mormon people — now rapidly increased to the number of 12,000 souls — to be admitted into the Union, and the protection of its troops against the Indians. This remarkable sect, has, since it was expelled from its first settlement on the Mississippi by the people of Illinois, wandered far out into the West beyond the Indian wilderness, Nebraska; and have founded a flourishing community, in a fertile valley bordering on a vast inland lake, called the great Salt Lake, in Upper California. I have not yet heard anything very creditable about the government or the customs of the people. Their bible, however, the Mormon Bible, I have been able to borrow here. It contains first the whole Christian Bible, after that an addition of some later pretended prophets, of whom Meroni and Mormon are the last.[18] In the prophecies of these men is given a closer and more definite prophecy of Christ, nay indeed, almost the whole of his history, and many of his words, but nothing new in religious doctrine, as far as I can discover. The peculiarity of the sect seems to be based upon the assertion, that their prophet Joe Smith is descended directly from these later Christian prophets, and has obtained, by miraculous communication, portions of their books as well also as of their spiritual gifts and power to communicate these gifts to others, by which means they are all brought into a closer .communication with Christ than any other Christians.

How a man, who evidently in many cases was a deceiver, could obtain so great an influence over thousands of people in the present Christian state of society, and was able to form them into a vast organised body, according to his law, seems scarcely comprehensible, unless it be by supposing that this man was really possessed of some extraordinary powers, partly of a prophetic kind, (and we hear of many such, similar to the oldest prophetic skill, even in the present day, as, for instance, the second-sight of the Scotch Highlanders), and partly of worldly prudence. He was shot during the war with Illinois, and he is said to have distinctly foretold the time, and the manner of his death — but the Mormon people continue to be led by men who adhere to his laws, and who pretend to be guided by his spirit. The habits and organisation of the community is said to be according to the Christian moral code, and extremely severe. ⸺

"In Charge was a Door-Keeper"

From *Things as They Are in America* by William Chambers.

William Chambers (1800-1883) was a Scot, a Fellow of the Royal Society of Edinburgh, and co-founder with his brother Robert of the 19th century publishing firm W. & R. Chambers, which, during the 1860s, would publish *Chambers's Encyclopædia*, then an essential English-language reference work.

In September, 1853, after a nearly calamitous experience aboard a Mersey tender, Chambers boarded the Cunard *America* in Liverpool, bound for Halifax, Nova Scotia. His circuit in the United States was similar to that of previous travelers; various stops in pre-Confederation Canada, select cities among the New England states, venturing no further south than Richmond, Virginia, and the obligatory stop in Washington, D.C., which, such as it is he observes, can be "seen in a single forenoon."

---

It was dark before the train reached Washington. About nine o'clock, it drew up at a handsome station,[1] outside of which were in waiting a string of carriages, invitingly open for passengers. By the recommendation of my new naval friend, I seated myself in that belonging to Willard's Hotel,[2] and was in a few minutes riding towards the further extremity of the city. The moon shone out as we passed the Capitol, and by its silvery light revealed a large white edifice, with a dome towering above us, on the summit of a commanding eminence. At the distance of a mile westward along Pennsylvania Avenue, the termination of my long day's journey was reached; and I thankfully sought refreshment and repose.

Travellers do not usually speak flatteringly of Washington. Everyone seems to think it his duty to have a slap at its pretensions, which fall so very far short of the reality. It is my misfortune in this, as in some other things, to differ from most of my predecessors, and to see little ground for either sarcasm or jocularity. All that can be said of Washington is, that it is a city in process of being built and occupied; and has already, since its commencement about sixty years ago, acquired a population of 40,000,[3] independently of an increase from members of the legislature with their families, and visitors, during the sessions of Congress. After the witticisms at its alleged spectral appearance, I was rather surprised to discover that, instead of a few mansions scattered about among trees, with miles of interval, it consisted of a number of streets lined with continuous rows of houses, several fine public buildings, and a fair show of stores and hotels. Why the Americans should aim at building a city specially for the accommodation of their government, is not quite clear to the minds of Europeans, who are accustomed to great overgrown capitals in which the wealth and grandeur of a nation are concentrated. Originating partly in the wish to remove the administration beyond the immediate action of popular influences, Washington, I believe, owes its rise chiefly to the desirableness of placing the political metropolis in a locality apart from, and independent of, any particular state. The situation, though no longer equidistant from the several states in the Union, was exceedingly well chosen by the great man whose name was given to the city.

The Chesapeake Bay, one of the largest inlets of the Atlantic, receives, about half-way up on the western side, the large river Potomac, itself for a long way up a kind of firth or sea two to three miles in width. Where it narrows to about a mile, at the distance of 290 miles from the Atlantic, the Potomac parts into two branches; and between these, on the left or eastern bank of the principal branch, Washington has been erected. The peninsula so selected, is spacious, with gentle slopes, and would afford accommodation for a city many miles in extent. On a central ridge of ground, with a stretch of open downs between it and the Potomac, stands the principal portion of the city; the Capitol, or seat of legislation, being at the eastern extremity, on a detached eminence, and the house of the President on the top of a rising-ground a mile westward.

Planned wholly on paper[4] before a single house was built, the thoroughfares have been arranged in parallel, rectangular, and diagonal lines: those which run in one direction being called from the letters of the alphabet; and those which cross them being named First, Second, Third Street; and so on.[5] The diagonal thoroughfares, the most important of all, are styled Avenues; and of these Pennsylvania may be considered the principal. I should think this is the widest street in the world. It measures 160 feet in width — the whole of the middle part for carriages being as well paved as the streets of London, and the foot-walks laid with stone or brick. Along the sides of these footpaths are rows of trees, imparting an agreeable shade in the heats of summer. Built of brick, red sandstone, or wood, the houses throughout the city are of the smart and tasteful kind seen in the northern states; and as there is plenty of space for mews-lanes, nothing incongruous is obtruded on the eye of the stranger, unless it be the number of negroes of both sexes, principally slaves. At the period of my visit, much was doing in the way of levelling and paving the streets; and I learned that the value of property had lately risen considerably.

Having surmounted the initiatory difficulties, Washington may now be said to be in a course of improvement creditable to the liberality of the nation; for all public works are undertaken at the expense of the Treasury. The district of Columbia, in which the city is placed — a small territory, formerly a part of Maryland, and possessing no separate political character — is under the administration of Congress. Complaints are occasionally heard of the expenses to which the country is put on account of Washington; but if the people only knew the sums lavished by parliament on the palaces, parks, and police of the British metropolis, at the cost of the entire United Kingdom, they would have reason to be thankful for being so mercifully dealt with.

As yet, comprehended within a narrow compass, and open in all quarters to visitors, Washington may be satisfactorily seen in a single forenoon. The first thing done is to visit the Capitol, which is observed standing proudly on its eminence, surrounded by an enclosed pleasure-ground, at the eastern extremity of Pennsylvania Avenue. In walking down this principal thoroughfare on the morning after my arrival, there was little bustle to remind one of being in a political metropolis of some celebrity. In the long line of street, there appeared only an omnibus on its way to George Town, in the vicinity, and one or two hackney-cabs. As the morning was fine, the steps of the various hotels were already crowded with lately arrived members of Congress; and the various parties clustering in debate, shewed that matters in connection with the approaching proceedings were in agitation. Built of light-coloured stone,[6] and in the Corinthian style of architecture, the Capitol, with its wings, hand-some portico, and lofty dome, is an edifice of imposing appearance. Advancing up the exterior flights of steps, and entering the portal, we are ushered into a central rotunda, ninety-five feet in diameter, and lighted from the cupola above. On the walls around this spacious vestibule, and on a level with the eye, are placed a series of large pictures representing scenes in American history; two of which, the surrender of Burgoyne and of Cornwallis, cannot but bring unpleasant recollections to the mind of the English visitor. Chairs are placed in front of the pictures, for the benefit of strangers, who are further accommodated with a printed key to the figures. At different points, doors lead to inner lobbies, whence access is gained to the Hall of the House of Representatives, and to the Senate-chamber, the Library, and other rooms — all so frequently described, that I spare any account of them on the present occasion. I must not omit, however, to mention one thing, from its extreme novelty. This is the perfect liberty to roam at will, without question and without payment, over the whole building. Nor is there any want of attendants ready and willing to afford any sort of information. By one of these, I was obligingly conducted to the top of the cupola, whence a splendid view was obtained of the city beneath; the two environing arms of the Potomac, beyond which were the woody hills of Virginia, forming a framework to the picture. On descending from this giddy altitude, I ventured to offer a gratuity to my conductor, which he respectfully refused, with an explanation worthy of recording: "I cannot take any money, sir, for doing my duty. I am a public officer, and paid by the public." If there be a door or gallery keeper in either House of Parliament, who would in this way refuse half-a-crown, let him by all means be named, for he must unquestionably be a prodigy!

The grounds around the building are prettily laid out with shady walks; and near the entrance is a sparkling fountain with a drinking-cup, to appease the insatiate craving for water, which seems a kind of disease among the Americans. In the grounds on the east, is the celebrated statue of Washington by Greenough;[7] it is of colossal size, in a sitting posture, and being executed in Parian marble, the effect is striking, though the spectator is not inclined to admire the exploded fancy of representing a modern soldier as a half-naked Roman. There are several other figures connected with the Capitol, but none which appears to require notice.

The public buildings I next visited were the Post-office and Patent-office, two remarkably fine edifices of white marble, near the centre of the town. The Patent-office contains a most extraordinary collection of models of articles which have been the subject of a patent; and no other spectacle could furnish so comprehensive a notion of the inventive faculties of the Americans. A spacious hall, with ranges of glass-cases lining the walls and projected across the floor, is full of every variety of object in mechanical art and science. Adjoining, are apartments devoted to the examination and enrolment of articles; and on the floor above, is a museum of natural history and objects of antiquarian interest. Compared with the treasures of the British Museum, the collection is insignificant; and as centralisation at the cost of a whole people is repugnant to the constitution of the States, it may be apprehended that the national museum will never attain the extent and grandeur exhibited in the collections of European capitals. The articles most worthy of notice are certain relics connected with American history — as, the dress, sword, and camp-equipage of General Washington, and the original document in vellum, declaratory of the independence of the States, bearing the autographs of the signers, very much faded. In a separate glass-case stands the old wooden printing-press at which Franklin wrought when a journeyman in London in 1725-6. Removed from the office in Wild Street, Lincoln's Inn Fields, where the young "American aquatic"[8] had laboured at his vocation, the machine underwent several changes of proprietors, till it was finally presented to the government of the United States by Mr. J. B. Murray of New York.[9] An inscription on a brass-plate narrates the circumstance of Franklin having visited the press in London in 1768, when he came to England as agent for Massachusetts. Among the latest additions to the attractions of Washington, the Smithsonian Institute is the most important; for it bears reference to the culture of general knowledge, on so liberal a scale as cannot but prove valuable to the community. Originating in the bequest of an English gentleman named Smithson,[10] in favour of the United States' government, a large sum has been appropriated to the erection of a building of red sandstone[11] in the Norman style of architecture, comprising a number of towers and pinnacles. The building occupies a favourable situation in the middle of a lawn, nineteen acres in extent, to the south of the city, near the road towards the Potomac. On visiting it, I found that it was not yet finished. But the main portions, consisting of a library and lecture-room, were open, both being free to all. Some valuable treatises have already appeared for general distribution at the expense of the institution. About a quarter of a mile westward, overlooking the Potomac, a gigantic obelisk was in course of erection to the memory of General Washington — to whom, with all deference, the multiplicity of such testimonials becomes a little tiresome, besides tending to suggest that America has never produced any other person worthy of commemoration. This enormous pile, which is designed to reach 600 feet from the ground, is reared by voluntary subscription throughout the United States. I suppose nothing since the days of the Pyramids has been built on so stupendous a scale.

When a stranger has seen these things, there is nothing left to do but take a look at the mansion of the President, and the adjoining buildings devoted to the Treasury and other administrative offices. To this quarter — the court end of the town, as I may call it — I now adjourned, for the purpose of calling on a gentle-man connected with the government. Here, I have pleasure in saying, I was received in the same perfectly urbane and unceremonious manner I had uniformly experienced in my interviews with officials in all the places I had visited. "You will call on the President, of course," said this newly acquired friend. "I should be glad to do so," I replied; "but I know no one to introduce me. I know nothing of the etiquette to be employed on the occasion." "Come along with me, and I will introduce you. The President is perfectly accessible." So saying, we set out immediately; and after crossing an enclosed patch of pleasure-ground, arrived at the White House, which has a fine look-out from the brow of an eminence, in a southerly direction, over the Potomac. The edifice, with a lofty portico of Ionic columns on its northern front, has a massive effect, with accommodation, I should think, for a large establishment. Neither as regards exterior nor interior appearances, however, was there anything to remind the stranger that the occupant was the head of a great nation. After seeing pretty nearly all the royal palaces in Europe, and being accustomed to observe that the persons of monarchs were surrounded, either for safety or distinction, with military guards, I was much struck with the total absence of force in any shape around the dwelling of the President; which, undefended from real or imaginary violence, can only, in the simplicity of its arrangements, be compared with a gentleman's residence in a quiet rural district. The only person in charge was a door-keeper, who admitted us to one of the lower reception-rooms—a large apartment, decorated in the French style—in which we paced about a few minutes till our cards were carried upstairs to the President, who was said to be engaged with his cabinet. "Mention to the President," said my conductor, in giving the cards, "that this is a gentleman from Europe."

Whether this recommendation had any effect, I know not; but after a short delay, we were requested to ascend. In going up stairs, my friend introduced me to several members of the House of Representatives, who were coming down. Two of them, I was after-wards informed, had been originally operative brick-layers, who, by a course of industry and self-culture, had raised themselves to an honourable position. Almost immediately on reaching the assigned apartment, General Pierce[12] entered from a side-room, and shaking hands, received me in a most agreeable manner; at the same time stating, that he was now much occupied, and hoped to have the pleasure of seeing me again before my departure from Washington. He was in a plain black dress, apparently about forty-five years of age, and I thought care-worn by the ceaseless and onerous duties he is called on to perform. I regret that the demands on my time did not permit my waiting for any of the soirees at the White House, which usually commence with the congressional sittings; and it was not, therefore, my good-fortune to see any more of the President, to whom I am, however, indebted for the affable manner in which he was pleased to receive me. Returning to my hotel, I pondered on the singularly simple forms by which the President of the United States regulates his personal intercourse with the world.

I spent another day in Washington, making inquiries of various kinds, and forming some agreeable acquaintances in the place. It had been suggested to me, that I should, as a matter of duty, call on the British minister.[13] I endeavoured to do so; but after wandering about for two hours in a straggling suburb, west from the President's house, where his excellency was said to dwell, I failed in discovering his residence; no one to whom I applied knowing anything at all about it.[14] In these and other rambles about Washington, the number of negro slaves, of both sexes and all ages, in the streets and doorways, and serving in various capacities, was exceedingly conspicuous; and this anomalous feature in the social condition of the capital, within the very precincts of the executive and legislature, was felt to lower the respect which, on general grounds, we are disposed to entertain towards the federal government. It would almost seem as if Congress were ashamed of the existence of slavery within the district over which it exercises a municipal sway.

"The Saddest Spot on Earth"

From *North America* by Anthony Trollope.

Anthony Trollope (1815-1882) was the son of that earlier and by now notoriously well-known visitor to the United States, Mrs. Francis Trollope. While the son is surely the better novelist (see *Barchester Towers* and the *Palliser* novels), he must have learned the value of prodigious output from his mother.

Anthony Trollope states in the Introduction to his *North American* that writing a book about America was a life-long ambition, and that he intended to describe the social and political state of the country as he found it. Perhaps by way of distinction, he also referred to his mother's *Domestic Manners of the Americans* as "essentially a woman's book."

Trollope covered a lot of ground in writing about the United States. That is to say, he visited much of the country, yes, but he also wrote at length about issues beyond mere touring, such as the federal government, the Congress, the Constitution, the causes of the Civil War, the military, slavery, the circumstances of women in American society, etc. He also wrote about the Post Office, the latter subject owing to the fact that he himself was at various times employed in this particular aspect of civil service back home.

Trollope's digressions into political and military matters and mostly excluded in the selections below in order to focus on his still lengthy ruminations about the nation's capital. Whether or not they are sufficiently representative of "a man's book" is left to the reader to decide.

---

The site of the present city of Washington was chosen with three special views; firstly, that being on the Potomac it might have the full advantage of water-carriage and a seaport; secondly, that it might be so far removed from the seaboard as to be safe from invasion; and, thirdly, that it might be central alike to all the States. It was presumed when Washington was founded that these three advantages would be secured by the selected position. As regards the first, the Potomac affords to the city but few of the advantages of a sea-port. Ships can come up, but not ships of large burthen. The river seems to have dwindled since the site was chosen; and at present it is, I think, evident that Washington can never be great in its shipping. *Statio benefida carinis*[1] can never be its motto. As regards the second point, singularly enough Washington is the only city of the Union that has been in an enemy's possession since the United States became a nation. In the war of 1812 it fell into our hands, and we burnt it. As regards the third point, Washington, from the lie of the land, can hardly have been said to be centrical at any time. Owing to the irregularities of the coast, it is not easy of access by railway from different sides. Baltimore would have been far better. But as far as we can now see, and as well as we can now judge, Washington will soon be on the borders of the nation to which it belongs, instead of at its centre. I fear, therefore, that we must acknowledge that the site chosen for his country's capital by George Washington has not been fortunate.

I have a strong idea, which I expressed before in speaking of the capital of the Canadas, that no man can ordain that on such a spot shall be built a great and thriving city. No man can so ordain even though he leave behind him, as was the case with Washington, a prestige sufficient to bind his successors to his wishes. The political leaders of the country have done what they could for Washington. The pride of the nation has endeavoured to sustain the character of its chosen metropolis. There has been no rival, soliciting favour on the strength of other charms. The country has all been agreed on the point since the father of the country first commenced the work. Florence and Rome in Italy have each their pretensions; but in the States no other city has put itself forward for the honour of entertaining Congress. And yet Washington has been a failure. It is commerce that makes great cities, and commerce has refused to back the General's choice. New York and Philadelphia, without any political power, have become great among the cities of the earth. They are beaten by none except by London and Paris. But Washington is but a ragged, unfinished collection of unbuilt broad streets, as to the completion of which there can now, I imagine, be but little hope.

Of all places that I know it is the most ungainly and most unsatisfactory; — I fear I must also say the most presumptuous in its pretensions. There is a map of Washington accurately laid down; and taking that map with him in his journeyings a man may lose himself in the streets, not as one loses oneself in London between Shoreditch and Russell Square,[2] but as one does so in the deserts of the Holy Land, between Emmaus and Arimathea.[3] In the first place no one knows where the places are, or is sure of their existence, and then between their presumed localities the country is wild, trackless, unbridged, uninhabited, and desolate. Massachusetts Avenue runs the whole length of the city, and is inserted on the maps as a full-blown street, about four miles in length. Go there, and you will find yourself not only out of town, away among the fields, but you will find yourself beyond the fields, in an uncultivated, undrained wilderness. Tucking your trousers up to your knees, you will wade through the bogs, you will lose yourself among rude hillocks, you will be out of the reach of humanity. The unfinished dome of the Capitol will loom before you in the distance, and you will think that you approach the ruins of some western Palmyra.[4] If you are a sportsman, you will desire to shoot snipe within sight of the President's house. There is much unsettled land within the States of America, but I think none so desolate in its state of nature as three-fourths of the ground on which is supposed to stand the city of Washington.

The city of Washington is something more than four miles long, and is something more than two miles broad. The land apportioned to it is nearly as compact as may be, and it exceeds in area the size of a parallelogram four miles long by two broad. These dimensions are adequate for a noble city, for a city to contain a million of inhabitants. It is impossible to state with accuracy the actual population of Washington, for it fluctuates exceedingly. The place is very full during Congress, and very empty during the recess. By which I mean it to be understood that those streets, which are blessed with houses, are full when Congress meets. I do not think that Congress makes much difference to Massachusetts Avenue. I believe that the city never contains as many as eighty thousand, and that its permanent residents are less than sixty thousand.

But, it will be said, — was it not well to prepare for a growing city? Is it not true that London is choked by its own fatness, not having been endowed at its birth or during its growth, with proper means for accommodating its own increasing. proportions? Was it not well to lay down fine avenues and broad streets, so that future citizens might find a city well prepared to their hand?

There is no doubt much in such an argument, but its correctness must be tested by its success. When a man marries it is well that he should make provision for a coming family. But a Benedict, who early in his career shall have carried his friends with considerable self-applause through half-a-dozen nurseries, and at the end of twelve years shall still be the father of one rickety baby, will incur a certain amount of ridicule. It is very well to be prepared for good fortune, but one should limit one's preparation within a reasonable scope. Two miles by one might perhaps have done for the skeleton sketch of a new city. Less than half that would contain much more than the present population of Washington; and there are, I fear, few towns in the Union so little likely to enjoy any speedy increase.

Three avenues sweep the whole length of Washington; — Virginia Avenue, Pennsylvania Avenue, and Massachusetts Avenue. But Pennsylvania Avenue is the only one known to ordinary men, and the half of that only is so known. This avenue is the backbone of the city, and those streets which are really inhabited cluster round that half of it which runs westward from the Capitol. The eastern end, running from the front of the Capitol, is again a desert. The plan of the city is somewhat complicated. It may truly be called "a mighty maze, but not without a plan." The Capitol was intended to be the centre of the city. It faces eastward, away from the Potomac, — or rather from the main branch of the Potomac, and also unfortunately from the main body of the town. It turns its back upon the chief thoroughfare, upon the Treasury buildings, and upon the President's house; and indeed upon the whole place. It was, I suppose, intended that the streets to the eastward should be noble and populous, but hitherto they have come to nothing. The building therefore is wrong side foremost, and all mankind who enter it, senators, representatives, and judges included, go in at the back-door. Of course it is generally known that in the Capitol is the Chamber of the Senate, that of the House of

Representatives, and the Supreme Judicial Court of the Union. It may be said that there are two centres in Washington, this being one, and the President's house the other. At these centres the main avenues are supposed to cross each other, which avenues are called by the names of the respective States. At the Capitol, Pennsylvania Avenue, New Jersey Avenue, Delaware Avenue, and Maryland Avenue converge. They come from one extremity of the city to the square of the Capitol on one side, and run out from the other side of it to the other extremity of the city. Pennsylvania Avenue, New York Avenue, Vermont Avenue, and Connecticut Avenue do the same at what is generally called President's Square. In theory, or on paper, this seems to be a clear and intelligible arrangement; but it does not work well. These centre depots are large spaces, and consequently one portion of a street is removed a considerable distance from the other. It is as though the same name should be given to two streets, one of which entered St. James's Park at Buckingham Gate, while the other started from the Park at Marlborough House.[5] To inhabitants the matter probably is not of much moment, as it is well known that this portion of such an avenue and that portion of such another avenue are merely myths, — unknown lands away in the wilds. But a stranger finds himself in the position of being sent across the country knee-deep into the mud, wading through snipe grounds, looking for civilization where none exists.

All these avenues have a slanting direction. They are so arranged that none of them run north and south or east and west; but the streets, so called, all run in accordance with the points of the compass. Those from east to west, are A Street, B Street, C Street, and so on, — counting them away from the Capitol on each side, so that there are two A Streets, and two B Streets. On the map these streets run up to V Street, both right and left, — V Street North and V Street South. Those really known to mankind are, E, F, G,

H, I, and K Streets North. Then those streets which run from north to south are numbered First Street, Second Street, Third Street, and so on, on each front of the Capitol, running to Twenty-fourth or Twenty-fifth Street on each side. Not very many of these have any existence, or I might perhaps more properly say, any vitality in their existence.

Such is the plan of the city, that being the arrangement and those the dimensions intended by the original architects and founders of Washington; but the inhabitants have hitherto confined themselves to Pennsylvania Avenue West, and to the streets abutting from it or near to it. Whatever address a stranger may receive, however perplexing it may seem to him, he may be sure that the house indicated is near Pennsylvania Avenue. If it be not, I should recommend him to pay no attention to the summons. Even in those streets with which he will become best acquainted, the houses are not continuous. There will be a house, and then a blank; then two houses, and then a double blank. After that a hut or two, and then probably an excellent, roomy, handsome family mansion. Taken altogether, Washington as a city is most unsatisfactory, and falls more grievously short of the thing attempted than any other of the great undertakings of which I have seen anything in the States. San José, the capital of the republic of Costa Rica in Central America, has been prepared and arranged as a new city in the same way. But even San José comes nearer to what was intended than does Washington.

For myself, I do not believe in cities made after this fashion. Commerce, I think, must select the site of all large congregations of mankind. In some mysterious way she ascertains what she wants, and having acquired that, draws men in thousands round her properties. Liverpool, New York, Lyons, Glasgow, Marseilles, Hamburg, Calcutta, Chicago, and Leghorn,[6] have all become populous, and are or have been great, because trade found them to be convenient for its purposes. Trade seems to have ignored

Washington altogether. Such being the case, the Legislature and the Executive of the country together have been unable to make of Washington anything better than a straggling congregation of buildings in a wilderness. We are now trying the same experiment at Ottawa in Canada, having turned our back upon Montreal in dudgeon. The site of Ottawa is more interesting than that of Washington, but I doubt whether the experiment will be more successful. A new town for art, fashion, and politics has been built at Munich, and there it seems to answer the expectation of the builders; but at Munich there is an old city as well, and commerce had already got some considerable hold on the spot before the new town was added to it.

The streets of Washington, such as exist, are all broad. Throughout the town there are open spaces, — spaces, I mean, intended to be open by the plan laid down for the city. At the present moment it is almost all open space. There is also a certain nobility about the proposed dimensions of the avenues and squares. Desirous of praising it in some degree, I can say that the design is grand. The thing done, however, falls so infinitely short of that design, that nothing but disappointment is felt. And I fear that there is no look-out into the future which can justify a hope that the design will be fulfilled. It is therefore a melancholy place. The society into which one falls there consists mostly of persons who are not permanently resident in the capital; but of those who were permanent residents I found none who spoke of their city with affection. The men and women of Boston think that the sun shines nowhere else; — and Boston Common is very pleasant. The New Yorkers believe in Fifth Avenue with an unswerving faith; and Fifth Avenue is calculated to inspire a faith. Philadelphia to a Philadelphian is the centre of the universe, and the progress of Philadelphia, perhaps, justifies the partiality. The same thing may be said of Chicago, of Buffalo, and of Baltimore. But the same thing cannot be said in any degree of Washington. They who belong to it turn up their noses at it. They feel that they live surrounded by a failure. Its grand names are as yet false, and none of the efforts made have hitherto been successful. Even in winter, when Congress is sitting, Washington is melancholy; — but Washington in summer must surely be the saddest spot on earth.

There are six principal public buildings in Washington, as to which no expense seems to have been spared, and in the construction of which a certain amount of success has been obtained. In most of these this success has been more or less marred by an independent deviation from recognized rules of architectural taste. These are the Capitol, the Post-office, the Patent-office, the Treasury, the President's house, and the Smithsonian Institute. The five first are Grecian, and the last in Washington is called — Romanesque. Had I been left to classify it by my own unaided lights, I should have called it bastard Gothic.

The Capitol is by far the most imposing; and though there is much about it with which I cannot but find fault, it certainly is imposing. The present building was, I think, commenced in 1815, the former Capitol having been destroyed by the English in the war of 1812-13. It was then finished according to the original plan, with a fine portico and well-proportioned pediment above it, — looking to the east. The outer flight of steps, leading up to this from the eastern approach, is good and in excellent taste. The expanse of the building to the right and left, as then arranged, was well proportioned, and, as far as we can now judge, the then existing dome was well proportioned also. As seen from the east the original building must have been in itself very fine. The stone is beautiful, being bright almost as marble, and I do not know that there was any great architectural defect to offend the eye. The figures in the pediment are mean. There is now in the Capitol a group apparently prepared for a pediment, which is by no means mean. I was informed that they were intended for this position; but they, on the other hand, are too good for such a place, and are also too numerous. This set of statues is by Crawford.[7] Most of them are well known, and they are very fine. They now stand within the old chamber of the Representative House, and the pity is, that if elevated to such a position as that indicated, they can never be really seen. There are models of them at West Point, and some of them I have seen at other places m marble. The Historical Society at New York has one or two of them. In and about the front of the Capitol there are other efforts of sculpture, — imposing in their size, and assuming, if not affecting, much in the attitudes chosen. Statuary at Washington runs too much on two subjects, which are repeated perhaps almost ad nauseam; one is that of a stiff, steady-looking, healthy, but ugly individual, with a square jaw and big jowl, which represents the great General; he does not prepossess the beholder, because he appears to be thoroughly ill-natured. And the other represents a melancholy, weak figure without any hair, but often covered with feathers, and is intended to typify the red Indian. The red Indian is generally supposed to be receiving comfort; but it is manifest that he never enjoys the comfort ministered to him. There is a gigantic statue of Washington, by Greenough, out in the grounds in front of the building.[8] The figure is seated and holding up one of its arms towards the city. There is about it a kind of weighty magnificence; but it is stiff, ungainly, and altogether without life.

But the front of the original building is certainly grand. The architect who designed it[9] must have had skill, taste, and nobility of conception; but even this was spoilt, or rather wasted, by the fact that the front is made to look upon nothing, and is turned from the city. It is as though the *façade* of the London Post-office had been made to face the Goldsmiths' Hall. The Capitol stands upon the side of a hill, the front occupying a much higher position than the back; consequently they who enter it from the back — and everybody does so enter it — are first called on to rise to the level of the lower floor by a stiff ascent of exterior steps, which are in no way grand or imposing, and then, having entered by a mean back-door, are instantly obliged to ascend again by another flight, — by stairs sufficiently appropriate to a back entrance, but altogether unfitted for the chief approach to such a building. It may, of course, be said that persons who are particular in such matters, should go in at the front door and not at the back; but one must take these things as one finds them. The entrance by which the Capitol is approached is such as I have described. There are mean little brick chimneys at the left hand as one walks in, attached to modern bakeries which have been constructed in the basement for the use of the soldiers; and there is on the other hand the road by which wagons find their way to the underground region with fuel, stationery, and other matters desired by senators and representatives, — and at present by bakers also.

In speaking of the front I have spoken of it as it was originally designed and built. Since that period very heavy wings have been added to the pile; wings so heavy that they are or seem to be much larger than the original structure itself. This, to my thinking, has destroyed the symmetry of the whole. The wings, which in themselves are by no means devoid of beauty, are joined to the centre by passages so narrow that from exterior points of view the light can be seen through them. This robs the mass of all oneness, of all entirety as a whole, and gives a scattered straggling appearance where there should be a look of massiveness and integrity. The dome also has been raised, a double drum having been given to it. This is unfinished and should not therefore yet be judged; but I cannot think that the increased height will be an improvement. This again, to my eyes, appears to be straggling rather than massive. At a distance it commands attention, and to one journeying through the desert places of the city gives that idea of Palmyra which I have before mentioned.

Nevertheless, and in spite of all that I have said, I have had pleasure in walking backwards and forwards, and through the grounds which lie before the eastern front of the Capitol. The space for the view is ample, and the thing to be seen has points which are very grand. If the Capitol were finished and all Washington were built around it, no man would say that the house in which Congress sat disgraced the city.

Going west, but not due west, from the Capitol, Pennsylvania Avenue stretches in a right line to the Treasury Chambers. The distance is beyond a mile, and men say, scornfully, that the two buildings have been put so far apart in order to save the Secretaries who sit in the bureaux from a too rapid influx of members of Congress. This statement I by no means indorse; it is undoubtedly the fact that both senators and representatives are very diligent in their calls upon gentlemen high in office. I have been present on some such occasions, and it has always seemed to me that questions of patronage have been paramount. This reach of Pennsylvania Avenue is the quarter for the best shops of Washington, — that is to say, the frequented side of it is so, — that side which is on your right as you leave the Capitol. Of the of the other side the world knows nothing. And very bad shops they are. I doubt whether there be any town in the world at all equal in importance to Washington, which is in such respects so ill provided. The shops are bad and dear. In saying this I am guided by the opinions of all whom I heard speak on the subject. The same thing was told me of the hotels. Hearing that the city was very full at the time of my visit — full to overflowing — I had obtained private rooms through a friend before I went there. Had I not done so, I might have lain in the streets, or have made one with three or four others in a small room at some third-rate inn. There had never been so great a throng in the town. I am bound to say that my friend did well for me. I found myself put up at the house of one Wormley,[10] a coloured man, in I Street, to whose attention I can recommend any Englishman who may chance to want quarters in Washington. He has an hotel on one side of the street, and private lodging-houses on the other in which I found myself located. From what I heard of the hotels I conceived myself to be greatly in luck. Willard's is the chief of these, and the everlasting crowd and throng of men with which the halls and passages of the house were always full, certainly did not seem to promise either privacy or comfort. But then there are places in which privacy and comfort are not expected, — are hardly even desired, — and Washington is one of them.

The Post-office and the Patent-office[11] lie a little away from Pennsylvania Avenue in F Street, and are opposite to each other. The Post-office is certainly a very graceful building. It is square, and hardly can be said to have any settled front or any grand entrance. It is not approached by steps, but stands flush on the ground, alike on each of the four sides. It is ornamented with Corinthian pilasters, but is not over ornamented. It is certainly a structure creditable to any city. The streets around it are all unfinished, and it is approached through seas of mud and sloughs of despond, which have been contrived, as I imagine, to lessen, if possible, the crowd of callers, and lighten in this way the overtasked officials within. That side by which the public in general were supposed to approach was, during my sojourn, always guarded by vast mountains of flour-barrels. Looking up at the windows of the building I perceived also that barrels were piled within, and then I knew that the Post-office had become a provision depot for the army. The official arrangements here for the public were so bad, as to be absolutely barbarous. I feel some remorse in saying this, for I was myself treated with the utmost courtesy by gentlemen holding high positions in the office, — to which

I was specially attracted by my own connection with the Post-office in England. But I do not think that such courtesy should hinder me from telling what I saw that was bad, — seeing that it would not hinder me from telling what I saw that was good. In Washington there is but one Post-office. There are no iron pillars or wayside letter-boxes, as are to be found in other towns of the Union; — no subsidiary offices at which stamps can be bought and letters posted. The distances of the city are very great, the means of transit through the city very limited, the dirt of the city ways unrivalled in depth and tenacity; and yet there is but one Post-office. Nor is there any established system of letter carriers. To those who desire it, letters are brought out and delivered by carriers who charge a separate porterage for that service; but the rule is that letters shall be delivered from the window. For strangers this is of course a necessity of their position; and I found that when once I had left instructions that my letters should be delivered, those instructions were carefully followed. Indeed nothing could exceed the civility of the officials within; — but so also nothing can exceed the barbarity of the arrangements without. The purchase of stamps I found to be utterly impracticable. They were sold at a window in a corner, at which newspapers were also delivered, to which there was no regular ingress, and from which there was no egress. It would generally be deeply surrounded by a crowd of muddy soldiers, who would wait there patiently till time should enable them to approach the window. The delivery of letters was almost more tedious, though in that there was a method. The aspirants stood in a long line, *en cue*, as we are told by Carlyle[12] that the bread-seekers used to approach the bakers' shops at Paris during the Revolution. This "cue" would sometimes project out into the street. The work inside was done very slowly. The clerk had no facility, by use of a desk or otherwise, for running through the letters under the initials denominated, but turned letter by letter through his hand. To one questioner out of ten would a letter be given. It no doubt may be said in excuse for this that the presence of the army round Washington caused at that period special inconvenience; and that plea should of course be taken, were it not that a very trifling alteration in the management within would have remedied all the inconvenience. As a building the Washington Post-office is very good; as the centre of a most complicated and difficult department, I believe it to be well managed: but as regards the special accommodation given by it to the city in which it stands, much cannot, I think, be said in its favour.

Opposite to that which is, I presume, the back of the Post-office, stands the Patent-office. This also is a grand building, with a line portico of Doric pillars at each of its three fronts. These are approached by flights of steps, more gratifying to the eye than to the legs. The whole structure is massive and grand, and, if the streets round it were finished, would be imposing. The utilitarian spirit of the nation has, however, done much toward marring the appearance of the building, by piercing it with windows altogether unsuited to it, both in number and size. The walls, even under the porticoes, have been so pierced, in order that the whole space might be utilized without loss of light; and the effect is very mean. The windows are small and without ornament, — something like a London window of the time of George III.[13] The effect produced by a dozen such at the back of a noble Doric porch, looking down among the pillars, may be imagined.

In the interior of this building the Minister of the Interior holds his court, and of course also the Commissioners of Patents. Here is, in accordance with the name of the building, a museum of models of all patents taken out. I wandered through it, gazing with listless eye, now upon this, and now upon that; but to me, in my ignorance, it was no better than a large toy-shop. When I saw an ancient dusty white hat, with some peculiar appendage to it which was unintelligible, it was no more to me than any other old white hat. But had I been a man of science, what a tale it might have told! Wandering about through the Patent-office I also found a hospital for soldiers. A British officer was with me who pronounced it to be, in its kind, very good. At any rate it was sweet, airy, and large. In these days the soldiers had got hold of everything.

The Treasury Chambers is as yet an unfinished building. The front to the south has been completed; but that to the north has not been built. Here at the north stands as yet the old Secretary of State's office. This is to come down, and the Secretary of State is to be located in the new building, which will be added to the Treasury. This edifice will probably strike strangers more forcibly than any other in the town; both from its position and from its own character. It stands with its side to Pennsylvania Avenue, but the avenue here has turned round, and runs due north and south, having taken a twist, so as to make way for the Treasury and for the President's house, through both of which it must run had it been carried straight on throughout. These public offices stand with their side to the street, and the whole length is ornamented with an exterior row of Ionic columns raised high above the footway. This is perhaps the prettiest thing in the city, and when the front to the north has been completed, the effect will be still better. The granite monoliths which have been used, and which are to be used, in this building are very massive. As one enters by the steps to the south there are two flat stones, one on each side of the ascent, the surface of each of which is about 20 feet by 18. The columns are, I think, all monoliths. Of those which are still to be erected, and which now lie about in the neighbouring streets, I measured one or two — one which was still in the rough I found to be 32 feet long by 5 feet broad, and 4½ deep. These granite blocks have been brought to Washington from the State of Maine. The finished front of this building, looking down to the Potomac, is very good; but to my eyes this also has been much injured by the rows of windows which look out from the building into the space of the portico.

The President's house — or the White House as it is now called all the world over — is a handsome mansion fitted for the chief officer of a great Republic, and nothing more. I think I may say that we have private houses in Loudon considerably larger. It is neat and pretty, and with all its immediate outside belongings calls down no adverse criticism. It faces on to a small garden, which seems to be always accessible to the public, and opens out upon that everlasting Pennsylvania Avenue, which has now made another turn. Here in front of the White House is President's Square, as it is generally called. The technical name is, I believe, La Fayette Square.[14] The houses round it are few in number, — not exceeding three or four on each side, but they are among the best in Washington, and the whole place is neat and well kept. President's Square is certainly the most attractive part of the city. The garden of the square is always open, and does not seem to suffer from any public ill-usage; by which circumstance I am again led to suggest that the gardens of our London squares might be thrown open in the same way. In the centre of this one at Washington, immediately facing the President's house, is an equestrian statue of General Jackson.[15] It is very bad; but that it is not nearly as bad as it might be is proved by another equestrian statue, — of General Washington, — erected in the centre of a small garden-plat at the end of Pennsylvania Avenue, near the bridge leading to Georgetown. Of all the statues on horseback which I ever saw, either in marble or bronze, this is by far the worst and most ridiculous. The horse is most absurd, but the man sitting on the horse is manifestly drunk. I should think the time must come when this figure at any rate will be removed.

I did not go inside the President's house, not having had while at Washington an opportunity of paying my personal respects to Mr. Lincoln. I had been told that this was to be done without trouble, but when I inquired on the subject I found that this was not exactly the case. I believe there are times when anybody may walk into the President's house without an introduction; but that, I take it, is not considered to be the proper way of doing the work. I found that something like a favour would be incurred, or that some disagreeable trouble would be given, if I made a request to be presented, — and therefore I left Washington without seeing the great man.

The President's house is nice to look at, but it is built on marshy ground, not much above the level of the Potomac, and is very unhealthy. I was told that all who live there become subject to fever and ague,[16] and that few who now live there have escaped it altogether. This conies of choosing the site of a new city, and decreeing that it shall be built on this or on that spot. Large cities, especially in these latter days, do not collect themselves in unhealthy places. Men desert such localities, — or at least do not congregate at them when their character is once known. But the poor President cannot desert the White House. He must make the most of the residence which the nation has prepared for him.

Of the other considerable public building of Washington, called the Smithsonian Institution,[17] I have said that its style was bastard Gothic; by this, I mean that its main attributes are Gothic, but that liberties have been taken with it, which, whether they may injure its beauty or no, certainly are subversive of architectural purity. It is built of red stone, and is not ugly in itself There is a very nice Norman porch to it, and little bits of Lombard Gothic have been well copied from Cologne. But windows have been fitted in with stilted arches, of which the stilts seem to crack and bend, so narrow are they and so high. And then the towers with high pinnacled roofs are a mistake, — unless indeed they be needed to give to the whole structure that name of Romanesque which it has assumed. The building is used for museums and lectures, and was given to the city by one James Smithson, an Englishman. I cannot say that the city of Washington seems to be grateful, for all to whom I spoke on the subject hinted that the Institution was a failure. It is to be remarked that nobody in Washington is proud of Washington, or of anything in it. If the Smithsonian Institution were at New York or at Boston, one would have a different story to tell.

There has been an attempt made to raise at Washington a vast obelisk to the memory of Washington, — the first in war and first in peace, as the country is proud to call him. This obelisk is a fair type of the city. It is unfinished, — not a third of it having as yet been erected, — and in all human probability ever will remain so.[18] If finished it would be the highest monument of its kind standing on the face of the globe, — and yet, after all, what would it be even then as compared with one of the great pyramids? Modern attempts cannot bear comparison with those of the old world in simple vastness. But in lieu of simple vastness, the modern world aims to achieve either beauty or utility. By the Washington monument, if completed, neither would be achieved. An obelisk with the proportions of a needle may be very graceful; but an obelisk which requires an expanse of flat-roofed, sprawling buildings for its base, and of which the shaft shall be as big as a cathedral tower, cannot be graceful. At present some third portion of the shaft has been built, and there it stands. No one has a word to say for it. No one thinks that money will ever again be subscribed for its completion. I saw somewhere a box of plate-glass kept for contributions for this purpose, and looking in perceived that two half-dollar pieces had been given; — but both of them were bad. I was told also that the absolute foundation of the edifice is bad; — that the ground, which is near the river and swampy, would not bear the weight intended to be imposed on it.

A sad and saddening spot was that marsh, as I wandered down on it all alone one Sunday afternoon. The ground was frozen, and I could walk dry-shod, but there was not a blade of grass. Around me on all sides were cattle in great numbers — steers and big oxen — lowing in their hunger for a meal. They were beef for the army, and never again I suppose would it be allowed to them to fill their big maws and chew the patient cud. There, on the brown, ugly, undrained field, within easy sight of the President's house, stood the useless, shapeless, graceless pile of stones. It was as though I were looking on the genius of the city. It was vast, pretentious, bold, boastful with a loud voice, already taller by many heads than other obelisks, but nevertheless still in its infancy, — ugly, unpromising, and false. The founder of the monument had said. Here shall be the obelisk of the world! and the founder of the city had thought of his child somewhat in the same strain. It is still possible that both city and monument shall be completed; but at the present moment nobody seems to believe in the one or in the other. For myself I have much faith in the American character, but I cannot believe either in Washington city or in the Washington monument. The boast made has been too loud, and the fulfilment yet accomplished has been too small!

Have I as yet said that Washington was dirty in that winter of 1861-1862? Or, I should rather ask, have I made it understood that in walking about Washington one waded as deep in mud as one does in floundering through an ordinary ploughed field in November? There were parts of Pennsylvania Avenue which would have been considered heavy ground by most hunting-men, and through some of the remoter streets none but light weights could have lived long. This was the state of the town when I left it in the middle of January. On my arrival in the middle of

December, everything was in a cloud of dust. One walked through an atmosphere of floating mud; for the dirt was ponderous and thick, and very palpable in its atoms. Then came a severe frost and a little snow; and if one did not fall while walking, it was very well. After that we had the thaw; and Washington assumed its normal winter condition. I must say that, during the whole of this time, the atmosphere was to me exhilarating; but I was hardly out of the doctor's hands while I was there, and he did not support my theory as to the goodness of the air. "It is poisoned by the soldiers," he said, "and everybody is ill." But then my doctor was perhaps a little tinged with southern proclivities.

... I have said that Washington was at that time, — the Christmas of 1861-1862, — a melancholy place. This was partly owing to the despondent tone in which so many Americans then spoke of their own affairs. It was not that the northern men thought that they were to be beaten, or that the southern men feared that things were going bad with their party across the river; but that nobody seemed to have any faith in anybody. Maclellan[19] had been put up as the true man — exalted perhaps too quickly, considering the limited opportunities for distinguishing himself which fortune had thrown in his way; but now belief in Maclellan seemed to be slipping away. One felt that it was so from day to day, though it was impossible to define how or whence the feeling came. And then the character of the ministry fared still worse in public estimation. That Lincoln, the President, was honest, and that Chase,[20] the Secretary of the Treasury, was able, was the only good that one heard spoken. At this time two Jonahs were specially pointed out as necessary sacrifices, by whose immersion into the comfortless ocean of private life the ship might perhaps be saved. These were Mr. Cameron,[21] the Secretary of War, and Mr. Welles,[22] the Secretary of the Navy. It was said that Lincoln, when pressed to rid his Cabinet of

Cameron, had replied, that when a man was crossing a stream the moment was hardly convenient for changing his horse; but it came to that at last, that he found he must change his horse, even in the very sharpest run of the river. Better that than sit an animal on whose exertions he knew that he could not trust. So Mr. Cameron went, and Mr. Stanton[23] became Secretary at War in his place. But Mr. Cameron, though put out of the Cabinet, was to be saved from absolute disgrace by being sent as Minister to Russia. I do not know that it would become me here to repeat the accusations made against Mr. Cameron, but it had long seemed to me that the maintenance in such a position, at such a time, of a gentleman who had to sustain such a universal absence of public confidence, must have been most detrimental to the army and to the Government.

Men whom one met in Washington were not unhappy about the state of things, as I had seen men unhappy in the North and in the West. They were mainly indifferent, but with that sort of indifference which arises from a break down of faith in anything. "There was the army! Yes, the army! But what an army! Nobody obeyed anybody. Nobody did anything! Nobody thought of advancing! There were, perhaps, two hundred thousand men assembled round Washington; and now the effort of supplying them, with food and clothing was as much as could be accomplished! But the contractors, in the meantime, were becoming rich. And then as to the Government! Who trusted it? Who would put their faith in Seward[24] and Cameron? Cameron was now gone, it was true; and in that way the whole of the Cabinet would soon be broken up. As to Congress, what could Congress do? Ask questions which no one would care to answer, and finally get itself packed up and sent home." The President and the constitution fared no better in men's mouths. The former did nothing, — neither harm nor good; and as for the latter, it had broken down and shown itself to be inefficient. So men ate, and drank, and laughed, waiting till chaos should come, secure in the belief that the atoms into which their world would resolve itself, would connect themselves again in some other form without trouble on their part.

And at Washington I found no strong feeling against England and English conduct towards America. "We men of the world," a Washington man might have said, "know very well that everybody must take care of himself first. We are very good friends with you, — of course, and are very glad to see you at our table whenever you come across the water; but as for rejoicing at your joys, or expecting you to sympathize with our sorrows, we know the world too well for that. We are splitting into pieces, and of course that is gain to you. Take another cigar." This polite, fashionable, and certainly comfortable way of looking at the matter had never been attained at New York or Philadelphia, at Boston or Chicago. The northern provincial world of the States had declared to itself that those who were not with it were against it; that its neighbours should be either friends or foes; that it would understand nothing of neutrality. This was often mortifying to me, but I think I liked it better on the whole than the *laisser-aller* indifference of Washington.

Everybody acknowledged that society in Washington had been almost destroyed by the loss of the southern half of the usual sojourners in the city. The senators and members of Government, who heretofore had come from the southern States, had no doubt spent more money in the capital than their northern brethren. They and their families had been more addicted to social pleasures. They are the descendants of the old English Cavaliers, whereas the northern men have come from the old English Roundheads. Or if, as may be the case, the blood of the races has now been too well mixed to allow of this being said with absolute truth, yet something of the manners of the old forefathers has been left. The southern gentleman is more genial, less dry, — I will not say more hospitable, but more given to enjoy hospitality than his northern brother; and this difference is quite as strong with the women as with the men. It may therefore be understood that secession would be very fatal to the society of Washington. It was not only that the members of Congress were not there. As to very many of the representatives, it may be said that they do not belong sufficiently to Washington to make a part of its society. It is not every representative that is, perhaps, qualified to do so. But secession had taken away from Washington those who held property in the South — who were bound to the South by any ties, whether political or other; who belonged to the South by blood, education, and old habits. In very many cases — nay, In most such cases — it had been necessary that a man should select whether he would be a friend to the South, and therefore a rebel; or else an enemy to the South, and therefore untrue to all the predilections and sympathies of his life. Here has been the hardship. For such people there has been no neutrality possible. Ladies even have not been able to profess themselves simply anxious for peace and goodwill, and so to remain tranquil. They who are not for me are against me, has been spoken by one side and by the other. And I suppose that in all civil war it is necessary that it should be so. I heard of various cases in which father and son had espoused different sides in order that property might be retained both in the North and in the South. Under such circumstances it may be supposed that society in Washington would be considerably cut up. All this made the place somewhat melancholy.

… Though I had felt Washington to be disagreeable as a city, yet I was almost sorry to leave it when the day of my departure came. I had allowed myself a month for my sojourn in the capital, and I had stayed a month to the day. Then came the trouble of packing up, the necessity of calling on a long list of acquaintances one after another, the feeling that bad as Washington might be, I might be going to places that were worse, a conviction that I should get beyond the reach of my letters, and a sort of affection which I had acquired for my rooms. My landlord, being a coloured man, told me that he was sorry I was going. Would I not remain? Would I come back to him? Had I been comfortable? Only for so and so or so and so, he would have done better for me. No white American citizen, occupying the position of landlord, would have condescended to such comfortable words. I knew the man did not in truth want me to stay, as a lady and gentleman were waiting to go in the moment I went out; but I did not the less value the assurance. One hungers and thirsts after such civil words among American citizens of this class. The clerks and managers at hotels, the officials at railway stations, the cashiers at banks, the women in the shops; — ah! they are the worst of all. An American woman who is bound by her position to serve yon, — who is paid in some shape to supply your wants, whether to sell you a bit of soap or bring you a towel in your bedroom at an hotel, — is, I think, of all human creatures, the most insolent. I certainly had a feeling of regret at parting with my coloured friend, — and some regret also as regards a few that were white.

As I drove down Pennsylvania Avenue, through the slush and mud, and saw, perhaps for the last time, those wretchedly dirty horse sentries who had refused to allow me to trot through the streets, I almost wished that I could see more of them. How absurd they looked, with a whole kit of rattletraps strapped on their horses' backs behind them, — blankets, coats, canteens, coils of rope, and, always at the top of everything else, a tin pot! No doubt these things are all necessary to a mounted sentry, or they would not have been there; but it always seemed as though the horse had been loaded gipsy-fashion, in a manner that I may perhaps best describe as higgledy-piggledy, and that there was a want of military precision in the packing. The man would have looked more graceful, and the soldier more warlike, had the pannikin[25] been made to assume some rigidly fixed position, instead of dangling among the ropes. The drawn sabre, too, never consorted well with the dirty outside woolen wrapper which generally hung loose from the man's neck. Heaven knows, I did not begrudge him his comforter in that cold weather, or even his long, uncombed shock of hair; but I think he might have been made more spruce, and I am sure that he could not have looked more uncomfortable. As I went, however, I felt for him a sort of affection, and wished in my heart of hearts that he might soon be enabled to return to some more congenial employment.

I went out by the Capitol, and saw that also, as I then believed, for the last time. With all its faults it is a great building, and, though unfinished, is effective; its very size and pretension give it a certain majesty. What will be the fate of that vast pile, and of those other costly public edifices at Washington, should the South succeed wholly in their present enterprise? If Virginia should ever become a part of the southern republic, Washington cannot remain the capital of the northern republic. In such case it would be almost better to let Maryland go also, so that the future destiny of that unfortunate city may not be a source of trouble, and a stumbling block of opprobrium. Even if Virginia be saved, its position will be most unfortunate.

"Fishing in Troubled Waters"

From *Six Months in the Federal States* by Edward Dicey.

Edward Dicey (1832-1911) came to America in the spring of 1862 as a special correspondent for two British publications: *Macmillan's Magazine* and the *Spectator* newspaper, the latter being decidedly pro-Union during the American Civil War. Dicey, then scarcely thirty years of age, had previously published *Rome in 1861* and *Cavour: A Memoir*, about the late Camillo Benso, Count of Cavour and first post-revolutionary Prime Minister of the united Kingdom of Italy.

In his *Preface*, Dicey states: "If anything that I have written should jar upon the feelings of my friends on either side the Atlantic, I can only beg them to believe that I have stated simply what I conceive to be the truth, in the earnest hope that, by so doing, I might render some little service towards creating a more friendly feeling between the two great English-speaking nations of the world."

Dicey, an experienced journalist with no small literary ability, dedicated his work, with permission, to a countryman, the 19th century liberal socio-political theorist and author of *On Liberty*, John Stuart Mill.

Washington

It was with an odd sensation of being for the first time in a strange society, of dwelling in a slave-owning city, that I became acquainted with the metropolis of the United States.

To a stranger, Washington must be a quaint residence, even in ordinary days. Had it progressed at the rate of ordinary Northern cities, it would have been by this time one of the finest capitals of the world; as it is, it was built for a city of the future, and the future has not yet been realized. It is still, as it was once called, the city of magnificent distances. On two low hills, a couple of miles apart, stand the white marble palaces of the Houses of Congress and the Government Offices. At their feet stretches the grand Potomac, just too far off to be visible as a feature in the town; and across the low, broken, marshy valley between them runs the long, broad, irregular Pennsylvania Avenue, a second hand Broadway[1] out at elbows. On either side hosts of smaller streets branch out for short distances, ending abruptly in brick-fields or in the open country; and that is all. If the plan of the city had ever been carried out, the Capitol would have been the centre of a vast polygon, with streets branching out from it in every direction. But owing to a characteristic quarrel between the Government and a private landowner,[2] which could never have occurred except in an Anglo-Saxon country, the plan was abandoned; the city sprawled out on one side only of the intended polygon, and left the Capitol stranded, so to speak, at the extremity of the town. So Washington has not the one merit of American architecture symmetry. The whole place looks run up in a night, like the cardboard cities which Potemkin[3] erected to gratify the eyes of his imperial mistress on her tour through Russia; and it is impossible to remove the impression that, when Congress is over, the whole place is taken down, and packed up again till wanted. Everything has such an unfinished "here for the day only" air about it. Everybody is a bird of passage at Washington. The diplomatic corps is transitory by its very nature. The senators, representatives, and ministers, reside there for two, four, possibly six sessions, as the case may be; and the fact of their being in Congress or in office now is rather a presumption than otherwise, that they will not be so again when their term expires. The clerks, officials, and government *employees* are all, too, mere lodgers. The force of necessity compels each Administration to reappoint a few of the subordinate clerks who understand the business of the office; but still, every official may be turned out in four years at the longest, and most of them know that they probably will be dismissed at the end of that period. There are no commercial or manufacturing interests to induce merchants or capitalists to settle here. The growth of Baltimore, and the filling-up of the Potomac, have destroyed what small prospect of commercial greatness Washington may ever have indulged in. There is nothing attractive about the place to make any one, not brought there by business, fix on it as a place of residence. With the exception of a few landowners who have estates in the neighbourhood, a score of lawyers connected with the Supreme Court, and a host of petty tradesmen and lodging-house keepers, there is nobody who looks on Washington as his home.

Hence nobody, with rare exceptions, has a house of his own there. Most of the members of Congress live in hotels or furnished lodgings. The wives and families of the married members (whose names are marked in the Congressional Directory, with a row of crosses corresponding to the number of womankind they bring with them) come to Washington for a few months or weeks during the session, and for the time of their stay a furnished house is taken. In consequence, there is no style about the mode of living. The number of private carriages is very few; and people are afraid of bringing good horses to be ruined by the rut tracks (for they are not worthy of the name of roads) which serve the purposes of streets in Washington. Public amusements of any kind are scanty and poor. There is a theatre about equal in size and merit to those of Margate or Scarborough[4] in the season; at the Smithsonian Institute (the barbarity of whose designation I am afraid is due to its English benefactor) there are frequent lectures, which, when they are not political demonstrations, are about as interesting, or uninteresting, as lectures on the Glaciers and the Tertiary Formation, *et hoc genus omne*,[5] are at home; and there are occasional concerts, dramatic readings, and pictorial exhibitions. But this, with the visit of an occasional circus, is all.

The city, in fact, is an overgrown watering-place. The roads appear to have been marked out and then left uncompleted, and the pigs you see grubbing in the main thoroughfares seem in keeping with the place. The broken-down ramshackle hackney-coaches (or hacks, as they are called), with their shabby negro drivers, are obviously brought out for the day, to last for the day only; the shops are of the stock Margate watering-place stamp, where nothing is kept in stock, and where what little there is is all displayed in the shop-windows. The private houses, handsome enough in themselves, are apparently stuck up anywhere the owner liked to build them, just as a travelling-van is perched on the first convenient spot that can be found for a night's lodging.

The grand hotels, too, which form a striking, if not an imposing feature in most American towns, are wanting in Washington. Even according to the American standard, there is not a decent hotel in the whole place. Willard's and the National are two huge rambling barracks where some incredible number of beds could be run up; but it is hard to say which is the shabbiest and dirtiest internally; and externally, neither of them have any pretensions to architectural grandeur. Of the lot, Willard's is the best, on the principle that if you are to eat your peck of dirt, you may as well eat it in as picturesque a form as possible. The aspect of this hotel during the time that the army was encamped before Manassas[6] was indeed a wonderful one. At all times Willard's is the house of call for everybody who has business in Washington. From early morning till late at night its lobbies and passages were filled with a motley throng of all classes and all nations. With the exception of the President, there is not a statesman or general, or man of note of any kind, in Washington, whom I have not come across, at different times, in the passages of Willard's. Soldiers in every uniform, privates and officers thrown together in strange confusion; Congressmen and senators, army contractors and Jews; artists, newspaper writers, tourists, prizefighters, and gamblers, were mixed up with a nondescript crowd of men, who seem to have no business except to hang about, and to belong to no particular nation, or class, or business. In the parlours, there was a like confusion. Half a dozen rough-looking common soldiers, with their boots encased in deep layers of Virginia mud, would be dozing with their feet hoisted on the high fenders before the fire. At the tables gentlemen, dressed in the mouldy black evening suits Americans are so partial to, would sit all day writing letters. Knots of three or four, belonging apparently to every grade of society, would be standing about the room shaking hands constantly with new comers, introducing everybody to everybody — "more Americano" — and adjourning, at intervals, in a body to the bar. Upstairs, on the floor above, splendidly-dressed ladies were strolling at all hours about the passages, chatting with friends, working, playing, and flirting with smartly-bedizened officers and gay young diplomatists.

In fact, barring the presence of the ladies, an ingredient we had little of there, I was constantly reminded of Naples in the Garibaldian days,[7] and, notably, of the Hotel

Victoria. There was the same collection of all sorts of men from every country, the same Babel of languages, the same fusion of all ranks and classes, the same ceaseless conversation about the war, the same preponderance of the military element, the same series of baseless contradictory rumours, and the same feverish restless excitement. Constantly, too, I came across well-remembered faces, and was saluted by acquaintances whose names I had forgotten, but whom I recollected at the camp before Capua,[8] and more frequently still about the *cafes* of Naples. What were they doing here? why they were employed here? what their rank might be? were all mysteries I did not care to fathom. I was content to answer by the expressive Italian formula of *Chi lo sa?*[9] It is good, I suppose, fishing in troubled waters.

As to the public buildings of Washington, they add little to the splendour of the town. Of the Capitol, I shall speak presently. The Treasury, a sort of white marble Madeleine, would be magnificent if it were finished. The White House is beautiful on a moonlight night, when its snowy walls stand out in contrast to the deep blue sky, but not otherwise. As to the Post Office, Patent Office, Smithsonian Institute, and the unfinished pedestal of the Washington monument, I must refer the curious to any handbook of travel. I am ashamed to say that I never visited either the curiosities of the Patent Office or of the Smithsonian; and I am still more ashamed to add that I do not regret my shortcomings. Stock sight-seeing is an amusement that, from some mental defect, I have an invincible aversion to.

Possibly this description does not do full justice to Washington. On a fine bright spring day, when the wooded banks that line the south side of the Potomac were in their early bloom, I have thought the city looked wondrously bright; but on nine days out of every ten the climate of Washington is simply detestable. When it rains, the streets are sloughs of liquid mud; and, by some miraculous peculiarity I could never get accounted for, even in the paved streets, the stones sink into the ground, and the mud oozes up between them. In a couple of hours from the time the rain ceases, the same streets are enveloped in clouds of dust. In spring time, the contrast between the burning sun and the freezing winds is greater than I ever knew it in Italy; and in summer, the heat is more dead and oppressive than in any place it has been my lot to dwell in. I had many friends in Washington, and my recollection of the weeks I spent there is a very pleasant one; but, as a place of sojourn, Washington seems to me simply detestable.

I recollect Mr. Hawthorne saying, that his impression on leaving Washington was, that if Washington were really the keystone of the Union, then the Union was not worth saving; and in this opinion I cordially agreed with him.[10]

## SOURCES

Books about Washington, D.C. are plentiful and increasingly informative in their topical diversity. Among general works about the nation's capital are a few that should be mentioned here. The best legislative history of the founding of Washington, D.C. appears in *Origin and Government of the District of Columbia* by William Tindall (Printed for Use of the Committee on the District of Columbia, House of Representatives. Washington: Government Printing Office, 1909). Wilhelmus Bogart Bryan's two-volume work, *A History of the National Capital* (New York: Macmillan, 1914-1916) is still useful for the depth of its original research but is woefully lacking in its treatment of slavery and the lives of the city's African-American residents. James Sterling Young's *The Washington Community: 1800-1828* (New York: Columbia, 1966) is an excellent period study of power and politics in the nation's capital but consequently intends no discussion of the powerless and the disenfranchised. Constance McLaughlin Green makes substantial progress in addressing the deficiencies in Bryan's *History* with her two-volume work, *Washington: A History of the Capital, 1800-1850* (Princeton University Press, 1962). Margaret Leech won her first Pulitzer Prize for History with *Reveille in Washington: 1860-1865* (New York: Harper, 1941), which for this reader is still the best book on the District during the Civil War, although there are commendable modern challengers. Randall Bond Truett produced an improved edition entitled *Washington, D.C.: A Guide to the Nation's Capital* (New York: Hastings House, 1968) which itself is a second revision of *Washington, City and Capital* (Washington: Government Printing Office, 1937). The latter is a doorstop of a book, arguably produced by committee under the auspices of the Works Progress Administration (WPA) and justly condemned for its often condescending tone. More recent works of general interest are the excellent *Washington: The Making of the American Capital* by Fergus M. Bordewich (New York: HarperCollins, 2008), the broad-brush *Washington: A History of Our National Capital* by Tom Lewis (New York: Basic Books, 2015), and the stylistically refreshing *Washington from the Ground Up* by James H. S. McGregor (Cambridge: The Belknap Press, 2007). Finally, *The A to Z of Washington, D.C.* by Robert Benedetto, Jane Donovan and Kathleen Duvall (Lanham, Maryland: The Scarecrow Press, 2005), remains an indispensable ready-reference.

---

Introduction: The summary of previous meeting places of Congress is adapted with minor alterations from Tindall's *Origin and Government of the District of Columbia*, pp. 13-14. The text of Article I: Section 8, Clause 17 of the Constitution of the United States is from *Constitution of the United States of America: With the Amendments Thereto: to Which are Prefixed the Declaration of Independence, the Articles of Confederation, and the Ordinance of 1787; and to Which are Added the Rules of the Senate, the Joint Rules of the Two Houses, and Jefferson's Manual of Parliamentary Practice. Revised and Enlarged Edition.* Washington: Government Printing Office, 1881. See p. 40. The text of Federalist XLIII by James Madison is from *The Federalist: a Commentary On the Constitution of the United States*, by John Jay, James Madison, and Alexander

Hamilton. Edited by Henry Cabot Lodge. New York: G. P. Putnam's sons, 1923. See pp. 267-269. Jefferson's description of the compromise that led to locating the capital on the Potomac appears in *The Complete Anas of Thomas Jefferson*, edited by Franklin B. Sawvel. New York: Round Table Press, 1903. See pp. 30-35. Brief descriptions of the events also appear in Bryan's *History*, Volume I: pp. 36-40; Lewis' *Washington*, pp. 3-10; and in *Alexander Hamilton* by Ron Chernow. New York: Penguin Press, 2004. See pp. 325-329. A more lengthy and textured narrative of the events appears in Bordewich's *Washington*. See "Dinner at Jefferson's, pp. 31-52.

I: *A Town of Any Importance* is excerpted from *Travels Through the States of North America, and the Provinces of Upper and Lower Canada, During the Years 1795, 1796, and 1797* by Isaac Weld, Jr. London: Printed for John Stockdale, 1799. See Volume I: Letter IV, pp. 49-53 and pp. 80-89. Details of Isaac Weld's life and career are from his biographical entry by Thomas Seccombe in the DNB: *Dictionary of National Biography*, 1885-1900, Volume 60, pp. 158-160.

II: *An Elegant Building* is excerpted from *Struggles Through Life, Exemplified in the Various Travels and Adventures in Europe, Asia, Africa, & America, of Lieut. John Harriott*. London Printed. Philadelphia Reprinted by James Humphreys, 1809. See Volume 2; pp. 196-201. Details of Harriott's life and career are from his biographical entry by Henry Manners Chichester in the DNB: *Dictionary of National Biography*, 1885-1900, Volume 24, pp. 439-440.

III: *Influx of Speculations* is excerpted from *Travels Through the United States of North America: the Country of the Iroquois, and Upper Canada, in the Years 1795,*

*1796, and 1797* by François-Alexandre-Frédéric La Rochefoucauld-Liancourt. 2nd ed. London: R. Phillips, 1800. See Volume III: "Federal City," pp. 622-632.

IV: *Obelisks in Trees* is excerpted from *Epistles, Odes and Other Poems* by Thomas Moore. London: Printed for James Carpenter, Old Bond Street, 1806. See pp. 209-215.

V: *A Place of Commerce* is excerpted from *The Stranger in America: Containing Observations Made during a Long Residence in that Country, on the Genius, Manners and Customs of the People of the United States* by Charles William Janson. London: Printed for James Cundee, 1807. See pp. 202-210. A contemporary review of Janson's book appears in *The Critical Review: Or, Annals of Literature.* Third Series: Volume 12, September-December, 1807. London: Printed for J. Mawman, 1808. See Article V, pp. 40-47. A brief history of Blodgett's Hotel appears in James M. Goode's *Capital Losses: A Cultural History of Washington's Destroyed Buildings*. Washington, D.C.: Smithsonian Institution Press, 1979. See pp. 160-161.

VI: *Drain the Swamp* is excerpted from *Travels in the United States of America, in the Years 1806 & 1807, and 1809, 1810, & 1811* by John Melish. Philadelphia: Published for the Author, 1812. See Volume I: Chapter XXXIII, "Interview with Mr. Jefferson," pp. 201-206. A summary of the life and career of John Melish appears in "John Melish and his Map of the United States" by Walter Ristow in *The Library of Congress Quarterly Journal of Acquisitions* 19 (1962), pp. 159-178.

VII: *Spoil of the Conqueror* is excerpted from *A Narrative of the Campaigns of the British Army at Washington and New Orleans, Under Generals Ross, Pakenham, and Lambert, in the Years 1814 and 1815* by George Robert

Gleig. London: John Murray, 1826. 2nd ed. See "Letter X," pp. 124-131. For a modern account of the burning of Washington, D.C., see Peter Snow's *When Britain Burned the White House: The 1814 Invasion of Washington*. New York: St. Martin's Press, 2013.

VIII: *America is Young* is excerpted from *Travels in Canada, and the United States, in 1816 and 1817* by Francis Hall. Boston: Re-published from the London edition by Wells and Lilly, 1818. See Chapter XXVIII: "Washington," pp. 196-202. A brief discussion of Benjamin Henry Latrobe's proposal for a national university on the National Mall appears in *The National Mall: Rethinking Washington's Monumental Core*, edited by Nathan Glazer and Cynthia R. Field. Baltimore: Johns Hopkins University Press, 2008. See pp. 15-18. A brief discussion of Benjamin Henry Latrobe's Massachusetts caryatid, modelled for inclusion in the capitol and referenced in Hall's *Travels*, appears in "From Roman Republicanism to Greek Democracy: Benjamin Henry Latrobe's Capitol" by Pamela Scott in *The Capitol Dome*, Volume 52, Number 3, Winter 2015-2016, pp. 25-28. A list of the investors who formed a stock company to build what became known as the Old Brick Capitol, constructed in large part to keep Congress in Washington, D.C. so the city would continue to function as the capital of the United States, appears in *A History of the National Capital: from its Foundation through the Period of the Adoption of the Organic Act* by Wilhelmus Bogart Bryan. New York: Macmillan, 1914. See Volume I: pp. 636-637.

IX: *Our Enlightened Countrymen* is excerpted from *Sketches of America: A Narrative of a Journey of Five Thousand Miles through the Eastern and Western States of America; Contained in Eight Reports Addressed to the Thirty-nine English Families by Whom the Author was*

*Deputed, in June 1817, to Ascertain Whether Any, and What Part of the United States Would be Suitable for their Residence* by Henry Bradshaw Fearon. London: Longman, Hurst, Rees, Orme, and Brown, 1818. See Fearon's "Introductory Remarks" and pp. 285-295. For the sale of Jefferson's books, see Library of Congress. Thomas Jefferson: Jefferson's Library, accessed May 11th, 2020, https://www.loc.gov/exhibits/jefferson/jefflib.html.

X: *The Aspect of the House* is excerpted from *Travels Through Part of the United States and Canada 1818 and 1819* by John M. (John Morison) Duncan. New York: W. Gilley, 1823. See Volume I: pp. 251-282. For information on Andrew Duncan as University Printer, see Special Collections: Glasgow University, "In Aedibus Academicis: The Glasgow University Press." *Special Collections: Part of the Library and University Services.* Accessed May 20th, 2020. www.gla.ac.uk....

XI: *Punishment is 20 Dollars* is excerpted from *An Historical, Topographical, and Descriptive View of the United States of America and of Upper and Lower Canada* by E. [Eneas] MacKenzie. 2nd ed. Newcastle upon Tyne: Mackenzie and Dent, 1819. See pp. 316-336. Few personal details about the author will be found in the DNB: *Dictionary of National Biography,* edited by Sidney Lee, Volume 35, London: Smith, Elder, 1893. See pp. 139.

XII: *The Custom is to Shake Hands* is excerpted from *An Excursion Through the United States and Canada During the Years 1822-1823* by An English Gentleman [William Newnham Blane]. London: Printed for Baldwin, Cradock and Joy, 1824. See pp. 37-51. The work was subsequently reprinted as *Travels Through the United States and Canada During the Years 1822-1823* [London: Printed for Baldwin and Co., 1828] and carried Blane's name as author on the title page. Blane's obituary notice [reprinted from the *Ayr Courier* of March 14] appears in *The Examiner*. London: John Hunt, 1826. See p. 222.

XIII: *God Bless the American People* is excerpted from *Lafayette in America In 1824 and 1825: Or, Journal of a Voyage to the United States* by Auguste Levasseur and [translator] John D. [Davidson] Godham. Philadelphia: Carey and Lea, 1829. See Volume II: pp. 241-254.

XIV: *Nobody Would Inhabit Such a Town* is excerpted from *Personal Narrative of Travels in the United States and Canada in 1826... With Remarks on the Present State of the American Navy* by Frederick Fitzgerald De Roos. London: William Harrison Ainsworth, Old Bond Street, 1827. See pp. 14-32. Biographical details for De Roos are from John Marshall's *Royal Naval Biography*. London: Longman, Hurst, Rees, Orme, Brown, 1835. See Volume IV, Part II, p. 261. The English translation of the Latin "eripuit cælo fulmen sceptrumque tyrannis" is from Google Translate.

XV: *Do You Mean to Buy the Lad, Sir?* is excerpted from *Travels in North America, in the Years 1827 and 1828* by Captain Basil Hall. 1st ed. Edinburgh: Cadell and Co.; London: Simpkin and Marshall, 1829. See Volume III: Chapters 1-3, pp. 1-68 [selections]. Personal details about Hall are from his DNB entry by John Knox Laughton. *Dictionary of National Biography*. London: Smith, Elder, 1893. See Volume 24: pp. 58-59.

XVI: *It Reminded Me Much of a Russian City* is excerpted from *Transatlantic Sketches: Comprising Visits to the Most Interesting Scenes in North and South America, and the West Indies. With Notes on Negro Slavery and Canadian*

*Emigration* by Capt. J. E. Alexander. Philadelphia: Key and Biddle, 1833. See Chapter XXXII: pp. 341-347.

XVII: *The Spitting was Incessant* is excerpted from *Domestic Manners of the Americans* by Mrs. Trollope. London: Printed for Whittaker, Treacher & Co., Ave-Maria-Lane, 1832. See Volume I: Chapter XX, pp. 305-336. An excellent summary of Mrs. Trollope's hardships in America appears in *Trollope: A Commentary* by Michael Sadleir. London: Constable, 1927. See pp. 72-83. For information on Thomas Newton Jr., see See History, Art & Archives, U.S. House of Representatives, "Fathers [and] Deans of the House," https://history.house.gov/Institution/Seniority/Deans-of-the-House/ (Accessed May 24, 2020). William Byrd's History of the Dividing Line Betwixt Virginia and North Carolina has been in print in various editions at least since the 1840s. A summary of Byrd's interest in draining the dismal swamp is found in *Description of the Dismal Swamp and a Proposal to Drain the Swamp* by William Byrd and E. G. [Earl Gregg] Swem. Metuchen, N.J.: Printed for C.F. Heartman, 1922.

XVIII: *To Dazzle with False Glitter* is excerpted from *Men and Manners in America* by Thomas Hamilton. Edinburgh: W. Blackwood, 1833. Hamilton's dedicatory remarks are in Volume I: p. iv. The selections from his work appear in Volume II: Chapter III, pp. 110-116 and Chapter IV, pp. 127-133.

XIX: *The Road to Washington* is excerpted from *Journal of a Residence and Tour in the United States of North America: From April, 1833, to October, 1834* by E. S. [Edward Strutt] Abdy. London: John Murray, Albemarle Street, 1835. Quotes regarding Abdy's purpose in visiting America are from his Introduction in Volume I. The subsequent selections from his work are from Volume II: Chapter XV, pp. 58-65 and Chapter XVI, pp. 95-98.

XX: *Ladies of America are Uncommonly Frank* is excerpted from *Impressions of America: During the Years 1833, 1834, and 1835* by Tyrone Power. Philadelphia: Carey, Lea & Blanchard, 1836. 2$^{nd}$ edition. See *Washington* and *Washington, Theatre*, Volume I: pp. 125-132 and *Impressions of Washington Society, Public and Private*, pp. 146-149. Montrose Jonas Moses' assessment of Power's *Impressions of America* appears in his brief biography of the Power family in *Famous Actor-Families in America* by Montrose Jonas Moses. New York: T. Y. Crowell & Company, 1906. See pp. 284-304. The editor's suggestion [read *guess*] at Power's first venue in Washington, D.C. is informed by an article of A. I. Mudd entitled "Early Theatres in Washington City," published in the *Records of the Columbia Historical Society*. See Volume 5: (1902), pp. 64-86.

XXI: *The Bottom of an Old Lake* is excerpted from *Travels in North America During the Years 1834, 1835 & 1836: Including a Summer of Residence with the Pawnee Tribe of Indians, in the Remote Prairies of the Missouri, and a Visit to Cuba and the Azore Islands* by Sir Charles Augustus Murray. 2$^{nd}$ ed. London: Richard Bentley, New Burlington Street, publisher in ordinary to Her Majesty, 1841. See Volume I: pp. 130-139 and pp. 143-146. Murray's recounting of the assassination attempt upon Andrew Jackson by Richard Lawrence is reasonably consistent with those of contemporary historians. Biographical details about Murray and his first wife are from Maxwell, H. E., and H. C. G. Matthew. "Murray, Sir Charles Augustus (1806–1895), diplomatist and author." Oxford Dictionary of National Biography. 23 Sep. 2004; Accessed 26 May. 2020.

https://www.oxforddnb.com/view/10.1093/ref:odnb/97801 98614128.001.0001/odnb-9780198614128-e-19596.

XXII: *The President Offered Me Bonbons* is excerpted from *Retrospect of Western Travel* by Harriet Martineau. London: Saunders and Otley; New York: Harper and Brothers, 1838. [Two Volumes]. See Volume I: *Life at Washington*, pp. 143-160 The identity of Harriet Martineau's traveling companion during her tour in the United States is from the publisher's announcement for G. Peter Winnington's *Harriet Martineau, Miss J and Ellen McKee*. Letterworth Press, 2019. Accessed 05/26/2020. https://www.theletterworthpress.org/Miss%20J/index.html. See also *Records of a Family, 1800-1933* by Herbert McLachlan. Manchester University Press, 1935, pp. 115.

XXIII: *A Subject of Grave Reflection* is excerpted from *A Diary in America: with Remarks on its Institutions* by Captain Marryat. Paris: A. and W. Galigniani, 1839. See Chapter XXII: pp. 115-123. The story of Lieutenant Drew and the *Caroline* appears in *Life of Frederick Marryat* by David Hannay. London: Scott, 1889. See pp. 105-107. The Latin *tam Marte quam Mercurio* was Englished by Google Translate.

XXIV: *Just One Month* is excerpted from *Souvenirs of a Diplomat: Private Letters from America During the Administration of Presidents Van Buren, Harrison, and Tyler* by Adolphe Fourier de Bacourt. Translated by Marie de Gonneville [Comtesse de Mirabeau]. New York: H. Holt, 1885. See Letters LV-LVI: pp. 164-170 and Letters LXVII-LXX: pp. 208-212. For the translator's relationship to the author, See her "Memoir of the Author" preceding the *Souvenirs*. See also "The Memoirs of Talleyrand" [Charles-Maurice de Talleyrand-Périgord] among the notices in *The Publisher's Weekly*, Volume 39, Number 1003, p. 572, dated April 18th, 1891.

XXV: *Magnificent ... Magnificent* is excerpted from *American Notes for General Circulation* by Charles Dickens. Boston: Ticknor and Fields, 1867. See Chapter VIII: pp. 60-67. Dickens apparently used William Elliot's *The Washington Guide: Containing Capt. John Smith's Account of the Chesapeake Bay.* Washington City: F. Taylor, 1837. See "East Front — Tympanum," *The Genius of America*, pp. 98-100. A recounting of the "Great Boz Ball" honoring Dickens in New York appears in *Account of the Ball Given in Honor of Charles Dickens In New York City, February 14, 1842.* Cedar Rapids, Iowa: Privately Printed [The Torch Press], 1908.

XXVI: *Every Species of Alcoholic Beverage* is excerpted from *The Western World, Or, Travels in the United States in 1846-47: Exhibiting Them in Their Latest Development, Social, Political, and Industrial, Including a Chapter on California, with a New Map of the United States, Showing Their Recent Territorial Acquisitions, and a Map of California*, by Alexander MacKay. London: R. Bentley, 1849. See Volume I: Chapters IX and X, pp. 165-191. Brief notes on Alexander MacKay's life are from his biographical entry by Gordon Goodwin in the DNB: *Dictionary of National Biography*, 1885-1900, Volume 35, pp. 117-118.

XXVII: *A Fit Act of Hero Worship* is excerpted from Lyell, Charles, Sir, 1797-1875. *A Second Visit to North America* by Sir Charles Lyell. 3rd ed. London: J. Murray, 1855. See Volume I: Chapter XIV, pp. 258-270. For biographical information on Francis Markoe, see his entry in Wilson, Wendell E. (2020), Mineralogical Record Biographical Archive, at www.mineralogicalrecord.com.

XXVIII: *We are the Same People* is excerpted from *Travels in the United States, etc., During 1849 and 1850* by Lady Stuart-Wortley. London: Richard Bentley, 1851. For Lady Stuart-Wortley's intentions in writing her *Travels*, see the Preface in Volume I. For her writing on Washington, See Volume I: Chapter XV, pp. 148-159. For more about Dr. Samuel Davies Heap and his relations, see "Heap Family of Philadelphia, Pennsylvania" by Lewis D. Cook which appears in *The Pennsylvania Genealogical Magazine*; September, 1953: PGM Volume 19, Number 2; pp 117-124. [Available by subscription at www.genpa.org].

XXIX: *No! No! ... No! No!* is excerpted from *The Homes of the New World: Impressions of America* by Fredrika Bremer. Translated by Mary Howitt. London: A. Hall, Virtue & Co., 1853. See Volume II: pp. 58-74. For a near contemporary text on Pocahontas and her descendants, see *Pocahontas: Alias Matoaka, and Her Descendants Through Her Marriage at Jamestown, Virginia, in April, 1614, with John Rolfe, Gentleman; Including the Names of Alfriend, Archer, Bentley, Bernard, Bland, Boling, Branch, Cabell, Catlett, Cary, Dandridge, Dixon, Douglas, Duval, Eldridge, Ellett, Ferguson, Field, Fleming, Gay, Gordon, Griffin, Grayson, Harrison, Hubard, Lewis, Logan, Markham, Meade, McRae, Murray, Page, Poythress, Randolph, Robertson, Skipwith, Stanard, Tazewel, Walke, West, Whittle, and Others,* by Wyndham Robertson. Richmond: J. W. Randolph & English, 1887.

XXX: *In Charge was a Door-Keeper* is excerpted from *Things as They Are in America* by William Chambers. Philadelphia: Lippincott, Grambo, 1854. For details about the beginning of his voyage, see Chapter I: pp. See pp. 257-266. The note on the Franklin nickname "American-Aquatic" is from *The True Benjamin Franklin* by Sydney

George Fisher. Philadelphia: J.B. Lippincott Company, 1899. See Fisher's Preface, p. 6. Information on the "Franklin" press is at National Museum of American History, "'Franklin' common press." Accessed 06/03/2020. https://americanhistory.si.edu/collections/search/object/nmah_882271. The location of British Ambassador John Crampton's residence and office is surmised from *The Washington and Georgetown Directory, Strangers' Guidebook for Washington, and Congressional and Clerks' Register* by Alfred Hunter. Washington: Printed by Kirkwood & McGill, 1853. See the Directory entry "British Minister (J. F. Crampton)," p. 12 and the Congressional Directory, Department of State entry "England," at p. 28.

XXXI: *The Saddest Spot on Earth* is excerpted from *North America* by Anthony Trollope. New York: Harper, 1863. See selections from Chapters XXI-XXIV, pp. 300-359. For a modern account of James Wormley, see *A Free Man of Color* by Carol Gelderman. Dulles, Virginia: Potomac Books, 2012.

XXXII: *Fishing in Troubled Waters* is excerpted from *Six Months in the Federal States* by Edward Dicey. London: Macmillan and Co., 1863. For the explanatory quote regarding his work, see Dicey's *Preface* in Volume I: p. viii. For the selection from his work, see *Washington*, Volume I: pp. 92-99. For Dicey's visit to Hawthorne, see *Concord*, Volume II, pp. 226-234. The full text of the Hawthorne essay "Chiefly About War Matters" appears in *The Atlantic* [online edition]. Accessed 05/29/2020. https://www.theatlantic.com/magazine/archive/1862/07/chiefly-about-war-matters/306159/. See also *The Complete Works of Nathaniel Hawthorne, with Introductory Notes by George Parsons Lathrop: Tales, Sketches, and Other Papers*. Riverside Edition. Boston: Houghton, Mifflin, 1883, Volume XII, pp. 299-345. ———

# NOTES

*Introduction*

[1] See Tindall, *Origin and Government of the District of Columbia*, pp. 13-14.
[2] *Constitution of the United States*, Article I: Section 8, Clause 17.
[3] See Lewis, *Washington*, p. 4.
[4] See *Federalist* XLIII (Madison), as edited by Henry Cabot Lodge, pp. 267-269.

*A Town of Any Importance*

[1] In an original footnote (omitted here), Weld repeats with some variation a familiar anecdote about Tiber Creek. A small tributary of the Potomac River, Tiber Creek, previously called Goose Creek, could once be seen meandering just south of the White House on its path from the Potomac to the Anacostia River. As the story goes, a certain Francis Pope owned a 400 acre tract of land near the White House. Pope called his land Rome. Goose Creek, renamed Tiber Creek, flowed through Rome. Thus, Pope had his Rome and Rome had its Tiber. Naming conventions notwithstanding, Tiber Creek eventually became the Washington City Canal, one of the city's greatest commercial failures. A portion of Tiber Creek flows under what is now Constitution Avenue, NW.
[2] Freestone is a common name for sandstone, which in this case was quarried from nearby Aquia Creek in what is now Stafford County, Virginia.
[3] Greenleaf's or Greenleaf Point was named for the early land speculator James Greenleaf (1765-1843). Now called Buzzard Point, it is located in Southwest Washington, D.C. at the confluence of the Potomac and Anacostia Rivers.
[4] Skilled workers; here Weld may be referring to both civilians and those in military service.

*An Elegant Building*

¹ The Patapsco River runs through Elkridge, Maryland, south of Baltimore, and empties into the Chesapeake Bay.
² Although no longer extant, Spurrier's Tavern was frequented by many travelers of the era, including George Washington. Spurrier's was located near what is now Jessup, Maryland along what is now U.S. Route 1, the main road between Washington, D.C. and Baltimore, Maryland.
³ A tributary of the Chesapeake Bay in the State of Maryland.
⁴ Bladensburg, Maryland, just east of Washington, D.C., was the site of the Battle of Bladensburg, also known as the "Bladensburg Races," during the War of 1812.
⁵ Sandstone quarried from Aquia Creek in what is now Stafford County, Virginia.
⁶ Early Washington, D.C. real estate speculator Thomas Law.
⁷ Early Washington, D.C. real estate speculator William Mayne *Duncanson*.
⁸ Law and Duncanson were Englishmen who had made early careers in the India trade, Law with the East India Company and Duncanson as a ship's captain.
⁹ Harriott likely references Samuel Blodget (or Blodgett), Jr.

*Influx of Speculations*

¹ Pennsylvania Signer of the Declaration of Independence, "Financier of the American Revolution," and one-time Washington, D.C. land speculator Robert Morris (1734-1806).
² John Nicholson and James Greenleaf, associates of Robert Morris.
³ President George Washington appointed three commissioners to carry out plans for the development of Washington, D.C. The original three commissioners were Daniel Carroll and Thomas Johnson, both of Maryland, and David Stuart of Virginia. Each was well-known to Washington.
⁴ Washington, D.C. is divided into four quadrants, designated Northeast (NE), Northwest (NW), Southeast (SE) and Southwest (SW).
⁵ Washington, D.C. land speculator Thomas Law.
⁶ Here the Duke likely references Washington, D.C. land speculator William Mayne Duncanson.
⁷ Likely John Eager Howard of Maryland (1752-1827) and Henry Lee III (1756-1818) of Virginia.

[8] Georgetown was founded in Maryland in 1751. An active Potomac River port town for much of the 18th century, Georgetown was incorporated into Washington, D.C. by Maryland's cessation of land for the founding of the capital city.
[9] Early Washington, D.C. real estate speculator Samuel Blodget (or Blodgett), Jr.
[10] *Greenleaf* or *Greenleaf's* Point, named for land speculator Thomas Greenleaf and located at the confluence of the Potomac and Anacostia Rivers in southwest Washington, D.C.

*Obelisks in Trees*

[1] A fellow Dubliner and Trinity College graduate.
[2] [Note in the original]. The "black Aspasia" of the present ********* of the United States, "inter Avernales baud ignotissima nymphas" has given rise to much pleasantry among the anti-democrat wits in America.
[3] [Note in the original]. "On the original location of the ground now allotted for the seat of the Federal City (says Mr. Weld) the identical spot on which the capitol now stands was called Rome. This anecdote is related by many as a certain prognostic of the future magnificence of this city, which is to be, as it were, a second Rome." Weld's Travels, Letter iv.
[4] [Note in the original]. A little stream runs through the city, which, with intolerable affectation, they have styled the Tiber. It was originally called Goose-Creek.
[5] [Note in the original]. "To be under the necessity of going through a deep wood for one or two miles, perhaps, in order to see a next-door neighbour, and in the same city, is a curious and I believe a novel circumstance." Weld, Letter iv.

The Federal City (if it must be called a city) has not been much increased since Mr. Weld visited it. Most of the public buildings, which were then in some degree of forwardness, have been since utterly suspended. The Hotel is already a ruin; a great part of its roof has fallen in, and the rooms are left to be occupied gratuitously by the miserable Scotch and Irish emigrants. The President's House, a very noble structure, is by no means suited to the philosophical humility of its present possessor, who inhabits but a corner of the mansion himself and abandons the rest to a state of uncleanly desolation, which those who are not philosophers cannot look at without regret. This grand edifice is encircled by a very rude pale, through which a common rustic stile introduces the visitors of the first man in America....

The private buildings exhibit the same characteristic display of arrogant speculation and premature ruin, and the few ranges of houses which were begun some years ago have remained so long waste and unfinished, that they are now for the most part dilapidated.

[6] [Note in the original]. The picture which [George Louis LeClerc] Buffon and [Abbé Cornelius] De Pauw have drawn of the American Indian, though very humiliating, is, as far as I can judge, much more correct than the flattering representations which Mr. Jefferson has given us. See the [Notes on the State of] Virginia, where this gentleman endeavours to disprove in general the opinion maintained so strongly by some philosophers, that nature (as Mr. Jefferson expresses it) belittles her productions in the western world. M. de Pauw attributes the imperfection of animal life in America to the ravages of a very recent deluge, from whose effects upon its soil and atmosphere it has not yet sufficiently recovered. See his Recherches sur les Americains, Part I. Tom. i. p. 102.

[7] [Note in the original]. On a small hill near the capitol there is to be an equestrian statue of General Washington [i.e. a monument to George Washington as envisioned by Pierre Charles L'Enfant].

*A Place of Commerce*

[1] Bladensburg, Maryland.
[2] Alexandria, Virginia.
[3] Blodgett's Hotel (no longer extant) was an ambitious project of real estate developer and speculator Samuel Blodgett, Jr. In spite of the name, the building was never used as a hotel. Eventually acquired by the Federal Government, Blodgett's Hotel once served as headquarters for the Patent Office, among other functions.
[4] Isaac Weld, Jr.
[5] See Isaac Weld's *Travels* excerpted in this volume.
[6] Theatre manager John William Green.
[7] Limestone quarried on the island of Portland in Dorset, England.
[8] Virginia plantation owner and politician Thomas *Mann* Randolph married Thomas Jefferson's daughter Martha Washington Jefferson who often served as White House hostess for her widower father.
[9] Virginia lawyer and politician John Wayles *Eppes* married Thomas Jefferson's daughter Mary Jefferson.
[10] Early Washington, D.C. real estate speculator Thomas Law.
[11] A stableman or tender of horses.

*Drain the Swamp*

¹ *On the Cause of the Yellow Fever* by Thomas Paine had been published the previous June and erroneously attributed the cause of the disease to "pernicious vapours" rising from exposed, low-lying riverbeds and swamps. During a major outbreak in Philadelphia in 1793, some 5,000 people, approximately ten percent of the population of what was then the capital of the United States, perished as a result of yellow fever. During the subsequent decades, other cities such as Baltimore and New York, where Paine resided, also suffered outbreaks of the disease.
² From Philadelphia, Pennsylvania to Washington, D.C.
³ The Non-Importation Act (1806) passed by Congress the previous April imposed trade restrictions on imports from Great Britain in part to combat that country's impressment of American sailors on the high seas, a precursor to the War of 1812.
⁴ English statesman of the Whig Party, the Honourable Charles James Fox (1749-1806).
⁵ William Eaton, Consul General to Tunis, active in the First Barbary War, and a witness in the treason trial of Vice President Aaron Burr.

*Spoil of the Conqueror*

¹ Major-General Robert Ross of the British Army.
² Gleig essentially enumerates here the United States Capitol, the White House and the Navy Yard.
³ Gleig served under Arthur Wellesley, 1ˢᵗ Duke of Wellington, during the siege of San Sebastián in Spain in the final years of the Peninsular War.

*American is Young*

¹ The August, 1814 battle in Bladensburg, Maryland which saw the Americans beat a hasty retreat from the field.
² *Marmion* by Walter Scott (1771-1832), a romantic poem set during the era of Henry VIII and published in 1808.
³ Benjamin Henry Latrobe (1764-1820), then serving for a second time as Superintendent of Buildings (i.e. Architect of the Capitol). Latrobe was re-hired to restore the building after it was burned by the British.
⁴ Latrobe suggested that a number of caryatids representing various characteristics of the states should be carved for the interior of the capital during its renovation. Massachusetts Congressman Timothy

Pickering (1745-1829) would later ridicule the very illustration to which Hall makes reference here. Congressional funding for Latrobe's caryatids was subsequently not forthcoming.
[5] Pennsylvania Avenue, NW.
[6] A holding place or planned location.
[7] George Washington had envisioned the founding of a national university in the capital city. In 1816, Benjamin Henry Latrobe, by direction of President James Madison, proposed such an institution to be located on the National Mall. Latrobe's proposal did not come to fruition.
[8] Commodore Stephen Decatur (1779-1820), veteran of the Barbary Wars and the War of 1812.
[9] José Correa de Serra (1750-1823), who famously called Washington, D.C. a "city of magnificent distances."
[10] Benjamin Williams Crowninshield (1772-1851).
[11] James Kirke Paulding (1778-1860).
[12] Enlightenment-era French author Guillaume Thomas François Raynal (1713-1796).
[13] i.e. *Goliaths*.
[14] From the Alexander Pope (1688-1744) translation of The Iliad of Homer.
[15] The Old Brick Capitol, constructed for the temporary use of Congress by local investors after the burning of Washington, D.C. in August, 1814, once stood on the current site of United States Supreme Court building.
[16] Representative William Gaston of North Carolina (1778-1844).
[17] Representative John C. Calhoun of South Carolina (1782-1850).
[18] Representative Daniel Webster of New Hampshire (1782-1852).
[19] Representative John Randolph of Virginia (1773-1833).
[20] Representative Thomas Peabody Grosvenor of New York (1778-1817).

*Our Enlightened Countrymen*

[1] i.e. the Grand Junction Canal in England.
[2] Following the original design of Dr. William Thornton (1759-1828), the north (Senate) wing was occupied in 1800 and the south (House) wing in 1807. Various stages of construction and renovation (after the War of 1812) continued for years. The two wings were joined and a dome completed atop the rotunda in the late 1820s.
[3] Congress, after some debate, purchased 6,487 books from Jefferson for $23,950 in 1815.

⁴ George Washington's estate, Mount Vernon, is about fourteen miles south of the Capitol on the Potomac River.
⁵ Generations later, the writer L. U. Reavis (1831-1889) would argue (unsuccessfully) for the removal of the United States Capital from Washington, D.C. to St. Louis, Missouri.
⁶ English singer Charles Incledon (1763-1826).
⁷ Sema Sama, aka Ramo Samee (or an imitator).

*The Aspect of the House*

¹ Here Duncan essentially summarizes several details of the L'Enfant Plan.
² [Note in the original]. I speak from recollection in calling these pilasters Corinthian. My memorandums are silent on the subject, and it is therefore not impossible that I may be wrong.
³ The iconic Lansdowne portrait of George Washington was executed by Gilbert Stuart (1755-1828) in 1796. A later copy hangs in the East Room of the White House. The National Portrait Gallery holds the original.
⁴ British-born Dr. William Thornton, who was also responsible for the design of the United States Capitol, was Superintendent of the Patent Office at the time.
⁵ [Note in the original]. Rapidity of publication is as well understood in America as anywhere. I copy the following from a New York newspaper which has recently reached me (May, 1823): —
"*Despatch in printing.* — The new novel, *Peveril of the Peak*, was received from England in New York on Monday at Ten A. M. and was printed, published, and sold on Tuesday, within 28 hours after the same was received. Another English copy of the same work was received per the Custom House, New York, at Twelve o'clock on Wednesday — at One o'clock forwarded to Philadelphia by the mail. In Philadelphia it was printed on Thursday, and on Friday 2000 copies were put in boards by Six o'clock in the morning. The English copy of Moore's Loves of the Angels was taken out of the Custom House in New York on a Monday in February last, at Eleven o'clock A. M.; was immediately sent to Philadelphia, and 250 copies of the work printed were received at New York on Thursday following by Eight o'clock A. M. and the same copies were sold and circulated that afternoon."
⁶ The "Old Brick Capitol," erected by local business leaders to provide Congress with a place to work (and to keep the Federal Government in residence in Washington, D.C.) after the burning of the Capitol in August, 1814.

⁷ [Note in the original]. The bill alluded to was afterwards thrown out in the House of Representatives, in consequence, as a member of the house told me, of it being somehow or other informal. I cannot help suspecting however, that disinclination to the object of the bill was the true cause.

⁸ Representative John *Sergeant*, Federalist of Pennsylvania.

⁹ [Note in the original]. Eight dollars, thirty six shillings sterling, for everyday that Congress sits, with an allowance of the same sum for every twenty miles that the member has to travel to and from Washington. A seat in Congress is worth rather more than two hundred pounds sterling a year.

¹⁰ Duncan witnessed some of the financial and legal convulsion in the capital that took place during the "Panic of 1819."

¹¹ John Trumbull (1756-1843) executed the *Declaration of Independence* in 1817. It still hangs in the rotunda of the United States Capitol.

¹² [Note in the original]. This brave officer has fallen in a duel since my return. That detestable practice is lamentably prevalent in America, and is some- times accompanied with circumstances of peculiar barbarity. In going the second time to Washington, I passed the ground where a duel was fought but a week or two before, with muskets, at ten paces distance; the one party was shot dead on the spot, the other dreadfully mangled, and I believe afterwards died. [Editor's note: Decatur died at home shortly after the duel. Barron would survive until 1851].

¹³ Duncan writes of Washington, D.C. resident (on Lafayette Square) Commodore Stephen Decatur, veteran of the American Revolution, the Barbary Wars and the War of 1812, and Commodore John Rogers (1772-1838), veteran of the latter two conflicts. Both were born Marylanders.

¹⁴ The Little Belt affair took place off the coast of North Carolina in May, 1811. Maritime historians acknowledge the British Commander Arthur Bingham (1784-1830) and his 20 gun Sloop-of-War *Little Belt* were clearly outgunned by Commander John Rogers and his 56 gun Frigate *President*.

*Punishment is 20 Dollars*

¹ George Washington was among those who capitalized on the abundance of fish in the Potomac River.

² Again, the scourge of Yellow Fever.

³ MacKenzie (here) omits statistics distinguishing among whites, slaves, and free blacks.

⁴ Surveyor of the City of Washington Andrew Ellicott (1754-1820).
⁵ MacKenzie appears to reference Johann Heinrich Lambert (1728-1777).
⁶ Dr. William Thornton (1759-1828) originally won the design contest for the United States Capitol building; Benjamin Henry Latrobe (1764-1820) subsequently superintended construction and would later contribute designs, primarily for the interior, after the burning of the Capitol by the British in August, 1814. Etienne Hallet, a.k.a. Stephen Hallet (1755-1825) and George Hadfield (1763-1826) were more involved with the construction of the building.
⁷ Leinster House currently serves as the Seat of the Irish Parliament and is the structure which informed the Irish architect James Hoban (1755-1831) in his contest-winning design of the White House.
⁸ Early Washington, D.C. real estate speculator Thomas Law.
⁹ American Colonization Society (ACS).
¹⁰ In his memoir *With Americans of Past and Present Days* the former French Ambassador to the United States Jean Jules Jusserand (1855-1932) attributes this quote to fellow countryman Jean-Jacques Ampère (1800-1864).
¹¹ Negus, a beverage consisting of hot water, wine, spices, and citrus.
¹² [In original text]… including the foundation walls of both wings, and of the centre or main building, and of alterations and repairs.

*The Custom is to Shake Hands*

¹ Major General Robert Ross (1766-1814), commander of the British forces that burned Washington, D.C. in August, 1814.
² Major Samuel Miller, United States Marine Corps.
³ Commodore Joshua Barney (1759-1818), United States Navy.
⁴ i.e. a fine marble such as that quarried in Brescia, Italy.
⁵ Associate Justice of the Supreme Court Bushrod Washington (1762-1829), George Washington's nephew, inherited Mount Vernon.
⁶ American artist John Trumbull (1756-1843).
⁷ Gaius Duilius (circa 3rd century BCE), Roman political figure and naval commander during the First Punic War.
⁸ Commodore John Rodgers (1772-1838), United States Navy.
⁹ A furlong is equivalent to 660 feet or 220 yards.

*God Bless the American People*

¹ The eldest son of sixth President John Quincy Adams (1767-1848) was George Washington Adams (1801-1829).

² Adams had just completed his tenure as James Monroe's Secretary of State. In his youth, Adams had accompanied his father, second President John Adams, during the latter's career in European diplomacy.

³ The election of 1824 saw Andrew Jackson gaining a majority of the popular vote over John Quincy Adams, but in what Jackson would call a "corrupt bargain," the final decision regarding the outcome of the election was taken up in the House of Representatives, which awarded a sufficient majority of electoral votes to Adams to install him as president. Jackson would go on to defeat Adams in 1828, relegating Adams to the highly exclusive club of one-term presidents, of which his father was founder.

*Nobody Would Inhabit Such a Town*

¹ Brown's Indian Queen Hotel, located on Pennsylvania Avenue between the White House and the Capitol.

² Sir Charles Richard Vaughan (1774-1849).

³ The French Minister in Washington, D.C. at that time was Joseph Alexandre Jacques Durant de Mareuil.

⁴ ... "seized the lightning and the scepter from tyrants."

⁵ St. John's Episcopal Church, at 17th and H Streets across Lafayette Square from the White House, was designed by Benjamin Henry Latrobe and scarcely a decade in existence when De Roos visited.

⁶ Richard Rush, son of Founding Father Benjamin Rush and at that time Secretary of the Treasury in the administration of John Quincy Adams.

⁷ The English actor-comedian John Liston (c1776-1846) frequently portrayed the minister character Mawworm [named for a parasitic intestinal worm] in "The Hypocrite" by John William Gear (1806-1866).

⁸ [Note in the original] Mississippi.

*Do You Mean to Buy the Lad, Sir?*

¹ Such was apparently the object of many foreign visitors to Washington, D.C.

² "FIERI FACIAS, usually abbreviated *fi. fa.* (Lat. "that you cause to be made"), in English law, a writ of execution after judgment obtained in action of debt or damages. It is addressed to the sheriff, and commands him to make good the amount out of the goods of the person against whom judgment has been obtained." (*Encyclopedia Britannica*; 11th Edition).

³ The practice continues today.
⁴ Born in South Carolina, Washington *Allston* (1779-1843) spent the last decades of his life in Cambridge, Massachusetts.
⁵ Washington's primary newspaper at the time, published from 1800 through 1870.

*It Reminded Me Much of a Russian City*

¹ Alexander refers here to John Gadsby (1766-1844) and his new Nation Hotel at Sixth Street and Pennsylvania Avenue (NW) in Washington, D.C. Gadsby also maintained hotels in Alexandria, Virginia and Baltimore, Maryland.
² Inspector General of the United States Army John E. Wool (1784-1869).
³ Any gathering of the Jackson family in the White House in this era would likely engender speculation among guests as to their identities. It appears [here with equal speculation] that in Captain Alexander's company on this occasion were Andrew Jackson Jr.; his wife, "young Mrs. (Sarah) Jackson" (née Yorke); "Mrs. Donaldson" whose husband Andrew Jackson Donaldson was then the president's private secretary; "Miss Eason," who would seem more likely to be Mrs. Peggy Eaton; and "Miss [Emma] Farquhar," who was a cousin of Mrs. Sarah Jackson. .
⁴ James Butler (died 1836).
⁵ Simón Bolívar the Liberator (1783-1830) led his native Venezuela and several other Central and South American countries to freedom from Spanish rule in the early 19th century.
⁶ New York Representative Congressman Aaron Ward (1790-1867).
⁷ The prolific New York author and historian Washington Irving served as aide-de-camp to the American Minister in London, Louis McLane, during the Jackson administration.
⁸ More likely Washington's step-grandson George Washington Parke Custis (1781-1857) as Washington's nephew Bushrod Washington had died in 1829.
⁹ The Washington Arsenal was at that time at Greenleaf's Point or the current Fort McNair.
¹⁰ The oldest Presbyterian Church in Washington, D.C. is located in Georgetown and was founded in 1790; however, additional congregations had begun to appear by the time of Alexander's visit.
¹¹ Charles Bankhead, later Chargé d'affaires in Mexico.
¹² Agustín de Iturbide (1783-1824) of Mexico.

[13] Alexander likely references the 15th century English character "Old Tom Parr."

*The Spitting was Incessant*

[1] [Note in the original]. The streets that intersect the great avenues in Washington are distinguished by the letters of the alphabet.
[2] Mrs. Trollope likely references the celebrated Washington, D.C. jeweler James Galt (1779-1847).
[3] American artist Charles Bird King (1785-1862).
[4] [Note in the original]. It has since been washed away by the breaking up of the frost of February, 1831.
[5] i.e. gentlemen's estates, plantations.
[6] [Note in the original]. As a proof of this defective hearing in the Hall of Congress, I may quote a passage from a newspaper report of a debate on improvements. It was proposed to suspend a ceiling of glass fifteen feet above the heads of the members. A member, speaking in favour of this proposal, said, "Members would then, at least, be able to understand what was the question before the House, an advantage which most of them did not now possess, respecting more than half the propositions upon which they voted."
[7] The "father" or "dean" of the House of Representatives was once an unofficial term of respect regarding the longest continually serving member of that legislative body. Here Mrs. Trollope likely refers to Representative Thomas Newton Jr. (1768-1847) who was born in Norfolk, Virginia and represented that state in Congress.
[8] References to draining the (dismal) swamp date back to William Byrd II (1674-1744) of Virginia in his *History of the Dividing Line* during a survey conducted in 1728. The Dismal Swamp straddles the Virginia-North Carolina border. George Washington, later an investor in the Dismal Swamp Canal Company, was of similar mind in terms of how best to utilize the swamp for commercial purposes. By 1805 the Dismal Swamp Canal would enable ships along the North Carolina coast to transfer and transport goods as far north as Norfolk, Virginia.
[9] In this era, the President's annual salary was fixed at $25,000.
[10] *Kalorama* was previously the estate of Jefferson confidante and supporter Joel Barlow (1754-1812).
[11] Now the site of Arlington National Cemetery.
[12] Swiss physiognomist and theologian Johann Kaspar Lavater (1741-1801).

*To Dazzle With False Glitter*

[1] New York-born Edward Livington (1764-1836).
[2] New Hampshire-born Daniel Webster (1782-1852).
[3] Robert Young Hayne (1791-1839) of South Carolina.
[4] Littleton Waller Tazewell (1774-1860) of Virginia.
[5] Samuel Smith (1752-1839) of Maryland.
[6] John Forsyth (1780-1841) of Georgia.
[7] i.e. ecclesiastical garb.

*The Road to Washington*

[1] "When suffering from a head cold..."
[2] Massachusetts Representative Edward Everett (1794-1865).
[3] [Note in the original]. "Another trait in their character is their great indulgence to their slaves. Though hunger and want be stronger than even the sacra fames auri [hunger for gold], the greatest pressure of these evils never occasions them to impose onerous labours on the negroes, or to dispose of them, though tempted by high offers, if the latter are unwilling to be sold." Notices of East Florida, with an Account of the Seminole Indians, by a recent traveller, &c., published at Charleston, S. Carolina, 1822. The description here given of the Indians, corresponds exactly with one I had from a Florida planter, (Mr. Kingsley), whom I met both in New York and at Philadelphia.
[4] [Note in the original]. The gold district, which now spreads over six or seven States, was supposed, in 1824, to be confined to a portion of N. Carolina. It produced in that year but 5,000 dollars; whereas the amount of what was obtained from it last year, was expected to be nearly 2,000,000 in value: 868,000 dollars in coined, and about as much in uncoined gold, having been the product in 1833.

*Ladies of America are Uncommonly Frank*

[1] i.e. clothing.
[2] i.e. chewing tobacco.
[3] [Note in the original]. Vermont is a State famous for its wild mountain scenery, and having a breed of horses unequalled for hardihood, fine temper, and bottom: they are found all over the States, and are everywhere in high esteem.
[4] [Note in the original]. The river Potomac is held to be the dividing line between the northern and southern States.

⁵ Power's vernacular use of *hirgo* (*large* in Latin; *wolf* in Irish and Scots-Gaelic) perhaps suggests he had lost his cigar but more likely that he could no longer keep up with Mr. Tolly atop the coachman's box. Power found his way inside at his next convenience.
⁶ In Greek mythology, a sea monster that dwells in the Strait of Messina; used often to describe a whirlpool. See Scylla and Charybdis.
⁷ Fuller's City Hotel, a predecessor to what is now the Willard Intercontinental Hotel at 14th Street and Pennsylvania Avenue, NW.
⁸ Although Power does not identify the venue, a likely candidate is the old American Theatre [or second Washington Theatre], then located on Louisiana Avenue near Capitol Hill.
⁹ The new National Theatre was constructed near Fuller's City Hotel, Power's aforementioned residence. The National Theatre first opened on December 7th, 1835. The most recent iteration of the National Theatre is located on the same spot at 1321 Pennsylvania Avenue, NW.

*The Bottom of an Old Lake*

¹ Brook's and White's are both historic London gentleman's clubs; the latter is the older.
² Henry Clay [1777-1852], then a Senator from Kentucky.
³ Daniel Webster [1782-1852], then a Senator from Massachusetts.
⁴ Charles Grey, 2nd Earl Grey [1764-1845].
⁵ Representative Warren Ransom Davis [1793-1835] of South Carolina.
⁶ Richard Lawrence [1800-1861] attempted [unsuccessfully] to assassinate then President Andrew Jackson on January 30th, 1835.
⁷ John C. Calhoun [1782-1850], then a Senator from South Carolina.
⁸ I have been informed that the rivalry and jealousy between the two towns of Alexandria and Georgetown was the real cause of the present location of the capital, each of them wishing to become the seat of government. Either of them would, in fact, be much more desirable situations: one from its commercial advantages, the other from its greater facility of inland communication and trade. As their disputes were irreconcilable, the capital was placed between them. I can scarcely conceive how the public, and the able men who then guided it, should allow their decision on so important a question to be influenced by the jealousies of these small towns; but my informant (Mr. L.) was a distinguished lawyer and senator, and his account deserves record. I cannot help believing that it was the intention of those who founded the Capital that it never should be a great manufacturing or commercial city, from a fear of its acquiring too great an influence, moral or physical, over the public councils. The reports that have attributed its

situation to the interested personal motives of General Washington, false and malignant as they are, drop harmless from the rocky integrity of his character.

*The President Offered Me Bonbons*

[1] Harriet Martineau was accompanied on her tour of America by Miss Louisa Caroline Jeffrey (1806-1887), who served both as companion and assistant to Martineau during her two-year visit.
[2] Warren Ransom Davis.
[3] Massachusetts-born Supreme Court Justice Joseph Story (1779-1845).
[4] Virginia-born Chief Justice of the Supreme Court John Marshall (1755-1835).
[5] Captain Toby Shandy is the uncle of the lead character in *The Life and Opinions of Tristram Shandy* (published 1759-1767) by the Irish-born novelist Laurence Sterne.
[6] The former Kentucky Representative and Senator of Kentucky Richard Mentor Johnson (1780-1850).
[7] Prolific writer and newspaper editor Amos Kendall (1789-1869).
[8] [Note in the original]. Society in America; vol. i., p. 60.
[9] The French newspaper *Le Moniteur Universel*.

*A Subject of Grave Reflection*

[1] Henry Stephen Fox (1791-1846), who, after his tenure as British Ambassador ended, died a recluse in Washington, D.C. and was buried in Congressional Cemetery.
[2] The House chamber in that era (now Statuary Hall) was known for its poor acoustics.
[3] Martin Van Buren (1782-1862) of New York was the eighth President of the United States and had served previously as Andrew Jackon's Vice-President. He served one term in both offices. Joel Roberts Poinsett (1779-1851) of South Carolina was Secretary of War in Van Buren's cabinet. John Forsyth (1780-1841) of Georgia was originally appointed by Andrew Jackson and continued as Van Buren's Secretary of State.
[4] Van Buren indeed lost to William Henry Harrison (1773-1841) of Virginia.
[5] American engineer Robert Fulton (1765-1815).
[6] American inventor Eli Whitney (1765-1825).
[7] The Graves Cilley duel involved William J. Graves (1805-1848), Representative of Kentucky and Jonathan Cilley (1802-1838),

Representative of Maine. Dueling was subsequently prohibited by legislation in Washington, D.C.

[8] "As much Mars as Mercury" or "As much by warfare as by skill."

*Just One Month*

[1] "Tippecanoe and Tyler Too."
[2] Lucius Quinctius Cincinnatus (c519-430 BCE), the Roman leader who beat his swords into plowshares, and for whom the Society of the Cincinnati, honoring the officers who served during the American Revolution under George Washington, is named.
[3] Pope Sixtus V (1521-1590), Bishop of Rome (1585-1590).
[4] Robert Tyler (1816-1877) and his wife Elizabeth Pricilla Cooper Tyler (1816-1899).
[5] [Note in the original]. In French means both represent and act.
[6] Samuel Lewis Southward (1787-1842) was President pro tempore of the Senate during the 27th Congress (March 4th, 1841-March 4th, 1843). He died in June, 1841. John Tyler had no Vice-President during his entire term.
[7] Alexander de Bodisco (1786-1854), Russian Ambassador to the United States from 1838 until his death in Georgetown, buried in Oak Hill Cemetery in Washington, D.C.

*Magnificent ... Magnificent*

[1] An area in London north of the River Thames, named for real estate developer Harry Penton (1736-1812).
[2] Mr. and Mrs. Dickens stayed at Fuller's City Hotel, the predecessor to The Willard Hotel at what is now Pennsylvania Avenue and 14th Street, NW.
[3] This expression is attributed to the Portuguese diplomat and scientist José Correia da Serra, the Abbé Correa (1750-1823).
[4] Dickens observes "The Genius of America" by Luigi Persico (1791-1860) in the tympanum over the east front of the Capitol.
[5] William Elliot's *The Washington Guide* (1837).
[6] i.e. "noblemen."
[7] Georgetown College (now Georgetown University), founded in 1789.
[8] The United States Marine Band, aka "The President's Own."
[9] Tenth President of the United States John Tyler (1790-1862) and his daughter-in-law, Elizabeth Priscilla Tyler, née Cooper, wife of Tyler's oldest son and private secretary Robert Tyler (1816-1877).

¹⁰ Dickens had briefly corresponded with and eventually met the equally prolific American novelist Washington Irving (1783-1859) in New York, where in February, 1842, a ball given in Dickens' honor. Their friendship apparently did not survive the publication of *American Notes*.

*Every Species of Alcoholic Beverage*

¹ Trinity House in Edinburgh, Scotland.
² The three buildings mentioned here, the Post Office, the Patent Office and the Treasury Department, were all designed by the America architect Robert Mills (1781-1855).
³ Faro or Pharaoh, then a popular card game whose participants included a banker and a number of players.
⁴ [Note in the original]. Since dead.
⁵ Formerly Vice-President under John Quincey Adams and Andrew Jackson, then Senator John C. Calhoun (1782-1850) of South Carolina, a vocal defender of the institution of slavery.

*A Fit Act of Hero Worship*

¹ Representative John Arnold Rockwell (1803-1861) of Connecticut.
² Representative Robert Charles Winthrop (1809-1894) of Massachusetts.
³ Senator Lewis Cass (1782-1866) of Michigan.
⁴ An ongoing boundary dispute between the Americans and the British, eventually resolved by treaty in June, 1846.
⁵ Then British Prime Minister Robert Peel (1788-1850) and his successor, John Russell (1792-1878).
⁶ George Hamilton-Gordon (1784-1860), 4$^{th}$ Earl of Aberdeen, Foreign Secretary under Prime Minister Robert Peel during negotiations that led to the Oregon Treaty of 1846.
⁷ Representative Stephen A. Douglas (1813-1861) of Illinois.
⁸ New Hampshire born Daniel Webster (1782-1852), then a Senator of Massachusetts.
⁹ Lyell appears to reference Justice John McLean (1785-1861) of Ohio.
¹⁰ i.e. Maryland and Virginia.
¹¹ Charles Wilkes (1798-1877) led the United States Exploring Expedition (1838-1842). Wilkes' *Narrative of the United States Exploring Expedition* was subsequently published in five volumes with an accompanying atlas. Among the plates subsequently mentioned by

Lyell to accompany the publication were reproductions of the work of artist Alfred Thomas Agate (1812-1846).

[12] James Dwight Dana (1813-1895) was an American geologist and member of the Exploring Expedition.

[13] English naturalist and author Charles Darwin (1809-1882) cited Lyell and his work on numerous occasions in *On the Origin of Species*.

[14] Literally the "great beast," in this case the fossil of a giant ground sloth.

[15] Georgia plantation owner and slaveholder James Hamilton Couper (1794-1866), at one time a correspondent of Sir Charles Lyell.

[16] A Mayan site near Chiapas in Mexico.

[17] American explorer John Lloyd Stephens (1805-1852) authored the seminal *Incidents of Travel in Central America, Chiapas and Yucatán*, published with illustrations by English artist Frederick Catherwood (1799-1854).

[18] First Lady Sarah Polk née Childress (1803-1891).

[19] Commanding General of the U.S. Army Winfield Scott (1786-1866).

[20] Secretary of the Navy George Bancroft (1800-1891).

[21] British Ambassador to the United States Richard Pakenham (1797-1868).

[22] Prussian Minister Plenipotentiary Frederich von Gerolt (1797-1879).

[23] American mineralogist Francis Markoe (1801-1872), was a lawyer who served with the United States Department of State and co-founded (with Joel Poinsett) the American Institute for the Promotion of Science, precursor to the Smithsonian Institution.

[24] British Ambassador to the United States Henry Stephen Fox (1791-1846).

[25] Alexander MacLeod (1796-1871), a Canadian arrested in America over issues relating to the "Caroline Affair," a diplomatic row between the U.S., Canada, and Great Britain stemming from the destruction of the ship *Caroline* over Niagara Falls.

[26] i.e. "governments within the government."

*We are the Same People*

[1] The phrase "City of Magnificent Distances" is attributed to José Correia da Serra, the Abbé Correa (1750-1823) of Portugal. English novelist Charles Dickens (1812-1870) would later paraphrase, calling Washington a "City of Magnificent Intentions."

[2] The character Stentor of the classical era engenders the expression "stentorian" for those who possess an exceptionally loud voice.

[3] The muezzin calls Muslims to prayer.

[4] Ángel Calderón de la Barca y Belgrano (1790-1861) was then Spain's Resident Minister in Washington, D.C. His second wife, Francis Erskine Inglis (1804-1882) authored *Life in Mexico*. Published in 1843, it recounts her time in Mexico with her diplomat husband.

[5] "The Discovery of America," a statuary group by the Italian Luigi Persico (1791-1860), was originally installed in 1844. During renovations of the East Front of the United States Capitol, which began in 1958, it was removed and placed in storage. See "Discovery of America, (sculpture)" in the Art Inventories Catalog, Smithsonian American Art Museum, Smithsonian Institution Research Information System (SIRIS). Control number 75002475. Accessed 05/31/2020. https://siris-artinventories.si.edu.... This information also appears in *Compilation of Works of Art and Other Objects in the United States Capitol* by the Architect of the Capitol. Washington, D.C. United States Government Printing Office, 1965. See pp. 365.

[6] [Note in the original]. Since the letters were written this has taken place.

[7] Dr. Samuel Davies Heap (1781-1853), formerly a surgeon in the United States Navy.

[8] i.e. the Monarch of Tunis.

[9] Sir Thomas Reade (1782-1849), once the British Consul-General in Tunis.

[10] A palace in Tunis, then residence of the British Consul.

[11] A moniker stemming from Taylor's role as a General in the Mexican American War.

[12] V — is for Victoria, Lady Welby-Gregory (1837-1912), the author's daughter and traveling companion during her tour in the United States.

[13] Zachary Taylor (1784-1850), 12th President of the United States, would die in office at the White House on July 9th, 1850.

[14] Mary Elizabeth Taylor Bliss (1824-1909), President Taylor's youngest daughter, acted as First Lady of the White House during Taylor's administration. She was the wife of West Point graduate William Wallace Smith Bliss (1815-1853) who then served as Taylor's secretary.

[15] A play on the daffodil, the subject of nursery rhymes, and a character in Nathaniel Hawthorne's 1843 story, "Little Daffydowndilly."

[16] American competitor to the British Cunard Line.

[17] i.e. "summer of St. Martin."

*No! No! ... No! No!*

[1] Joel Roberts Poinsett (1779-1851) of South Carolina.
[2] Senator Henry Clay (1777-1852) of Kentucky.
[3] i.e. the District of Columbia.
[4] New Hampshire born Senator for Massachusetts Daniel Webster (1782-1852).
[5] John Parker Hale (1806-1873).
[6] Samuel Houston (1793-1863).
[7] Thomas Corwin (1794-1865) and Salmon Portland Chase (1808-1873).
[8] William Henry Seward (1801-1872).
[9] John MacPherson *Barrien* (1781-1856).
[10] James *Shields* (c1806-1879) and Stephen Arnold Douglas (1813-1861).
[11] Thomas Hart Benton (1782-1858).
[12] The Benton-Lucas duel took place on August 12th, 1817 between Thomas Hart Benton and Charles Lucas (1792-1817), both Missourians.
[13] Pierre Soulé (1801-1870).
[14] Ms. Bremer appears to mis-identify this person.
[15] Jefferson Davis (1808-1889).
[16] Henry Stuart Foote (1804-1880).
[17] The two Senators representing Virginia at that time where Robert Mercer Taliaferro Hunter (1809-1887) and James Murray Mason (1798-1871). The former is the more likely candidate regarding this anecdote.
[18] *Moroni* and Mormon.

*In Charge was a Door-Keeper*

[1] The new Washington Depot, constructed for the Baltimore and Ohio railroad and then located at New Jersey Avenue and C Street, NW. below Capitol Hill, is no longer extant.
[2] Located at Pennsylvania Avenue between 14th and 15th Streets, NW.
[3] This number is an accurate reflection of the 1850 Census: The Seventh Census of the United States, exclusive of Georgetown and the "remainder" of the District of Columbia (i.e. land in the Territory of Columbia outside the City of Washington). The number can be further delineated as follows: 29,730 "whites," 8,158 "free colored," and 2,113 "slaves," for a total of 40,001 persons. Alexandria, that portion of the

District of Columbia initially ceded by Virginia, had been retroceded to that state in 1846.
[4] Chambers references the L'Enfant Plan of Pierre Charles L'Enfant (1754-1825).
[5] Numbered streets run north and south, lettered streets run east and west.
[6] Aquia Creek sandstone or "freestone," quarried in Virginia.
[7] Massachusetts born American sculptor Horatio Greenough (1805-1852).
[8] Benjamin Franklin, in his Autobiography, states that his fellow printers called him the "Water-American" because he drank only water at work while many co-workers drank beer. The nickname "American-Aquatic" has been attributed to Mason Locke Weems (1759-1825) by Sydney George Fisher (1856-1927).
[9] The Smithsonian Institution identifies "American banker John B. Murray" as the individual who acquired the "Franklin" press.
[10] James Smithson (1765-1829).
[11] Red sandstone from the quarries in Seneca, Maryland.
[12] New Hampshire born Franklin Pierce (1804-1869), 14th President of the United States.
[13] Then British Ambassador to the United States John Crampton (1805-1886).
[14] Crampton's residential address was then listed as K Street between 24th and 25th Streets, NW, and his official offices listed as 23rd and K Streets, NW.

*The Saddest Spot on Earth*

[1] i.e. "for the benefit of shipping."
[2] Shoreditch is a district in London's East End; Russell Square is in Bloomsbury.
[3] Ancient biblical towns.
[4] An ancient city in what is now Syria.
[5] St. James's Park in Central London
[6] An English name for Livorno, Italy.
[7] Trollope references Thomas Crawford (1814-1857) and the statues in his monumental *Progress of Civilization*, displayed as he indicates before they were installed in the tympanum over the Senate chamber entrance on the east side of the Capitol.
[8] Trollope references the much criticized statue of George Washington (in a toga) by Horatio Greenough (1805-1852) which has traveled from

inside and outside the Capitol to the Smithsonian Castle and is now displayed in the Smithsonian's National Museum of America History.
[9] Dr. William Thornton (1759-1828), though not a trained architect, won the contest for the design of the new Capitol building in 1793.
[10] James Wormley (1819-1884) was a free person of color in Washington, D.C. and a respected hotelier.
[11] Both designed by the American architect Robert Mills (1781-1855), the former is now a hotel, the latter houses two Smithsonian museums, the National Portrait Gallery and the American Art Museum.
[12] British historian Thomas Carlyle (1795-1881).
[13] George III (1738-1820), British monarch during the American Revolution.
[14] Originally the northern portion of "President's Park," subsequently named in honor of Gilbert du Mortier, the Marquis de Lafayette.
[15] The equestrian statue of Andrew Jackson in Lafayette Square and that of George Washington in what is now Washington Circle are both by the self-taught sculptor Clark Mills (1810-1883).
[16] The enduring scourge of yellow fever.
[17] The original "Smithsonian Castle" by the American architect James Renwick (1818-1895).
[18] Construction of the Washington Monument, also designed by Robert Mills, began in 1848, paused in 1854, and resumed in earnest in 1879 with the dedication taking place in 1885.
[19] George Brinton *McClellan* (1826-1885), then Commanding General of the United States Army.
[20] Salmon Portland Chase (1808-1873), formerly a Senator from Ohio.
[21] Simon Cameron (1799-1889), formerly a Senator from Pennsylvania.
[22] Gideon Welles (1802-1878) of Connecticut.
[23] Edwin McMasters Stanton (1814-1869) of Ohio.
[24] Secretary of State William Henry Seward (1801-1872)
[25] A small drinking cup.

*Fishing in Troubled Waters*

[1] Dicey spent the first days of his American visit in New York.
[2] David Burnes (died 1799), a contemporary of George Washington and one of the last holdouts among landowners in the newly surveyed Federal City.
[3] Grigory Potemkin (1739-1791), a Russian builder of cities for Catherine the Great.
[4] Both English towns on the North Sea coast.
[5] i.e. "and all this sort of thing."

[6] Dicey refers to the Second Battle of Manassas, late August, 1862.
[7] Italian General Giuseppe Maria Garibaldi (1807-1882).
[8] An Italian city just north of Naples.
[9] "Who knows?"
[10] Dicey, in the company of the celebrated American author Nathaniel Hawthorne, among others, made an excursion from Washington, D.C. to Alexandria, Virginia in the spring of 1862. He subsequently visited Hawthorne at his home in Concord, Massachusetts. Although Hawthorne's comment appears otherwise undocumented, it does reflect the spirit of a controversial Hawthorne essay entitled "Chiefly About War Matters," published in the July, 1862 issue of *The Atlantic* under the pseudonymous authorship of "A Peaceable Man."

Made in the USA
Middletown, DE
20 July 2020